The Life and Ideas of
Robert Owen

INTERNATIONAL PUBLISHERS
381 Park Avenue South
NEW YORK, N.Y. 10016

The Life and Ideas of
Robert Owen
by
A. L. Morton

The Life and Ideas of
Robert Owen
by
A. L. Morton

International Publishers
New York

This book was first published by
Lawrence and Wishart, London, in 1962.
This new and revised Edition, the first
in paperback, is published simultaneously
by International Publishers, New York,
Lawrence & Wishart, London,
and Seven Seas Books, Berlin, 1969
Second printing by
International Publishers,
New York, 1978

Dedicated
to those who prefer a system of society
which will ensure the happiness of the human race
throughout all future ages,
to a system which
so long as it shall be maintained,
must produce misery to all.

Owen's Dedication to
THE BOOK OF THE NEW MORAL WORLD, 1836

Contents

CONTENTS

Foreword

The object of this book is to give a general account of the life and work of Robert Owen by means of extracts from his own writings. For this purpose they have been grouped in sections covering the main stages of his career and the main aspects of his thought. A certain overlapping is unavoidable, especially as Owen was an extremely diffuse writer, whose leading ideas were formed early and who was never afraid of repeating them. Except for the development of details, and for some eccentricities which appeared in old age, there is little in his later works which has not been said, and as a rule said better, in the writings of his New Lanark period (1813—21). It is upon them, therefore, that I have drawn most heavily, though passages from later books have been included where they seemed helpful. An exception is his autobiography, published at the very end of his life, though perhaps partly written earlier. This I have used freely, as it gives the most vivid impression of his work and character.

Owen, I think, is one of the few writers who really gains more than he loses by being read in selections. His books taken as a whole are so verbose and rhetorical that the core of wisdom and good sense, seldom absent, is often lost in a desert of words. In selection it is possible to see much more clearly what he was aiming at and what is new and valuable in his thought.

In my last section I have given a number of estimates

of Owen—favourable and otherwise—made by contemporaries. And in a few places I have included passages, not by Owen but by his son Robert Dale Owen and others, which seemed to throw useful light on his work.

My introduction does not pretend to give a detailed account of his life—that has been done elsewhere, or of his thought—that I hope is done by the extracts which follow it. It aims rather at supplying the information necessary to make the extracts intelligible. I have referred throughout to those extracts which relate to particular passages in the introduction. These will be found enclosed in brackets: thus (X, 3) would be extract No. 3 in Chapter X.

While a detailed bibliography would be out of place here, a short note on books for further reading may be helpful. Apart from Owen's own writings, there is much information in the autobiography of his son, Robert Dale Owen. *Threading My Way* (New York, 1847). This, however, has little for the period after the New Harmony experiment, as Robert Dale took American citizenship and remained in the U.S.A. *The History of Co-operation* by G. J. Holyoake (Revised ed. 1906) is a ramshackle and not always reliable book, but contains a great deal about people and events of which Holyoake had personal knowledge. Of later books, the most convenient biography is *The Life of Robert Owen* by G. D. H. Cole (Revised ed. 1930) *Revolution 1789 to 1906* (1920) and *The Builders' History* (N.D.), both by R. W. Postgate, are useful for the Trade Union period (1833—4), and *William Thompson* by R. K. P. Pankhurst (1954) for the early Co-operative Movement. *Heavens Below* by W. H. G. Armytage (1961) may be consulted for the Owenite Communities. Other books which may be used for the general background are *A History of British Socialism* by Max Beer (1940), *The Early English Socialists* by H. L. Beales (1933), and *The British Labour Movement, 1770–1920* by A. L. Morton and George Tate (1956).

I have made use of the following abbreviations:

New View. 'A New View of Society: or Essays on the Principle of the Formation of Human Character.' 1813.

Observations. 'Observations on the Effect of the Manufacturing System.' 1815.

New Lanark. 'An Address to the Inhabitants of New Lanark.' 1816.

Relief of Poor. 'Report to the Committee for the Relief of the Manufacturing Poor.' 1817.

Catechism. 'A Catechism of the New View of Society and Three Addresses.' 1817.

Development. 'Further Development of the Plan for the Relief of the Poor and the Emancipation of Mankind.' 1817.

Children. 'On the Employment of Children in Manufactories.' 1818.

Manufacturers. 'To the British Master Manufacturers.' 1818.

Working Classes. 'An Address to the Working Classes.' 1819.

Report. 'Report to the County of Lanark.' 1821.

Dialogue. 'A Dialogue in Three Parts, between the Founder of "The Association of all Classes of all Nations", and a Stranger.' 1838.

Address. 'An Address to all Classes, Sects and Parties.' 1840.

Marriages. 'Lectures on the Marriages of the Priesthood of the Old Immoral World.' 4th ed. with an Appendix. 1841.

Revolution. 'The Revolution in the Mind and Practice of the Human Race.' 1849.

Millennial Gazette. 'Robert Owen's Millennial Gazette,' No. 11, August 1st, 1857.

Life. 'The Life of Robert Owen by Himself.' 1857. (Reprinted by G. Bell, 1920. References are to this edition.)

Life, 1A. 'A Supplementary Appendix to the First Volume of the Life of Robert Owen.' 1858.

Cole. 'A New View of Society and Other Writings.' Robert Owen. Ed. G. D. H. Cole. Dent, Everyman Library, 1927. (This volume contains a number of Owen's important writings, and when quoting these I have given page references from this edition as being more accessible than earlier ones.)

Buonarroti. 'Buonarroti's History of Babeuf's Conspiracy for Equality.' Translated by Bronterre O'Brien. 1836. (O'Brien printed several of Owen's writings to show the similarity of his views to those of Babeuf.)

T.M.W. 'Threading My Way,' by Robert Dale Owen. New York. 1847.

PART ONE

Owen's Life and Work

1

England in 1785

About the year 1785 England, and more especially Lancashire, stood at the edge of a period of unprecedented industrial development. This affected all branches of the economy—mining, metallurgy, transport, agriculture—but most of all it affected the new manufacturing industry of cotton textiles. Here the rate of growth was greatest. New machinery was used most widely, the new industrial towns were most rapidly enlarged, the vastest fortunes were made. Cotton was only one part of the Industrial Revolution, but it may justly be regarded as the most typical part, the one in which its character was most fully embodied.

A decade earlier—between 1766 and 1785—the series of inventions associated with the names of Hargreaves, Arkwright and Crompton had been developed: these were now beginning to be put to use on a mass scale, and both in Lancashire and in Lanark, along the Clyde, numbers of new spinning mills worked by water power were being built. The new methods were being applied, of course, also to other textile industries, but here they had to overcome long-established prejudices and productive relationships. Cotton, a new industry with few traditions, was speedily and completely conquered. Further, cotton goods were cheap and suitable for mass production and export. They therefore began to replace woollens as Britain's leading export. One set of figures will sufficiently indicate the rapidity of the advance. In 1780, 6,700,000 pounds of raw cotton were imported; in 1790, over 30,000,000; in 1801, over 50,000,000 and in 1810, over 123,000,000.

In 1785, also, two other new developments had their beginning. In this year the first steam-driven spinning mill was opened, and within a generation steam had virtually replaced water as a source of power, making possible larger units, greater efficiency and a greater concentration of production. The factory could now move from the hillside, to which workers had to be brought, into the towns themselves, so that industry at last became fully urban. And second, in 1785 Edward Cartwright invented the power loom, which, while it took longer to become widely used, was in the end to revolutionise weaving, the other branch of the textile industry.

All this was not merely a *technical* revolution. It was a social transformation in which, as Marx said, 'entire classes of the population disappear and new ones with new conditions of existence and new requirements take their place'. A new bourgeoisie and a new working class, the proletariat in the modern, scientific sense of the word, were created. New possibilities of wealth, new methods of exploitation and new forms of struggle appeared. Britain, which had been unique in Europe only in its political structure, now became unique also economically. It was the land of developed capitalism, of machinery and of industrial mass production, dominating the markets of the entire world.

It must be remembered, also, that this advance took place under abnormal conditions. From 1793 to 1815 Britain was waging a war against revolutionary and imperial France on a scale previously unknown, and war, though it disturbs and distorts industrial growth, is also a forcing house. Large quantities of certain types of goods are in urgent demand, rising prices encourage enterprise and speculation, and the sense of national crisis may be used to break down established customs and enforce changes to which in other circumstances there would be the greatest opposition.

Such, very briefly, were the changes taking place or foreshadowed in 1785. And in this year the young Robert Owen came to Manchester, the very heart and centre of the new England.

II

Early Life 1771–1800

Owen had been born in a different time and in very different surroundings. His father was ironmonger and postmaster at Newtown, a small, sleepy market town in central Wales, hardly touched even by the changes whose beginnings were becoming evident elsewhere. The only new feature, perhaps, was the intellectual and moral ferment of Methodism, by which Wales was deeply affected. Robert was the sixth of seven children, and neither his parents nor any of his brothers or sisters seem to have had any ability out of the ordinary. After his early boyhood he appears to have had little contact with any of them. He was a precocious child, as may be seen from his *Life* (II, 2): at the age of seven he had learnt all the village schoolmaster had to teach him, and it was an important part of his make-up that he was in all essentials entirely self-educated. All he learnt he learnt for himself and it became a part of his own thought. This was to be a source both of strength and weakness in later life. Because his ideas were based so directly on his personal experience he held to them with immense tenacity, but he never learnt to evaluate them properly.

When he was ten he left home for good, as he tells us, with forty shillings in his pocket, and henceforth was self-supporting. He went first to London and then to Stamford in Lincolnshire where he was apprenticed to a draper with a well-established, rather aristocratic business. Here he was kindly treated, not overworked, and found time to read a great deal—about five hours a day, he tells in his *Life*. If he was an omnivorous reader as a boy, he seems to have abandoned the habit early. His son, Robert Dale Owen says that 'he read a good deal, but it was chiefly one or two London dailies, with other periodicals as they came out. . . . He usually glanced over books without mastering them.'[1] Thus his mind closed early, and while he made important deductions from his personal experience he lacked the field of reference for his ideas which serious study might have given him. It is probably true to say that never in his whole life did he doubt the absolute truth of his convictions (I, 5 ; IX, 9).

In 1784 he left Stamford and became an assistant to a large firm of London drapers, Flint and Palmer. Here the work was hard and the hours long, and the next year he found a third employer, a Mr. Slatterfield of Manchester (II, 3). Manchester, as we have said, was at the heart of the Industrial Revolution just entering its period of greatest advance. Owen was now well qualified to make use of the abundant opportunities which were opening before him. True, he knew nothing of industry or of machines, but he knew textiles and he knew the market. He was industrious, ready to learn, ready to take chances and bursting with self-confidence. All around him people were talking about the cotton trade, the new machinery and the profits that might be made from them. It was a time when anyone who could command even a small capital could hope to make a fortune.

Owen's life during the next few years might almost have been invented to illustrate this phase of capitalist development. With a borrowed capital of only £100 he embarked with a rather dubious partner in the making of spinning machinery: when the partnership broke up Owen was left with three of these 'mules'. Setting them to work

[1] *T.M.W.*, 90.

he was soon making a net profit of £300 a year. We can see from this both the fantastic rate of profit that could be obtained and the degree of exploitation which made this possible. Employing only three workmen, Owen was able to extract a clear £2 a week profit from each of them. (II, 4). These super-profits in a period when machine reproduction was still not general, help to account for the rapid accumulation of capital and the expansion of production in the early stages of the Industrial Revolution. Robert Dale Owen writes of this time: 'Yarn, of a quality which in 1815 was sold for three shillings a pound, brought, in the infancy of the manufacture, as high as thirty shillings.'[1]

Before long Owen abandoned this project to become, at the age of twenty, manager of a large spinning mill employing 500 workers, and soon, he says, 'my name was now up for being the first fine cotton spinner in the world, and this was my standing as long as I remained the manager of Mr. Drinkwater's factory.'[2] After a few years a disagreement arose and Owen was able to take a new step forward by becoming partner as well as manager of a newly formed firm. In 1797, while on a business visit to Glasgow, he met Anne Caroline Dale, daughter of David Dale, owner of the great spinning mill at New Lanark, which Dale had built with Arkwright some seventeen years before. Friendship with Miss Dale led to a proposal of marriage, and this, in turn, to a train of events which ended in Owen and his Manchester partners buying the New Lanark Mill. At the beginning of 1800 he moved to Scotland to take over the management of the establishment (II, 5).

With this move a new stage in his life began. Hitherto his had been a success story, remarkable enough but not exceptional in the England of his time. At New Lanark he became a national figure and began to put into practice the ideas which have made him famous.

[1] T.M.W., 34. [2] Life, 48.

III

Owen at New Lanark

The New Lanark Mills, employing some thousand workers, were among the largest in Britain. Owen has given a
graphic and no doubt honest account of the conditions as
he found them there, but it is only fair to add that under
Dale this was generally regarded as a model establishment.[1] Nevertheless we must accept Owen's description
of the situation at New Lanark as correct in essentials,
and this may be taken as an indication of the terribly low
level that was then taken for granted in such places. It
seems likely, also, that Dale, who had a number of other
business interests, and was in 1800 an elderly man on the
way to retirement, did not in these last years give close
personal supervision to the Mill. His benevolent intentions were perhaps less fully realised than he had
imagined.

It is clear from Owen's own statement (II, 5) that he
went to New Lanark with the formed and conscious purpose of putting into practice what were already clear and
definite ideas about man and his environment. These
ideas are fully explained by Owen in numerous writings
at all stages of his life and only a few comments need be
made here to supplement his own exposition (I). They
are based upon two propositions which he was never tired
of repeating: 'Man's character is made for and not by

[1] (III, 1.) Compare G. J. Holyoake, *Self Help a Hundred Years
Ago* (1890), 128-134.

him,' and 'Any character from the worst to the best, from the most ignorant to the most enlightened, may be given to any community, even to the world at large, by applying certain means, which are to a large extent at the command, and under the control, or easily made so, of those who possess the government of nations.' It was this statement which he placed upon the title page of his first important book, *A New View of Society*, in 1813.

The deductions which he drew from these propositions were directly contrary to the orthodox thinking of his time and class. It was for them an article of faith that the masses were poor because they were idle, vicious, intemperate and ignorant. Their poverty was therefore a just consequence of their sins and a part of the divine order of the world. Owen thought that in so far as the masses were idle, vicious, intemperate and ignorant it was because they were poor. As they were lifted out of their poverty, as they were better housed, fed and clothed, and given cultural and educational opportunities, so their character would be transformed. He began with this conviction and, testing it at New Lanark, he found that it worked (III, 2, 3; VII, 1).

The great element of truth in Owen's theory is no less evident than its one-sidedness. Yet his thinking was less naïve than is sometimes supposed. He wrote that 'any character may be given to any *community*', not that it may be given to any individual, though at times he both wrote and acted as if he believed this also. Yet, as his account of his proceedings at New Lanark shows, he had a very shrewd estimate of the difficulties and the limits of what could be expected at this stage (III, 2, 3).

His true weakness, and one to which his position as manager and employer contributed, was his inability to see that the new environment must be created by the efforts and struggles of the working people themselves. He, Owen, had changed the environment at New Lanark with startlingly benefical results: he, Owen, could instruct his fellow employers and managers, and under his instruction they also could change the environment of the whole working population with equally benefical results. And while he did gain a certain degree of practical insight into the minds of his workpeople (though never to the extent that he imagined), he never understood the ruling class and, despite endless disappointments, never lost his belief in their benevolence and convincibility. A politician had only to show polite interest in whatever he had to say and he was convinced that he had won a firm disciple. He never learnt to recognise a polite brush-off, though he must have met with more of these than any other man in history, nor did he learn the futility of bombarding monarchs and ministers with long manifestoes calling upon them to transform the world (VIII, 3, 8, 9; IX, 1). The Revolution by Reason upon which he pinned his hopes always involved the possibility of persuading the rich and powerful to give up their privileges.

Yet all this lay in the future, and in the twenty years following his arrival at New Lanark one success followed another. Overcoming the natural suspicion which the workers felt for a 'foreign' employer, he gradually won their confidence. Their houses, all owned by the Company, were enlarged, sanitation improved, hours of labour shortened and conditions of work improved, shops were opened at which cheap and good quality food and clothes could be bought, continually improving educational and cultural facilities were provided—and used. In the course of years New Lanark became known all over Europe as a model community to which hundreds, and finally thousands, of visitors came every year. It should, however, be noted that, contrary to what has sometimes been said, money wages were not greatly above the normal. The deputation which visited New Lanark in 1819, sent from Leeds under the leadership of the well-known Liberal newspaper owner Edward Baines, whose report was in general enthusiastic, even declared that 'among us their wages would be thought low', though we must make allowance for the different level of prosperity in Scotland and the West Riding at that time (III, 5). Still, there were sufficient other reasons for Owen's employees to consider themselves exceptionally fortunate. Perhaps the greatest benefits from his work were enjoyed by the children, at this time perhaps the most cruelly exploited section of the working population.

IV

Education and the Factory Children

One of the results of the mechanisation of spinning was the increase in the number of women and children employed. Statistics from both Scotland and Lancashire show that almost half the employees in spinning mills were children, and, of the adults, by far the greater number were women. Men, as a rule, were employed for skilled work or as supervisors. And since water was the power first used to drive the machines, factories had to be built where a sufficient force of water existed, often at a distance from any centre of population. In order to meet the labour problem so created, the system of taking on pauper apprentices grew up. Workhouse children were virtually sold to the millowners by public authorities who were too glad to get them off their hands to inquire closely what happened to them afterwards. What this meant for children who came into the hands of brutal or unscrupulous employers can well be imagined, and even under the best circumstances, as Owen shows, the sytem was extremely unsatisfactory (III, 1; VI, 1, 2). Many other children employed were, of course, sent to the factories by their parents, and while some parents accepted this as natural and inevitable, many hated the necessity and only sent their children as a consequence of their own poverty (VI, 3).

Owen found both pauper apprentices and other children working at New Lanark and as soon as he was able he began to improve their conditions. We do not know just how fast he was able to move. When considering his New Lanark activities it is important to remember that he never had a completely free hand. He was manager and part owner, but had always to convince and carry with him partners whose ideas were very different from his own. He formed in all three partnerships, and in the first two his partners were business men to whom profits were the main consideration and who were reluctant to spend anything on education or social welfare. It was not till his third partnership, formed in 1813, and consisting largely of Quakers, but including also the utilitarian philosopher Jeremy Bentham, that he had partners who were content with a fixed return of 5 per cent on their capital and were prepared to give him a fairly free hand (III, 4). And with these he ran into a new kind of difficulty, since some of the Quakers, when they found that the education of the children included dancing and music, concluded that Owen was imperilling their immortal souls.

Paradoxically, I think that the very difficulties Owen had to overcome, especially in his first two partnerships, were among the reasons for his success at New Lanark as compared with later failures. They kept him firmly on the ground, forced him to take one step at a time and to grapple constantly with objective difficulties and problems imposed from the outside. Later, without such restraints, he tended to lose all sense of his limitations and leapt from one grandiose plan to another less practical. Or, to put it another way, the problems he was set at New Lanark were just those which a self-educated, empirical industrialist, trained in the practical school of Manchester, was best capable of solving. Perhaps his early success came too easily, for he came to believe that all problems could be solved in the same way and no amount of failures could persuade him that it was not so. The contrast between his uninterrupted success till about 1820 and his repeated failure after is striking: but it may be that the later failures were part of the price he had to pay for his early success, which gave him a false impression both of his own powers and of the difficulties he would have to face.

At any rate he had to proceed gradually at New Lanark, but the children were certainly his first concern. This was partly because he believed, rightly, that the characters of children could be much more easily formed than those of adults (VII, 3), but also because he really loved children and wanted them to be happy. And he believed that without a happy childhood they would not grow up to be rational, properly balanced men and women. His first step was to reduce hours of work and get the very young children out of the factory. This he did by stages, till none were employed before ten years old. The working day was reduced to ten and three-quarter hours, as compared with fourteen or more hours then often worked. He would have liked to make the age for starting work later, but this was as far as any of his partners would follow him. At least it left a number of years in which the basis of education was possible.

Owen's work as a pioneer of education has perhaps received less recognition than it deserved. In general, of course, his theories were those of the Enlightenment. But he put them into practice on a large scale and with resounding success. And the contrast between Owen's practice and that of his contemporaries in Britain was complete. Their method may be summed up by saying, 'Take a child and drill, or, more usually, beat a number of facts into it—Greek and Latin for the upper classes, a minimum of literacy for the lower.' The most fashionable method among those who thought of themselves as advanced, that of Joseph Lancaster, was a fantastic attempt to apply the technique of mass production to education. A master would instruct selected pupils by rote and these in turn would mechanically pass on their newly acquired knowledge to others. In this way, it was hoped, a single teacher could 'educate' a thousand or more children. The results of the system may easily be imagined.

At one time even Owen was disposed to favour it, but soon discarded it when he came to develop his own schools. He believed that the object of education was not to cram a child with facts but to prepare it for life by developing its character and personality (VII, 4). Therefore children must not be abused or frightened, but surrounded from the start with love and understanding, they must be kept interested and drawn out to desire knowledge, and this knowledge must be given to them in a simple, practical way. Books should be used sparingly (Owen says not till after the tenth year, perhaps forgetting for a moment his own youthful passion for reading) and at all stages lesson and play should go together. Dancing, singing, and physical exercise was an essential part of the New Lanark education (VII, 1). And, since the imparting of knowledge had only a minor place in Owen's conception of education, he was ready to take children at a much earlier age than was then usual. As soon as infants could be brought to the school they were received, encouraged to play happily, and were well looked after. In this way they began to learn and to acquire confidence very young. They were also saved from the terrible neglect that was the fate of nearly all young children whose parents were both working long hours in the factories.

After the formation of his third partnership in 1813 Owen was able to carry out his educational plan more fully. He enlarged his schools, improved the equipment, and on January 1st, 1816, the school became the nucleus of his Institute for the Formation of Character, designed, as he said in a speech to the people of New Lanark, 'to effect a complete and thorough improvement in the *internal* as well as the *external* character of the whole village'. It was a large two-storey building used as a school for the children by day and a club, adult education centre, dance hall and concert room in the evenings.

Owen, intensely serious as he was, was no enemy of enjoyment (XIII, 3). In an age when long hours were seriously defended on the grounds that unless employed the workers would inevitably be misusing their time (VI, 5), he believed that leisure and recreation were necessary both for children and adults. Some visitors to New Lanark were, indeed, critical of this side of his work, finding it too worldly, too much concerned with the good of the body and too little with the salvation of the soul. For Owen, these were two aspects of the same thing. And certainly in his last years at New Lanark the overwhelming majority of the thousands of visitors, who included, as Owen wrote, beside the Tsar Nicholas, 'Princes John and Maximilian of Austria, Foreign Ambassadors, many bishops, and clergy innumerable—almost all our own nobility—learned men of all professions from all countries—and wealthy travellers for pleasure and knowledge of every description,'[1] went away amazed and enthusiastic. Owen began to be a figure of international reputation.

In 1815 he began his first public campaign—for a Bill to regulate the employment of young people in textile factories. He began by calling a meeting of Glasgow cotton magnates, at which he proposed resolutions asking the Government to remove the tax on imported raw cotton and to pass an Act to improve the position of the factory children. The first was carried enthusiastically, the second failed to find a single supporter. Owen then approached Sir Robert Peel (father of the Prime Minister of the same name) who promised to introduce a bill which Owen drafted. This prohibited the employment of children under ten in textile factories, reduced hours to ten and a half per day for all under eighteen, for whom night work was

[1] *Life,* 203.

31

also forbidden, and set up a system of Inspection, without which, as was later discovered, any such measure would be ineffective.

Owen seems to have expected little opposition to his Bill, but he soon found it was attacked from all sides and he himself subjected to the most unscrupulous personal abuse (VI, 5). Every possible delay was created, and in the end it was not till 1819 that a Bill, so mutilated as to be virtually useless, was passed through Parliament (VI, 2, 3, 4). Almost its sole importance was in establishing a precedent for Government interference with industry, and in fact it was the first of many such Acts. In this respect, as well as in the field of education, Owen occupies a distinguished place among the early defenders of the rights of children. However, he was so disgusted at the delays and manoeuvres which he had encountered, that long before 1819 he had left the conduct of his Bill to Richard Oastler and others and had turned his attention elsewhere.

V

A New View of Society

The ending of the long war against Imperial France in 1814-15 precipitated a general economic crisis. The artificial market created by the war vanished, and some time elapsed before new markets could be developed. Thousands of demobilised soldiers and sailors were flung upon the labour market. Prices fell, production was cut down as stocks of unsold goods piled up, unemployment reached unprecedented levels, everywhere there were riots and disorders, while political agitation, which had been forced below the surface during the war, flared up as millions saw in a corrupt and oligarchic society the cause of their hunger and sufferings.

The ruling class was thoroughly alarmed. The Tory Government of the time, headed by such men as Liverpool, Eldon, Sidmouth and Castlereagh, was possibly the most callous and reactionary that Britain has ever known, nor did it at all understand the changes which had come over the country during the last generation. One problem which attracted immediate attention was that of the rapidly rising poor-rate. Poor relief was then organised on a parochial basis, every parish being responsible for the relief of its own poor. In those areas and parishes where unemployment was concentrated this was becoming a crushing burden, all the more so since the system was most inefficiently administered. About the middle of 1816 a meeting was called in London, attended by many of the bishops and aristocracy, to discuss the question. Owen also was there.

As we have seen, his work at New Lanark had made him widely known. He was the benevolent Mr. Owen, the philanthropic millowner, whose schools and welfare schemes were universally admired. And a few years earlier, in 1813-14, he had published his first important book, *A New View of Society*, sometimes known as *Essays on the Formation of the Human Character*. Though most of Owen's later ideas are implicit in this book the more alarming of them are not obtruded: Owen is dealing mainly with generalities about character and environment, the importance of proper education and the advantages of humane treatment of workpeople. The book is dedicated to, among others, Wilberforce and the Prince Regent (later George IV). Consequently, though *A New View* had attracted considerable attention and helped to increase Owen's reputation, it had not alarmed the ruling class. When the meeting decided to set up a Committee, under the chairmanship of the Archbishop of Canterbury, to raise a fund to relieve distress and to consider possible remedies, Owen was included.

When it met he was probably its only member with practical experience of industrial conditions, and was therefore listened to with marked respect. When he declared that he had a positive remedy, the Committee invited him to prepare a written report explaining it. This document, *Report to the Committee for the Relief of the Manufacturing Poor* (1817), was the first statement of Owen's famous Plan, to the advocacy of which the rest of his life was to be devoted and which has given him his place among the pioneers of socialism.

Details of the Plan are given below in Owen's words and need not be elaborated here (X, XI). Broadly, he proposed that instead of pouring out money unproductively on Poor Relief, the Government should raise a fund to establish village settlements, each with around 1,200 inhabitants, in which the unemployed could maintain themselves and add to the wealth of the nation. In many respects these villages were to resemble his own establishment at New Lanark, with the important difference that while that was purely industrial, these were to have sufficient land to produce their own food: Owen always regarded a unity of manufacture and agriculture as the ideal basis for any community.

At this stage, it should be noted, Owen's object was the limited one of meeting the crisis and relieving unemployment: he had not yet begun to think of the villages as the basis for a new kind of society based on co-operation instead of competition. They were, therefore, not to be self-governing or socialist in any proper sense, but controlled by officers appointed by the public bodies, or groups of public-spirited capitalists by whom they might be established (X, 3). Soon, however, as the idea grew clearer in Owen's mind, he felt that life in these villages would be in every way better than life under any existing circumstances, and then, 'of course no part of society will long continue in a worse condition than the individuals within such proposed establishments. . . . The change from the *old* system to the *new* must be universal' (X, 5). In Owen's later writings, from his *Report to the County of Lanark* (1820) onwards, though the technical details of the Plan do not greatly change, many details are developed, more and more stress is laid on the necessity for equality and self-government, and the questions of the relations between the villages, their grouping into an all-embracing national, and, finally, international structure, are increasingly insisted upon (X, 67; XI, 1, 5).

When Owen presented his *Report,* as he says, 'the Archbishop and the Committee appeared to be taken by surprise, and appeared at a loss what to say or do.'[1] After a little thought they decided that such a plan fell outside

[1] *Life,* 182.

the scope of their avowedly charitable objects, and they passed him and his Plan on to a Parliamentary Committee which had been set up to consider the revision of the Poor Laws. But they, too, found the plan embarrassing, and after keeping Owen waiting about for two days, informed him that they would not hear his evidence. He was naturally indignant, and attributed their refusal to the influence of the ideas of Malthus, with which he strongly disagreed (V, 6). He did not understand that the ruling class could never accept a Plan which threatened their dominant position in society, but attributed every rebuff to some misunderstanding, to particular stupidity, or to the intrigue of some personal enemy. At this particular time, far from intending to do anything to improve the condition of the workers, the Government was more and more turning to open violence, repressive legislation and the wholesale use of spies and provocateurs to crush the growing revolt. Owen could not see this, and he continued for years to press his Plan upon all sorts of prominent people (VIII, 5).

At the same time, he did begin to realise that he must now appeal to a wider public, and on August 14th, 1817, held the first of a series of large and enthusiastic public meetings in London at which he explained his ideas. He accompanied these with a publicity campaign by pamphlets and through the press (VIII, 1). It was at the second of this series of meetings, on August 21st, that he made the famous attack on religion which he always regarded as one of the turning points of his life (XIII, 1).

This laid him open to what were then the most damaging attacks, and Owen always believed that it was this action which lost him the support of most of his 'respectable' backers. This, perhaps, is only partly true. No doubt it was at about this time that many former friends began to abandon him, but this happened only gradually and it seems likely that the increasingly clearly socialist and subversive nature of his Plan was in the long run more responsible. The charge of 'infidelity' might be a convenient excuse for those who wished to withdraw on other grounds. Engels is perhaps more correct when he attributes Owen's loss of upper-class support to his triple attack on private property, religion, and bourgeois marriage (XVII, 4).

As late as 1820 he was invited by the County of Lanark to submit a plan for 'relieving Public Distress and Removing Discontent, by giving permanent, productive Employment to the Poor and the Working Classes'. His *Report to the County of Lanark* is in many ways the clearest and best reasoned statement of his Plan. Like his earlier proposals it was politely received and promptly shelved.

Between 1817 and 1824 Owen was constantly in the public eye, addressing meetings, issuing a stream of pamphlets and travelling incessantly. He visited Europe (VIII, 6) and Ireland and became acquainted with many of the leading personalities of his time. As yet, however, he had no connexion with the working class or their radical leaders (VIII, 4). He appealed, as indeed he continued to do throughout his life, to the men of enlightened good will in all classes (IX, 6).

With all these activities Owen obviously had less time to give to New Lanark, and after about 1817 the detailed supervision of his factory was increasingly left to subordinates. Some of his partners, too, especially the Quaker William Allen, were alarmed by his religious unorthodoxy, and insisted on modifications to his plans—something that Owen was the last man to accept readily. Besides all this there was the growing sense of the inadequacy of what could be done under the conditions imposed upon him there. Owen was a perfectionist and New Lanark was obviously still far from perfect (III, 5). All these factors combined to lessen Owen's interest, and in 1825 he ceased to be manager of the New Lanark Mills, though he kept his financial interest till 1828.

VI

Owen in the New World

As the hope of securing official backing for his Plan receded Owen began to turn to the idea of himself establishing a model community whose success could act as an example and inspiration for others. At first he hoped to act through the agency of the benevolent rich.

In 1819 a Committee was set up, under the Chairmanship of the Duke of Kent and including the Duke of Sussex, Sir Robert Peel, senior, and the economist David Ricardo, with the object of raising £100,000 to set up an Owenite community. It was proposed to pay 5 per cent interest on all capital subscribed. In its address to the public the Committee thought it necessary to reply to certain objections, and the passage in which it did so gives an interesting glimpse of the grounds upon which Owen was already being attacked:

'The private opinions which Mr. Owen has been supposed to entertain on matters of religion form one of such objections. This is a point on which it has not been thought fit to require Mr. Owen to make any public declaration; it is deemed sufficient to have ascertained that Mr. Owen is not known to have in any one instance endeavoured to alter the religious opinions of persons in his employment; that the desires of his workmen to attend their respective places of worship are complied with and aided to the utmost extent; that a minister has long been paid by the proprietors of the manufactory under Mr. Owen's management for performing Divine service, in the Gaelic tongue to the Highland workmen; that Mr. Owen's own house is a house of daily prayer; that he is father of a large well-regulated moral family; that his conduct appears to be free from reproach, and that his character is distinguished by active benevolence, perfect sincerity, and undisturbed tranquility of temper.

'Several other objections rest upon a supposition that Mr. Owen's plans necessarily involve a community of goods; this is a great mistake or misrepresentation. In the establishment which is now proposed there would be no community of goods nor any deviation from the established laws of property. Mr. Owen has expressed on a former occasion some opinions in favour of a state of society in which a community of goods should exist, but he has never considered it as essential to the success of such an establishment as is now proposed, nor required it as a condition of his superintendance. Mr. Owen's opinion upon this matter need scarcely be regarded with apprehension by any part of society, when it is considered that the present laws of real property make a community of profits from land quite impossible, and that the legislature are not likely to alter the laws of the land in this respect upon any suggestion of Mr. Owen's.

'It has also been said that these plans have a tendency to the equalisation of ranks. This notion is connected with, and depends upon, the erroneous one that they involve a community of goods. If the laws of property are preserved, and the plan rests, as it does, upon the supposition of its being a profitable mode of investing capital, it has no other tendency to equalisation than all plans which have for their object the extension of the comforts, the intelligence, and the virtues of the poorer classes of society.'[1]

[1] *Life, IA,* 245-6.

After several months less than £8,000 had been subscribed, and the Committee decided to wind up its affairs and dissolve. A second appeal launched by a similar Committee in 1822 was little more successful. Owen now began to turn his thoughts to the possibility of a more radical experiment, more directly under his control and in a new land where the laws of real property were less restrictive. The U.S.A. was not only such a land, it was also widely regarded a this time as the world's potential Utopia, a place where the corrupting traditions of Europe had never penetrated and where it was possible to make a really new start under the most favourable conditions. It was a promised land to which thousands of emigrants were already making their way from Europe. Already a number of Utopian communities, mostly on a religious basis, had been established there, and as early as 1817 Owen had published an account of one of these groups, the Shakers, sent to him by a Philadelphian Quaker, with an introductory note calling it, 'a simple but convincing proof of the effects of the principle of combined labour and expenditure'.[1]

In 1824, therefore, Owen went to the U.S.A. with the belief that here was the best promise for his great experiment. He met with an enthusiastic welcome and lectured successfully in all parts of the country, illustrating his lectures with a scale model of his proposed community. This model is lost, but we know from drawings by Stedman Whitwell that it was an impressive quadrangle rather like one of the Oxford or Cambridge colleges on a grand scale. Owen was now a rich man, but his wealth was still not sufficient to start on quite this style. However, he found that the Rappites, another group of religious communists, were anxious to leave their settlement of Harmony, Indiana. Owen could buy the well-constructed village and 30,000 acres of good land, much of it

[1] *Life, IA,* 146.

already under cultivation, for £30,000. On this venture he risked the whole of his considerable fortune and ultimately lost the greater part of it.

Owen now issued a general invitation to 'the industrious and well-disposed of all nations' to come and join in the first step towards a new civilisation. By May 1st, 1825, about 800 had assembled and New Harmony was officially inaugurated. Its first constitution gave him complete control for a preliminary period of three years. Shortly after the opening Owen returned to England for some months. During this period New Harmony appears to have developed fairly satisfactorily, and on his return in January 1826 with a number of distinguished supporters, he proposed a new constitution based on complete equality and self-government. This was the second of seven constitutions adopted within a space of two years. The result was disappointing: quarrels, the formation of factions leading to secessions and the formation of break-away communities followed. It would be pointless to trace these events in detail, but by the spring of 1827 New Harmony virtually came to an end. Only the school, which had all along been its most successful feature, survived in a modified form.

Robert Dale Owen, who had played a leading part in the experiment, has some interesting reflections on its failure:

'My father made another still greater mistake. A believer in the force of circumstances and of the instinct of self interest to reform all men, however ignorant or vicious, he admitted into his village all comers, without recommendatory introduction or any examination whatever. This error was the more fatal, because it is in the nature of any novel experiment, or any putting forth of new views which may tend to revolutionize the opinions or habits of society, to attract to itself (as the Reformation did three hundred years ago, and as spiritualism

41

does today) waifs and strays from the surrounding so-
ciety; men and women of crude, ill-considered, extra-
vagant notions; nay, worse, vagrants who regard the
latest heresy but as a stalking-horse for pecuniary gain,
or a convenient cloak for immoral demeanor.'[1]

There is no doubt that the absence of any attempt to
select members was not accidental but the result of
Owen's oversimplified views of the effect of environment
on character: he genuinely thought that it would not much
matter who came because, once there, all would be
speedily transformed. Today, while we may accept in
principle the correctness of belief that human nature is a
product of human life, we have learnt from experience
that the transformation is a long, complex and difficult
process. At New Harmony, at any rate, there was no time
for the process even to begin. The community was over-
weighted from the start with middle-class intellectuals
who were incapable of sustained manual labour or regarded it as beneath them, and they and the working-class
members were never able to pull together.

Owen was not really discouraged by his failure, but
began at once to negotiate with the Mexican Government
for concessions of territory 'one hundred and fifty miles
in breadth from the Gulph of Mexico to the Pacific
Ocean',[2] on which the Plan might indeed have been
carried out on a stupendous scale. Perhaps understandably, nothing came of this project and after some more
lecturing and debating in the U.S.A. Owen returned to
England in 1829. While he still did not doubt in the
slightest the correctness of his ideas, he was in a mood
to consider other means of realising them.

[1] *T.M.W.*, 259. [2] *Revolution*, 128.

VII

Owen Among the Workers

The years during which Owen had been chiefly in the U.S.A. had been a time of remarkable advance for the working-class movement in Britain. The repeal of the Combination Acts in 1824 had legalised trade unions, though leaving them still under great legal disabilities, and they had grown everywhere in numbers and power. The political movement for democratic reform, which had receded in the years immediately following the Peterloo Massacre (1819) revived again as Britain approached the crisis that secured the first Reform Bill (1832). And in this revival the workers began to take a more independent part, throwing up their own leaders and looking for their own distinctive ideas. A left-wing press that had a *class* as distinct from a purely radical outlook came into being leading up to the founding of the *Poor Man's Guardian* in 1830. It was in these years, too, that many of the books of the early English socialists were published, and the term socialist (at this time used as a synonym for Cooperative) was then first coined. William Thompson published his *Inquiry into the Principles of the Distribution of Wealth* in 1824. In 1825 both John Grey's *Lecture on Human Happiness* and Thomas Hodgskin's *Labour Defended* appeared, while Thompson replied to the latter in his *Labour Rewarded* in 1827.

All these works were broadly Owenite in character, though by no means merely derivative. This is especially true of Thompson, whose *Inquiry* made an important advance by linking Owen's Plan to the idea of exploitation. Owen is known to have read and admired this book and his thinking was perhaps influenced by it: it is certainly from about this date that the conception of his Plan as a means of ending exploitation begins to emerge.

So in these years—1825 to 1830—Owenism, which before had been a general idea operating outside class, now began to appear in a new, working-class form. I think this was less in spite of than because of Owen's absence from the country. So long as he was conducting the campaign he did it in his own benevolently dictatorial way. There could be no real movement, only Owen and his disciples who accepted all he said and did and left him to make all the decisions. He could never learn to work with others as an equal: he must be totally right, and if so, what other men thought or desired could not be of any importance (XVII, 3).

But in his absence a broader, genuinely democratic movement could develop, with no one leader but a number of active figures—Thompson, Minter Morgan, William Pare, Dr. King, Benjamin Warden, William Lovett, to name only a few of the better known.

From about 1826 Co-operative Societies began to be formed, mainly by groups of skilled artisans in London and other towns. These Societies differed greatly from the Societies we know today. They were definitely Owenite in the sense that the objective was the setting up, eventually, of a co-operative community. But as they were formed by poor men, the problem of finding initial capital had to be faced. So they began to engage in retail trade among themselves, hoping in time to accumulate a common fund with which, in the end, a community could be started. Meanwhile, they were pleased to be keeping in their own hands profits that would otherwise have gone to some middleman. A little later groups of trade unionists, or sometimes of self-employing artisans, began to set up Productive Societies, with the idea that instead of working for some capitalist master or merchant they should combine to produce goods and sell them direct to the public. In a few years a large number of Co-operatives of both these types, as well as some combining features of each, were in existence. A natural further step was to combine these local Societies into some sort of federation for mutual help and encouragement. Such was the stage which the movement had reached when Owen returned in 1829.

Owen at first, Lovett tells us, 'looked somewhat coolly on these Trading Associations.' He had always been accustomed to work on the grand scale and through the medium of statesmen and influential people. These little trading ventures among the workers seemed mean and unpromising to a man who always believed he was about to change the whole world within a few years (IX, 6; XII, 2). Holyoake, quoting from *The New Moral World*, tells us that Owen,

> '*related that on his journey to New Lanark he passed through Carlisle. Devoting Tuesday and Wednesday* "*to seeing the friends of the system, and those whom I wish to make its friends: to my surprise I found there are six or seven co-operative societies, in different parts of the town, doing well, as they think, that is, making some profit by joint-stock retailing. It is, however, high time to put an end to the notion very prevalent in the public mind, that this is the social system which we contemplate, or that it will form any part of the arrange-ments in the* New Moral World".'[1]

But more than this was involved.

Owen's previous contact with workers had been at New Lanark, where he was in authority—a just, kindly

[1] *History of Co-operation*, I, 141.

ruler, but an absolute one. It was for him to benefit the masses, for the masses to respond gratefully. And the New Lanark workers were politically backward and quite unorganised. There is nothing in Owen's writings to suggest that he had even heard of trade unions before this time, though presumably he must have done so.

Now he had to deal with the skilled London craftsmen, the proudest, most articulate, most politically developed section of the working class at that time, even if not in the long run the most militant. They had behind them generations of struggle and conscious radicalism and were accustomed to think of themselves as the natural leaders of their class. Where Owen had previously commanded he must persuade and convince, a thing he had never learnt to do. The London artisans were ready to admire and respect Owen, they had already learnt much from him—but they were not prepared to surrender their mental independence. It was inevitable that a partnership between them would be stormy and impermanent. It was also inevitable that such a partnership should be attempted.

Owen had failed in his attempts to convince the rich and powerful. He had failed at New Harmony. He was no longer the rich millowner of New Lanark. And here were the workers, whom he genuinely wished to benefit, accepting his teachings, and trying, no doubt inadequately, to put them into practice. He would go to them and show them how to do better.

The next stage was that of Co-operative Congresses and Labour Exchanges or Co-operative Bazaars. The first Congress was held in Manchester in May 1831. It proposed that a sum of £30 should be raised from each of 200 local Societies to establish a Community to which each subscribing Society could nominate one of its members. Owen opposed the scheme on the ground that its scale and resources would be quite inadequate, but it was nevertheless adopted by the Congress.

In this difference of opinion we may perhaps see the beginning of a conflict between Owen and Thompson. Thompson was unquestionably the other outstanding figure in the movement at the time, with a prestige almost equal to that of Owen and a greater ability to work on terms of equality with others. In his *Labour Rewarded* he had expressed his support for manhood suffrage and, outlining a plan for a co-operative community similar to that of Owen, he had given it a democratic structure quite foreign to Owen's outlook. And, while he regarded a community of about 2,000 as ideal, he had written in the *Co-operative Magazine* suggesting that a start might be made with as few as ten families and a quite small working capital. He knew at least that there was no possibility of accumulating within the existing movement, almost entirely working class, capital on the scale which Owen believed necessary.

This was, indeed, unhappily demonstrated, for a year later it was found that only a few pounds had been subscribed and the project had to be abandoned. While the individual societies maintained the objective of establishing communities, in practice the struggle to survive swallowed up all available funds.

At the third Congress (April 1833) the differences were even more acute. Thompson again advocated a small-scale venture suited to their limited resources, Owen a grand scheme, for which, he said, money could be borrowed on the Stock Exchange. He suggested that only he had the necessary knowledge and experience and should be given a free hand. The Congress decided in favour of Thompson's proposals, and also took the more practical step of appointing a number of 'missionaries' to carry on Co-operative propaganda in all parts of the country. These disputes, though they bulk large in the Co-operative literature of the time, were in themselves perhaps healthy: they reflect the growing pains of a real movement in which difference and argument were possible. It would seem that Thompson was the only figure in this movement who had the ability and prestige to stand up to Owen, and the indications are that he was carrying it with him. But he was already in bad health and died in the following spring.

Meanwhile a good deal of the movement's effort was being directed to the formation of Labour exchanges. The first of these was set up in London in 1830, and others followed in London, Birmingham and Liverpool. The largest and best known was the National Equitable Labour Exchange set up by Owen himself in 1832 in the Grays Inn Road.

The idea was that co-operators in all branches of production should bring the articles they had made to the central Exchanger or Bazaar, where they could be credited with Labour Notes based on the estimated cost of the raw materials and the amount of time taken for their manufacture. Apparently the maker's own estimate of the time was accepted and little attempt was made to differentiate between the value of the time taken in different forms of production. Consequently, some articles were valued much above and others much below the normal market price. The natural result was that the undervalued goods were immediately sold and the overvalued accumulated in the store. In this way a steadily worsening financial position might be concealed for a time by brisk sales. By 1834 the National Equitable Labour Exchange, now transferred to new premises in Charlotte Street, which were for a long time to be the Owenite headquarters, was running into difficulties. What might have happened to it cannot be known, since it, like many other Co-operative enterprises, was caught up and overwhelmed in the great crisis of that year.

VIII

Owen as Trade Union Leader

The growth of the Co-operative Movement has been outlined as if it was the only important development of these years, and this, I think, is how it probably appeared to Owen himself, who hardly seems to have noticed the intense political excitement that centred around the struggle for the Act of 1832 for the reform of Parliament. But of course it was not the only development, since these were years of bitter struggle, disillusionment, and the growth of a new political understanding among the masses. The Whigs had mobilised these masses behind the slogan of Parliamentary Reform, but the most advanced sections of the workers, organised by the National Union of the Working Classes and Others, whose leaders included Lovett, Hetherington and a number of others actively engaged in the Co-operative Movement, were already moving in the direction of independent working-class politics which led a few years later to Chartism.

The sense of betrayal which followed the passing of the Reform Act of 1832 greatly strengthened this tendency, but it led also, and more immediately, to a parallel movement in the direction of revolutionary Trade Unionism, the idea that a new society could be secured by industrial action. Owen's connexion with the Labour Exchanges had brought him into close contact with trade unionists, not only in London but also in provincial centres to which he went on propaganda tours. Trade Unionists began to form the bulk of his audiences, and in some cases it was the Unions which organised his meetings. He found an England in an extraordinary ferment of mingled hopes and despairs which made men eager to consider new solutions to their problems.

For a number of years, and especially since the repeal of the Combination Acts in 1824, the idea of a Trades Union had been gaining ground. At this time most existing unions were not only confined to a particular craft but to a particular locality or area—the idea of a national union covering all workers in a single craft or industry was only beginning to arise, and such national unions as did exist tended to be temporary and far from inclusive. In the industrial struggles of the time these local craft unions found they were seldom strong enough to defeat the much better organised employers, especially as these usually had the active support of the State apparatus. So attempts were constantly made, like that of John Doherty, a convinced Owenite who was the outstanding figure in Lancashire trade unionism, to form a Trades Union, on a federal basis, which would eventually include all workers of all industries in all parts of Britain.

They did not meet with much success, but attempts to form a national organisation for a single industry fared better, especially among the Builders, who in 1830 formed a Builders' Parliament which included not only all sections of craftsmen but attempted to organise on the one hand the architects and on the other the labourers. It was to these provincial workers that Owen's ideas made the strongest appeal. They were, on the whole, of a different stamp from the London artisans with whom he had been dealing, less sophisticated, less sceptical and perhaps also less limited in their outlook. They were also poorer and more exploited, and so less ready to await the outcome of a slow process of education and propaganda.

Their attitude to Owen was consequently much less

critical. James Morrison, one of the most capable of the Builders' leaders, wrote to him:

> 'I hope you will not hesitate to tell me my errors, my prejudices and my natural discrepancies. Your doctrines have made me a better and happier being. . . . Be then my Physician—I put my case in your hands. Give me your counsel—your practice inspires my perfect confidence.'[1]

Similarly Joseph Hansom, a Birmingham architect who played a leading part in forming the Builders' Guild, writes to Owen in 1833:

> 'We have been reading your Manifesto [XII, 3] this morning together, and were particularly struck with the force of its truth. There does indeed seem to be a new life producing to us, and a new light wherewith to see things . . . The Builders are a beautiful class of men to operate, with their minds less sophisticated than others, yet tutored to a great extent in practical knowledge.'[2]

This receptive and explosive world of trade unionism, so new to Owen, must have intoxicated him and sent his hopes soaring with the possibility of using the movement as a means of establishing his socialist commonwealth. He began to dream of a society in which the unions became productive bodies, dominating the industries which they covered, and ultimately replacing the State by a network of inter-related producers' co-operatives. He believed that this could be done quite peacefully, and opposed any idea of class struggle. The workers, inevitably, saw things differently. While they were, many of them, ready to welcome Owen's utopian vision with enthusiasm, they were in practice engaged in class struggle every day of their

[1] R. W. Postgate, *The Builders' History*, 83. [2] ibid., 85.

lives, and for them the unions remained, as they had always been, primarily a means of defending or improving their actual conditions of life, an aspect of things with which Owen hardly concerned himself at all.

In the long run, therefore, conflict between Owen and the mass of his followers was inevitable, but this was not immediately apparent, and Owen's great national prestige made him at the outset a welcome and universally respected leader. It is hardly an exaggeration to say that his adhesion gave trade unionism a new national standing.

The first steps were taken by the builders. In September 1833 the Builders' Parliament met at Manchester and heard Owen expound his plans. The Union virtually transformed itself into a National Guild, which planned to organise production in such a way as to make the capitalist master builders superfluous, to improve the living standards of its members, and to begin the 'reeducation' of them and their children which would 'enable them to become better Architects and Builders of the human character, intellectually and morally, than the world has yet known or even deemed to be practicable.'[1] (XII, 3.)

The Guild secured a few small contracts and began to build a Guildhall in Birmingham which would serve as a national headquarters. From the start, however, it met with opposition from the masters, who in many places refused to employ anyone who would not sign a declaration, known as 'the Document', that they were not members of the Union and would not support it in any way. In other places the Union made demands for higher wages, or for control of the conditions under which contracts were accepted. All over the country there were local, stubbornly contested strikes and lockouts, which soon strained the resources of the Union to the utmost.

The Builders were only a part of a much wider movement. In October Owen presided at a conference in

[1] Postgate, op. cit., 465.

London which decided to form the all-embracing Trades Union which later adopted the name of the Grand National Consolidated Trades Union. Within a short time it claimed half a million members, and the total number of trade unionists throughout the country was estimated at a million. Many of these, no doubt, were members of existing unions which affiliated to the new organisation, but a great many new members were certainly made, often in areas and trades where unionism had previously been almost unknown. Quite early differences began to show themselves. The October Conference decided to call a further conference in the following March to draw up a formal constitution: in the event, a conference was called in February on Owen's personal initiative, an ominous indication of his impatience and disregard of democratic decisions. It was probably for this reason that the Builders did not attend and some other powerful groups were not represented on the Executive Council of the Consolidated Union. Nevertheless the conference was representative and enthusiastic, and adopted a constitution whose general aims clearly reflect Owen's views and influence, declaring,

'That, although the design of the Union, is, in the first instance, to raise the wages of the workmen, or prevent any further reduction therein, and to diminish the hours of labour, the great and ultimate object of it must be to establish the paramount rights of Industry and Humanity, by instituting such measures as shall effectually prevent the ignorant, idle, and useless part of society from having that undue control over the fruits of our toil, which through the agency of a vicious money system, they at present possess; and that, consequently, the Unionists should lose no opportunity of mutually encouraging and assisting each other in bringing about a different state of things, *in which the really useful and intelligent part of society only shall have*

*the direction of affairs, and in which well-directed
industry and virtue shall meet their just distinction and
reward, and vicious idleness its merited contempt and
destitution.'*[1]

There was a clearly expressed belief that the Union
would develop in such a way as to replace the existing
State and render it superfluous:

*'If every member of the Union be a constituent, and
the Union itself become a vital member of the State,
it instantly erects itself into a House of Trades which
must supply the place of the present House of Commons, and direct the commercial affairs of the country,
according to the will of the trades which compose the
associations of industry.'*[2]

Soon, however, the Union was facing external and
internal problems. In March the arrest and transportation
of six Dorset farm workers from the village of Tolpuddle
for the crime of administering oaths while forming a
branch showed that the Government meant to act forcibly
against what it regarded as a serious menace. The case
aroused general indignation, uniting all sections of the
working-class and radical movements from Cobbett and
Fielden to O'Connor and the Owenites and trade
unionists. At the same time, more strikes and lockouts
were taking place everywhere, and all those involved
expected help from the Union which it had no funds to
give.

Meanwhile, an open quarrel deloped, with Owen
opposed to James Morrison, editor of *The Pioneer*, the
Union's journal, and to J. E. Smith, editor of *The Crisis*,

[1] G. D. H. Cole, *Life of Robert Owen*, 335.

[2] *The Pioneer*, May 31st, 1834. From Max Morris: *From Cobbett to
the Chartists*.

which was more directly controlled by Owen. Owen accused them of preaching crude class hatred instead of concentrating on the peaceful transformation of society XII, 5). Smith wrote in *The Pioneer*:

'He means to work behind the curtain and yet be dictator. Now our move is to prevent this dictatorship, for we know it cannot be tolerated.'

By the summer Owen had closed down both journals and Smith and Morrison were driven out of the movement.

By this time the G.N.C.T.U. was virtually dead, destroyed by the attacks of employers and government, by the inadequacy of its organisation and by the confusion of its ideas. Owen acknowledged this, in effect, by calling a congress of his supporters in August to set up a new organisation, The British and Foreign Consolidated Association of Industry, Humanity and Knowledge, whose avowed purpose was to affect a reconciliation of classes throughout the country. Closing down *The Crisis*, he declared that its purpose had been served. The crisis was over, and the old world was about to pass away through a great moral revolution of the human mind. This new stage he proposed to signalise by a new journal, to be called *The New Moral World*.

His trade union supporters could not follow him on the new course. The G.N.C.T.U. continued for a few months in rapid decline till it finally disappeared, and with it ended Owen's influence over the mass of the workers. Henceforward Owenism was to continue as a sect, active and lively, but outside the main stream of working-class life. During the next few years there was a slow recovery of the trade union movement from the defeat of 1834, and a great political advance which led to the Chartist movement of 1837—48. With neither of these was Owen in any way directly concerned, though many Chartists as individuals were still influenced by his socialist ideas and looked towards some sort of Co-operative Commonwealth as an ultimate ideal. But they rejected his tactics, seeing that the first step was to win control of the State, and that this could only be done through political struggle. In this new stage, Owenism began to seem irrelevant to the great majority of the people.

Nevertheless it would be a mistake to regard this episode as effort wasted. For the first time the conception of the possibility of a completely new kind of society, based on equality and co-operation, had been put forward and had been accepted by thousands, perhaps by millions. The means by which Owen proposed to reach such a society were impracticable, the necessary conditions and forms of organisation did not yet exist, but the idea had been implanted and was never entirely to die. It is one of Owen's great positve achievements to have given to the masses in Britain their first conception of Socialism.

IX

Owen's Last Years

Owen was sixty-three in 1834: he was to live another twenty-four years, but it is important to remember that in 1834 he was already an old man by the standards of his time, and it is by the work he had done in these first sixty-three years, and not by the eccentricities of his old age, that he ought to be judged. And that work was surely substantial enough. Socialist thinker, enlightened industrialist, factory reformer, pioneer of education, founder, if almost by accident, of the Co-operative Movement, leader of a great episode in our trade union history: for any one of these things he would have deserved a place in history. Taken together they constitute a truly remarkable achievement, and we have no right to complain if he did not add anything significant to them in his last years.

Owenism, as an organised movement, now assumed a mainly propagandist character. The fall of the G.N.C.T.U. had brought down with it the Labour Exchanges, already in difficulties, and the productive Co-operative Societies which had throughout been closely connected with the trade unions. Some of the trading Co-operatives lasted longer, but very few survived to the time when Trading Co-operative Societies revived in a new form in the 1840's. The last of the series of Co-operative Congresses, which had begun in 1830, was the seventh in the spring of 1835, and both this and the sixth (March 1834) seem to have been quite small as compared with their predecessors. It is true they were succeeded by a series of Socialist Congresses, but whereas the Co-operative Congresses had been composed in the main of delegates from Societies, these latter were little more than public meetings of individual followers of Owen.

Nevertheless, it would be a mistake to underrate the extent and activity of the Owenite agitation. Active branches existed in scores of towns all over Britain, a number of full-time 'missionaries' were employed in lecturing and organisation, journals, pamphlets and leaflets were produced and distributed in large numbers and in the most important centres the Owenites had their own meeting places, often newly built and commonly known as Halls of Science. Holyoake, himself one of the most vigorous of these missionaries, writes of this time:

> *'In two years and a half two millions of tracts were circulated. At Manchester one thousand were distributed at public meetings every Sunday. In London 40,000 were given away in one year. During the Birmingham Congress half a million were dispersed. Fifty thousand copies of Mr. Owen's manifesto in reply to the Bishop of Exeter were sold. The outline of the rational system was translated into German, Polish and Welsh. At one meeting £50 was received for the sale of pamphlets. During one year fifty formal discussions were held with the clergy. During another 1,450 lectures were delivered, of which 604 were upon theology and ethics. Three hundred and fifty towns were regularly visited by missionaries, and the country was divided into fourteen missionary districts.'*[1]

As a result of all this, socialist and secularist ideas were widely circulated and influenced, directly or indirectly, a large part of what Engels calls the 'most educated and

---

[1] *History of Co-operation,* I, 244.

solid elements' of the working class. But far from being able, as Engels hoped in 1844, to advance to the standpoint of the working-class, Owenite Socialism as the years went by became more abstract and remote from reality. This is perhaps reflected in the grandiose titles of the organisations which succeeded one another but which in fact were only the same group under another name. Thus, the British and Foreign Consolidated Association of Industry, Humanity and Knowledge, formed in 1834, was replaced in 1835 by the Association of All Classes of All Nations, and this in 1839 by the Universal Community Society of Rational Religionists.

Meanwhile Owen, who since the *Report to the County of Lanark* had written little but a stream of manifestoes and addresses, began to produce a new series of books and pamphlets. The most substantial of these was *The Book of the New Moral World,* which appeared in parts between 1836 and 1844. It became a sort of sacred text for the Owenites, but in fact really adds nothing to what Owen had already written. Generally speaking, all his later books were more verbose and less carefully planned than those of the New Lanark period. The one which attracted most hostile attention was a pamphlet *The Marriages of the Priesthood of the Old Immoral World* (1835), expounding his unorthodox views about marriage and the family (XIV). Like his religious beliefs (XIII) these were made the excuse for the most unjust attacks upon Owen, and upon his Socialist ideas with which, in fact, they have little connexion.

Owenism also returned to the old idea of establishing a Community. Once again subscriptions were collected from the Owenite bodies all over the country, and more substantial sums were given by well-to-do-disciples. In 1839 about 500 acres of rather poor land were leased at Queenwood in Hampshire, and a start was made. Owen at first opposed the project on the grounds that the capital available was inadequate: he now said that £250,000 was the lowest sum with which a successful experiment could be made. Despite this, the attempt was made but soon began to encounter difficulties. In 1840 Owen formed a new body—the Home Colonisation Society—to raise additional capital, and in 1841 became Governor of the Community.

With the architect Joseph Hansom, who had earlier helped to form the Builder's Guild, he began construction at Queenwood on a magnificent scale. Both men were accustomed to think big, and they decided that every-thing about the new venture should be of the best: only the finest materials and craftsmanship were allowed, an excellent principle which swallowed up money as fast as Owen could collect it. At no time did the community ever approach the position of being self-supporting: few of the members, though they seem to have been of a better quality than those of New Harmony, were accustomed to the agricultural work, the necessary basis for such a venture.[1]

By 1844 the Owenite societies were becoming restive at the apparently never-ending demands Queenwood made upon them. At a Congress held in that year John Finch was elected President—a post hitherto automat-ically occupied by Owen—and resolutions were passed criticising Owen's administration. He at once resigned, and went to join his sons in the U.S.A. where he remained till 1847. In 1845 Queenwood was dissolved and the last and most ambitious experiment of its kind in Britain ended in a rather sordid legal squabble over the remain-ing assets.

---

[1] It is worth observing that the only community on Owenite lines which looked like being a success was that founded at Ralahine in Ireland under the influence of William Thompson. This was composed entirely of peasants, accustomed to hard work and plain living. It came to an end in 1833 only because the sympathetic land-owner on whose estate it was formed had to sell it to pay his gambling debts.

The failure of Queenwood and the dissatisfaction which accompanied it virtually ended Owenism as a serious movement. When Owen returned from the U.S.A. he continued to hold meetings, wrote books, organised conferences and sent out addresses to all and sundry (IX, 1, 2, 3) but less and less attention was paid to them and the number of his supporters steadily diminished.

While Queenwood, the last of the old-style Co-operative ventures, was struggling for life, the first venture in the new style was opening in the North. In 1843 a few weavers in Rochdale, Lancashire, Owenites and Chartists, opened a small shop for the sale of groceries. It was on the face of it, a typical enterprise like hundreds that had begun and ended during the previous dozen years. Its rules even contained the usual hope 'that as soon as practicable the Society shall proceed to arrange the powers of production, distribution, education and government; or, in other words, to establish a self-supporting home-colony of united interests, or to assist other Societies in establishing such colonies.[1]

While the Rochdale Pioneers thus paid tribute to Owenite orthodoxy they made it an empty tribute by arranging to pay out their profits in the form of a dividend on purchases to their members. This innovation proved a success, the society flourished, and during the next decade scores of similar societies grew up, established themselves permanently, and were the true originators of the Co-operative Movement in the form which we know today. With all this Owen had no direct connexion: as we have seen he took little interest in, and even despised, such trading concerns as a petty travesty of his great Plan for world regeneration. Yet it was the work of his followers, and without his inspiration they could never have moved. The vast movement which grew up from these beginnings is right in thinking of Owen as its founder, though he

[1] G. D. H. Cole, *Life of Robert Owen*, 303.

would probably have thought poorly of it if he could have seen how it was to develop. As it grew, many of those who had been his intimate followers turned towards the new Co-operation, especially after his death when there was not even the shadow of an Owenite movement in the old sense.

In Owen's old age the Messianism which lies at the back of all utopianism grew stronger (XVI, 2, 3). The true second coming, a universal Jerusalem, spirit forces guiding the rulers of the world, his old supporter the Duke of Kent making appointments with him through mediums (VIII, 4; XVI, 4), became hopelessly confused with the realities of everyday life. Yet Owen was never at any stage insane, and in these very years he wrote his best and most readable book, *The Life of Robert Owen written by Himself,* which appeared only a year before his death. This, I think, is one of the great autobiographies, and it is unfortunate that it was unfinished, taking the account only to about the end of the New Lanark period. It is a narrative which helps us to understand why Owen, with all his failings, some of which must have been infuriating, was not only respected but loved by everyone who knew him. Even those who disagreed or had quarrelled with him seldom spoke of him afterwards with anything but affection.

Up to the end he went on writing and speaking: in 1857 he presided at and constantly addressed a 'Congress of Advanced Minds' which was held in London and fully reported in his last periodical *The Millennial Gazette.* In 1858 he was interested in the formation of the National Association for the Promotion of Social Science, in which Lord Brougham was a leading spirit.[1] At the end of October, though ill, he insisted on travelling to Liverpool to address its annual conference. After doing so he was

[1] Lord Brougham, Lord Chancellor in the Whig government of 1830-5, an old friend of Owen.

escorted or carried out and had to be put to bed. Recovering, he suddenly decided to visit his birthplace, Newtown, which he had not seen since his boyhood. There he immediately began to arrange a series of lectures, but was clearly dying.

'Shortly before his death the local clergyman came to his bedside to offer him religious consolation. Owen declined the offer in the most decided manner, and when the minister asked him whether he did not regret having wasted his life in fruitless efforts, he made the proud rejoinder: "My life was not useless; I gave important truths to the world, and it was only for want of understanding that they were disregarded. I have been ahead of my time."'[1]

Shortly after, on November 17th, 1858, he died.

[1] Max Beer, *History of British Socialism*, II, 174.

X

Owen and the French Utopians

Owen was convinced of the absolute originality of his plan and of his ideas about human nature and society. All the same, as Engels has pointed out, these ideas derived to a great extent from the work of the French philosophers of the Enlightenment. Owen shared with them the conviction that the interests of the individual and society ought to coincide and that only a rational reorganisation of society could produce this result. He shared their complete confidence in the powers of reason, their rational and secularist optimism, and, finally, their certainty that education is capable of changing man and society. There is, he constantly declared, no obstacle but ignorance.

It is difficult to say to what extent this coincidence of views was due to his reading. We have no evidence to show that Owen had ever read, for example the works of Helvetius or Holbach, or even those of Volney, whose book, *The Ruins, or Meditations on the Revolutions of Empires* enjoyed a considerable popularity at the beginning of the nineteenth century. Yet he may very well have read at any rate some of these things, for a number were published in English in this period and quite widely discussed.

The question is anyhow of minor importance. The fact that the ideas of the Enlightenment were widely discussed is sufficient reason for us to assume that they were familiar to him, if only at second hand. In his early days he had been an active member of the Philosophical Society in Manchester, and one of his most important characteristics was his ability to grasp and assimilate any idea he needed for his special purposes. If he encountered these ideas in conversation rather than in books it would be all the easier to convince himself they had originated in his own mind. In this connexion the talks he had with the philosopher Godwin, with whom he became friendly in London in 1813, were perhaps of the greatest importance.

In the same kind of way Owen and the French utopian socialists, Saint-Simon and Fourier, would seem to have developed independently along paths that were often closely similar. Fourier, indeed, made some rather condescending remarks about Owen, and Fourier's system was the subject of a critical article in Owen's journal *The New Moral World* written by the young Owenite Goodwyn Barmby who had visited France and was well acquainted with French socialist writings. These comments, however, belong to a period well after the formation of Owen's ideas, and are no evidence that he had known of either Saint-Simon or Fourier during his experiments at New Lanark or when he was formulating his Plan for villages of co-operation.

Nevertheless the similarities remain striking and could have resulted from an infiltration of French utopian thinking, from the necessity of solving similar social problems, or, indeed, from a combination of both factors. A few of the more outstanding of these may be noted.

The first lies at the root of their social criticism. Owen condemned existing society, just as Saint-Simon and Fourier did, because of its irrationality. It is to this that they ascribe the origin of all human miseries. All other causes are secondary and derived. The remedy was the complete reconstruction of society on a new, rational basis.

Next we may note the insistence with which Owen declares that the old house must not be abandoned till the new one is ready (VIII, 5b) and compare this with the minute detail in which Fourier elaborates the features of his ideal phalanstery.

Another significant point is that they all, Saint-Simon and Fourier even more completely than Owen, rejected the conception of a class struggle. Like him they saw no need for political democracy and hoped confidently to win the support of governments and of the rich. In this respect Owen, at least during the period when he was engaged with the trade union movement and in close contact with working-class co-operators, was in advance of the French utopian socialists.

Finally, and this is perhaps a universal characteristic of utopians, all three were convinced that they alone, by an extraordinary effort of their own reasoning powers, had discovered the final solution to all the problems which confronted the human race. Fourier wrote, for example: 'I alone have confounded twenty centuries of political stupidity, and it is to me alone that present and future generations will owe the foundation of their immense happiness.'[1] This messianic streak has made it dificult for utopian socialists to admit, even to themselves, that they have any ideological ancestors.

One more relationship may be noted, that between Owen and Cabet. We know that during his exile in England from 1834 to 1839 Cabet had many contacts and discussions with Owen and his disciples. Even if he drew his inspiration more directly from Fourier, his system includes a number of features which show Owenite influence. These include his insistence upon rational dress and communal meals, both of which points are developed by Cabet with the utmost detail. At a somewhat later date Cabet's ideas in turn had some influence in England and were assimilated into the stream of Owenism.

[1] *Textes Choisis,* ed. Félix Armand, 11.

XI

Conclusion

It is illuminating to compare the estimates of Owen and his work made by Engels in 1844 and in 1878 (XVII, 7). At first sight they seem contradictory, till we remember the circumstances in which they were written. In 1844 Engels was actively involved in the struggles of Chartism, in the actual development of a political movement and a political party among the British workers. From this point of view, Owenite socialism, standing apart from and claiming to be above the struggle, had to be criticised: only by descending into the arena and accepting the standpoint of the masses could the positive side of Owenism be developed. In fact, as we have seen, it proved unable to do this, and socialism *in this form* virtually disappeared. Socialism reappeared a generation later only in a new, Marxist, form, into which the positive side of Owenism had been absorbed.

Yet without this positive side it would not now be remembered, and Engels writing in 1878, on the eve of the rebirth of socialism in Britain, realises that this is the side on which it is now useful to dwell, that the mistakes which destroyed it are no longer a source of weakness to the movement and may be ignored. Engels now insists on Owen's greatness and the contributions he made to the advance of the working class in a whole number of fields. In a sense, it is a question of the stages of development of the working class.

Utopian socialism is a natural product of the first stage of growth, when the working class is 'just separating itself from the propertyless masses as the nucleus of a new class, as yet quite incapable of independent political action, [and] appeared as an oppressed, suffering estate of society, to which, in its incapacity to help itself, help could be brought at most from outside, from above'.[1] At this stage Owen had a real contribution to make. He set before the masses the conception of a different social order, based on co-operation and not on competition. He showed that the growth of machine production and large-scale industry, far from being an evil in itself, made the advance to this new society both necessary and possible. He put forward the idea, developed by Thompson and others, that labour is the source of wealth and the measure of value. He put forward also the idea that labour was not necessarily man's curse but could be made a source of fuller life and happiness. In advocating the abolition of the antagonism between town and country and of the excessive division of labour Owen was sketching the new conception of the role and purpose of labour which Marx and Morris were later to extend. Owenite socialism, like Marxist socialism, leads us to see man as the measure and master of things, not as their victim or slave.

By doing all this he played a great part in the development of the working class itself, helping it to a better understanding of society and of its own tasks. In the generation after Owen began to write (1815-45) the British working class was able to make an immense advance, in organisation, in clarity of ideas, in confidence. It ceased to be merely 'a suffering estate' and began to make history, to set itself the objective of conquering State power as a means of transforming the conditions of life.

In reaching this stage it owed much to Owen, but by reaching it it outgrew him. As we have seen, his mind was

[1] *Anti-Dühring*, 290-1.

formed early and it is not really surprising, or greatly to his discredit, that he was unable to develop his ideas to keep pace with the development of the working class. In 1834, his utopian socialism, based on abstract reason, and to be imposed from above by a benevolent dictatorship, had ceased to correspond to the needs and realities of the situation.

It is perhaps also true that Owen's mechanical determinism led inevitably to a growing rigidity. He saw man as the product of his environment, his character automatically shaped by his heredity and environment. And of course, as compared with the theories that human nature is unchangeable or that man is inherently sinful, there is a side of Owen's idea which is both true and progressive. But such a doctrine cannot really account for change: if man is wholly the product of his circumstances, how can he transform them? Owen attempted to get round this problem by supposing that to him alone the truth had been opened, and if mankind would listen to him this truth would set it free.

He never realised, and indeed this was something not yet understood, that man and his environment are dialectically related, that man by his struggle with his environment transforms both himself and it, that history is, in fact, a process in which human struggle, and in particular the struggle of classes, leads from one stage to the next.

Owen lived in an age of bitter and increasing class struggles, but he never understood them. For him class struggle was merely the outcome of ignorance and could be abolished by demonstrating that it was unreasonable. For this reason, though the workers were attracted by the prospect of socialism as he presented it, he was never able to be an effective leader of a class on the move. It has often been said that on his return from the U.S.A. in 1829 Owen turned to the workers—this is true in the sense that he came to see the organised workers as a means of realising his Plan. But it is at least as true to say that the workers came to Owen, drawing him towards them, and, for a time, carrying him to an understanding which he would not otherwise have reached. They took from him not what he wished to give, nor what he thought he was giving, but what they needed from him—a confidence that if they were prepared to help themselves they could create a new society, and a conception of the shape which that society might take.

I have mentioned already the particular fields in which Owen was a pioneer, and in all these his contribution was important and will be remembered. But I think that in the end his place in the history of the Labour Movement will rest upon his part in developing the confidence and maturity of the British working class, the most advanced of its time in the world, at a critical stage of its growth.

PART TWO

Selected Writings

I

First Principles:
Human Nature and Environment

[All Owen's ideas were based on a few simple principles about human character, which can be summed up in his dictum that man's character is formed for him and not by him. He believed that to change environment was speedily and directly to transform human nature. This belief, supported by his experiences at New Lanark, remained unaltered by any subsequent experience.]

1* MAN'S CHARACTER IS FORMED FOR HIM

From the earliest ages it has been the practice of the world to act on the supposition that each individual man forms his own character, and that therefore he is accountable for all his sentiments and habits, and consequently merits reward for some and punishment for others. Every system which has been established among men has been founded on these erroneous principles. When, however, they shall be brought to the test of fair examination, they will be found not only unsupported, but in direct opposition to all experience, and to the evidence of our senses.

This is not a slight mistake, which involves only trivial consequences; it is a fundamental error of the highest possible magnitude, it enters into all our proceedings regarding man from his infancy; and it will be found to be the

* *New View*, Cole, 44-5.

true and sole origin of evil. It generates and perpetuates ignorance, hatred and revenge, where, without such error, only intelligence, confidence, and kindness would exist. It has hitherto been the Evil Genius of the world. It severs man from man throughout the various regions of the earth; and it makes enemies of those who, but for this gross error, would have enjoyed each other's kind offices and sincere friendship. It is, in short, an error which carries misery in all its consequences.

This error cannot much longer exist; for every day will make it more evident *that the character of man is, without a single exception, always formed for him; and that it may be, and is, chiefly created by his predecessors that they give him, or may give him, his ideas and habits, which are the powers that govern and direct his conduct. Man, therefore, never did, nor is it possible that he ever can, form his own character.*

The knowledge of this important fact has not been derived from any of the wild and heated speculations of an ardent and ungoverned imagination; on the contrary, it proceeds from a long and patient study of the theory and practice of human nature, under many varied circumstances; and it will be found to be a deduction drawn from such a multiplicity of facts, as to afford the most complete demonstration.

2* TRUE AND FALSE PRINCIPLES

Every society which now exists, as well as every society history records, has been formed and governed on a belief in the notions, assumed as *first principles:*

First—That it is in the power of every individual to form his own character.

Hence the various systems called by the name of religion, codes of law and punishments. Hence also the angry

* *New Lanark,* Cole, 109-110.

passions entertained by individuals and nations towards each other.

Second—That the affections are at the command of the individual.

Hence insincerity and degradation of character. Hence the miseries of domestic life, and more than one half of the crimes of mankind.

Third—That it is necessary that a large portion of mankind should exist in ignorance and poverty, in order to secure the remaining part such a degree of happiness as they now enjoy.

Hence a system of counteraction in the persuits of man, a general opposition among individuals to the interests of each other, and the necessary effects of such a system— ignorance, poverty, and vice.

Facts prove, however—

First—that character is universally formed *for,* and not *by* the individual.

Second—That *any* habits and sentiments may be given to mankind.

Third—That the affections are *not* under the control of the individual.

Fourth—That every individual may be trained to produce far more than he can consume, while there is a sufficiency of soil left for him to cultivate.

Fifth—That nature has provided means by which populations may be at all times maintained in the proper state to give the greatest happiness to every individual, without one check of vice or misery.

Sixth—That any community may be arranged, on a due combination of the foregoing principles, in such a manner, as not only to withdraw vice, poverty, and, in a great degree, misery, from the world, but also to place *every* individual under such circumstances in which he shall enjoy more permanent happiness than can be given to *any* individual under the principles which have hitherto regulated society.

Seventh—That all the assumed fundamental principles on which society has hitherto been founded are erroneous, and may be demonstrated to be contrary to fact. And—

Eighth—That the change which would follow the abandonment of these erroneous maxims which bring misery to the world, and the adoption of principles of truth, unfolding a system which shall remove and for ever exclude that misery, may be effected without the slightest injury to any human being.

3* CONDITIONS FOR HAPPINESS

A rational government . . . will know that the following conditions are requisite to the attainment of happiness by human nature:

1st. To have a good organisation at birth; and to acquire an accurate knowledge of its organs, faculties, propensities, and qualities.

2nd. To have the power of procuring at pleasure whatever is necessary to preserve the organisation in the best state of health; and to know the best mode by which to produce and distribute these requisites, for the enjoyment of all.

3rd. To receive from birth the best cultivation of our natural powers—physical, mental, moral, and practical —and to know how to give this training and education to others.

4th. To have the knowledge, the means, and the inclination, to promote continually, and without exception, the happiness of our fellow-beings.

5th. To have the inclination and means to increase continually our stock of knowledge.

6th. To have the power of enjoying the best society—

* *Revolution,* 53-4.

and more especially of associating, at pleasure, with those for whom we feel the greatest regard and affection.

7th. To have the means of travelling at pleasure, with pleasure.

8th. To have full liberty to express our thoughts upon all subjects.

9th. To have the utmost individual freedom of action, compatible with the permanent good of society.

10th. To have the character formed for us to express the truth only, in look, word, and action, upon all occasions—to have pure charity for the feelings, thoughts and conduct of all mankind—and to have a sincere good-will for every individual of the human race.

11th. To be without superstition, supernatural fears, and the fear of death.

12th. To reside in a society well situated, well organised, and well governed, whose laws, institutions, and arrangements, are all in unison with the laws of human nature; and to know the best means by which, in practice, to combine all the requisites to form such society.

4* OWEN'S MILLENNIUM

What ideas individuals may attach to the Millennium I know not; but I know that society may be formed so as to exist without crime, without poverty, with health greatly improved, with little, if any, misery, and with happiness increased a hundred-fold; and no obstacle whatsoever intervenes at this moment, except ignorance, to prevent such a state of society from becoming universal.

5** OWEN'S ENLIGHTENMENT

Causes, over which I have no control, removed in my early days the bandage which covered my mental sight. If I

* *New Lanark*, Cole, 108.   ** *New Lanark*, Cole, 106.

have been enabled to discover this blindness with which my fellow-men are afflicted, to trace their wanderings from the path which they were most anxious to find, and at the same time to perceive that relief could not be administered to them by any premature disclosure of their unhappy state, it is not from any merit of mine; nor can I claim any personal consideration whatever for having been myself relieved from this unhappy situation. But, beholding such truly pitiable objects around me, and witnessing the misery which they hourly experienced by falling into the dangers and evils by which, in these paths, they were on every side surrounded, could I remain an idle spectator? Could I tranquilly see my fellow-men walking like idiots in every imaginable direction, except that alone in which the happiness they were in search of could be found?

6* CHARACTER AND ENVIRONMENT: A PRISON EXPERIENCE

Having heard from various quarters what highly beneficial effects had been produced by Mrs. Fry, of St. Mildred's Court, Poultry, among the female prisoners in Newgate, I yesterday by previous appointment, accompanied that Lady, and was conducted by her through all the apartments of the prison occupied by the unfortunate females of every description. I shall not easily, if ever, forget the impressions I experienced; they were of a mixed and very opposite nature. In passing from room to room we were met in every instance (there was not one exception) with kind looks and the most evident feelings of affection in every prisoner towards Mrs. Fry. Not a feature in the countenance of any, however hardened they might have been on entering the prison, that did not evince, in strongest expression than language can define, their love and admiration for what she had done for them. With an

* *Catechism,* Cole, 185-7.

alacrity and pleasure that could be commended in the best-trained children in attending to parental requests, they were ready and willing to comply with her advice. It was evidently a heartfelt consolation to these poor creatures to know her wishes, that they might show their gratitude by an immediate compliance with them. She spoke in manner and voice the language of confidence, kindness, and commiseration to each; and she was replied to in such accordant feelings as are, and ever will be, produced in human beings, whenever they shall be spoken to and treated thus rationally. On quitting the prison the eyes of all were directed towards her until she was no longer in their sight. The apartments and the persons of the prisoners were clean and neat; order, regularity, decency and almost cheerful content pervaded the whole of these heretofore miserable and degraded wretches! With the constant habit, for years, of reading the mind in the countenance among the lower classes, I could not discover, throughout the numerous apartments we visited, one line of feature that denoted any inclination to resist, in the slightest degree, Mrs. Fry's wishes; but, on the contrary, the looks and manner of each female prisoner strongly indicated a full acquiescence in this new government of well-directed kindness. The only regret I heard expressed was by those who were unemployed, 'that they had no work'. All who had something to do were far more cheerful than I had previously supposed human beings could be in the situation, with the accommodation and under the circumstances here described. We next proceeded to the female school; and, on entering, every eye was fixed on their benefactress. The little girls, children of the prisoners and convicts, looked on her as human creatures might be imagined to look upon beings of a superior, intelligent, and beneficent nature. They were all clean and neat; and some of their countenances very interesting. The school was in excellent order, and appeared to be under good management.

I could not avoid contrasting the present with the former situation of all these poor unfortunates. What a change they must have experienced! from filth, bad habits, vice, crime—from the depth of degradation and wretchedness—to cleanliness, good habits, and comparative comfort and cheerfulness! Had not certain experience long made known to me the simplicity and certain effects of the principles which had here been carried into practice, I might have been led to inquire what profound statesman had been here? What large sums had been expended, How many years of active and steady perseverance had been necessary to accomplish this extraordinary improvement, which had foiled even the British Government and Legislature to effect during the centuries they have existed? And what would have been my astonishment at the simple narrative which was told me? That this change, from the depth of misery to the state described, was effected by Mrs. Fry and a few benevolent individuals of the Society of Friends, in three months, without any increased expense, and with feelings of high gratification to herself!

We left the female side of the prison, and passed to the rooms, courts, &c., occupied by the males. We went first to the boys' court, and found the school, which was formed at Mrs. Fry's request, had just been dismissed. The person acting as master asked if he should muster the boys; to which she consented, and it was instantly done. What a melancholy sight did they offer! A collection of boys and youths with scarcely the appearance of human beings in their countenance; the most evident sign that the Government to which they belong had not performed any part of its duty towards them. For instance; there was one boy, only sixteen years of age, double-ironed! Here a great crime has been committed, and a severe punishment has been inflicted, which under a system of proper training and prevention would not have taken place.

Lord Sidmouth will forgive me, for he knows I intend no personal offence. His dispositions are known to be mild and amiable; but the Chief Civil Magistrate of the country, in such a case, is far more guilty than the boy; and, in strict justice, if a system of coercion and punishment be rational and necessary, he ought rather to have been double-ironed, and in the place of the boy. The Secretary of State for the Home Department has long had the power, and ought to have used it, to give that boy, and every other boy in the Empire, better habits, and to place them under circumstances that would train them to become moral.

We left these boys, and visited the men who were yet to be tried, those who had been tried, and others under sentence of death. Everything of this side of the prison was most revolting to common sense and human feelings; but it serves to exhibit the contrast between the practice that results, and will ever result, from acting upon rational and irrational principles. I wish the Members of Government would now investigate these extraordinary facts. If they were to inspect them, with this benevolent female, I am sure they would learn the principles which have guided her practice, and adopt them in all their future measures. They would then enjoy only the highest satisfaction.

It was admitted by the attendants of the prison, that a few months ago the women were more depraved than the men are now; they were both proclaimed to be irreclaimable: but the state of the female prison has been entirely changed, and that in the short space of three months; notwithstanding this fact, the men are still pronounced to be irreclaimable!

7* OUR SOCIETY MANUFACTURES CRIMINALS

How much longer shall we continue to allow generation after generation to be taught crime from their infancy, and

* *New View*, Cole, 25.

when so taught, hunt them like beasts of the forests, until they are entangled beyond escape in the toils and nets of the law? when, if the cxircumstances of those poor unpitied sufferers had been reversed with those who are even surrounded with the pomp and dignity of justice, these latter would have been at the bar of the culprit, and the former would have been at the judgement seat.

Had the present Judges of these realms been born and educated among the poor and profligate of St. Giles, or some similar situation, is it not certain, inasmuch as they possess native energies and abilities, that ere this they would have been at the head of their *then* profession, and, in consequence of that superiority and proficiency, would already have suffered imprisonment, transportation or death? Can we for a moment hesitate to decide, that if some of those men whom the laws dispensed by the present Judges have doomed to suffer capital punishments, had been born, trained and circumstanced as these Judges were born, trained and circumstanced, that some of those who had so suffered would have been the identical individuals who would have passed the same awful sentences on the present highly esteemed dignitaries of the law.

8* WOULD OWEN'S PLAN CREATE PAUPERISM?

[Owen here replies to Cobbett and other critics. Cobbett had described his village communities as 'parallelograms of paupers'. See also XVII, 2.]

I would here beg leave to ask these gentlemen—

If to train a child carefully and well, from earliest infancy, be a likely means to create, increase and perpetuate pauperism?

If to instruct a child in accurate and correct knowledge of facts be a likely means to create, increase and perpetuate pauperism?

* *Catechism*, Cole, 195-6.

If to give a child health, kind and benevolent dispositions, other good habits, and an active and cheerful industry, be a likely means to create, increase and perpetuate pauperism?

If, among the working classes, to instruct each male in the practice and knowlede of gardening, of agriculture, and in at least some one other trade, manufacture or occupation—if to instruct each female in the best method of treating infants and training children, in all the usual domestic arrangements to make themselves and others comfortable—in the practice and knowledge of gardening, and in some one useful, light and healthy manufacture; I ask if all or any of these parts of the plan be a likely means to create, increase and perpetuate pauperism?

If to remove the causes of ignorance, anger, revenge and every evil passion, be a likely means to create, increase and perpetuate pauperism?

If to train the whole population of a country to be temperate, industrious, and moral, be a likely means to create, increase and perpetuate pauperism?

If to unite in cordial union and mutual co-operation, without one feeling of distrust on the part of any, be a likely means to create, increase or perpetuate pauperism?

If to increase the wealth of the world fourfold, perhaps tenfold, not improbably a hundredfold—be a likely means to create, increase or perpetuate pauperism?

But I might proceed to ask these gentlemen many other questions, and to which, perhaps, they would not make so ready a reply as to those now put: one, however, shall suffice.

How do they propose to relieve the people from the ignorance, distress, and immorality with which the country abounds; and which, if not speedily checked, must soon overwhelm all ranks in one general scheme of confusion, disorder, and ruin?

II

Boyhood and Early Life

[In Owen's early life we can see the formation of many of the traits so characteristic of his maturity. Everything he did and was, was based on his personal experiences.]

1* OWEN LOOKS BACK AT HIS LIFE

The mission of my life appears to be, to prepare the population of the world to understand the vast importance of the second creation of Humanity, from the birth of each individual, through the agency of man, by creating entirely new surroundings in which to place all through life, and by which a new human nature would appear to arise from the new surroundings.

In taking a calm retrospect of my life from the earliest remembered period of it to the present hour, there appears to me to have been a succession of extraordinary or out-of-the-usual events, forming connected links of a chain, to compel me to proceed onward to complete a mission, of which I have been a compelled agent, without merit or demerit on my part.

That mission has been to point out to humanity the way to remove from it the cause of sin and misery, and how in place thereof to attain for all our race in perpetuity a new existence of universal goodness, wisdom and

* *Life,* xii.

happiness, and to withdraw from man all unkindness to man and even to animal life over the earth, so far as may be consistent with his own happy progress while upon it.

2 CHILDHOOD IN NEWTON

(a)* In schools in these small towns it was considered a good education if one could read fluently, write a legible hand, and understand the fiirst four rules of arithmetic. And this I have reason to believe was the extent of Mr. Thickness's qualifications for a schoolmaster—because when I had acquired these small rudiments of learning, at the age of seven, he applied to my father for permission that I should become his assistant and usher, as from that time I was called while I remained at school. As I remained at school about two years longer, those two years were lost to me, except that I thus early acquired the habit of teaching others what I knew.

But at this time I was very fond of and had a strong passion for reading everything which fell my way. As I was known to and knew every family in the town, I had the libraries of the clergyman, physician, and lawyer—the learned men of the town—thrown open to me, with permission to take home any volume which I liked, and made full use of the liberty given to me.

Among the books I selected at this period were *Robinson Crusoe, Philip Quarle, Pilgrim's Progress, Paradise Lost,* Harvey's *Meditations among the Tombs,* Young's *Night Thoughts,* Richardson's, and all the other standard novels. I believed every word of them to be true, and was therefore deeply interested; and I generally finished a volume daily. Then I read Cook's and all the circumnavigators' voyages—*The History of the World*, Rollin's *Ancient History*—and all the lives I could meet with of the philosophers and great men.

* *Life,* 3-4.

(b)*   During my childhood, and for many years afterwards, it never occurred to me that there was anything in
my habits, thoughts, and actions different from those of
others of my age; but when looking back and comparing
my life with many others, I have been induced to attribute
my favourable difference to the effects produced at the
early period when my life was endangered by the spoon-
ful of scalding flummery. Because from that time I was
compelled to notice the effects produced by different kinds
of food on my constitution, which had been also deeply
injured in its powers of digestion. I could not eat and
drink as others of my age, and I was thus compelled to
live in some respects the life of a hermit as regards tem-
perance. I entered, however, into the amusements of those
of my own standing, and followed the games played by
boys of that period in that part of the country—such as
marbles, hand and foot ball, etc. I also attended the dancing school for some time, and in all those games and exercises I excelled not only those of my own age, but those
two or three years older, and I was so active that I was
the best runner and leaper, both as to height and distance,
in the school. I attempted also to learn music, and to play
upon the clarionet, and during my noviciate, as my father's
house was in the middle of the principal street, I fear I
must have annoyed all the neighbourhood—for my
'God Save the King' and similar tunes were heard all
over the town. But I do not recollect that any formal complaint was ever made. I was too much of a favourite with
the whole town for my benefit, and was often pitted
against my equals, and sometimes against my superiors in
age—sometimes for one thing and sometimes for another.
I have often since reflected how unjust such proceedings
are in principle, and how injurious in practice. One instance of this made a deep impression on my mind. Some
party bet that I could write better than my next eldest

* *Life*, 3-6.

86

brother John, who was two years older; and upon a formal trial, at which judges were appointed, it was decided that my writing was better, although so far as I could then form an opinion I thought my brothers' was as good as my own. From that day I do not think my brother had as strong an affection for me as he had before this unwise competition.

3* APPRENTICE TO FLINT AND PALMER ON LONDON BRIDGE

I was lodged and boarded in the house, and had a salary of twenty-five pounds a year, and I thought myself rich and independent, for I had more than sufficient to supply all my personal wants. Soon, however, as the spring advanced, I found this was a different situation to the one I had enjoyed at Stamford. The customers were of an inferior class—they were treated differently. Not much time was allowed for bargaining, a price being fixed for everything, and, compared with other houses, cheap. ... But to the assistants in this busy establishment the duties were very onerous. They were up and breakfasted and were ready to receive customers in the shop at eight o'clock; and dressing then was no slight affair. Boy as I then was, I had to wait my turn for the hairdresser to powder and pomatum and curl my hair, for I had two large curls on each side, and a stiff pigtail, and until all this was very nicely and systematically done, no one could think of appearing before a customer. Between eight and nine the shop began to fill with purchasers, and their number increased until it was crowded to excess, although a large apartment, and this continued until late in the evening; usually until ten, or halfpast ten, during all the spring months. Dinner and tea were hastily taken—two or three, sometimes only one, escaping at a time to take what he or she could most

* *Life*, 25-7.

easily swallow, and returning to take the place of others who were serving. The only regular meals at this season were our breakfasts, except on Sundays, on which days a good dinner was always provided, and was much enjoyed. But when the purchasers left at ten or halfpast ten, before the shop could be quite clear a new part of the business was commenced. The articles dealt in as haberdashery were innumerable, and these when exposed to the customers were tossed and tumbled and unfolded in the utmost confusion and disorder, and there was not time to put anything right and in order during the day. This was a work to be performed with closed doors after the customers had been shut out at eleven o'clock; and it was often two o'clock in the morning before the goods in the shop had been put in order and replaced to be ready for the next day's similar proceedings. Frequently at two o'clock in the morning, after being actively engaged on foot all day from eight o'clock in the morning, I have scarcely been able with the aid of the banisters to go upstairs to bed. And then I had about five hours for sleep. . . .

The spring trade ceased, and the business gradually became less onerous. We could take our meals with some comfort, and retire to rest between eleven and twelve, and by comparison this became an easy life. I was kindly treated.

4 THE GROUND FLOOR OF THE
INDUSTRIAL REVOLUTION

(a)*   [Owen, now a draper's apprentice in Manchester, meets mechanic named Jones.]

. . . and he begins to tell me about the great and extraordinary discoveries that were beginning to be introduced

* *Life*, 30-36.

into Manchester for spinning cotton by new and curious machinery. . . . At length he told me he had succeeded in seeing these machines at work, and he was sure he could make them and work them. He had, however, no capital, and he could not begin without some. He said that with one hundred pounds he could commence and soon accumulate capital sufficient to proceed; and he ended by saying that if I would advance one hundred pounds, I should have one half of the great profits that were to result if I would join him in partnership. . . . I wrote to my brother William in London, to ask him if he could conveniently advance me the sum required, and he immediately sent me the hundred pounds. . . . We had shortly about forty men at work to make machines, and we obtained wood, iron, and brass, for their construction, upon credit.

I soon found however that Jones was a mere working mechanic, without any idea how to manage workmen, or how to conduct a business on the scale on which we had commenced.

I had not the slightest knowledge of this new machinery —had never seen it at work. . . . I looked very wisely at the men in their different departments, although I really knew nothing. But by intensely observing everything, I maintained order and regularity throughout the establishment, which proceeded under such circumstances far better than I had anticipated. We made what are technically called 'mules' for spinning cotton, sold them, and appeared to be carrying on a good business; while, having discovered the want of business capacity in my partner, I proceeded with fear and trembling. [Jones soon found a new partner and Owen was squeezed out of the business.]

They offered to give me for my share in the business six mule machines such as we were making for sale, a reel and a making up machine, with which to pack the yarn when finished in skeins into bundles for sale. I had now, when about nineteen years of age, to begin the world on my own account, having the promise of the machinery named to commence with. . . .

From Jones and his new partner I received *three* out of *six* mule machines which were promised, with the reel and making up machine. . . . Seeing I was not likely to obtain more machinery from my former partner I made up my mind to do as well as I could with that amount which I had obtained. With the three men spinning for me, reeling, and making up that which they spun, and by selling it weekly to Mr. Mitchell, I made on the average six pounds of profit a week and deemed myself doing well for a young beginner. . . .

About this period cotton spinning was so profitable that it began to engage the attention of many parties with capitals.

(b)* [A Mr. Drinkwater advertised for a manager for a big new spinning mill.]

I put on my hat and proceeded straight to Mr. Drinkwater's counting-house, and boy, and inexperienced, as I was, I asked him for the situation for which he had advertised. . . . He said immediately—'You are too young'—and at that time being fresh coloured I looked younger than I was. I said, 'That was an objection made to me four or five years ago, but I did not expect it would be made to me now.' 'How old are you?' 'Twenty in May this year'—was my reply. 'How often do you get drunk in the week?' (This was a common habit with almost all persons in Manchester and Lancashire at that period.) 'I was never', I said, 'drunk in my life'—blushing scarlet at this unexpected question. My answer and the manner of it made, I suppose, a favourable impression; for the next question was—'What salary do you ask?' 'Three hun-

* *Life,* 37.

dred a year'—was my reply. ' What?' Mr. Drinkwater said, with some surprise, repeating the words—'Three hundred a year! I have had this morning I know not how many seeking the situation, and I do not think that all their askings together would amount to what you require.' 'I cannot be governed by what others may ask,' said I, 'and I cannot take less. I am now making that sum by my own business.' 'Can you prove that to me?' 'Yes, I will show you the business and my books.' 'Then I will go with you, and let me see them', said Mr. Drinkwater. [Owen proved his profits, got the job, and made a great success of it.]

(c)* Some idea may be formed of the success of the manufacture in which I was engaged for Mr. Drinkwater from the fact that I gave five shilling a pound for cotton, which, when finished into fine thread for the muslin weaver, extending to near 250 hanks in the pound, I sold for £9/18/6 per pound. This was sold at the commencement of 1792 to Alexander Speirs of Kilbarchan, who made it into muslins, the first piece of which he sent as a present, as the greatest curiosity of British manufacture, to old Queen Charlotte. I extended afterwards the fineness of the thread to upwards of 300 hanks in the pound, and if this had been sold at the same period, it would have brought upwards of thirty-six pounds sterling for one pound of the yarn; but this prosperity in the manufacture was checked by the war with France, and the same high prices were I believe never afterwards obtained for the same fineness or number of hanks.

My name was now up for being the finest cotton spinner in the world, and this was my standing as long as I remained the manager of Mr. Drinkwater's factory.

* *Life,* 48.

(a)* I have mentioned my knowledge of Mr. Robert Spear, the Manchester cotton, broker, who sent me the first two bags of American Sea Island cotton imported into this country. He had a sister, whom I also knew, and who was living with him in Manchester. This sister happened to be on a visit to the family of Mr. Dale, who was then one of the most extraordinary men in the commercial world of Scotland—an extensive manufacturer, cotton spinner, merchant, banker and preacher. He had five daughters—the eldest then about nineteen. While I was one day walking in Glasgow, near to the Cross, the most public place in the city, I met Miss Spear in company with Miss Dale. Miss Spear was glad to meet one whom she knew from Manchester, and stopped me, introducing me at the same time to Miss Dale. I conversed some time with Miss Spear concerning our friends in Manchester. After a short time Miss Dale asked me if I had seen the Falls of Clyde and her father's mills, for if I had not, and wished to see them, she would give me an introduction to her uncle who was one of the managers of the mills and who lived there. I thanked her, and said I had a friend with me in Glasgow, and we should both like to see the falls and the mills. She said she would like to know what we thought of them after we had seen them and returned. The introduction was sent for me and my friend, and we visited this to us new scenery, and inspected the mills under the guidance of Mr. James Dale, who, I learned, was half-brother to Mr. David Dale, the father of Miss Dale. When I had inspected the establishment which was called the 'New Lanark Mills', and which then consisted of a primitive manufacturing Scotch village and four mills for spinning cotton, I said to my friend, as I stood in front of the establishment, 'Of all places I have

* *Life*, 63.

yet seen, I should prefer this in which to try an experiment I have long contemplated and have wished to have an opportunity to put into practice; not in the least supposing at the moment that there was the most distant chance that the wish would ever be gratified.

(b)* [A] second visit to Glasgow I found was beginning to create other feelings than those of mere business. As I was now established as a partner in one of the most respectable firms in Manchester, and with every appearance of being successful, I felt inclined to look out for a wife. But I was yet a novice, and backward in forming acquaintance with women and was much too sensitive in my feelings to make any progress with them except I received encouragement to overcome my diffidence. [Later, Miss Spear spoke to Owen about Miss Dale, saying] 'When we parted, she asked me who you were, and all respecting you that I knew, and when I had satisfied her inquiries, she said, "I do not know how it is—but if I ever marry, that is to be my husband." I tell you this because I know you will make only a proper use of it.' . . . . Without this knowledge I do not think I should ever have ventured to think of Miss Dale for a wife.

[Mr. Dale was at first opposed to Owen as a son-in-law, and it was in the course of pressing his suit that Owen in partnership with some Manchester business men, acquired the New Lanark Mills. He married on September 30th, 1797.]

* *Life,* 65, 69.

III

Owen at New Lanark

[Owen went to New Lanark an unknown Manchester manufacturer: it was his work there which made him a nationally famous figure and gave him an audience for his social theories. See also Chapters VI, for pauper apprentices, and VII for the New Lanark schools.]

1 WHAT OWEN FOUND AT NEW LANARK

(a)*   In the year 1784 the late Mr. Dale, of Glasgow, founded a manufactory for spinning cotton, near the falls of the Clyde, in the county of Lanark, in Scotland; and about that period cotton mills were first introduced into the northern part of the kingdom.

It was the power which could be obtained from the falls of water that induced Mr. Dale to erect his mills in this situation; for in other respects it was not well chosen. The country around was uncultivated; the inhabitants were poor and few in number; and the roads in the neighbourhood were so bad, that the Falls, now so celebrated, were then unknown to strangers. It was therefore necessary to collect a new population to supply the infant establishment with labourers. . . . Those who have a practical knowledge of mankind will readily anticipate the

* *New View,* Cole, 26-7.

character which a population so collected and constituted would acquire.

(b)*   I soon found that I had every bad habit and practice of the people to overcome. They were intemperate and immoral, with very few exceptions, throughout the whole establishment. The brother of one of the chief managers was in the frequent practice of taking what is called a *'spree'*—that is being intoxicated day after day weeks together, without attending to his occupation during the whole period. Theft was very general, and was carried on to an enormous and ruinous extent, and Mr. Dale's property had been plundered in all directions, and had been considered almost public property. The population had been collected from anywhere and anyhow, for it was then most difficult to induce any sober, well-doing family to leave their home to go into cotton mills as then conducted.

(c)**   The population of New Lanark at this period consisted of about 1,300, settled in the village as families, and between 400 and 500 pauper children, procured from the parishes, whose ages appeared to be from five to ten —but said to be from seven to twelve. These children were by Mr. Dale's directions well lodged, fed, and clothed, and there was some attempt made to teach them to read and to teach some of the oldest to write, after the business of the long day was over. But this kind of instruction, when the strength of the children was exhausted, only tormented them, without doing any real good—for I found that none of them understood anything they attempted to read, and many of them fell asleep during the school hours.

The instructor was a good schoolmaster, on the old mode of teaching, and kind and considerate to the chil-

* *Life,* 79-80. ** *Life,* 83-4.

dren, but what could he do with 400 or 500 of them under such circumstances? The whole system, although most kindly intended by Mr. Dale, was wretchedly bad, and the establishment had been constructed and managed by ordinary minds, accustomed only to very primitive proceedings. I determined therefore that the engagements made by Mr. Dale with the parishes, should run out; that no more pauper children should be received; that the village houses and streets should be improved, and new and better houses erected to receive new families to replace the pauper children; and that the interior of the mills should be rearranged, and the old machinery replaced by new. But these changes were to be made gradually and to be effected by the profits of the establishment.

2* OWEN'S FIRST STEPS

In addition to these evil conditions around the workpeople, I found it necessary, as the foundation of all future success, to make the establishment not only selfsupporting, but also productive of sufficient surplus profit to enable me to effect the changes to the improved conditions which I contemplated. My partners were all commercial men, and expected a profit in addition to interest for their capital. I had therefore to readjust the whole business arrangements, and to make great alterations in the building and gradually to change the whole machinery of the mills.

The work-people were systematically opposed to every change which I proposed, and did whatever they could to frustrate my object. . . . My intention was to gain their confidence, and this, from their prejudice to a stranger from a foreign country, as at this time the working class of Scotland considered England to be, was extremely

* *Life,* 86-8.

difficult to attain. My language was naturally different from their Lowland Scotch and the Highland Erse, for they had a large number of Highlanders among them. I therefore sought out the individuals who had the most influence among them from their natural powers or position, and to these I took pains to explain what were my intentions for the changes I wished to effect. . . .

By these means I began slowly to make an impression upon some of the least prejudiced and most reasonable among them; but the suspicions of the majority, that I only wanted, as they said, to squeeze as much gain out of them as possible, were long continued. I had great difficulty also in teaching them cleanly habits, and order and system in their proceedings. Yet each year a sensible general improvement was effected.

The retail shops, in all of which spirits were sold, were great nuisances. All the articles sold were bought on credit at high prices, to cover great risks. The qualities were most inferior, and they were retailed out to the work-people at extravagant rates. I arranged superior stores and shops, from which to supply every article of food, clothing, etc., which they required. I bought everything in the first markets, and contracted for fuel, milk, etc., on a large scale and had the whole of these articles of the best qualities supplied to the people at cost price. . . .

The effect of this soon became visible in their improved health and superior dress, and in the general comfort of their houses.

[In 1806 a trade crisis gave Owen his opportunity. Instead of closing the mills, he says,] I therefore concluded to stop all the machinery, retain the people, and continue to pay them their full wages for only keeping the machinery clean and in good working condition . . . . and during that period the population of New Lanark received more than seven thousand pounds sterling for their unemployed time, without a penny being deducted from the full wages of anyone.

These proceedings won the confidence and hearts of the whole population, and henceforward I had no obstructions from them in my progress of reform, which I continued in all ways, as far as I thought my monied partners would permit me to proceed, and indeed until their mistaken notions stopped my further progress.

[David Dale had acted in a similar manner some years earlier, when part of the mills was destroyed by fire.]

3* THE SILENT MONITOR

I was greatly averse to punishments, and much preferred as far as possible simple means to render punishment unnecessary, as it is always unjust to the individual. To prevent punishment by the overlooker and masters of departments who had been accustomed to whip and strap the young people, and who often from ignorance abused their authority, I invented what the people soon called a telegraph.

This consisted of a four-sided piece of wood, about two inches long, and one broad, each side coloured—one side black, another blue, the third yellow, and the fourth white, tapered at the top, and finished with wire eyes, to hang upon a hook with either side to the front. One of these was suspended in a conspicious place near to each of the persons employed, and the colour at the front told the conduct of the individual during the preceding day, to four degrees by comparison. Bad, denoted by black, indifferent by blue, good by yellow and excellent by white.**

This was the preventer of punishment. There was no beating—no abusive language. I passed daily through all the rooms, and the workers observed me always to look at these telegraphs—and when black I merely looked at the person and then a the colour—but never said a word to one of them by way of blame. And if any one

* *Life,* 188-9.   ** This paragraph is interpolated from *Life,* 111.

thought the inferior colour was not deserved by him as given, it was desired that complaint should be made to me. But this seldom occurred. Now this simple device and silent monitor began to show its effects upon the character of the workers. At first a large proportion daily were black and blue, few yellow and scarcely any white. Gradually the black were changed for blue, the blues for yellow, and the yellows for white. And for many years the permanent daily conduct of a very large number of those who were employed, deserved and had No. 1 placed as their character on the books of the establishment. Soon after the adoption of this telegraph I could at once see by the expression of the countenance what was the colour which was shown. As there were four colours there were four different expressions of countenance most evident to me as I passed along the rooms.

Never perhaps in the history of the human race has so simple a device created in so short a period so much order, virtue, goodness, and happiness, out of so much ignorance, error, and misery.

[It is often said that in this, and other ways, Owen treated his work-people as if they were children. There is some truth in this, but it must be remembered that a large proportion of them *were* children. And it was always with children that Owen was most successful.]

4* OWEN AND HIS PARTNERS

[Owen was constantly frustrated by partners who only wanted the maximum profit. After various changes he found a new group, including Jeremy Bentham the philosopher, and several Quakers, who were ready to give him a free hand. His old partners were unaware of this,

* *Life*, 121-8.

and hoped to buy Owen out at a bargain price. The sale took place in 1813.]

Previous to the sale they took measures to circulate reports to deteriorate the value of my New Lanark establishment, and to lower my character as manager of it. They stated that I had visionary and wild schemes for the education of the children and the improvement of the character of the people—schemes that no one but myself ever thought or believed to be practicable. They said they had given eighty-four thousand pounds for the establishment, and they did not think it now worth forty thousand pounds, and should be too happy to obtain that sum at the coming sale. . . .

I did not meet them until the morning of the sale, to decide upon what should be what is called the upset price [reserve price]. The first question which I asked them was —'What do you propose shall be the upset price?' They said, as I expected, forty thousand pounds. I said—'Will you now take sixty thousand pounds for the property?' 'No—we will not,' was their immediate reply. 'Then it shall be put up at sixty thousand pounds.' And they were under the necessity in consequence of their reply to admit of this decision.

My proposed new partners while we were all met in London asked me the price which I thought the property was now worth. I said we should not let it be purchased from us at less than one hundred and twenty thousand pounds. And it was concluded that I should be empowered to bid to that amount.

[At the auction Owen's agent bought the property for £114,100 much to the disgust of his former partners.]

Mr. John Atkinson, who had been a partner with me in the establishment from the beginning, and who therefore knew its value, went immediately from the sale room, while his feelings were highly excited . . . and said, with great emphasis—'Confound that Owen! He has bought it and twenty thousand pounds too cheap!' There were the partners who for so many months had been crying down the value of the establishment, and saying they would be glad to get forty thousand pounds for it!

[That night they were dining with a Colonel Hunter.]

The Colonel was a straightforward, bold, honest man and feared no one; and he was determined to make these parties feel the new position in which they had placed themselves. He therefore asked permisson to propose a toast, which was readily acceded to, and he gave 'Success to the parties who had this morning sold a property by public sale for one hundred and fourteen thousand one hundred pounds, which a little time ago they valued only at forty thousand pounds!' adding. 'Fill a bumper to a success so wonderful and extraordinary!' His toast, however, instead of arousing the spirits of my opponents, acted, I was told, as an additional damper.

5* THE FINAL LESSON OF NEW LANARK

The real cause of this happiness was unknown to them and to the public; but so obvious were the beneficial results even to passing strangers, that the establishment and its appendages became familiarly known as 'The Happy Valley'. . . .

In a few years I had accomplished for this population as much as such a manufacturing system would admit of; and although the poor work-people were content, and, by contrast with other manufacturing establishments and all other work-people under this old system, deemed themselves so much better treated and cared for, and were highly satisfied, yet I knew it was a miserable existence compared with that which, with the immense means at the control of all governments, might now be created for every population over the world.

I could do no more for mere manufacturing popula-

* *Revolution*, 16-17.

tion, for manufacturers are not the true foundation of society. And, after all, what had I done for these people? —what was their real condition, even with all the expenditure which had been incurred, and the measures which had been adopted to improve it?

The people were slaves at my mercy; liable at any time to be dismissed; and knowing that, in that case, they must go into misery, compared with such limited happiness as they now enjoyed.

And yet the working part of this population of 2,500 persons was daily producing as much real wealth for society, as, less than half a century before, it would have required the working part of a population of 600,000 to create. I asked myself what became of the difference between the wealth consumed by 2,500 persons and that which would have been consumed by 600,000; and the consideration enforced upon me even more powerfully than I had previously appreciated them, the errors and gross irrationality of the present system, in inflicting so much misery upon all, but more especially upon the producing classes, while such enormously superabundant means to produce wealth and happiness for all, are at the control of society and utterly neglected.

6* A REPORT ON NEW LANARK

[Owen's claims about the change he made at New Lanark are confirmed by the evidence of many visitors, like the deputation sent in August 1819 by the Guardians of the Poor in Leeds. It reported:]

Mr. Owen's establishment at Lanark is essentially a manufacturing establishment, conducted in a manner superior to any other the deputation ever witnessed, and dispensing more happiness than perhaps any other institu-

* *Life, IA,* 254-6.

tion in the kingdom where so many poor persons are employed; and is founded on an admirable system of moral regulation. . . .

In the education of the children the thing that is most remarkable is the general spirit of kindness and affection, which is shown towards them, and the entire absence of everything that is likely to give them bad habits—with the presence of whatever is calculated to inspire them with good ones; the consequence is, that they appear like one well-regulated family, united together by the ties of the strongest affection. . . .

In the adult inhabitants of New Lanark we saw much to commend. In general they appeared clean, healthy and sober. Intoxication, the parent of so many vices and so much misery, is indeed almost unknown here. The consequence is that they are well clad, and well fed, and their dwellings are inviting. . . .

In this well-regulated colony, where almost everything is made, wanted by either the manufactory or its inhabitants, no cursing or swearing is any where to be heard. There are no quarrelsome men or brawling women.

These effects arise partly out of the moral culture of the place—partly from the absence of public houses, as we have before said—and partly from the seclusion of the inhabitants from the rest of the world, if that can be called seclusion where 2,500 persons are congregated within the narrow compass of a quarter of a square mile.

High wages, it is manifest, are not the cause of the comfort which prevails here. Among us their wages would be thought low. The wages of those under eighteen years of age, per week, are, for the males that work by the day, 4s. 3d.; for the females 3s. 5d.; and for those that work by the piece, 5s. 4d. for the former and 4s. 7d. for the latter. The average weekly wages for those above eighteen years of age are, for men, 9s. 11d.; for women, 6s. by the day; and 14s. 10d. for the former, and 8s. for the latter by the piece.

IV

The Industrial Revolution

[Owen was among the first to understand the nature of the Industrial Revolution, with its vast possibilities of increased wealth and the actual misery it brought to the masses. He certainly took too rosy a view of the past, but he knew the England of his day. The strength and weakness of his analysis may best be judged by comparing it with that of *The Communist Manifesto*.]

1* CONSEQUENCES OF THE INDUSTRIAL REVOLUTION

Not more than thirty years since, the poorest parents thought the age of fourteen sufficiently early for their children to commence regular labour: and they judged well; for by that period of their lives they had acquired by play and exercise in the open air, the foundations of a sound robust constitution; and if they were not all initiated in book learning, they had been taught the far more useful knowledge of domestic life, which could not but be familiar to them at the age of fourteen, and which, as they grew up and became the heads of families, was of more value to them (as it taught them economy in the expenditure of their earnings) than one half of their wages under the present circumstances.

* *Observations,* Cole, 122-7.

It should be remembered also that twelve hours per day, including the time for regular rest and meals, were then thought sufficient to extract all the working strength of the most robust adult; when it may be remarked local holidays were much more frequent than at present in most parts of the kingdom.

At this period, too, they were generally trained by the example of some landed proprietor, and in such habits as created a mutual interest between the parties, by which means even the lowest peasant was generally considered as belonging to, and forming somewhat of a member of, a respectable family. Under these circumstances the lower orders experienced not only a considerable degree of comfort, but they had also frequent opportunities of enjoying healthy rational sports and amusements; and in consequence they became strongly attached to those on whom they depended; their services were willingly performed; and the mutual good offices bound the parties by the strongest ties of human nature to consider each other as friends in somewhat different situations; the servant indeed often enjoying more solid comfort and ease than his master.

Contrast this state affairs with that of the lower orders of the present day—with human nature trained as it now is, under the new manufacturing system.

In the manufacturing districts it is common for parents to send their children of both sexes at seven or eight years of age, in winter as well as summer, at six o'clock in the morning, sometimes of course in the dark, and occasionally amidst frost and snow, to enter the manufactories, which are often heated to a high temperature, and contain an atmosphere far from being the most favourable to human life, and in which all those employed in them very frequently continue until twelve o'clock at noon when an hour is allowed for dinner, after which they return to remain, in the majority of cases, till eight o'clock at night.

The children now find they must labour incessantly for

their bare subsistence: they have not been used to innocent, healthy, and rational amusements; they are not permitted the requisite time, it they had been previously accustomed to enjoy them. They know not what relaxation
means, except by the actual cessation from labour. They
are surrounded by others similiarly circumstanced with
themselves; and thus passing on from childhood to youth,
they become gradually initiated, the young men in particular, but often the young females also, in the seductive
pleasures of the pot-house and inebriation; for which their
daily hard labour, want of better habits, and the general
vacuity of their minds, tend to prepare them.

Such a system of training cannot be expected to produce
any other than a population weak in bodily and mental
faculties, and with habits generally destructive of their
own comforts, of the well-being of those around them,
and strongly calculated to subdue all the social affections.
Man so circumstanced sees all around him hurrying forward, at a mail coach speed, to acquire individual wealth,
regardless of him, his comforts, his wants, or even his sufferings, except by way of a *degrading parish charity* fitted
only to steel the heart of man against his fellows, or to
form the tyrant and the slave. Today he labours for one
master, tomorrow for a second, then for a third, and a
fourth, until all the ties between employers and employed
are frittered down to the consideration of what immediate
gain each can derive from the other.

[Owen goes on to propose, as remedy, an Act of Parliament to regulate factory hours and conditions.]

Those measures, when influenced by no party feelings
or narrow mistaken notions of immediate self-interest,
but considered solely in a national view, will be found
beneficial to the child, to the parent, to the employer, and
to the country. . . .

I do not anticipate any objection from employers to the
age named [ten years] for the admittance of children into

their manufactories; or to the children being previously trained in good habits and the rudiments of common learning; for upon an experience abundantly sufficient to ascertain the fact, I have uniformly found it to be more profitable to admit children to constant daily employment at ten years old than at any earlier period; and that those children, or adults, who had been the best taught, made the best servants, and were by far the most easily directed to do everything that was right and proper for them to perform. The proprietors of expensive establishments may object to the reduction of the *now* customary hours of labour. The utmost extent, however, of their argument is, that the rent or interest of the capital expended in forming the establishment is chargeable on the quantity of its produce—and if, instead of being permitted to employ their work-people within their manufactories so long as fourteen or fifteen hours per day, they shall be restricted to twelve hours of labour per day from their work-people, then the prime cost of the article which they manufacture will be increased by the greater proportion of the rent or interest which attaches to the smaller quantity produced. If, however, this law shall be, as it is proposed, general over England, Scotland, and Ireland, whatever difference may ultimately arise in the prime cost of the articles produced in these manufactories, will be borne by the consumers, and not by the proprietors of such establishments. And, in a national view, the labour which is exerted twelve hours per day will be obtained more economically than if stretched to a longer period.

I doubt, however, whether any manufactory, so arranged as to occupy the hands employed in it twelve hours per day, will not produce its fabric, even to the immediate proprietor, nearly if not altogether as cheap as those in which the exertions of the employed are continued to fourteen or fifteen hours per day.

Should this, however, not prove to be the case to the extent mentioned, the improved health, the comforts, useful acquirements of the population, and the diminution of the poor-rates, naturally consequent upon this change in the manners and habits of the people, will amply compensate the country for a mere fractional addition to the prime cost of any commodity.

And is it to be imagined that the British Government will ever put the chance of a trivial pecuniary gain to a few, in competition with the solid welfare of so many millions of human beings?

[Owen's arguments have proved correct, but he was soon to discover that he was wrong in thinking the manufacturers would not object to such regulations, or that the Government would put the welfare of the workers before the employer's demand for unlimited profit. So stubborn was the opposition that it was some half century before the measures Owen proposed could be secured. See Chapter VI.]

2* THE PHILOSOPHY OF HIGH WAGES

Every master manufacturer is most anxious to have his work cheaply performed, and as he is perpetually exerting all his faculties to attain this object, he considers low wages to be essential to his success. By one master or another, every means are used to reduce wages to the lowest possible point, and if one succeeds the others must follow in their own defence. Yet when the subject is properly considered, no evil ought to be more dreaded by master manufacturers than low wages of labour, or a want of means to procure reasonable comfort among the working class. These, in consequence of their numbers, are the greatest consumers of all articles; and it will always be found that when wages are high the country prospers;

* *Manufacturers*, Cole, 143-4.

and when they are low, all classes suffer, from the highest to the lowest, but more particularly the manufacturing interest; for food must be first purchased and the remainder only of the labourer's wages can be expended in manufactures. It is therefore essentially the interest of the master manufacturer that wages of the labourer should be high, and that he should be allowed the necessary time and instruction to enable him to expend them judiciously —which is not possible under the existence of our present practices. . . .

The most substantial support of the trade, commerce and manufactures of this and of any other country are the labouring classes of its population: and the real prosperity of any nation may be at all times accurately ascertained by the amount of wages, or the extent of the comforts which the productive classes can obtain in return for their labour. . . .

But when ignorance, overwork and low wages are combined, not only is the labourer in a wretched condition, but all the higher classes are essentially injured, although none will suffer in consequence more severely than the master manufacturer, for the reason which has been before stated.

3* CAUSES OF THE POST-WATERLOO CRISIS

The immediate cause of the present distress is the depreciation of human labour. This has been occasioned by the general introduction of mechanism into the manufactures of Europe and America, but principally into those of Britain, where the change was greatly accelerated by the inventions of Arkwright and Watt.

The introduction of mechanism into the manufacture of objects of desire in society reduced their price; the reduc-

* *Relief of Poor,* Cole, 156-8.

tion of price increased the demand for them, and generally to so great an extent as to occasion more human labour to be employed after the introduction of machinery than had been employed before.

The first effects of these new mechanical combinations were to increase individual wealth, and to give a new stimulus to further inventions.

Thus one mechanical improvement gave rise to another in rapid succession; and in a few years they were not only generally introduced into the manufactures of these kingdoms, but were eagerly adopted by other nations of Europe, and by America. . . .

The war itself, when it had extended its ravages over Europe, to Asia and to America, seemed but a new stimulus to draw forth our endless resources; and in its effects the war did so operate. The destruction of human life in its prime, which it caused throughout the world, and the waste of all the materials necessary for war on so large a scale—perhaps unparalleled in ancient or modern times—created a demand for various productions, which the overstrained industry of British manufacturers, added by all the mechanism they could invent and bring into action, was hardly competent to supply.

But peace at length followed, and found Great Britain in possession of a new power in constant action, which, it may be safely stated, exceeded the labour of *one hundred millions* of the most industrious human beings, in the full strength of manhood. : . .

Thus our country possessed, at the conclusion of the war, a productive power, which operated to the same effect as if her population had been actually increased fifteen or twentyfold; and this has been chiefly created within the preceding twenty-five years. The rapid progress made by Great Britain, during the war, in wealth and political influence, can therefore no longer astonish: the cause was quite adequate to the effect.

Now, however, new circumstances have arisen. The

war demand for the productions of labour having ceased, markets could no longer be found for them; and the revenues of the world were inadequate to purchase that which a power so enormous in its effects did produce: a diminished demand consequently followed. When, therefore, it became necessary to contract the sources of supply, it soon proved that mechanical power was much cheaper than human labour; the former, in consequence, was continued at work, while the latter was superseded; and human labour may now be obtained at a price far less than is absolutely necessary for the subsistence of the individual in ordinary comfort.

V

Economic Theory

[In Owen's writings we can find the first expression of many ideas which were elaborated by such English socialists as Gray, Hodgskin and Thompson and were to play a great part in the development of socialist theory. Among them were the ideas of labour as the source of wealth and the measure of value, and of the abolition of the opposition between town and country. Owen's refutation of Malthus is also notable.]

1* LABOUR THE SOURCE OF WEALTH

The evil for which your Reporter has been required to provide a Remedy, is the general want of employment at wages sufficient to support the family of a working man benefically to the community.

After most earnest consideration of the subject he has been compelled to conclude that such employment cannot be procured through the medium of trade, commerce, or manufactures, or even of agriculture, until the Government and the Legislature, cordially supported by the country, shall previously adopt measures to remove obstacles which, without their interference, will now permanently deteriorate all the resources of the empire.

* *Report*, Cole, 245-8.

Your reporter has been impressed with the truth of this conclusion by the following considerations:

First—That manual labour, properly directed, is the source of all wealth, and of national prosperity.

Second—That, when properly directed, labour is of far more value to the community than the expense necessary to maintain the labourer in considerable comfort.

Third—That manual labour, properly directed, may be made to continue this value in all parts of the world, under any supposable increase in its population, for many centuries to come.

Fourth—That, under a proper direction of manual labour, Great Britain and its dependencies may be made to support an incalculable increase of its population, most advantageously for all its inhabitants.

Fifth—That when manual labour shall be so directed, it will be found that population cannot, for many years, be stimulated to advance as rapidly as society might be benefitted by its increase. . . .

Your reporter directed his attention to the consideration of the possibility of devising arrangements by means of which the whole population might participate in the benefits derivable from the increase of scientific productive power; and he has the satisfaction to state to the meeting, that he has strong grounds to believe that such arrangements are practicable.

His opinion on this important part of the subjects is founded on the following considerations:

First—It must be admitted that scientific or artificial aid to man increases his productive powers, his natural wants remaining the same; and in proportion as his productive powers increase he becomes less dependent on his physical strength and on the many contingencies connected with it.

Second—That the direct effect of every addition to scientific or mechanical and chemical power is to increase wealth; and it is found, accordingly, that the immediate causes of the present want of employment for the working classes is an excess of production of all kinds of wealth, by which, under the existing arrangements of commerce, all markets of the world are overstocked.

Third—That, could markets be found, an incalculable addition might yet be made to the wealth of society, as is most evident from the number of persons who seek employment, and the far greater number who, from ignorance, are inefficiently employed, but still more from the means we posses of increasing, to an unlimited extent, our scientific powers of production.

Fourth—That the deficiency of employment for the working classes cannot proceed from a want of wealth or capital, or of the means of greatly adding to that which now exists, but from some defect in the mode of distributing that extraordinary addition of new capital throughout society, or, to speak commercially, from the want of a market, or means of exchange, co-extensive with the means of production.

Were effective measures devised to facilitate the distribution of wealth after it was created, your Reporter could have no difficulty in suggesting the means of beneficial occupation for all who are unemployed, and for a considerable increase to their number.

2* LABOUR AS THE TRUE STANDARD OF VALUE

One of the measures which he thus ventures to propose, *to let prosperity loose on the country* (if he may be allowed the expression) is *a change in the standard of value*.

It is true that in the civilized parts of the world gold and silver have long been used for this purpose; but these metals have been a mere artificial standard, and they have performed the office very imperfectly and inconveniently. . . .

* *Report*, Cole, 248-51.

A temporary expedient was thought of and adopted, and Bank of England paper became the British legal standard of value—a convincing proof that society may make any artificial substance, whether possessing intrinsic worth or not, a legal standard of value. . . .

Your Reporter, then, after deeply studying these subjects, practically and theoretically, for a period exceeding thirty years, and during which his practice without a single exception has confirmed the theory which practice first suggested, now ventures to state, as one of the results of this study and experience,

THAT THE NATURAL STANDARD OF VALUE IS, IN PRINCIPLE, HUMAN LABOUR, OR THE COMBINED MANUAL AND MENTAL POWERS OF MEN CALLED INTO ACTION.

And that it would be highly benefical, and has now become absolutely necessary, to reduce this principle into immediate practice.

It will be said, by those who have taken a superfical or mere partial view of the question, that human labour or power is so unequal in individuals, that its average amount cannot be estimated.

Already, however, the average physical power of man as well as of horses (equally varied in the individuals), has been calculated for scientific purposes, and both now serve to measure inanimate powers.

On the same principle the average of human labour or power may be ascertained, and as it forms the essence of all wealth, its value in every article of produce may also be ascertained, and its exchangeable value with all other values fixed accordingly; the whole would be permanent for a given period.

Human labour would thus acquire its natural or intrinsic value, which would increase as science advanced; and this is, in fact, the only really useful object of science.

The demand for human labour would no longer be subject to caprice, nor would the support of human life be made, as at present, a perpetually varying article of commerce, and the working classes made the slaves of an artificial system of wages, more cruel in its effects than any slavery ever practised by society, either barbarous or civilized.

3* UNITY OF AGRICULTURE AND MANUFACTURE

Society, ever misled by closet theorists, has committed almost every kind of error in practice, and in no instance perhaps a greater, than in separating the workman from his food, and making his existence depend upon the labour and uncertain supplies of others, as is the case under our present manufacturing system; and it is a vulgar error to suppose that a single individual more can be supported by such a system than without it; on the contrary, a whole population engaged in agriculture, with manufactures as an appendage, will, in a given district, support many more, and in a much higher degree of comfort, than the same district could do with its agriculture separate from its manufacturing population.

Improved arrangements for the working classes will, in almost all cases, place the workman in the midst of his food, which it will be as beneficial for him to create as to consume.

Sufficient land, therefore, will be allotted to these cultivators, to enable them to raise an abundant supply of food and the necessaries of life for themselves, and as much additional agricultural produce as the public demands may require from such a portion of the population.

Under a well-devised arrangement for the working classes they will all procure for themselves the necessaries

* *Report,* Cole, 266-7.

and comforts of life in so short a time, and so easily and pleasantly, that the occupation will be experienced to be little more than a recreation, sufficient to keep them in the best health and spirits for rational enjoyment of life.

The surplus produce from the soil will be required only for the higher classes, those who live without manual labour, and those whose nice manual operations will not permit them at any time to be employed in agriculture and gardening.

Of the latter, very few, if any will be necessary, as mechanism may be made to supersede such operations, which are almost always injurious to health.

4* PRINCIPLES OF EXCHANGE

Society has been hitherto so constituted that all parties are afraid of being over-reached by others, and, without great care to secure their individual interests, of being deprived of the means of existence. This feeling has created a universal selfishness of the most ignorant nature, for it almost *ensures* the evils which it means to prevent.

These new associations can scarcely be formed before it will be discovered that by the most simple and easy regulations all the natural wants of human nature may be abundantly supplied; and the principle of selfishness (in the sense in which the term is here used) will cease to exist for want of an adequate motive to produce it.

It will be quite evident to all, that wealth of that kind which will alone be held in any estimation amongst them may be so easily created to exceed all their wants, that every desire for individual accumulation will be extinguished. To them individual accumulation of wealth will appear as irrational as to bottle up or store water in

* *Report*, Cole, 288-90.

situations where there is more of this invaluable fluid than all can consume.

With this knowledge, and the feelings that will arise from it, the existing thousand counteractions to the creation of new wealth will also cease, as well as those innumerable motives to deception which now pervade all ranks in society. A principle of equity and justice, openness and fairness, will influence the whole proceedings of these societies. There will, consequently, be no difficulty whatever in the exchange of the products of labour, mental or manual, among themselves. . . .

The peculiar produce to be raised in each establishment, beyond the general supply of the necessaries and comforts of life, which, if possible, will be abundantly created in each, will be adapted to afford the greatest variety of intrinsically valuable objects to exchange with each other; and the particular surplus products which will serve to give energy and pleasure to the industry of the members of each association will be regulated by the nature of the soil and climate and other local capabilities of the situation of each establishment. In all these labour will be the standard of value, and as there will always be a progressive advance in the amount of labour, manual, mental, and scientific, if we suppose population to increase under these arrangements, there will be in the same proportion a perpetually extending market or demand for all the industry of society, whatever may be its extent. Under such arrangements what are technically called 'bad times' can never occur. . . .

A paper representative of the value of labour, manufactured on the principle of the new notes of the Bank of England, will serve for every purpose of their domestic commerce or exchanges, and will be issued only for intrinsic value received and in store.

Many of you have long experienced in your manufacturing operations the advantages of substantial, well-contrived, and well-executed machinery.

Experience has also shown you the difference of the results between mechanism which is neat, clean, well arranged, and always in a high state of repair; and that which is allowed to be dirty, in disorder, and without the means of preventing unnecessary friction, and which therefore becomes, and works, much out of repair.

In the first case the whole economy and management are good, every operation proceeds with ease, order, and success. In the last, the reverse must follow, and a scene be presented of counteraction, confusion, and dissatisfaction among all the agents and instruments interested or occupied in the general process, which cannot fail to create great loss.

If, then, due care as to the state of your inanimate machines can produce such beneficial results, what may not be expected if you devote equal attention to your vital machines, which are far more wonderfully constructed?

When you shall acquire a right knowledge of these, of their curious mechanism, of their self-adjusting powers; when the proper mainspring shall be applied to their various movements—you will become conscious of their real value, and you will readily be induced to turn your thoughts more frequently from your inanimate to your living machines; and you will discover that the latter may be easily trained and directed to procure a large increase of pecuniary gain, while you may also derive from them a high and substantial satisfaction.

Will you then continue to expend large sums of money

---

* *New View* (Dedication to the Superintendents of Manufacturers), Cole, 8-9.

to procure the best devised mechanisms of wood, brass, or iron; to retain it in perfect repair; to provide the best substance for the prevention of unnecessary friction, and to save it from falling into premature decay? Will you also devote years of intense application to understand the connection of the various parts of these lifeless machines, to improve their effective powers, and to calculate with mathematical precision all their minute and combined movements? And when in these transactions you estimate time by minutes, and the money expended for the chance of increased gain by fractions, will you not afford some of your attention to consider whether a portion of your time and capital would not be more advantageously applied to improve your living machines? From experience which cannot deceive me, I venture to assure you, that your time and money so applied, if directed by a true knowledge of the subject, would return you, not five, ten, or fifteen per cent, for your capital so expended, but often fifty, and in many cases a hundred per cent.

6 THE FALLACY OF MALTHUSIANISM

(a)* All men may, by judicious and proper laws and training, readily acquire knowledge and habits which will enable them, if they be permitted, to produce far more than they need for their support and enjoyment: and thus any population, in the fertile parts of the earth, may be taught to live in plenty and happiness, without the checks of vice and misery.

Mr. Malthus is, however, correct when he says that the population of the world is ever adapting itself to the quantity of food raised for its support; but he has not told us how much more food an intelligent and industrious

* *New View,* Cole, 85-6.

people will create from the same soil, than will be produced by one ignorant and ill-governed. It is, however, as one to infinity.

For man knows not the limit of his power of creating food. How much has that power been latterly increased in these islands? And in them such knowledge is in its infancy. Yet compare even this power of raising food with the efforts of the Bosgemens or other savages, and it will be found, perhaps, as one to a thousand.

Food for man may also be considered as a compound of the original elements, of the qualities, combinations, and control of which, chemistry is daily adding to our knowledge; nor is it yet for man to say to what this knowledge may lead or where it may end.

The sea, it may be remarked also, affords an inexhaustible source of food. It may then be safely asserted that the population of the world may be allowed naturally to increase for many thousand years; and yet, under a system of government founded on the principles for the truth of which we contend, the whole may continue to live in abundance and happiness, without one check of vice or misery; and under the guidance of these principles, human labour properly directed, may be made far more than sufficient to enable the population of the world to live in the highest state of human enjoyment.

(b)*   Every agriculturalist knows that each labourer now employed in agriculture can produce five or six times more food than he can eat; and therefore, even if no other facilities were given to him than those we now possess, there is no necessity in nature for 'the population to press against subsistence', until the earth is fully cultivated. There can be no doubt that it is the artificial law of supply and demand, arising from the principles of individual gain in opposition to the general well-being of society,

* *Catechism*, Cole, 181.

which has hitherto compelled population to press upon subsistence. The certain effect of acting upon the principle of individual gain is, ever to limit the supply of food, in an average season, to a sufficiency, according to the customs of the times, for the existing inhabitants of the earth.

VI

Owen and the Factory Children

[Owen's first great public campaign was for the regulation of the condition of children employed in the factories. His experiences of the system of pauper apprenticeship, and other evils, had shown him the necessity for this. The first passage describes the situation at New Lanark.]

1* PAUPER APPRENTICES

It is not to be supposed that children so young could remain, with the intervals of meals, from six in the morning until seven in the evening, in constant employment, on their feet within cotton mills, and afterwards acquire much proficiency in education. And so it proved; for many of them became dwarfs in body and mind, and some were deformed. Their labour throughout the day and their education at night became so irksome, that numbers of them continually ran away, and almost all looked forward with impatience and anxiety to the expiration of their apprenticeship of seven, eight, and nine years, which generally expired when they were from thirteen to fifteen years old. At this period of life, unaccustomed to provide for themselves, and unacquainted with the world, they usually went to Edinburgh or Glasgow, where boys and girls were soon assailed by the innumerable temptations

* *New View,* Cole, 28.

which all large towns present, and to which many of them fell sacrifices.

Thus Mr. Dale's arrangements, and his kind solicitude for the comfort and happiness of these children, were rendered in their ultimate effects almost nugatory. They were hired by him and sent to be employed, and without their labour he could not support them; but, while under his care, he did all that any individual circumstanced as he was, could do for his fellow-creatures. The error proceeded from the children being sent from the workhouses at an age much too young for employment. They ought to have been detained four years longer, and educated; and then some of the evils which followed would have been prevented.

If such be a true picture, not overcharged, of parish apprentices to our manufacturing system, under the best and most humane regulations, in what colours must it be exhibited under the worst?

2 THE BILL OF 1815

[In 1815 Owen prepared a Bill to regulate the labour of children in textile mills. Sir Robert Peel, father of the future Prime Minister and himself a leading spinner, promised to introduce it into Parliament. Owen visited mills throughout the country, collecting evidence.]

(a)* I thus saw the importance of the machinery employed in these manufactures and its rapid annual improvements. I also became vividly alive to the deteriorating conditions of the young children and others who were made slaves of these new mechanical powers. And whatever may be said to the contrary, bad and unwise as American slavery is and must continue to be, the white

* *Life*, 155-6.

slavery in the manufactories of England was at this unrestricted period far worse than the house slaves whom I afterwards saw in the West Indies and in the United States, and in many respects, as regards health, food, and clothing, the latter were much better provided for than were these oppressed and degraded children and work-people in the home manufactories of Great Britain.

(b)*   At the commencement of these proceedings I was an utter novice in the manner of conducting the business of this country in Parliament. But my intimate acquaintance with these proceedings for the four years during which this Bill was under the consideration of both Houses, opened my eyes to the conduct of public men, and to the ignorant vulgar self-interest, regardless of the means to accomplish their object, of trading and mercantile men, even of high standing in the commercial world. No means was left untried by these men to defeat the object of the Bill, in the first session of its introduction, and through four years in which, under one futile pretext and another, it was kept in the House of Commons.

Children at this time were admitted into the cotton, wool, flax, and silk mills, at six and sometimes even at five years of age. The time of working, winter and summer, was unlimited by law, but usually it was fourteen hours per day—in some fifteen, and even, by the most inhuman and avaricious, sixteen hours—and in many cases the mills were artificially heated to a high state most unfavourable to health.

The first plea of the objectors to my Bill was, that masters ought not to be interfered with by the legislators in any way in the management of their business.

After long useless discussions, kept up to prolong time, this was at length overruled.

The next attempt was to prove that it was not injurious

* *Life,* 161-2.

to employ these young children fourteen or fifteen hours per day in overheated close rooms, filled often with the fine fibre of the material used, particularly in cotton and flax spinning mills. Sir Robert Peel most unwisely consented to a committee being appointed to investigate this question, and this committee was continued for two sessions of Parliament before these wise and honest men, legislating for the nation, could decide that such practices were detrimental to the health of these infants.

The Bill as I prepared it was assented to by all the leading members of both Houses, except the trading and manufacturing interests, including cotton, wool, flax, and silk mill-owners. Sir Robert yielding to the clamour of the manufacturers, first gave up wool, flax, and silk, and they were struck out, although at that time flax spinning was the most unhealthy of the four manufactures.

(c)*   I was so disgusted at the delays created by these interested members, and at the concessions made to them by Sir Robert Peel during the progress of the Bill through the House of Commons, that after attending the committee every day of its sitting during two long sessions, I took less interest in a Bill so mutilated and so unlike the Bill which had been prepared by me. . . .

It may be remarked here, that this Bill has since been almost continuously before Parliament for improvement after improvement, and yet it has not been suffered by the master cotton-spinners to attain the full benefits contained in the Bill when first introduced at my instance. . . . But in this and all other cases between the tyranny of the masters and the sufferings of their white slaves, the error is in reality in the system of society, which creates the necessity for tyrants and slaves, neither of which could exist in a true and rational state of society.

* *Life,* 167-8.

[Owen took his son, Robert Dale Owen, then fourteen, on his tour of the mills. What he saw left a lasting impression on the boy.]

The facts we collected seemed to me terrible almost beyond belief. Not in exceptional cases, but as a rule, we found children of ten years old worked regularly fourteen hours a day, with but half an hour's interval for the midday meal, which was eaten in the factory. In fine yarn cotton mills they were subjected to this labour in a temperature usually exceeding seventy-five degrees; and in all the cotton factories they breathed atmosphere more or less injurious to the lungs, because of the dust and minute cotton fibres that pervaded it. . . . It need not be said that such a system could not be maintained without corporal punishment. Most of the overseers openly carried stout leather thongs, and we frequently saw even the youngest children severely beaten. We sought out the surgeons who were in the habit of attending these children, noting their names and the facts they attested. Their stories haunted my dreams. In some large factories, from one-fourth to one-fifth of the children were cripples or otherwise deformed, or permanently injured by excessive toil, sometimes by brutal abuse. The younger children seldom held out more than three or four years without serious illness, often ending in death. When we expressed surprise that parents should voluntarily condemn their sons and daughters to slavery so intolerable, the explanation seemed to be that many of the fathers were out of work themselves, and so were, in a measure, driven to the sacrifice for lack of bread; while others, imbruted by intemperance, saw with indifference an abuse of the infant faculties compared to which the infanticide of China may almost be termed humane.

* *T.M.W.*, 125-6.

I have no doubt the honourable member who first introduced this Bill into Parliament, and who has devoted so much time to the subject, is aware that these enactments are very inadequate to meet the existing evils.

He is probably afraid to ask more, lest he should increase the opposition of those who think themselves interested in perpetuating an oppression of their fellow creatures, worse than any slavery of the same extent with which the human race has been hitherto afflicted. . . .

I am fully aware of the clamour these propositions will at first call forth from the blind avarice of commerce; for commerce, my Lord, trains her children to see only their immediate or apparent interest; their ideas are too contracted to carry them beyond the passing week, month, or year at the utmost.

They have been taught, my Lord, to consider it to be the essence of wisdom to expend millions of capital, and years of extraordinary scientific application, as well as to sacrifice the health, morals, and comforts of the great mass of the subjects of a mighty empire, that they may uselessly improve the manufacture of and increase the demand for, pins, needles, and threads—that they may have the singular satisfaction, after immense care, labour, and anxiety on their own parts, to destroy the real wealth and strength of their country by gradually undermining the morals and physical vigour of its inhabitants, for the sole end of relieving other nations of their due share of this enviable process of pin, needle, and thread making.

I trust, my Lord, it is not by such men that our great national concerns are henceforth to be directed.

* *Children* (To the Earl of Liverpool), Cole, 37-8.

[Owen published some of the objections raised by the factory owners to his Bill.]

This Bill might be characterised as one to reduce the productive labour of the country; to prevent large families from supporting themselves by their joint industry; as lessening their independence and comforts; as directly increasing the Poor's Rates (one of the most alarming features of this Bill is the certainty of its increasing the Poor's Rates in every district where it will operate), by compelling such families to resort to them to make up defective earnings; as injuring their morals, by throwing them idle and disorderly on the community too early in the evenings; as depriving the heads of families of their natural control over their children, and of their proper discretion as to their employment; and as superseding parental by legislative authority; and finally, as burdening the counties with additional Rates altogether unnecessary.

[But the feature most bitterly opposed by the owners was the proposal to appoint Factory Inspectors.]

The appointment of Stipendiary Visitors would expose the secrets of every man's business; his premises would become public; he would be liable to continual intrusions and informations; the more intrusive and litigious a Visitor might be, the more merit would he lay claim to in the discharge of his duty—a duty, the very nature of which is repulsive to those who are qualified to discharge, and attractive only to such as are unfit for it. The power to be given to them would fix a deep and unmerited stigma on the principal employers of the national industry.

* *Life*, IA., 30.

VII

Pioneer of Education

[Though Owen's theories of education were not original, he was the first to put them into practice on a large scale —and they proved brilliantly successful. At New Lanark, as in his later communities of New Harmony and Queenwood, the schools were the most outstanding and successful feature. And schools feature largely in all his plans for proposed Villages of Co-operation.]

1 THE NEW LANARK SCHOOLS

(a)*   I had before this period acquired the most sincere affection of all the children. I say all—because every child above one year old was daily sent to the schools. I had also the hearts of all their parents, who were highly delighted with the improved conduct, extraordinary progress, and continually increasing happiness of their children. . . .

It was in vain to look to any old teachers upon the old system of instruction by books . . . and I had to seek among the population for two persons who had a great love for and unlimited patience with children, and who were thoroughly tractable and willing unreservedly to follow my instructions. The best to my mind in these respects that I could find in the population of the village

* *Life,* 191-4.

was a poor, simple-hearted weaver, named James Buchanan, who had been previously trained by his wife to a perfect submission to her will, and who could gain but a scanty living by his now dying trade of weaving common plain cotton goods by hand. But he loved children strongly by nature and his patience with them was inexhaustible. [Owen found for the infants a young woman] about seventeen years of age, known familiarly among the villagers as 'Molly Young', who of the two, in natural powers of the mind, had an advantage over her companion in an office perfectly new to them both.

The first instruction which I gave them was, that they were on no account ever to beat any one of the children, or to threaten them in any manner of word or action, or to use abusive terms; but were always to speak to them with a pleasant countenance, and in a kind manner and tone of voice. That they should tell the infants and children (for they had all from one to six years old under their charge) that they must on all occasions do all they could to make their playfellows happy—and that the older ones, from four to six years of age, should take especial care of the younger ones, and should assist to teach them to make each other happy. . . .

The schoolroom . . . was furnished with paintings, chiefly of animals, with maps, and often supplied with natural objects from the gardens, fields, and woods—the examination and explanation of which always excited their curiosity and created an animated conversation between the children and their instructors, now themselves acquiring new knowledge by attempting to instruct their young friends, as I always taught them to think their pupils were, and to treat them as such. . . .

It was most encouraging and delightful to see the progress which these infants and children made in real knowledge without the use of books. And when the best means of instruction or forming character shall be known, I doubt whether books will be ever used before children attain their tenth year. And yet without books they will have a superior character formed for them at ten, as rational beings, knowing themselves and society in principle and practice, far better than the best-informed now know these subjects at their majority, or the mass of the population of the world ever know them at any age.

(b)* I said to the public—'Come and see, and judge for yourselves.' And the public came—not by hundreds but by thousands annually. I have seen as many at once as seventy strangers attending the early morning exercises of the children in the school. At this period the dancing, music, military discipline, and geographical exercise were especially attractive to all except 'very pious' Christians. Yet even these latter could not refrain from expressing their wonder and admiration at the unaffected joyous happiness of these young ones—children of the common cotton spinners.

Being always treated with kindness and confidence, and altogether without fear, even of a harsh word from any of their numerous teachers, they exhibited an unaffected grace and natural politeness, which surprised and fascinated strangers, and which new character and conduct were for most of them so unaccountable, that they knew not how to express themselves, or how to hide their wonder and amazement.

These children, standing up, seventy couples at a time, in the dancing room, and often surrounded with many strangers, would with the utmost ease and natural grace go through all the dances of Europe, with so little direction from their master, that strangers would be unconscious that there was a dancing master in the room.

In their singing lesson, one hundred and fifty would sing at the same time—their voices being trained to harmonize; and it was delightful to hear them sing the

* *Life,* 197-9.

old popular Scotch songs, which were great favourites with most strangers, from the unaffected simplicity and heart feeling with which these songs were sung by the children, whose natures had been naturally and rationally cultivated.

In their military exercises they went through their evolutions with precision equal, as many officers of the army stated, to some regiments of the line; and at the head of their marchings were six and sometimes eight young fifers, playing various marches. The girls were thus disciplined, as well as the boys, and their numbers were generally nearly equal. And it may be here remarked, that being daily brought up together, they appeared to feel for and treat each other as brothers and sisters of the same family; and so they continued until they left the day schools at the age of twelve.

Their lessons in geography were no less amusing to the children themselves and interesting to strangers. At a very early age they were instructed in classes on maps of the four quarters of the world. ... The lookers on were as much amused, and many as much instructed, as the children, who thus at an early age became so efficient, that one of our Admirals, who had sailed round the world, said he could not answer many of the questions which some of these children not six years old readily replied to, giving the places most correctly.

2* AN EXPERIMENT THAT FAILED

[A number of eminent men, including Lord Brougham and James Mill, decided to open a school in London on Owen's model.]

They asked me whether I would give them James Buchanan to be the master of their school. I replied—

* *Life*, 196, 210.

'Most willingly, for I have pupils who can take his place without any injury to my school.' . . .

But great were my surprise and horror when I visited the second infant school, which was situated in Westminster, and was under the auspices of great names and good men, but who themselves knew nothing of the requisite practice, and could not therefore give poor Buchanan the aid and support which he required, and without which it was now evident to me that he could do little or nothing that was efficient. On entering the school, the first object I saw was *Mrs.* Buchanan, whom I had never seen in the New Lanark School, brandishing a whip, and terrifying the children with it! Buchanan I saw in another part of the room, apparently without authority or influence, and as much subject to his wife as the children. Upon my unexpected appearance an attempt was made to hide the whip, but the countenances of the children were so different from the open, frank, and happy expressions of my children at New Lanark, that they at once told me of their position, and the extent of the ignorant management to which they had to submit.

3* CHILDREN CAN BE MOULDED

Children are, without exception, passive and wonderfully contrived compounds; which, by an accurate previous and subsequent attention, *founded on a correct knowledge of the subject,* may be formed collectively to have any human character. And although these compounds, like all the other works of nature, possess endless varieties, yet they partake of that plastic quality, which, by perseverance under judicious management, may be ultimately moulded into the very image of rational wishes and desires.

In the next place, these principles cannot fail to create feelings which, without force or the production of any

* *New View,* Cole, 22-3.

counteracting motive, will irresistably lead those who possess them to make due allowance for the difference of sentiments and manners, not only among their friends and countrymen, but also among the inhabitants of every region of the earth, even including their enemies.

4* EDUCATION – A PREPARATION FOR LIFE

Whatever knowledge may be attained to enable man to improve the breed of his progeny at birth, facts exist in endless profusion to prove to every mind capable of reflection, that men may now possess a most extensive control over those circumstances which affect the infant after birth; and that, as far as such circumstances can influence human character, the day has arrived when the existing generation may so far control them, that the rising generations may become in character, without any individual exceptions, whatever man can now desire them to be, that is not contrary to human nature.

It is with reference to this important consideration that your Reporter, in the forming of these new arrangements, has taken so much pains to exclude every circumstance that could make an evil impression on the infants and children of this new generation.

And he is prepared, when others can follow him, so to combine new circumstances, that vice, or that conduct which creates evil and misery in society, shall be utterly unknown in these villages, to whatever number they may extend.

Proceeding on these principles, your Reporter recommends arrangements by which the children shall be trained together as though they were literally all of one family.

For this purpose two schools will be required within the interior of the square, with spacious play and exercise grounds.

* *Report,* Cole, 279-84.

These schools may be conveniently placed in the line of the buildings to be erected across the centre of the parallelograms, in connexion with the church and places of worship.

The first school will be for the infants from two to six years of age. The second for children from six to twelve. . . .

The children in these schools should be trained systematically to acquire useful knowledge through the means of sensible signs, by which their powers of reflection and judgement may be habituated to draw accurate conclusions from the facts presented to them. This mode of instruction is founded in nature, and will supersede the present defective and tiresome system of book learning, which is ill calculated to give either pleasure or instruction to the minds of children. When arrangements founded on these principles shall be judiciously formed and applied to practice, children will, with ease and delight to themselves, acquire more real knowledge in a day than they have attained under the old system in many months. They will not only thus acquire valuable knowledge, but the best habits and dispositions will be at the same time imperceptibly created in every one; and they will be trained to fill every office and to perform every duty that the well-being of their associates and the establishments can require. It is only by education, rightly understood, that communities of men can ever be well governed, and by means of such education every object of human society will be attained with the least labour and the most satisfaction.

It is obvious that training and education must be viewed as intimately connected with the employments of the association. The latter, indeed, will form an essential part of education under these arrangements. Each association, generally speaking, should create for itself a full supply of the usual necessaries, conveniences and comforts of life. . . .

It has been a popular opinion to recommend a minute division of labour and a division of interests. It will presently appear, however, that this minute division of labour and division of interests are only other terms of poverty, ignorance, waste of every kind, universal opposition throughout society, crime, misery, and great bodily and mental imbecility.

To avoid these evils, which, while they continue, must keep mankind in a most degraded state, each child will receive a general education, early in life, that will fit him for the proper purposes of society, making him the most useful to it, and the most capable of enjoying it.

Before he is twelve years old he may with ease be trained to acquire a correct view of the outline of all the knowledge which men have yet attained.

By this means he will early learn what he is in relation to past ages, to the general period in which he lives, to the circumstances in which he is placed, to the individuals around him, and to future events. *He will then only have any pretension to the name of a rational being.* . . .

Instead of being the unhealthy pointer of a pin— header of a nail—piecer of a thread—or clodhopper, senselessly gazing at the soil around him, without understanding or rational reflection, there would spring up a working class full of activity and useful knowledge, with habits, information, manners and dispositions that would place the lowest in the scale many degrees above the best of any class which has yet been formed by the circumstances of past or present society.

VIII

Owen as a Public Figure

[Owen's success at New Lanark gave him a reputation that ensured his views on social questions wide attention, though not acceptance. For a number of years after 1817 he became an internationally celebrated public figure, on friendly terms with the most distinguished men of the time. His great failure to see that reason has a class basis, which led him to imagine that the ruling class could be persuaded to inaugurate socialism, is dealt with in greater detail in the next chapter.]

1* OWEN PREACHES HIS GOSPEL

I have now to narrate the public proceedings which by my means were set in action in 1817, and which aroused the attention of the civilized world, alarmed the governments, astounded the religious sects of every denomination, and created an excitement in all classes, such as seldom occurs, except in cases of revolution. It was the public announcement of a new and strange system of society, by an ordinarily educated cotton-spinning manufacturer. It was a proceeding unprecedented in the annals of history, and its consequences have been fermenting to this day, and are continuing to ferment, throughout society, and will now advance without retrogression until they shall so regenerate

* *Life,* 212-3.

the human mind, that it shall be 'born again', and will entirely change society all over the world, in spirit, principle, and practice, giving new surroundings to all nations, until not one stone of the present surroundings of society shall be left upon another. For in consequence of this change 'old things will entirely pass away and all will become new'.

The proceedings which first publicly announced to the world the rational and only true system of society for the human race, occupied the excited attention of the civilized world especially during the summer and autumn of 1817, and to a considerable extent afterwards, until I left this country in 1824, to go to the United States to sow the seeds of it in that new fertile soil—new for material and mental growth—the cradle of the future liberty of the human race—a liberty yet so little understood by the present population of the United States, as well as by that of *all the old states*. *Liberty* is a word continually used, but nowhere yet understood. For true liberty can exist only in a society based on a true knowledge of humanity, and constructed to be consistent with that foundation, in all its parts and as a whole. This will constitute the rational system of society, which is to give practically the greatest individual liberty that human nature can enjoy. Because it will of necessity make each one good, wise, and happy; and such only can ever be trusted with the full amount of individual liberty.

2* HIS ASSURANCE OF SUCCESS

It is an extraordinary fact, that under the innumerable contests in which I was destined to encounter the prejudices or superstition of all parties for so many years, I never once felt the slightest misgiving or doubt that I should in the course of time overcome every obstacle, and

* *Life*, 263.

that sooner or later the population as one man would admit the great and all-important truth for the permanent progress and happiness of all the human kind, 'that the character of man is before and from birth formed for him', and that, with this knowledge, comprehended in all its bearing, a good, useful, and most valuable character might with ease and pleasure be formed by society for everyone from birth, and to some important extent even before birth, in an increasing ratio through every succeeding generation.

With this impression deeply seated in the inmost recesses of my mind, no obstacle, no temporary defeat, no abuse from the press or religions, created the slightest discouragement to my onward progress. Knowing how the characters of all were formed *for* them, their abuse and violence only created a sympathy for them in proportion to their ignorance, and to the misery which that ignorance necessarily inflicted upon them.

3 OWEN AND THE POLITICIANS

[Owen never lost his belief that the Tory Government, headed by such arch-reactionaries as Castlereagh, Sidmouth and Lord Liverpool (Prime Minister, 1812—27), were genuinely eager to support his proposals and were only prevented from doing so by some unaccountable accident. The extracts which follow illustrate some of his views and experiences of the ruling class in England and abroad.]

(a)*   The Government had been on all occasions most friendly to me, and afterwards learned from the Dean of Westminster, who had been private secretary to Lord Liverpool for some time, that his Lordship and many of

* *Life,* 217.

his Cabinet were converts to the New Views which I advocated.

(b)* Lord Liverpool gave me a seat, and with a considerable diffidence and agitation in his manner, said, 'Mr. Owen, what is your wish?'—in a tone of voice and with an expression of countenance as much as to say, 'Your wishes shall be gratified.' And I believe the Government would have given me any place or station, or almost anything I should ask; for it was evident that they felt they were at my mercy. . . . I therefore replied to his Lordship's question, that all I desired was, that his Lordship and his Cabinet would allow their names to be upon the committee of investigation which I should propose at the meeting the next day, with an equal number of disunion, to saturate society at all times with wealth, if my proposed resolutions should be carried.

On my saying this I never saw anyone so immediately relieved from an apparent great anxiety—and his Lordship replied in the most confiding manner, 'Mr. Owen, you shall have full liberty to make any use of our names you desire and which you may think useful to your views, short of implicating us as a Government.'

(c)** [At Frankfort Owen met M. Gentz, Secretary to the Congress of Sovereigns to be held at Aix. They discussed Owen's proposals.]

I stated that now, through the progress of science, the means amply existed in all countries, or might easily be made to exist on the principle of union for the foundation of society, instead of its present foundation of disunion, to saturate society at all times with wealth, sufficient to amply supply the wants of all through life. What was my surprise to hear the reply of the learned secretary! 'Yes,' he said, and apparently speaking for the

* *Life,* 218-20.   ** *Life,* 253.

governments, 'we know that very well; but we do not want the mass to become wealthy and independent of us. How could we govern them if they were?'

(d)*   [Owen attempted to present a copy of his memorials to the Emperor.]

. . . but his dress fitted so tightly to his person, that, having no pockets, he had no place in which he could put so large a packet. He was evidently annoyed by the circumstance, and said, as I thought angrily. 'I cannot receive it—I have no place to put it in. Who are you?' 'Robert Owen,' was my reply. 'Come to me in the evening at Mr. Bethman's,' and he passed on.

I did not like his manner of speaking to me, and did not go; which I afterwards regretted, for he was naturally amiable, and as kind-hearted as the surroundings of despotism would admit, and I might have influenced him to some beneficial purpose, for my influence among European governing parties was, as I learned afterwards, far greater than I was conscious of. . . .

I may here remark, that in all my intercourse with the Ministers of despotic powers, I uniformly found them in principle favourably disposed to the introduction of the new system of society, and that they gave me all the facilities and aid which their position would admit.

(e)**   As soon as the Sovereigns met I hastened to Aix-la-Chapelle, and there completed the two memorials to the governments of Europe and America. I then applied to Lord Castlereagh, the representative, with the Duke of Wellington, of the British Government at this Congress. Lord Castlereagh, in the most friendly manner promised to present these documents to Congress under the most favourable circumstances. He did so, and it was stated to

* *Life*, 255-6.   ** *Life*, 257.

142

me in confidence on my return to Paris, by one of the Ministers of the Government, that these two memorials were considered the most important documents which were presented to the Congress.

(f)*   In the House of Lords it was evident that Lord Liverpool and the leading members of his Cabinet were favourable to the full investigation of the subject, and the debate was taking that turn, when Lord Lauderdale arose, and with marked emphasis in his manner and tone of voice, said, 'My Lords, I know Mr. Owen, and I have examined his plan for the relief of the working classes, as he has published it to the world, and I tell your Lordships, that if you countenance Mr. Owen and his new views, there is no government in Europe that can stand against them.'

This declaration from a peer of the highest influence in the House, decided the course which the Government must take in both Houses, much to their regret, for they heartily inclined to have the principles and plans I had so openly placed before the public, fairly tried under the auspices of their administration.

4 OWEN AND THE DUKE OF KENT

[One of the oddest features of Owen's life was his friendship with the Duke of Kent, son of George III and father of Queen Victoria. In his later years Owen became an ardent spiritualist and claimed to have had many conversations with the dead Duke. See Chapter XVI.]

(a)**   The most valuable of [my supporters], while he lived was His Royal Highness the late Duke of Kent, whose real character for the last four years of his life is yet but little known to the public. His letters addressed to me, about thirty of them, will show the power and good-

* *Life*, 299.   ** *Life*, 266-7.

ness of that mind which, had he lived to reign, would have given all his influence to have peaceably established truth in principle, spirit, and practice throughout the British Empire, and by the success of such a change in governing, would have induced all the other governments to imitate his. . . .

Their Royal Highnesses the Dukes of Kent and Sussex, who at this period were much united in affection and pursuits, occasionally looked in upon me to study the model I had, of the first new surroundings in which I proposed to place the poor and working classes, to train them out of their inferior habits and to give good and superior ones to their children; and also to see and draw their own conclusions from inspecting the cubic proportions of the different classes of society, which I had directed to be made to exhibit to the eye the contrast between the amount in numbers of the governing and the governed classes.

On some of these visits the royal dukes would bring with them some members of the higher nobility. On one occasion the Duke of Kent observed one of them to point very significantly to the great difference between the very small cube which represented the governing powers (the Royal Family and the House of Peers), and the various classes governed by them, and looking at the Duke, as much as to say, 'Is not this rather a dangerous and levelling exhibition?' The Duke caught the expression, and said, 'I see you imagine I have not studied this subject, and that I do not foresee its ultimate results. I know these will be a much more just equality of our race, and an equality that will give much more security and happiness to all, than the present system can give to any; and it is for this reason that I so much approve of it and give it my support.'

(b)* [Owen claimed to have had 'communications with the spirits of many past worthies'.]

* *Life*, 275.

144

Among these, in an especial manner, I have to name the apparent very anxious feelings of the spirit of His Royal Highness the Duke of Kent (who early informed me there were no titles in the spiritual spheres into which he had entered), to benefit, not a class, a sect, a party, or any particular country, but the whole of the human race throught futurity. And in this feeling he seemed to be strongly united with the spirit of my friend and warm disciple President Jefferson, and his particular friend the celebrated Benjamin Franklin. These three spirits have frequently come together to communicate to me the most interesting and valuable knowledge, with occasional notices of persons who when living were dear to these superior spirits. But never upon any occasion was there a trivial idea expressed by either of them.

At one important *seance* these three spirits came in company with the spirits of Channing, Chalmers, Shelley, Byron, and several of the old prophets; and on this occasion the spirits of eight of my deceased relatives were also present.

(c)*   The Duke of Kent's whole spirit proceeding with me has been most beautiful; making his own appointments; meeting me on the day, hour, and minute he named; and never in one instance (and these appointments were numerous as long as I had mediums near me upon whom I could depend) has this spirit not been punctual to the minute he had named.

5 OWEN AND THE WORKERS

[Owen was indifferent, and even hostile, to the proposals for political reform advocated by the Radicals and Chartists of the time.]

* *Life*, 316.

(a)* At this period [about 1817] I had had no public intercourse with the operatives and working classes in any part of the two Islands—not even in the metropolis. They were at this time strangers to me and to all my views and future intentions. I was at all periods of my progress, and from my earliest knowledge and employment of them, their true friend. While their democratic and much mistaken leaders taught them that I was their enemy, a friend to all in authority, and that I desired to make slaves of them in these villages of unity and mutual co-operation.

On the other hand, my opponents had been most industrious in marshalling their forces, and they were led to the meeting by the popular orators of the day, and these were encouraged in their opposition by the leading active members of the then popular school of modern political economy.

(b)** As you proceed in these inquiries, you will find that mankind cannot be improved or rendered reasonable by force or contention; that it is absolutely necessary to support the old systems and institutions under which we now live, until another system and another arrangement of society shall be proved by practice to be essentially superior. You will, therefore, still regard it as your duty to pay respect and submission to what is established. For it would be no mark of wisdom to desert an old house, whatever may be its imperfections, until a new one shall be ready to receive you, however superior to the old that new one may be when finished.

Continue to obey the laws under which you live; and although many of them are founded on principles of the grossest ignorance and folly, you obey them—until the government of the country (which I have reason to believe is in the hands of men well disposed to adopt a

* *Life*, 221.   ** *New Lanark*, Cole, 118-9.

system of general improvement) shall find it practicable to withdraw those laws which are productive of evil, and introduce others of an opposite tendency.

6* OWEN AND THE REFORMERS

Among the leading Radical reformers who were personally very friendly, but yet were opposed to my *New View of Society,* were Sir Francis Burdett, M.P.; Major Cartwright; Henry Hunt, M.P.; William Cobbett, M.P.; Feargus O'Connor, M.P.; Mr. John Frost; Mr. Ernest Jones; and many others.

My knowledge of the formation of character enabled me to know how their characters were formed, and therefore enabled me to differ from them in opinion and yet do justice to their good intentions, although their measures always appeared to me to arise from want of a comprehensive knowledge of human nature and society, and from their supposing that violence and force could effect any permanent good, while mind remained unconverted.

7** A VISIT TO FRANCE, 1817

Shortly after this came Professor Pictet, the celebrated savant of Geneva . . . to invite me to France and to Switzerland and the Continent generally. He said that his particular friend Cuvier, the celebrated French naturalist, and secretary to the French Academy in Paris, would come over and meet us in London, and we could return with him to Paris. . . .

My first visit was to the Duke of Orleans, to whom the Duke of Kent's letter gave me a ready and welcome introduction. The Duke received me more as a friend than a stranger . . . and then entered familiarly into a narrative,

* *Life,* 292.   ** *Life,* 229-35.

confidential at that period, of the delicate position which he held in relation to the other and then reigning branch of the Bourbon family.

The Duke said—'The reigning family are jealous of me. They are afraid of my liberal principles. I am watched, and I feel it necessary to be guarded in my private and public conduct. I therefore live very quietly and take no active part in any of the movements of the day. But I observe all that takes place, and the day may come when I may have more liberty to act according to my views of the necessities of the times.' He was at this time a thoughtful, watchful character and rather timid than otherwise. My views were too well known, he said, to allow him to appear openly to countenance me. . . .

I was next introduced by my friends, Cuvier and Pictet, to La Place, the wide-world-known astronomer. And then to Alexander von Humboldt, who was then in Paris pursuing his scientific investigations.

And we four—La Place, Cuvier, Pictet, and myself—afterwards often met at the house of one or other of the two first to converse freely upon public affairs interesting to the population of all countries. . . . And I was now considered by these men as the advanced mind in a practical knowledge of human nature and the science of society. It was to me at first astonishing to discover, in La Place and Cuvier especially, but less so in Pictet, their childish simplicity on all subjects relative to human nature and to the science of society. They sought my society eagerly, to question me on these subjects, apparently quite new to their study, they having so long had their minds fixed on their own respective sciences, that they had never entered the field of investigation of these subjects, so familiar to me.

Professor Pictet seemed to be much respected by all parties, and he was on friendly terms with the leaders of the more liberal view. . . . Some of these names I especially remember. One was Count de Boissy d'Anglas, who, upon my being introduced to him, received me, to my no little surprise, with open arms and a salute on each cheek, from a rougher chin than I had ever so encountered —for he was the first man from whom I received such a salute. I found he was a warm and ardent disciple of mine—open, frank, and honest in his avowal of his principles, and in his adherence to rational liberty.

Another was Camille Jourdain, so well known through all the stages of the Revolution. . . .

A third on my memory was the Duke de la Rochefoucault, who had from patriotic motives established on his estate in the country, what at that time in France was considered a large cotton-spinning manufactory. He wished me to see it, and took me with him into the country. I examined the whole business as then carried on at the Duke's risk and with his capital. I found by this investigation, that I was manufacturing the same number of fineness of thread, but of much better quality, at the New Lanark establishment in Scotland, at fourpence a pound cheaper than the Duke's. One penny per pound upon the annual produce at that time at New Lanark, was £8,000 sterling—which sum multiplied by four gives a gain upon the same quality, of the Duke's, of thirty-two thousand pounds per year. Evidently therefore the Duke required a high duty on British cottons to enable him, and all similarly situated to proceed. But it was equally evident that the French people had to pay this duty to their own manufacturers to enable them to continue their work. . . .

And thus for six weeks did the Professor and myself luxuriate amidst the *élite* of the most distinguished men then in Paris; and I lost no opportunity of obtaining the best thoughts of these superior characters. . . . And from one cause or another I was made during this period, through the Professor's means and others, the lion of Paris. Knowing the defects of my early education, the little instruction I had received from others, of the little

I really knew of the mind, habits, and manners of the great world, and being then and for a long time afterwards unconscious of the deep and widespread impressions which had been made by my publications on the formation of character, my practical measures, so long pursued at New Lanark, and latterly my public meetings and proceedings in London—I was continually at a loss to account for the extraordinary deference and respect which was paid to me by all these parties. But so it was.

8* IN GENEVA

Among many others, I was introduced during this visit to Madame Necker, the sister of Mademe de Staël.... The Professor had made my *New View of Society* very popular at Geneva, and they were always the favourite topic of conversation with Madame Necker and the Professor's daughters, who were never tired of pursuing it through all its ramifications, to its beautiful results, ending in the practice of the Millennium over the Earth, and the cordial union of the race as one superior and enlightened family.

9** INTERNATIONAL SUCCESS OF OWEN'S WRITINGS

These works had also been translated into foreign languages, and very many editions were published in the United States, where also they had prepared for me a warm national reception. For, as I have already stated, in 1816, when John Quincey Adams was the United States Ambassador in London, he applied to me ... to know if I wished them to be introduced into the United States, for if I did, he would shortly return there, and if I would entrust him with copies for the President and his Cabinet,

* *Life*, 237.   ** *Life*, 278-9.

and for the Governor of each State in the Union, he would assure me that they should be faithfully delivered. ... They gave me a ready introduction to all the Presidents of the Republic, from John Adams downwards, and with him Jefferson, Madison, Munroe, John Quincey Adams, General Jackson, and Mr. Van Buren, by all of whom I was admitted into their confidence, and from whom I obtained their best thoughts, and the unbiased results of their valuable experience.

These works, imperially bound, were also gladly received by every sovereign in Europa, and by Napoleon the First when in the Island of Elba, in which he had time to study them, and did so, as I was afterwards informed by Major-General Sir Neil Campbell. ... It was stated that these works, in which the erroneous warlike proceedings of Napoleon were animadverted upon, had so far changed his views, that he said, should he be allowed by the other European powers to remain quiet on the throne of France, he would do as much for peace as he had previously done in war.

10* OWEN IN THE U.S.A.

[This passage illustrates both the attention which Owen received in official circles and his tendency to mistake polite interest for conviction.]

My first visits were to John Adams, to Thomas Jefferson, to James Madison and to James Munroe—the two latter, the fourth and fifth presidents. George Washington, the first president of the republic, had died before my first visit to the United States. ...

After a full explanation of my views to the four Presidents of the United States, they regularly, one after

* *Millennial Gazette,* 52-6.

the other, admitted the truth of the fundamental principle on which the new dispensation must be raised. But they one and all said, we do not see how these principles, true and beautiful as they are, can be applied to practice. . . .

I then stated in what manner I had then for thirty years applied them to practice. . . .

They said you have now so much practical knowledge of the application of these new principles to practice that our want of experience must yield to your experience. . . .

There was at this period a friendship established between the ex-President, the existing President, Mr. Munroe, and his successor John Quincey Adams, the son of President Adams; and I had every reason to suppose that the ex-President, whom I had thus visited, communicated his ideas and impressions to all of them; for from that period I had the full confidence of the United States Government, through the administrations of Mr. Munroe, Mr. John Quincey Adams, General Jackson, and Mr. Van Buren; the interesting particulars of which will be given in detail in my life which I am now engaged in writing.

11 ADDRESS TO CONGRESS

[On February 25th and March 7th, 1825, Owen gave two lectures in Washington to an audience including members of both Houses of Congress, the President of the U.S.A., members of the Cabinet and other distinguished persons. These were published under the title *A Discourse on a New System of Society*. Much Owen said dealt with his general ideas and the details of his Plan along lines covered elsewhere in this volume. I give a few extracts in which he discusses the special application of the Plan to American conditions and a short account of New Harmony which was opened a few months later.

My quotations are made from a typescript copy of the

very rare original edition, for the use of which I am much indebted to the American Institute for Marxist Studies.]

(a) Man, through ignorance, has been, hitherto, the tormentor of man.

He is *here*, in a nation deeming itself possessed of more privileges than all other nations, and which pretensions, in many respects, must be admitted to be true. . . .

If the leading men of these states, forgetting every little and unworthy party and sectarian distinction, will now cordially unite, they may, with ease, break asunder the bonds of ignorance, superstition, and prejudice, and, by thus acting, they could not fail to dispel error, and to give and secure mental freedom and happiness to the world. . . .

The Government and Congress of this new empire have only, now, as I have previously stated, to will this change, and it will be at once effected; and, by such act, they will give and secure liberty, affluence, and happiness, to America and to the world.

I have said, give liberty to America; but the natives of this empire have been taught to believe, that they already possess full liberty. I know it is *not* so; and, in proof of this denial, permit me to ask, how many present feel they possess the power to speak their real sentiments, freely and openly, on subjects the most important to themselves and to the well being of society? Until this can be done, and done without any disadvantages whatever to those who do it, liberty has not been attained, and you have yet to work out for yourselves this, the most precious and valuable part of liberty. . . . By a hard struggle you have attained political liberty, but you have yet to acquire real mental liberty, and if you cannot possess yourselves of it, your political liberty will be precarious and of much less value. The attainment of political liberty is however, a necessary step towards the acquirement of real mental liberty, and as you have obtained the former, I have come here to assist you to secure the latter. For, without mental liberty, there can be no sincerity; and without sincerity devoid of all deception, there can be no real virtue or happiness among mankind.

(b) With this view, I have purchased from the Harmonite Society, the settlement and property of Harmony, in the states of Indiana and Illinois. The settlement, or town of Harmony, is upon the Wabash, in Indiana; it is composed of log, weather boarded, and brick dwelling houses of infant manufactures, of wool, cotton, leather, hats, pottery, bricks, machinery, grain, distilleries, breweries &c. &c. with granaries and two large churches, and other public buildings, laid out in regular squares like all the modern American towns. It does not, however, form such a combination as the model before you represents, and, therefore, it will serve only a temporary, but yet a useful temporary purpose, for the objects which I have in view. It will enable me to form immediately a preliminary society in which to receive a new population, and to collect, prepare, and arrange the materials for erection of several such combinations, as the model represents, and of forming several independent, yet united associations, having common property, and one common interest. These new establishments will be erected upon the highlands of Harmony, from two to four miles from the river, and its Island, of which the occupants will have a beautiful and interesting view, there being several thousand acres of well cultivated land, on a rich second bottom, lying between the highlands and the river. And here it is, in the heart of the United States, and almost the centre of its unequalled internal navigation, that that power which directs and governs the universe and every action of man, has arranged circumstances which were far beyond my control, to permit me to commence a new empire of peace and good will to man, founded on other principles, and leading to other practices than those of the past or present, and which principles, in due season, and in the allotted time, will lead to that state of virtue, intelligence, enjoyment and happiness, in practice, which as has been foretold by the sages of past times, would, at some distant period, become the lot of the human race!

IX

Revolution by Reason

[When Owen spoke of Revolution by Reason he meant a revolution in which class and class conflict had no part. This chapter gives something of his attitude to the popular movements and demands of his time, and of his views about the relation of classes.]

1* FORCE OR REASON

[Owen seldom referred directly to Chartism, but his views can be inferred indirectly from this Proclamation issued by the Congress of the Universal Community Society of Rational Religionists in May 1840.]

The progress of machinery and of scientific knowledge has made a revolution, either by force or reason, unavoidable in the whole business of life.

A revolution by *force* will be *injurious to all*.

A revolution by *reason* will be *beneficial to all*.

The British Empire is the most advanced in the *progress of machinery and in scientific knowledge;* and, in consequence, now experiences the strongest necessity for this change; and it should, therefore, lead the revolution by reason, that the revolution by force may be avoided. . . .

* *Address*, 7-8.

It is most irrational to suppose that the millions will continue to starve in the midst of plenty, and in the midst of means permanently to ensure that plenty for all. . . .

Nor is it now practicable to maintain this degraded and miserable state of existence; for, unless a wise direction shall be given to machinery and scientific knowledge, and attention paid to the better formation of the character of individuals and of society, the masses—the millions—will be goaded on by desperation to the commission of acts of the most frightful violence. For it is impossible to suppose that men can longer submit to be kept in ignorance and poverty, and in the midst of every vicious and injurious external circumstance; while now, with so much ease, they may be filled with the most useful and valuable knowledge, and be made permanently wealthy, and surrounded with the most virtuous, elevating, and beneficial external circumstances that the human mind, in its highest and best state, can desire.

But, it will be asked, how can this change be made by reason, when the history of man declares that hitherto all revolutions have been effected by force?

We reply, that the world has advanced to an entirely new position; that a benefical revolution cannot now be effected by violence, and that all the means are prepared to accomplish this mighty change in the condition of the human race, without force or fraud of any kind, and without injury to a single individual.

2 TWO DEDICATIONS

[Owen's book *The Revolution in the Mind and Practice of the Human Race*, contains two introductory addresses, the first, 'To Her Majesty, Victoria, Queen of the British Empire, and to Her Responsible Advisers', the second, 'To the Red Republicans, Communists and Socialists of Europe'. The date—1849—gives them a special interest.]

(a)*   The extended and increasing misery of the human race, arising from the want of requisite knowledge to trace its cause, and provide a remedy, calls loudly for the simple and plain language of truth, in the spirit of charity and kindness, to declare both cause and remedy to the authorities of the world. . . .

The enormous power of the British Empire, for good or for evil, and its present peaceful and secure position, compared with other nations, call upon it to take a friendly direction to assist those nations out of the miserably entangled state into which they have fallen. . . .

The British Empire is now generally admitted to be the most advanced, and next to the United States, the most secure, of all nations; but all nations at this crisis, are subject to manifold casualties at home and abroad.

Great Britain is now, with the most ample means to create illimitable wealth, and to make its dominions an example of high prosperity and wealth, involved, like other nations, in a complicated system of error in principle and practice; which makes it a glaring example of poverty, crime, disease, and misery among the majority of its population, while the few are deeply injured by an excess of wealth and luxury, and of injustice to the many. . . .

Will you now investigate this all-important subject, and, if you find that I have declared that only which is true, good, and practical, will you adopt the principles and practices now recommended?

(b)**   Friends and Fellow Men—The excited feelings aroused by the sufferings of the industrious masses, and now existing throughout Europe, between the Aristocracy and Democracy, are producing a desolating conflict between parties whose real interests are the same.

The existing system of society, in all its varieties

* *Revolution,* xi-xvi.
** *Revolution,* xvii-xxiii.

throughout the world, is based on falsehood—is, therefore artificial, and opposed to the eternal laws of humanity; it has always been degrading, unjust, and cruel, to the mass of mankind; and the sooner it can be made to terminate, the better it will be for all now living and those who will live hereafter. . . .

It is this impulse to overcome evil which now agitates the populations of Europe, and alarms the governing powers.

This was the true cause of the French revolution in February last, and of all the revolutions which have previously or since occurred over the world. Nor will these revolutions now cease until there shall be an entire change in the whole system of society, both in principle and practice. . . .

You desire to change to a better system, but see no mode of succeeding, except through violence.

I equally desire to see the change for the better accomplished; but it seems to me impossible to effect a beneficial, permanent change, through violence. . . .

Last year you had the power of Europe at your control; you lost it, not from the power of your opponents, but, from your want of knowing how to use power, when, through great difficulties, you had attained it. Were you again to acquire it, you would, from your want of knowledge of human nature, and of the true science of society, again allow it to be taken from you by the present aristocracy, who are experienced in governing, although upon false, injurious, and most cruel principles; but, taught as they have been, they know no other system. . . .

Without this knowledge you cannot proceed one step rationally towards the construction of a permanently prosperous and happy state of society.

The want of this knowledge was *alone* the cause of the failure of your efforts last year in France; it is the only cause of the present involved state of Europe, and of the irrational, or truly insane, conduct of so many contending nations at this moment; all of which are acting in direct opposition to their own well-being, interest and happiness.

While you know not the true mode of forming a good character for all; or the means to obtain these results—to form revolutions will be useless and injurious to all. For, when successful, they will only increase the miseries of the mass, and make democrats into aristocrats, and thus keep society in a continual circle of contention and turmoil.

3* MANHOOD SUFFRAGE – A BAUBLE

Public attention has long been directed to a reform in Parliament as a panacea for all political evils, in which the expectants will be sadly disappointed, for it can effect no good or evil. A Parliament elected by manhood suffrage, things remaining as they are, would make little or no change for the better to the working classes, but would create perhaps more useless debates on subjects little understood by the new debaters. It would, however, be wisdom in the government to bring in and pass a bill for reform on the most liberal conditions—however liberal it will be harmless, and it will prevent more waste of invaluable time.

As members elected to the House of Commons have been prejudiced from birth by their erroneous training, education, and surroundings, they can see and comprehend private interests only; they are unprepared to legislate for the general public good; and such would be the case with the elected members under the full manhood suffrage. This result is demonstrated by the manhood elected members of the Congress of the United States, where an entire reform in the character and condition of the mass of the

* *Life, IA.,* xxi-xxii. (Memorial to the Right Honourable the Lords of Her Majesty's Treasury. 1858.)

people is quite as much required as in the British dominions.

But as manhood suffrage is at present a popular bauble, that will do neither good nor harm in its practical results, it will satisfy the most energetic but least experienced of the population of these islands to have it made a law of the constitution of this country, and it may now be safely granted to them.

4* THE RICH MUST ALWAYS GOVERN

Stranger: What hope have you then of a change, seeing that the rich and powerful will always, in the nature of things, govern the world?

Founder: My sanguine expectation of a speedy and extensive change rests upon the knowledge that the rich and powerful must always govern the world, and that they will govern it in accordance with what they are taught to believe will contribute most to their interest and happiness.

Stranger: Have they not always acted upon this principle, are they not now acting upon it? And if they must always persevere in this course, whence is this unheard-of change to proceed, and who are they who are to effect this mighty revolution in all human affairs?

Founder: This great change ... must and will be accomplished by the rich and powerful. There are no other parties to do it, for those who can obtain the direction of public affairs, must be the most powerful, and the most powerful will soon make themselves the most wealthy. . . .

Stranger: Then you think that it is a waste of time, talent and pecuniary means, for the poor to contend in opposition to the rich and powerful?

Founder: I do; because if these who are poor today become powerful and succeed to the government tomor-

* *Dialogue,* 18-20.

it, recur to the past, in which all have been compelled to act an irrational part; but we will earnestly apply ourselves to the future; and having discovered the light of true knowledge, we will henceforth walk by it.'

6* TO WHOM CAN MY PLANS BE SUBMITTED?

Not to the mere commercial character, in whose estimation to forsake the path of immediate individual gain would be to show symptoms of a disordered imagination; for the children of commerce have been trained to direct all their faculties to buy cheap and sell dear; and consequently, those who are the most expert and successful in this wise and noble art, are, in the commercial world, deemed to possess foresight and superior acquirements; while such as attempt to improve the moral habits and increase the comforts of those whom they employ, are termed wild enthusiasts.

Nor yet are they to be submitted to the mere men of the law; for these are necessarily trained to endeavour to make wrong appear right, or to involve both in a maze of intricacies, and to legalize injustice.

Nor to the mere political leaders or their partizans, for they are embarrassed by the trammels of party, which mislead their judgement, and often constrain them to sacrifice the real well-being of the community and of themselves, to an apparent but most mistaken self-interest.

Nor to those termed heroes and conquerors, or to their followers; for their minds have been trained to consider the infliction of human misery, and the commission of military murders, a glorious duty, almost beyond reward.

Nor yet to the fashionable or splendid in their appearance; for these are from infancy trained to deceive and to be deceived, to accept shadows for substances, and to

* *New View,* Cole, 61-2.

live a life of insincerity, and of consequent discontent and misery.

Still less are they to be exclusively submitted to the official expounders and defenders of the various opposing religious systems throughout the world; for many of these are actively engaged in propagating imaginary notions, which cannot fail to vitiate the rational powers of man, and to perpetuate his misery.

These principles, therefore, and the practical systems which they recommend, are not to be submitted to the judgement of those who have been trained under, and continue in, any of these unhappy combinations of circumstances. But they are to be submitted to the dispassionate and patient investigation and decision of those individuals of every rank and class and denomination of society, who have become in some degree conscious of the errors in which they exist; who have felt the thick mental darkness by which they are surrounded; who are ardently desirous of discovering and following truth wherever it may lead; and who can perceive the inseparable connexion which exists between individual and general, between private and public good!

7* OWEN'S OPPONENTS

[Owen's refutation of Malthus is given in Chapter V. Here it may be noted that on the whole he has more confidence in the Tories than in either Whigs or Radicals. His attitude to the Radicals, and later to the Chartists, was one of the main barriers between him and the working class.]

Those who opposed the principles and plan I advocated were some of the younger disciples of the much-dreaded

* *Catechism*, Cole, 205-7.

is my confidence in the truth of the principles on which the system I am about to introduce is founded, that I hesitate not to assert their power heartily to incline all men to say, 'This system is assuredly true, and therefore eminently calculated to realize those invaluable percepts of the Gospel—universal charity, goodwill, and peace among men. Hitherto we must have been trained in error; and we hail it as the harbinger of that period when our swords shall be turned into ploughshares, and our spears into pruning-hooks; when universal love and benevolence shall prevail; when there shall be but one language and one nation; and when fear of want or of any evil among men shall be known no more.'

Acting, although unknown to you, uniformly and steadily upon this system, my attention was ever directed to remove as I could prepare means for their removal, such of the immediate causes as were perpetually creating misery amongst you, and which, if permitted to remain, would to this day have continued to create misery. I therefore withdrew the most pernicious incitements to falsehood, theft, drunkenness, and other pernicious habits, with which many of you were familiar: and in their stead I introduced other causes, which were intended to produce better *external* habits. I say better *external* habits, for to these alone have my proceedings hitherto been intended to apply. What has yet been done I consider as merely preparatory.

9* ENTIRELY RIGHT OR ENTIRELY WRONG

Stranger: Since we parted I have had time to reflect upon our last conversation, and reflection has only increased the magnitude of the importance which I attach to a right consideration of those principles which you ad-

* *Dialogue,* 8-9.

vocate. I, therefore, repeat, that you are entirely wrong in the foundation and superstructure of your New Moral World, or we of the old world must be so; for principles and practices more opposed to each other the human mind cannot conceive.

Founder: This is the view of the subject which I wish you to take; for I, at once, admit that I am entirely wrong or entirely right; and that, if I am right, you of the old world are wrong in all your views of human nature and of society; that is, of man in his individual state, and as a being associated with his fellows to promote their mutual happiness.

The plan represented is on a scale considered to be sufficient to accommodate about 1,200 persons.

And these are to be supposed men, women, and children, of all ages, capacities and dispositions; most of them very ignorant; many with bad and vicious habits, possessing only the ordinary bodily and mental faculties of human beings, and who require to be supported out of the funds appropriated to the maintenance of the poor—individuals who are at present not only useless and a direct burden on the public, but whose moral influence is highly pernicious, since they are the medium by which ignorance and certain classes of vicious habits and crimes are fostered and perpetuated in society.

It is evident that while the poor are suffered to remain under the circumstances in which they have hitherto existed, they and their children, with very few exceptions, will continue unaltered in succeeding generations.

In order to effect any radically beneficial change in their character, they must be removed from the influence of such circumstances, and placed under those which, being congenial to the natural constitution of man and the well-being of society, cannot fail to produce that amelioration in their condition which all classes have an interest in promoting.

2* HOW CAN SUCH VILLAGES BE ESTABLISHED

[Owen estimated the initial cost of setting up one of these villages at about £100,000.]

There are several modes by which this plan may be effected.

It may be accomplished by individuals—by parishes —by counties—by districts, &c., comprising more coun-

* *Relief of Poor*, Cole, 164-5.

ties than one—and by the nation at large through its Government. Some may prefer one mode, some another; and it would be advantageous certainly to have the experience of the greatest variety of particular modes, in order that the plan which such diversified practice should prove to be the best might afterwards be generally adopted. It may therefore be put into execution by any parties according to their own localities and views.

The first thing necessary is, to raise a sum of money adequate to purchase the land (or it may be rented)—to build the square, manufactories, farm-houses, and their appendages—to stock the farm—and to provide everything to put the whole in motion.

Proper persons must be procured to superintend the various departments, until others should be trained in the establishment to supply their places.

The labour of the persons admitted may then be applied to procure a comfortable support for themselves and their children and to repay, as might be required, the capital expended on the establishment.

When their labour shall be thus properly and temperately directed, under an intelligent system, easy of practice, it will soon be found to be more than sufficient to supply every reasonable want of man. . . . The period is also arrived when the state of society imperiously requires the adoption of some measures to relieve the wealthy and industrious from the increasing burdens of the poor's rate, and the poor from their increasing misery and degradation.

3* GOVERNMENT OF THE COMMUNITIES

The peculiar mode of governing these establishments will depend on the parties who form them.

Those formed by landowners and capitalists, public

* *Report*, Cole, 287.

one particle of interest in all those nameless associations which had been formed by and with the departed object; and at the same time liable to insult, poverty, and every kind of oppression, and no one inclined to help or relieve. All are individualized, cold, and forbidding; each being compelled to take an hundred-fold more care of himself than would be otherwise necessary; because the ignorance of society has placed him in direct opposition to the thousands around him.

Under the proposed scheme, what a reverse will take place in practice when any of these dispensations of life occur! In these happy villages of unity, when disease or death assail their victim, every aid is near; all the assistance that skill, kindness and sincere affection can invent, aided by every convenience and comfort, are at hand. The intelligent resigned sufferer waits with cheerful patience, and thus effectually parries every assault of disease, when unaccompanied by his fell companion, death; and when death attacks him, he submits to a conqueror who he knew from childhood was irresistible, and whom for a moment he never feared! He is gone! The survivors lose an intelligent, a sincere and truly-valued friend; a beloved child; they feel their loss, and human nature must ever regret it; but the survivors were not unprepared, or unprovided, for this natural event. They have, it is true, lost one endeared and beloved object; and endeared and beloved in proportion as it was intelligent and excellent; but they have consolation in the certain knowledge that within their own immediate circle they have many, many others remaining; and around them on all sides, as far as the eye can reach, or imagination extend, thousands on thousands, willing to offer them aid and consolation. No orphans left without protectors; no insult or oppression can take place, nor any evil result whatever, beyond the loss of one dear friend or object among thousands who remain, dear to us as ourselves. Here may it be truly said, 'O death, where is thy sting? O grave, where is thy victory?'

It may be useful here to remark, that the plan developed in my Report to the Committee of the Association for the Relief of the Manufacturing and Labouring Poor, and of the House of Commons on the Poor Laws, was intended for the parish poor *only;* and of course no part of society will long continue in a worse condition than the individuals within such proposed establishments. Under these arrangements the parish poor will soon lose their ignorant and vulgar habits, and acquire such an improved character as the new circumstances will imperceptibly and speedily give them. When these results irresistibly force themselves on the minds of all, the meanest and most miserable beings now in society will thus become the envy of the rich and indolent under the existing arrangements. The change from the *old* system to the *new* must become universal. To resist the introduction of this plan, in any part of the world, will *now* be as vain and useless, as for man by his puny efforts to preclude from the earth the vivifying rays of the sun.

6** A TEN YEARS' PLAN

All the means requisite to effect this change over Europe and America in five years from its commencement, and over the world in less than ten, are now at the control of society; and they will be thus applied as soon as measures shall be adopted to make society so far rational as to understand their own permanent interest.

And if the governments and peoples of Europe and America will now enter cordially into these measures, the populations of both continents may with ease, through a right direction of the daily and other periodical publica-

* *Development*, Cole, 231-2.
** *Revolution*, 48-9.

tions, and by other teachings, be made to become rational; and the dark glass of error, through which everything is now seen and mystified, will be removed, and they may be enabled to see things as they are, and prepared to act rationally, in less than one year.

Such is the simplicity and power of truth.

7* THE SYSTEM WILL BE WORLD WIDE

It is the interest of each one of the human race that there should be but one interest, one language, one general code of laws, and one system of administering them. These unions offer the most natural, easy, and speedy mode of effecting these great and always to be desired results. The federative connection of these Townships, by tens for more limited local objects, by fifties or hundreds for more enlarged operations, and by thousands for the most extended interests, to ensure peace and goodwill through every district and clime, will be effected without difficulty. For it will be discovered that the highest and most permanent interest of each one over the world, will be most effectually secured by these Townships and federations of Townships, without limit, until the population of the globe shall be cordially united as members of one family, all actively engaged in promoting the happiness of each other. These Townships, thus separate and united, will form palaces, surrounded with gardens, pleasure-grounds, and highly cultivated estates, on each side of all the railways, which will traverse each country in the most convenient directions for all general purposes.

* *Revolution,* 74.

XI

Some Features of the Plan

Under this head are to be noticed, the amount and collection of the revenue, and the public or legal duties of the associations in peace and war.

Your Reporter concludes that whatever taxes are paid from land, capital, and labour under the existing arrangements of society, the same amount for the same proportion of each may be collected with far more ease under those now proposed. The Government would, of course, require its revenue to be paid in the legal circulating medium, to obtain which, the associations would have to dispose of as much of their surplus produce to common society for the legal coin or paper of the realm as would discharge the demands of Government.

In time of peace these associations would give no trouble to Government; their internal arrangements being founded on principles of prevention, not only with reference to public crimes but to the private evils and errors which so fatally abound in common society. Courts of law, prisons, and punishments would not be required. These are requisite only where human nature is greatly misunderstood; where society rests on the demoralizing system of individual competition, rewards, and punishments—they are necessary only in a stage of existence

* *Report,* Cole, 291-2.

previous to the discovery of the science of the certain and overwhelming influence of circumstances over the whole character and conduct of mankind. Whatever courts of law, prisons, and punishments have yet effected for society, the influence of other circumstances, which may now be easily introduced, will accomplish infinitely more; for they will effectually prevent the growth of those evils of which our present institutions do not take cognizance till they are already full formed and in baneful activity. In times of peace, therefore, these associations will save much charge and trouble to Government.

In reference to war also, they will be equally beneficial. Bodily exercises, adapted to improve the dispositions and increase the health and strength of the individual, will form part of the training and education of the children. In these exercises they may be instructed to acquire facility in the execution of combined movements, a habit which is calculated to produce regularity and order in time of peace, as well as to aid defensive and offensive operations in war. The children, therefore, at an early age, will acquire, *through their amusements,* those habits which will render them capable of becoming, in a short time, at any future period of life, the best defenders of their country, if necessity should ever arise to defend it; since they would, in all possibility, be far more to be depended upon than those whose physical, intellectual, and moral training had been less carefully conducted. In furnishing their quotas for the militia or common army they would probably adopt the pecuniary alternative; by which means they would form a reserve that, in proportion to their numbers, would be a great security to the nation's safety. They would prefer this alternative, to avoid the demoralizing effects of recruiting.

But knowledge of the science and influence of circumstances over mankind will speedily enable all nations to discover not only the evils of war, but the folly of it. Of all modes of conduct adopted by mankind to obtain advantages in the present stage of society, this is the most certain to defeat its object. It is, in truth, a system of direct demoralization and of destruction; while it is the highest interest of all individuals and of all countries to *remoralize and conserve*. Men surely cannot with truth be termed rational beings until they shall discover and put in practice the principles which shall enable them to conduct their affairs without war. The arrangements we are considering would speedily show how easily these principles and practices may be introduced into general society.

From what has been stated it is evident that these associations would not subject the Government to the same proportion of trouble and expense that an equal population would do in old society; on the contrary, they would relieve the Government of the whole burthen; and by the certain and decisive influence of these arrangements upon the character and conduct of the parties, would materially add to the political strength, power, and resources of the country into which they shall be introduced.

2* WAR AND MILITARY TRAINING: A CITIZEN ARMY

Were all men trained to be rational, the art of war would be rendered useless. While, however, any part of mankind shall be taught that they form their own characters, and shall continue to be trained from infancy to think and act irrationally—that is, to acquire feelings of enmity, and to deem it a duty to engage in war against those who have been instructed to differ from them in sentiments and habits—even the most rational must, for their personal security, learn the means of defence; and every community of such characters, while surrounded by men who have been thus improperly taught, should acquire a

* *New View*, Cole, 57-8.

knowledge of this destructive art, that they may be enabled to over-rule the actions of irrational beings, and maintain peace.

To accomplish these objects to the utmost practical limit, and with the least inconvenience, every male should be instructed how best to defend, when attacked, the community to which he belongs. And these advantages are only to be obtained by providing proper means for the instruction of all boys in the use of arms and the arts of war.

As an example how easily and effectually this might be accomplished over the British Isles, it is intended that the boys trained and educated at the Institution at New Lanark shall be thus instructed; that the person appointed to attend the children in the playground shall be qualified to drill and teach the boys the manual exercise, and that he shall be frequently so employed; that afterwards, fire-arms, of proportionate weight and size for the age and strength of the boys, shall be provided for them, when also they might be taught to practise and understand the more complicated military movements.

This exercise, properly administered, will greatly contribute to the health and spirits of the boys, give them an erect and proper form, and habits of attention, celerity, and order. They will, however, be taught to consider this exercise, an art rendered absolutely necessary by the partial insanity of some of their fellow-creatures, who by the errors of their predecessors, transmitted through preceding generations, have been taught to acquire feelings of enmity, increasing to madness, against those who could not avoid differing from them in sentiments and habits; that this art should never be brought into practice except to restrain the violence of such madmen; and, in these cases, that it should be administered with the least possible severity, and solely to prevent the evil consequences of those rash acts of the insane, and, if possible, to cure them of their disease.

Thus, in a few years, by foresight and arrangement, may almost the whole expense and inconvenience attending the local military be superseded, and a permanent force created, which in numbers, discipline and principles, would be superior, beyond any comparison, for the purpose of defence; always ready in case of need, yet without the loss which is now sustained by the community of efficient and valuable labour. The expenditure which would be saved by this simple expedient, would be far more than competent to educate the whole of the poor and labouring classes of these kingdoms.

3* ADVANTAGES OF COMMUNAL MEALS

It is upon these principles that arrangements are now proposed for the new agricultural villages, by which the food of the inhabitants may be prepared in one establishment, where they will eat together as one family.

Various objections have been urged against this practice; but they have come from those only who, whatever may be their pretensions in other respects, are mere children in the knowledge of the principles and economy of social life.

By such arrangements the members of these new associations may be supplied with food at far less expense and with far more comfort than by any individual or family arangements; and when the parties have been once trained and accustomed, as they easily may be, to the former mode, they will never afterwards feel any inclination to return to the latter.

If a saving in the quantity of food—the obtaining of a superior quality of prepared provisions from the same materials—and the operation of preparing them being effected in much less time, with far less fuel, and with greater ease, comfort, and health to all the parties

* *Report,* Cole, 275.

employed—be advantages, these will be obtained in a remarkable manner by the new arrangements proposed.

And if to partake of viands so prepared, served up with every regard to comfort, in clean, spacious, well-lighted and pleasantly-ventilated apartments, and in the society of well-dressed, well-trained, well-educated, and well-informed associates, possessing the most benevolent dispositions and desirable habits, can give zest and proper enjoyment to meals, then will the inhabitants of the proposed villages experience all this in an eminent degree.

When the new arrangements shall become familiar to the parties, this superior mode of living may be enjoyed at far less expense and with much less trouble than are necessary to procure such meals as the poor are now compelled to eat, surrounded by every object of discomfort and disgust, in the cellars and garrets of the most unhealthy courts, alleys, and lanes, in London, Dublin, and Edinburgh, or Glasgow, Manchester, Leeds, and Birmingham.

4 RATIONAL DRESS

(a)* Food and lodging being thus provided for, the next consideration regards dress.

This, too, is a subject, the utility and disadvantages of which seem to be little understood by the Public generally; and, in consequence, the most ridiculous and absurd notions and practices have prevailed concerning it.

Most persons take it for granted, without thinking on the subject, that to be warm and healthy it is necessary to cover the body with thick clothing and to exclude the air as much as possible; and first appearances favour this conclusion. Facts, however, prove that under the same circumstances, those who from infancy have been the most lightly clad, and who, by their form of dress, have

* *Report,* Cole, 276-7.

been the most exposed to the atmosphere, are much stronger, more active, in better health, warmer in cold weather, and far less incommoded by heat, than those who from constant habit have been dressed in such description of clothing as excludes the air from their bodies. The more the air is excluded by clothing, although at first the wearer feels warmer by each additional covering he puts on, yet in a few weeks, or months at most, the less capable he becomes of bearing cold than before.

The Romans and the Highlanders of Scotland appear to be the only two nations who adopted a national dress on account of its utility, without, however, neglecting to render it highly becoming and ornamental. The form of the dress of these two nations was calculated first to give strength and manly beauty to the figure, and afterwards to display it to advantage. The time, expense, thought, and labour now employed to create a variety of dress, the effects of which are to deteriorate the physical powers, and to render the human figure an object of pity and commiseration, are a certain proof of the low state of intellect among all classes in society. The whole of this gross misapplication of the human faculties serves no one useful or rational purpose. On the contrary, it essentially weakens all the physical and mental powers, and is, in all respects, highly pernicious to society.

All other circumstances remaining the same, sexual delicacy and virtue will be found much higher in the nations among whom the person, *from infancy,* is the most exposed, than among those people who exclude from sight every part of the body except the eye.

(b)* [Nearly all Owen's theories arise directly from personal experience. This is illustrated by a comparison between the passage above and the following from his Autobiography.]

* *Life,* 8-9.

My cousin and I read and thought much, and yet we were both generally very active. But one very hot day in hay-harvest time we both felt ourselves, being overclothed, quite overcome with heat while we sauntered from the house towards a large field where numerous haymakers were actively at work. They appeared to us, who had been doing nothing and yet were overcome with heat, to be cool and comfortable. I said 'Richard! how is this? These active work-people are not heated, but are pleasantly cool, and do not suffer as we do from the heat. There must be some secret in this. Let us try to find it out. Let us do exactly as they do, and work with them.' He willingly agreed. I was, I suppose, between nine and ten years of age, and he was between eight and nine. We observed that all the men were without their coats and waistcoats, and had their shirts open. We adopted the same practice, procured the lightest rakes and forks—for both were used occasionally—and Richard and I, unburthened of our heavy clothing, led the field for several hours, and were cooler and less fatigued than when we were idle and wasting our time. This became ever afterwards a good *experience* and lesson to both; for we found ourselves much more comfortable with active employment than when we were idle.

5 OTHER ASPECTS OF THE PLAN

(a)* No Government Will Resist

Let a rational plan, in principal and practice, be now proposed to the existing governments, in a rational manner and a right spirit, by their peoples, and let governments be requested to carry the proposed plan into practice, with order, in peace, and consistently or rationally, and it will be found that no government can or will resist such application; and because, as previously stated,

* *Revolution,* 36.

it will be obviously for the interests of the governors as well as of those whom they govern, to adopt such plans without contest or delay.

(b)* How to Begin

To proceed rationally with the practical measures of transition, the existing governments, remaining undisturbed, like the old roads during the formation of the railways which were to supersede them, should select a certain number—say seven, more or less—of the most intelligent practical men they can find, to be called a committee, or council, or by any other name, who should have entrusted to them the creation of the new arrangements, under which, in the new state of society, all the business of life is to be conducted. . . .

This committee should begin the change by appointing competent officers, properly instructed, to direct the domestic, educational, mechanical, agricultural, and all other required operations.

They should enlist from the unemployed, or inefficiently employed, of the working classes, those who are willing to support themselves by their own properly directed industry, under the newly created superior arrangements; to be formed into a civil army, to be trained under the new arrangements, in order that they may create their own supplies of every description, be reeducated, become defenders of their country in case of invasion, and maintain peace and order at home; while the regular army shall be employed abroad, as long as a regular army shall be necessary.

(c)** Forming New Townships

When the numbers increase in any given Township beyond the population that it will maintain in the highest state of comfort, a new Township must be commenced

* *Revolution,* 36-7. ** *Revolution,* 39.

187

upon a new site; and this process must be continued until all the land of the earth shall be covered with these federative Townships. This period will probably never arrive; but if it should, as the population of the world will be then highly good, intelligent, and rational, they will know far better than the present most irrational generation, how to provide for the occurrence. But for men now, when the earth is comparatively a waste and a forest for want of people to drain and cultivate it, to suppose that population is already, or is likely for ages to become, superabundant, is one of the thousand insanities with which the present generation is afflicted.

(d)* *Self-Sufficiency*

Each of these Townships should be devised to be self-educating, self-employing, self-supporting, and self-governing. Any arrangements short of this result will be inefficient, and not in accordance with the fundamental principle of the new system of universality, and will be deficient in forming the superior independent character which should be given to these Townships.

(e)** *Equality of Condition*

Every member of the Township must be *well and equally accommodated according to age.* For there must be, as a leading principle for practice, perfect equality of condition, according to age, throughout the whole proceedings of each Township; for without this equality properly carried out among all the members of each Township, there can be no justice, no unity, no virtue, no permanent happiness. But as long as external arrangements are made to be unequal, there can be no equality in practice.

Those who have been trained in a system of inequality, have no conception of the unnecessary misery which it in-

* *Revolution,* 40. ** *Revolution,* 42.

flicts upon rich and poor; or of the enormous injustices which it creates, or of the endless irrationalities to which it gives rise.

(f)* *All or None*

It is an Almighty decree, *'that all of the human race shall be happy, or none'*. . . . 'All or none' will ere long become, first the watchword of democracy, and then the universal motto of men of every country or clime.

* *Revolution*, 57-8.

XII

The Trades Union

[When Owen returned from the U.S.A. in 1829 he found a growing co-operative movement stemming from his own principles. This brought him for the first time into contact with the workers except as their employer. When the great upsurge of Trade Unionism began in 1833 he welcomed it as a possible means of putting his Plan into practice. Yet this involved him in a class struggle, of which, as we have seen, he disapproved in principle, and he soon came into conflict with the left wing of the movement, represented by James Morrison and J. E. Smith. This conflict is reflected in the fourth and last extracts in this Chapter.]

1* AN APPEAL TO THE RICH

We, *the producers of all real wealth,* have been, and now are, held in disesteem; while the *unproductive,* useless and injurious members of society, riot to their own hurt in riches, and are trained to consider us their servants and slaves. By these ignorant and unnatural proceedings, the Earth and his own nature have been made the perpetual source of evil instead of good to men.

* *A manifesto of the productive classes of Great Britain and Ireland, to the governments and people of the continents of Europe, and of North and South America. May 13, 1833.* Buonarroti, 446-8.

We *will*, that this irrational state of society shall now cease, and that, henceforth, *all* except those of the present generation too far advanced in life for the change, shall be trained to become producers of physical wealth or of intellectual gratification, and that none shall maintain who are not occupied in producing or acquiring that which will benefit society, or be deemed equivalent to their consumption of its productions.

We know that all will become far better and happier, by being made to be producers, physically or intellectually, or both, of the means of gratification to society, than they can be by living a life of idleness and uselessness. . . .

Come then, and for your own happiness, co-operate with us as friends. We are the producers of all the wealth and means of comfort you have hitherto possessed—we can make arrangements by which, in future, you may enjoy these good things in safety, and without fear; but, were we so inclined, we could effectually withhold them from you and your children; and force applied to us would demonstrate only the weakness and folly of our mistaken opponents. The reign of terror, of carnal arms, or of physical force of any kind or description in opposition to public opinion, has for ever ceased. It is now useless to speak of these old wornout means to effect any great or permanent object. We discard them as being worse than useless; as means of power gone by, never more to be called into action by *beings* claiming a rational nature.

We call upon you to discard them also, and to turn your thoughts from the destruction of your fellow men, and of their wealth, to the acquisition of that knowledge which will enable you to assist materially to improve the former, and greatly increase the latter. To act thus is your duty and your interest, for it is the only course that can insure your permanent satisfaction, or that can now give you a chance of happiness.

The turn-out of the building operatives, and the existing differences with their masters, will, I doubt not, tend to effect a permanent good for both parties. It affords a fair opportunity to you, the producing classes (and masters and men are producers), quietly, calmly, and most effectively, to make a stand, at once, and put yourselves in your right position, and thereby gradually accomplish the great change required; that is, that individual competition, the bane of the producing class, shall cease among you. . . .

Now as you perceive that you alone have been taught to do anything beneficial for society, decide at once to form new arrangements, to reorganise yourselves, to produce and obtain a full supply of the best of everything for the whole population of Great Britain and Ireland, yourselves enjoying, as well as the upper and middle classes, superior food, houses, furniture, clothes, instruction for yourselves and children, and daily rational recreation, such as will improve your health and contribute to your happiness.

This you may now do and you can accomplish this change for the whole population of the British Empire in less than five years, and *essentially* ameliorate the condition of the producing class *throughout Great Britain and Ireland* in less than *five months*.

3** THE BUILDERS' GUILD

[While we cannot be certain that this Manifesto was written by Owen, both ideas and style are essentially his.]

* 'Address to the Operative Builders', August 26, 1833, from R. W. Postgate, *Revolution from 1789 to 1906*, 90.

** 'Friendly declaration of the Delegates of the Lodges of the Building Branches of the United Kingdom, held in Manchester. ... Addressed to their Fellow Subjects throughout the British Dominions', September, 1833, from R. W. Postgate, *The Builders' History*, 463-6.

After the most mature and grave deliberation in Council among ourselves, we have come to the conclusion that we and you are in false positions and that the real interests of all parties are sacrificed to the errors of those who do not understand the resources of our country or the means of advantageously calling them into action. . . .

It is now evident to us that those who have hitherto advised the Authorities of these realms in devising the Institutions of our country were themselves ignorant of the first principles requisite to be known to establish and maintain a prosperous and superior state of society.

Knowing this and seeing no prospects of any improvement in our condition, being also conscious that our most valuable materials are ignorantly wasted by being senselessly scattered throughout the four quarters of the world and that our industry and skill and unlimitable powers of invention are now most grossly misdirected; we, without any hostile feelings to the government or any class of persons, have been compelled to come to the conclusion that no party can or will relieve us from the tremendous evils which we suffer and still greater which are coming upon us, until we begin in good earnest to act for ourselves and at once adopt the recommendation of Sir Robert Peel, 'to take our affairs into our own hands.'

[The Manifesto announces the formation of a National Building Guild of Brothers, including among its objectives the following:]

9th—We will exhibit to the world, in a plain and simple manner, by our quiet example, how easily the most valuable wealth may be produced in superfluity beyond the wants of the population of all countries; also how beneficially, for the Producing Classes (and all classes will soon perceive their interest on becoming superior producers) the present artificial, inaccurate and therefore injurious circulating medium for the exchange of our riches, may be superseded by an equitable, and therefore rational representation of real wealth, and as a consequence of these important advances the causes which generate the bad passions and all the vices and corruptions attributed to human nature, shall gradually diminish until they all die a natural death and be known no more, except as matter of past history, and thus by contrast, be the cause of everlasting rejoicing.

10th—We shall by these and other means now easy of adopting speedily open the road to remove the causes of individual and national competition, of individual and national contests, jealousies and wars, and enable all to discover their true individual interests and thereby establish peace, goodwill and harmony, not only among the Brethren of the Building Guild, but also by their example among the human race for ever.

4* AT THE HEIGHT OF THE CRISIS

[Owen issued this statement when the struggle of the Consolidated Trades Union had reached a climax with the conviction and sentence of the Tolpuddle labourers. This event is the 'circumstances' to which Owen refers in the fourth paragraph.]

Under this system, the idle, the useless, and the vicious govern the population of the world; whilst the useful and truly virtuous, so far as such a system will permit men to be virtuous, are by them degraded and depressed. . . .

Men of industry, and good and virtuous habits! this is the last state to which you ought to submit, nor would I advise you to allow the ignorant, the idle, the presumptuous, and the vicious, any longer to lord it over the well-

---

* *The Legacy of Robert Owen, To the Population of the World,* Buonarroti, 435-6.

being, the lives, and happiness, of yourselves and families, when by *three days* of such idleness as constitutes the whole of their lives, you would for ever convince each of these mistaken individuals that you now possess the power to compel *them* at once to become the abject slaves, and the oppressed portion of society, as they have hitherto made *you*.

But all the individuals now living are the suffering victims of this accursed system, and all are objects of pity: you will, therefore, effect this great and glorious revolution without, if possible, inflicting individual evil. You can easily accomplish this most-to-be-desired object. Proceed with your Union on the principles you have latterly adopted; they are wise and just; and wisdom and justice, combined with your Union, will be sure to render it for ever legal.

Men of industry, producers of wealth and knowledge, and of all that is truly valuable in society! *unite your powers to create a new and righteous state of human existence; a state in which the only contest shall be, who shall produce the greatest amount of permanent happiness for the human race.* You have all the requisite materials awaiting your proper application of them to effect this change, and circumstances have arisen within the last week to render delay a dereliction of the highest duty which you have to perform to yourselves, to your families, and to the population of the world.

Men of industrious habits, you who are the most honest, useful, and valuable parts of society, by producing for it all its wealth and knowledge, *you have formed and established the Grand National Consolidated Trades' Union of Great Britain and Ireland, and it will prove the palladium of the world.* All the intelligent, well-disposed, and superior minds among all classes of society, male and female, will now rally round the Consolidated Union, and become members of it; and if the irrationality of the present degraded and degrading system render it necessary, you will discover the reasons why you should willingly sacrifice all you hold dear in the world, and life itself, rather than submit to its dissolution or slightest depression.

For your sakes I have become a member of your Consolidated Union; and while it shall be directed with the same wisdom and justice that it has been from its commencement, and its proceedings shall be made known to the public as you intend them to be, my resolve is to stand by your order, and support the Union to the utmost of my power. It is this Consolidated Union that can alone save the British Empire from greater confusion, anarchy, and misery than it has ever yet experienced. It is, it will daily become more and more, *the real conservative power of society;* for its example will be speedily followed by all nations, and through its beneficial example the greatest revolution ever effected in the history of the human race will be commenced, rapidly carried on, and completed over the world, without bloodshed, violence, or evil of any kind, merely by *an overwhelming moral influence;* which influence individuals and nations will speedily perceive the folly and uselessness of attempting to resist.

Experience has forced these important truths into my mind, and I give them now to the population of the world as the *most valuable legacy that man can give to man.*
                                                            March 30, 1834.

5* AGAINST CLASS ANTAGONISM

It is time the official organ of the Consolidated Union [*The Pioneer*] should cease uselessly to irritate other classes of society: this is not the mode to serve any cause, but to create unnecessarily greater obstacles to retard the progress of the sacred cause of human amelioration, under-

* 'A Lecture': April 27th, 1834 from R. W. Postgate, *Revolution from 1789 to 1906,* 100.

taken by the National Consolidated Union. No man, who understands what human nature is, and how in each individual, it is formed to become what we find it at maturity, and who comprehends the elements of which all society is formed, and how they must be combined to produce any permanent good for the mass of the people, can continue to write to irritate. . . .

Let, therefore, reason and sound argument, and not passion and prejudice, or party or petty proceedings of any kind, be now the characteristic of the official and public organ of the Consolidated Union. Not an article should be in it which ought not to be calmly considered by the Executive and marked as having received their deliberate sanction.

XIII

Owen on Religion

1 OWEN DENOUNCES ALL RELIGIONS

[Owen always regarded the moment when, at a meeting in the City of London Tavern, on August 21st, 1817, he publicly declared all religions to be erroneous, as one of the turning points in his life, and, indeed, in the history of the world. Below is the text of his statement, and an account, from his Autobiography, of its reception.]

(a)* On this day—in this hour—even now—shall these bonds be burst asunder, never more to reunite while the world shall last. What the consequences of this daring deed shall be to myself, I am as indifferent about as whether it shall rain or be fair tomorrow. Whatever may be the consequences, I shall now perform my duty to you, and to the world; and should it be the last act of my life, I shall be well content, and know that I have lived for an important purpose.

Then, my friends, I tell you, that hitherto you have been prevented from even knowing what happiness really is, solely in consequence of the errors—gross errors—that have been combined with the fundamental notions of every religion that has hitherto been taught to men. And, in consequence, they have made man the most in-

* *Catechism,* Cole, 216.

consistent, and the most miserable being in existence. By the errors of these systems he has been made a weak, imbecile animal; a furious bigot and fanatic; or a miserable hypocrite; and should these qualities be carried, not only into the projected villages, but *into Paradise itself, a Paradise would no longer be found!*

In all the religions which have hitherto been forced on the minds of men, deep, dangerous, and lamentable principles of disunion, division and separation have been fast entwined with all their fundamental notions; and the certain consequences have been all the dire effects which religious animosities have, through all the past periods of the world, inflicted with such unrelenting stern severity or mad and furious zeal!

If, therefore, my friends, you should carry with you into these proposed villages, of intended unity and unlimited mutual co-operation, one single particle of *religious intolerance,* or sectarian feelings of *division* and *separation*—maniacs only would go there to look for harmony and happiness; or *elsewhere,* as long as such insane errors shall be found to exist!

I am not going to ask impossibilities from you—I know what you *can* do; and I know also what you *cannot* do. Consider again on what grounds each man in existence has a full right to the enjoyment of the most unlimited liberty of conscience. I am not of your religion, nor of any religion yet taught in the world! to me they all appear united with much—yes, with very much—error!

(b)* I commenced my address, and continued amidst much applause and cheering from the friends of the cause which I advocated, until I approached that part in which I denounced all the religions of the world as now taught; when by my manner I prepared the audience for some extraordinary proceeding. . . .

* *Life,* 222-7.

The meeting here became excited to the highest pitch of expectation as to what was to follow; and a breathless silence prevailed, so that not the slightest sound could be heard. I made a slight pause, and, as my friends afterwards told me, added a great increase of strength and dignity to my manner, of which at the time I was wholly unconscious, and in that state of mind I finished my statement and I then again paused for some seconds, to observe the effects of this unexpected and unheard-of declaration and denouncement of all existing religions, in one of the most numerous public meetings of all classes ever held in the British metropolis under cover and at midday.

My own expectations were, that such a daring denouncement in opposition to the deepest prejudices of every creed, would call down upon me the vengeance of the bigot and superstitious, and that I should be torn to pieces at the meeting. But great was my astonishment at what followed. A pause ensued, of the most profound silence, but of noiseless agitation in the minds of all— none apparently knowing what to do or how to express themselves. All seemed thunderstruck and confounded. My friends were taken by surprise, and were shocked at my temerity, and feared for the result. Those who came with the strongest determination to oppose me, had, as they afterwards stated to me, their minds changed as it were by some electric shock, and the utmost mental confusion seemed to pervade the meeting, none venturing to express their feelings; and had I not purposely paused and waited for some demonstration from the audience, I might have continued my address in the astonished silence which I had produced. [Some clergymen attempted] to lead the meeting by a few low hisses. But these, to my great astonishment, were instantly rebutted by the most heartfelt applause from the whole of the meeting, with the exception stated, that I ever witnessed, before or since, as a public demonstration of feeling.

I then said to the friends near me—'The victory is gained. Truth openly stated is omnipotent.' . . .

My friend Henry Brougham, since known as Lord Brougham, and Lord Chancellor of England, saw me the day after the meeting walking in the streets of the metropolis, and came to me, saying—'How the devil, Owen, could you say what you did yesterday at your public meeting! If any of us (meaning the then so-called Liberal party in the House of Commons) had said half as much, we should have been burnt alive—and here are you quietly walking as if nothing had occurred!'

2 THE RATIONAL RELIGION

[Owen was often accused of atheism: in fact he was a deist, much as Tom Paine was, and his deism, like Paine's, allowed of a thorough-going materialism. He lays down the following Laws for his Townships on religious matters.]

(a)* 1st. Everyone shall have an equal and full liberty to express the dictates of his conscience on religious and all other subjects.

2nd. No one shall have any other power than fair and friendly argument to control the opinions and beliefs of another.

3rd. No praise or blame, no merit or demerit, no reward or punishment shall be awarded for any opinions or belief.

4th. But all, af every religion, shall have equal right to express their opinions respecting the Incomprehensible Power which moves the atoms and controls the universe; and to worship that power under any form or in any manner agreeable to their consciences—not interfering with any others.

* *Revolution*, 108.

(b)*   [Owen sets out 'The Principles and practices of the Rational Religion' in ten 'Laws'. The first three, which contain the main substance of his views, are given below.]

Law 1. That all facts yet known to man, indicate that there is an external or internal Cause of all existences, by the fact of their existence; that this all-pervading Cause of motion and change in the universe, is that Incomprehensible Power which the nations of the world have called, God, Jehovah, Lord, etc.; but that the facts are yet unknown to man which define what that Power is.

Law 2. That it is a law of nature, obvious to our senses, that the internal and external character of all that have life upon the earth, is formed *for* them and not *by* them; that, in accordance with this law, the internal and external character of man is formed *for* and *not by* him, as hitherto most erroneously imagined; and therefore, he cannot have merit or demerit, or deserve praise or blame, reward or punishment, in this life, or in any future state of existence.

Law 3. That the knowledge of this fact, with its all-important consequences, will necessarily create in everyone a new, sublime, and pure spirit of charity, for the convictions, feelings and conduct of the human race, and dispose them to be kind to all that have life—seeing that this varied life is formed by the same Incomprehensible Power that has created human nature, and given man his peculiar faculties.

3** SUNDAY – A DAY FOR ENJOYMENT

Those, then, who desire to give mankind the character which it would be for the happiness of all that they should possess, will not fail to make careful provision for their amusement and recreation.

* *Revolution,* 109-13.   ** *New View,* Cole, 42.

The Sabbath was originally so intended. It was instituted to be a day of universal enjoyment and happiness to the human race. It is frequently made, however, from the opposite extremes of error, either a day of superstitious gloom and tyranny over the mind, or of the most destructive intemperance and licentiousness. The one has been the cause of the other; the latter the certain and natural consequence of the other. Relieve the human mind from useless and superstitious restraints; train it on those principles which facts, ascertained from the first knowledge of time to this day, demonstrate to be the only principles which are true; and intemperance and licentiousness will not exist; for such conduct in itself is neither the immediate nor the future interest of man; and he is ever governed by one or other of these considerations, according to the habits which have been given him from infancy.

The Sabbath, in many parts of Scotland, is not a day of innocent and cheerful recreation to the labouring man; nor can those who are confined all the week to sedentary occupations, freely partake, without censure, of their air and exercise to which nature invites them, and which their health demands.

4* AN ATTEMPTED CONVERSION

[Owen's children were brought up in orthodoxy by their pious mother, and Robert Dale Owen describes an attempt to convert his free-thinking father in a passage that tells us much both about Owen's religion and his attitude to his children.]

I sounded my father by first asking him what he thought about Jesus Christ. His reply was to the effect that I would do well to heed his teachings, especially those relating to charity and to our loving one another.

* *T.M.W.*, 83-4.

This was well enough, as far as it went; but it did not at all satisfy me. So, with some trepidation, I put the question direct, whether my father disbelieved that Christ was the Son of God?

He looked a little surprised and did not answer immediately. 'Why do you ask that question, my son?' he said at last.

'Because I am sure—' I began eargerly.

'That he *is* God's Son?' asked my father, smiling.

'Yes, I am.'

'Did you ever hear of the Mahometans?' said my father, while I paused to collect my proofs.

I replied that I had heard of such people who live somewhere, far off.

'Do you know what their religion is?'

'No.'

'They believe that Christ is not the Son of God, but that another person, called Mahomet, was God's chosen prophet.'

'Do they not believe the Bible?' asked I, somewhat aghast.

'No. Mahomet wrote a book called the Koran; and Mahometans believe it to be the word of God. That book tells them that God sent Mahomet to preach the gospel to them and to save their souls.'

Wonders crowded fast upon me. A rival Bible and a rival Saviour. Could it be? I asked. 'Are you *quite* sure this is true, papa?'

'Yes, my dear, I am quite sure.'

'But I suppose there are very few Mahometans: not near—*near* so many as there are of Christians.'

'Do you call Catholics Christians, Robert?'

'O no, papa. The Pope is Antichrist.'

My father smiled. 'Then by Christians you mean Protestants.'

'Yes.'

'Well, there are many more Mahometans than Protestants in the world: about a hundred and forty million Mahometans and less than a hundred million Protestants.'

'I thought almost everyone believed in Christ, as mama does.'

'There are probably twelve hundred millions of people in the world. So, out of every twelve persons only one is a Protestant. Are you quite sure that the one is right and the eleven wrong?'

My creed, based on authority, was toppling. I had no answer ready. . . . And so ended this notable scheme of mine for my father's conversion.

XIV

Marriage and the Family

[Owen's denunciation of bourgeois marriage, often rather violently expressed, exposed him to even more unscrupulous abuse than his attacks on religion. Yet, as may be seen from Extract 7, his practical proposals were both moderate and sensible.]

1* EVIL EFFECTS OF THE MARRIAGE SYSTEM

And now I tell you, and through you, the population of all the nations of the earth, that the present marriages of the world, under the system of moral evil in which they have been devised and are now contracted, are the sole cause of all the prostitution, of all its incalculable grievous evils, and of more than one half of all the vilest and most degrading crimes known to society. And that, until you put away from among you and your children for ever, *this accursed thing,* you will never be in a condition to become chaste or virtuous in your thoughts and feelings, or to know what real happiness is. For now almost all who are in the married state are daily and hourly practising the deepest deception, and living in the grossest prostitution of body and mind; and misery is multiplied by it beyond any of your feeble powers, in your present irrational state, to estimate. . . . It is a Satanic device of

* *Marriages,* 7-8.

the Priesthood to place and keep mankind within their slavish superstitions, and to render them subservient to all their purposes; and until you can acquire fortitude and moral courage to look this subject fairly in the face and meet it fully on the ground of common sense and right reason, and can show it to be, as it is, in direct opposition to the laws of your Organization, it is eminently calculated to make you, in the greatest extreme, ignorantly selfish, wretchedly vicious, and most unhappy.... It is now ascertained that you have not been organized to feel or not to feel at your pleasure. You, therefore, commit a crime against the everlasting laws of your nature when you say that you will 'love and cherish' what your organization may compel you to dislike and loathe, even in a few hours.

2 CELIBACY A CRIME

(a)* *Let it now be known to all,* that when the mind of man shall be regenerated, and he shall enter upon the state of moral good, in an association of sufficient numbers to support and protect itself, and its rising generation, against the ignorance and consequent prejudices of moral evil; that *celibacy,* beyond the period plainly indicated for its termination by nature (although esteemed a high virtue under the reign of moral evil), will be known to be a great crime, necessarily leading to disease of body and mind....

Also, in the present state of moral evil, it is esteemed a high and superior virtue to be chaste, according to the unnatural notions of a most degraded order of men, called the Priesthood, who, in various parts of the world, have taken upon themselves to direct the opinions and feelings of the human race, as though they were themselves divinities. ... This order of men, to whose oppres-

* *Marriages,* 10-11.

sions of body and mind no rational being will longer submit, have chosen to make chasity to consist in having sexual intercourse in accordance only with *their* most fantastic whims and unnatural notions; and whom they discordantly join, *'let'* say they *'no man put asunder!'* This human decree of the Priesthood is the origin of all prostitution, and of all the endless crimes, evils, and sufferings; and of all impure thoughts and desires, and of all the known and unknown, and almost unimagined crimes and miseries of the present married life.

(b)* The priest's and the rich man's laws of chastity are very different to Nature's laws of chastity. . . .

The chastity of Nature, then, or real chastity—that chastity which alone is virtuous—consists in the intercourse of the sexes when there is a pure and genuine sympathy or sincere affection between the parties; when the physical, intellectual, and moral feelings of the one are in perfect accordance with those of the other; when, in fact, their natures are so happily blended, that together they form but one harmonious whole, and become, when thus united in heart and soul, or body and mind, one being, whose feelings and interests are identified, and who are thus made capable of enjoining these sympathies and affections so long as Nature has designed them to remain, and thus to experience the full happiness of their nature, or of a virtuous mode of existence.

3 THE FAMILY IN BOURGEOIS SOCIETY

(a)** The first effect of these artificial marriages is to make it necessary for the newly married couple to have a single-family establishment, varied in detail, according to the class or rank of life of the parties. Within these new arrangements the husband and wife place themselves,

* *Marriages*, 75-6.   ** *Marriages*, 26-7.

to provide for their family, to the utmost extent of their powers and capacities to advance themselves and children towards the highest pinnacles of society, and thus they are at once placed in direct or indirect contest with all other families having the same laudable object, as it is now termed, in view.

Now this single-family arrangement is one of the most unfortunate and vicious for the husband and wife, for the children, and for society, that could be devised. It is calculated, in the first place, to make the husband, wife, children, and the public, most ignorantly selfish, and to make the greatest mistakes relative to their individual interest. It next places the husband and wife under such unfavourable circumstances relative to each other, that there are many, many chances, considering the erroneous notions respecting themselves and human nature, which they have been forced from infancy to receive, that they will speedily create an unfavourable difference of feeling for each other, on account of some of these single-family arrangements, or daily and hourly transactions and proceedings. Then this mode of life is highly injurious for the well training and educating of the children. The family arrangements are made to be as convenient as the parties know how, for the adult part of it, and they thus become most inconvenient for the children. The whole furniture of the house of a single-family establishment, in all ranks of life, is itself a most vicious and undesirable circumstance placed around the children from their birth.

(b)* The single-family arrangements are hostile to cultivation in children of any of the superior and ennobling qualities of human nature. They are trained by them to acquire all the most mean and ignorant selfish feelings that can be generated in human character. The children within those dens of selfishness and hypocrisy are taught

* *Marriages,* 36.

to consider their own little individual family their own world, and that it is the duty and interest of all within that little orb to do whatever they can to promote the advantages of all the legitimate members of it. Within these persons, it is *my* house, *my* wife, *my* estate, *my* children, or *my* husband; *our* estate, and *our* children; or *my* brothers, *my* sisters; and *our* house and property. This family party is trained to consider it quite right, and a superior mode of acting, for each member of it to seek, by all fair means, as almost any means, except *direct* robbery, are termed, to increase the wealth, honour, and privileges of the family, and every individual member of it.

Now, all other families are so placed and taught that they also feel a similar desire to promote, by the same *fair* means, as they are called, the interests of every individual relative within the family circle.

4* END SECRECY AND SHAME

Then now I tell you, and through you, the whole of the human race, that man and woman have been made perfect; that each part of them is an essential part of their existence; that nature never intended that they should always remain ignorant of each other; or that secrecy, or mystery of any kind, should permanently exist between the two sexes: that the time is arrived when whatever secrecy and mystery have been engendered between the sexes, through ignorance of their real nature, should now terminate for ever; and that arrangements should be formed, as speedily as possible, to enable them to return, in all their ideas and feelings, to the innocency and simplicity of their former condition, in these respects, before the priesthood of the world introduced their ignorant mysteries, which created the real fall of man.

* *Marriages, 43-5.*

The fall of man from innocency and from the plain and direct road of intelligence and happiness occurred when the priesthoods of the world induced some of our ignorant ancestors to feel ashamed of any part of their nature. That this feeling is altogether an artificial and false shame may be ascertained by observing how difficult it is to impress the necessity for it upon all children, and to notice the different habits respecting it which obtain among various nations and tribes, and how much the people of our country condemn the notions of others upon the practices which, in these respects, are national in various districts of the world. . . .

And will this change from gross ignorance to real knowledge, respecting ourselves and human nature, destroy true delicacy of feeling in man and woman, for themselves and for each other?

It is only those who have been grossly irrational, that imagine this false shame is necessary to create true delicacy of feeling, or insure a virtuous or healthy and happy intercourse between the sexes.

5* MARRIAGE AND PROSTITUTION

It is said that the chastity of woman could not be secured without the legal bond of marriage. It may with much greater truth be said, that it can never be secured with the legal bond of marriage. Has this bondage hitherto secured it? Was there ever a period in the history of man when the vilest prostitution was so universal over the world as at present? And is there a single vice in the whole catalogue of crimes which so degrades the human character, or inflicts the same extent of misery on its votaries, and upon society in general, as prostitution? No: but the miseries engendered by prostitution, and suffered by individuals and their families, friends, and connections, are

* *Marriages*, 49.

generally hidden from public gaze and inspection, and are covered by the darkness of night, or concealed in dens of wretchedness. No security for the chastity of woman! What blasphemy against nature which has provided the most ample security in the innocent affections of the female and in the cultivated feelings of the male, whenever ignorant inexperienced men shall permit these virtues their free and natural course of action.

The pure and genuine chastity of nature is to have connection only with affection; and prostitution arises only when connection is induced or forced without affection; and it is always induced or forced by artificial causes, or forced by some necessity of law or custom, when it takes place without affection.

6* MONOGAMY AND POLYGAMY

Now we have had great experience of the two first artificial customs, and probably the population of the world is at present nearly equally divided between these two very opposite practices; and yet both modes are said by their respective priests to be of God's appointment. . . .

The human law which binds one man to the same woman, and the woman to the man through life, whether or not they can retain an affection for each other, has produced more hatred, and destroyed more love between these parties than would otherwise have taken place, probably many thousand-fold.

Then the Eastern legal custom of one man having permission to have as many wives as he can maintain, although, perhaps, less injurious in some respects than the customs of Christians, especially as it materially diminishes promiscuous intercourse, is, nevertheless, a most unfortunate device for mankind. It tends powerfully to make men and women weak, jealous, irrational beings. It destroys

* *Marriages*, 66-8.

the confidence of man in woman, and woman in man; and makes woman a mere slave to man's sexual propensity; it tends to perpetuate woman in a state of mental childhood.

7* OWEN'S PRACTICAL PROPOSALS

In the present absence of real knowledge, derived from experience, and with the existing irregular feelings of the population of the world, created by a false education, we propose that the union and disunion of the sexes should take place under the following regulations—

MARRIAGE

Announcement—'Persons having an affection for each other, and being desirous of forming a union, first announce such intention publicly in our Sunday assemblies.

Preliminary Period—'If the intention remain at the end of *three months,* they make a second public declaration.

Marriage—'Which declarations being registered in the books of the Society will constitute their marriage.'

OBJECT OF MARRIAGE

'Marriages will be solely formed to promote the happiness of the sexes; and if this end be not obtained, the object of the unions is defeated.'

DIVORCE
FIRST — WHEN BOTH PARTIES DESIRE TO SEPARATE

Announcement—'Should both parties, after the termination of *twelve months at the soonest,* discover that their dispositions and habits are unsuited to each other, and that there is little or no prospect of happiness being

* *Marriages,* Appendix, 88-9.

derived from their union, they are to make a public declaration as before, to that effect.

Preliminary Period—'After which they return and live together *six months longer;* at the termination of which, if they still find their qualities discordant, and both parties unite in the declaration, they make a second declaration.

Divorce—'Both of which being duly registered and witnessed, will constitute their legal separation.'

SECOND—WHEN ONE ONLY DESIRES A SEPARATION

Preliminary Period—'Should one alone come forward upon the last declaration, and the other object to the separation, they would be required to live together another *six months,* to try if their feelings and habits could be made to accord, so as to promote happiness.

Divorce—'But if at the end of *the second six months,* the objecting party shall still remain of the same mind, the separation shall then be final.'

POSITION OF THE PARTIES AFTER DIVORCE

'The parties may, without diminution of public opinion, form new unions more suited to their dispositions.'

PROVISION FOR THE CHILDREN

'As all the children of the new world will be trained and educated under the superintendance and care of the Society, the separation of the parents will not produce any change in the condition of the rising generation.'

XV

A Plan for India

[The following proposals* were put forward in January 1858, during the War of Independence. While certainly in advance of much that was being said at the time, they may also be compared with the full support for the Indian struggle that Ernest Jones was giving in *The People's Paper*.]

1st. That India be made an empire or kingdom, under one of our young princes, with an upper and lower house of assembly, the members of both to be elected after the model of the United States.

2nd. That this empire or kingdom be hereditary, and the king or governor be assisted by a cabinet, not exceeding twelve appointed by the crown, but made strictly responsible to the two houses of legislation for their proceedings.

3rd. That until the young sovereign shall attain the age of twenty-one, India shall be governed by the British Government, on the principles afterwards stated, and that when the sovereign shall have attained his majority, British Rule shall cease, and a treaty of federation on equal terms be made between Great Britain and this new Indian government.

* 'Memorial to the Right Honourable the Lords of Her Majesty's Treasury,' *Life, IA.,* xx-xxi.

4th. That from the majority of the sovereign of India, its government shall be independent and self-supported, except being federatively united with Great Britain in peace and war and commerce.

5th. That, for a period to be fixed, the bank notes of the Bank of England shall be legal tender in all payments; but as soon as the new Indian government shall be sufficiently established, it shall establish a Bank of the Indian Empire, based on the credit of India.

6th. That British subjects in India shall have all the rights of Indian subjects, while all Indian subjects shall have the full rights of British subjects throughout the British Empire.

7th. That the officers and soldiers employed to regain, and to retain India until the Indian government can support itself, shall be entitled according to rank and service to certain portions of land in India—their proportions to be decided by the British Parliament.

8th. That the government of India shall be by British born subjects, until the sovereign shall be of age; after which period the natives of India to have the full rights of subjects, except to the high offices of government and to the two houses of assembly,—and to these also in ten years from the time when they give their adhesion to the new government.

9th. That the directors of the East India Company and its shareholders shall be amply compensated for their present interests in the company; but all their rights to rule India to cease for ever.

10th. That during the period while the sovereign shall be attaining his twenty-first year, the British government shall take into its most grave consideration the best practical means, as the opportunity is so peculiarly favourable for the purpose, to arrange new surroundings in which to place the native subjects of the new Indian Empire while under the British rule. These surroundings to be scientifically combined through a knowledge of the social science, in such a manner as shall secure to all, by their own well-directed industry within these surroundings, the means by which they shall all, at all times, be well-fed, clothed, lodged, trained, educated, occupied, amused, and locally well governed by themselves.

XVI

Eccentricities

[In many ways Owen was a man of outstandingly good
sense, but, as was the case with many of the Utopians,
this sense was oddly streaked with a dogmatic crankiness,
which increased as he grew older. It must be noted that
all the eccentricities quoted below belong to his last years
—and that even at his wildest, good sense keeps breaking in.]

1* AS IN THE BEST ASYLUMS

[Owen's inability to see the people as a positive historical
force finds striking expressions here. It was perhaps his
greatest single weakness.]

The good effects of the decrease of punishment in lunatic
asylums and schools, are beginning to be seen and acknowledged. In the best of both, physical punishments now
scarcely exist. The time approaches when it will be discovered that the speediest mode to terminate the
innumerable diseases—physical, mental, and moral—
created by the irrational laws invented and introduced
by men during their irrational state of existence in progress towards rationality, will be to govern or treat all
society as the most advanced physicians govern and treat

* *Revolution,* 71-2.

their patients in the best arranged lunatic hospitals, in which forbearance and kindness, and full allowance for every paroxysm of the peculiar disease of each, govern the conduct of all who have the care of these unfortunates—unfortunates made to become so through the irrationality and injustice of the present most irrational system of society.

2* THE TRUE SECOND COMING

[The next two extracts have a peculiar interest because of the large part played by Millennial speculation in English Radical thought from the time of the Revolution in the seventeenth century. Owen's language here, and especially his use of the Jerusalem symbolism, is strikingly similar both to that of many of the left-wing sects of the seventeenth century and of his great contemporary William Blake.]

Thus, in the due order of nature, will *truth*, or pure Christianity reconcile man to man, overcome all evil, establish the reign of peace and harmony, and happiness will prevail and reign over the earth for ever.

Say not that these heavenly results are unattainable on earth. They are only so under the Satanic system of individual selfishness, ignorance of the laws of humanity, and obstruction to the practice of universal love and charity for all men, the divine principles taught by Jesus of Nazareth, or the Great and Glorious *Truth* which was the *First Coming* of Christ among men.

The *Second Coming* is the yet greater and more glorious Truth, given in this our day, of the science by which to make the *First Truth* universal in practice. And thus will be fulfilled the promise to the Jews of the Coming Messiah to overcome and conquer the world of evil; and to

* *Millennial Gazette*, 39.

the Christians, of the Second Coming of Christ to overcome and conquer all error. Thus will be united Jew and
Gentile and all the nations of the earth, into one family
of good, wise, and happy, well-formed men and women,
having one language, interest, and feeling, all superior in
their individual qualities, yet no two the same, but the
combined distinct qualities of all contributing to constitute the one great humanity of the earth.

3* THE NEW JERUSALEM

The population at the termination of this period will be
actively engaged in extending the City of the New
Jerusalem, which will extend over the earth, and in which
there will be no streets, lanes, courts, or alleys—all these
being inferior or injurious surroundings. . . .

The earth will be laid out to form, over its whole extent, one City, to be composed of separate townships with
their required appliances; and each will be a paradise of
a township, connected with all other such townships over
the globe, until they will form the earth gradually into
this one great city, which may be called the New Jerusalem, or united earthly paradise.

The spaces between the townships will be laid out in
gardens, groves, fertile fields, to be as beautiful as human
knowledge and scientific means can make them.

The City, containing all the inhabitants of the earth,
will be occupied by a thoroughly developed and regenerated race of human beings, governed solely by God's
Laws, speaking the same language, and that, the language
of truth only ['The Anglo-Saxon language, improved to
the utmost, will be taught to all in its purity from birth.'
Millennial Gazette, 127.] having one interest and one feeling, to promote each other's happiness; all filled from
birth with the spirit of universal charity and love for one

* *Millennial Gazette,* 117-19.

another, and applying those divine qualities to their every-day practice through life. . . .

The travelling over seas and oceans will be on well constructed large islands, formed by men, and navigated by the aid of steam, if better and superior motive powers may in future not be discovered and brought into use. Thus travelling will always be performed on dry land, unless the means for superior safe arrival by *aerial navigation* may be discovered and introduced into practice; and this discovery, under the new dispensation of unity of mind and interests, may, indeed, be reasonably antic-ipated; for under the united system of truth and good-ness for forming the character and governing the world, men will be enabled not only to remove mountains and fill up valleys, when useful, but to do far greater things than these.

4 SPIRITUALISM

(a)* This great change, the wonder of all nations and people, will be effected through the medium of the, to many, strange and yet little understood *Spiritual Mani-festations.*

The spirits of just men made perfect, will assist, guide, and direct the way to the full and complete reformation and regeneration from ignorance to the wisdom of the races of man, thus preparing, through a new practical religion, a new earth, and a new sphere in heaven for those thus reformed and thus regenerated.

There are Spirits now round and about us, Spirits who, through the aid of superior intelligence and power, have been purified and perfected, who are now deeply inter-ested in forming and carrying forward various measures in different parts of the world, to bring about this great and glorious change of humanity—this new dispensa-

* *Millennial Gazette,* 83.

tion, and permanent happy existence of man upon the earth, to prepare him at once for the higher enjoyments of superior spheres in heaven.

(b)* I have received communications from various influences calling themselves the Spirits of departed friends and relatives, in whom when living I had full and perfect confidence in their integrity, and as each made their communications to me in the character, strongly exhibited, which they possessed when living on the earth, I am compelled to believe their testimony as thus given; and as these communications have a good and high character in testifying now to the active exertions made by superior Spirits to assist developed man now to reform and regenerate the human races, I think their direct and uniform statements respecting themselves, are far more worthy of credit, than the random suppositions of those who are evidently ignorant of the whole subject of Spiritualism, and who by their previously acquired prejudices are strongly opposed to admit the existence of spirits, against any evidence that can be testified by human means to the contrary.

But as this is yet a subject which is generally so little understood, and which in irrational minds excites only irrational feelings of anger and ridicule, let it remain in abeyance until experience shall give us more facts and knowledge on this complex subject, and let us apply our attention to practical measures of deep and lasting interest to all of our race. This is *now our* business; and the Spirits, by the unchanging laws of their *will power,* shall ceaselessly take care of their own, and certainly perform their duties to us.

* *Millennial Gazette,* 95-6.

The new Spiritual Manifestations are now powerfully influencing the ruling earthly powers to stand still their irrational and evil career, to look around them to know what they should do to avert a storm such as men have not yet encountered, and fearful to contemplate. . . .

The Spirits are more especially occupied in preparing the British, Russian and French governments to this change. The British to commence now in India; the Russians and Indians being well prepared for this new mode of domestic colonising. And the French population has for some time had a strong liking for some such change. Her British Majesty and Royal Consort, with their Imperial Majesties of Russia and France, are at this time much under the influence and inspiration of superior Spirits, to induce them to unite and lead in this great change, and then to induce all other governments to follow their example.

6** PHRENOLOGY

[The pseudo-science of phrenology was, in Owen's time, and long after, taken very seriously, especially in 'advanced' circles. Owen's attitude to it was less uncritical than that of many of his contemporaries.]

Stranger: Pray inform me what you consider to be the practical utility of phrenology.

Founder: Most willingly. But first I must do justice to the founders of phrenology, and especially to Dr. Spurzheim, who I knew from his first arrival in this country, and for whom I have always entertained the greatest regard. I believe he was a most conscientious, estimable

---

* 'Second Letter to the Ruling Powers of the World,' Jan., 1, 1858, *Life, IA.,* xxxvi-xxxvii.
** *Dialogue,* 11-12.

man, and most certainly he has done much, in connexion with Dr. Gall, to promote a knowledge of the structure of the brain, and to remove much rubbish that was in the way of a fair investigation of the human powers, physical, intellectual, and moral. . . . Dr. Spurzheim, however, knew little compared with what should be known of either the theory or practice of education to enable any one to instruct the human race upon the formation of character, the most important and least known of all subjects.

Stranger: But surely his followers and disciples in this and other countries have done much to elicit additional facts relative to this subject, and have reasoned well and fairly respecting them?

Founder: They have elicited important facts, and reasoned as well respecting them as could have been anticipated from their want of higher knowledge, and of extensive experience in practice upon the subject; but owing to their deficiency in these essential qualifications, they are, at this moment, unintenionally leading the public much astray. . . .

Stranger: I am desirous of learning your opinion of the present state of phrenology.

Founder: It is easily given. Those among the professors of it who have the soundest judgements and most experience, can give a shrewd guess, by examination of the head, of what nature at birth, and the impressions of external objects from birth, have effected in forming the character of the individual; but from such an examination, it can never give more than a shrewd guess. For, where the organs of the brain are so numerous, and varied as they are in the human subject, and being, as they are, in a different combination of proportions in each individual, no man from external appearances alone, can ever do more than make a probable conjecture of the real internal character of the individual, and, to form this conjecture is the province of phrenology.

XVII

Some Contemporary Estimates
of Robert Owen

[The writers quoted in this chapter are all in their way representative of some section of the Radical or Socialist movements. Place and Cobbett are outstanding in the earlier Radical movement, Place in its philosophical, Benthamite wing, Cobbett in the more practical and empirical popular field, with even some vestiges of Tory thinking. Lovett and O'Brien were leaders of Chartism, Lovett of the right wing among the London artisans, O'Brien the theoretician of the left, at any rate in the early days of Chartism. Buonarroti was a survivor of the extreme socialist left of the French Revolution. Holyoake was in his youth an Owenite 'missionary' and survived to play a leading part in the Co-operative movement for another fifty years. The two passages from Engels are interesting as having been written in very different times and under very different circumstances.]

1 FRANCIS PLACE

He introduced himself to me, and I found him a man of kind manners and good intentions, of an imperturbable temper and an enthusiastic desire to promote the happiness of mankind. A few interviews made us friends. . . .

Mr. Owen then was, and is still, persuaded that he was the first who had ever observed that man was the creature of circumstances. On this supposed discovery he founded his system. Never having read a metaphysical book, not held a metaphysical conversation, nor having even heard of the disputes concerning freewill and necessity, he had no clear conception of his subject, and his views were obscure. Yet he had all along been preaching and publishing and projecting and predicting in the fullest conviction that he could command circumstances or create them, and place men above their control when necessary. He was never able to explain these absurd notions, and therefore always required assent to them, telling those who were not willing to take his words on trust that it was their ignorance which prevented them from at once assenting to these self-evident propositions.

From Graham Wallas, *Life of Francis Place*, 63-4.

2 WILLIAM COBBETT

A Mr. Owen, of Lanark, has, it seems, been before the committee with his schemes, which are nothing short of a species of *monkery*. This gentleman is for establishing innumerable *communities* of paupers! Each is to be resident in an *inclosure*, somewhat resembling a barrack establishment, only more extensive. I do not clearly understand whether the sisterhoods and brotherhoods are to form distinct communities, like nuns and friars, or whether they are to mix promiscuously; but I perceive that they are all to be under a very *regular discipline;* and that wonderful peace, happiness, and national benefit are to be the result! How the little matters of black eyes, bloody noses, and pulling off of caps are to be *settled,* I do not exactly see, nor is it explicitly stated whether the novices, when once they are confirmed, are to regard their character of paupers as indelible, though this is a point of great importance. Mr. Owen's scheme has, at any rate, the recommendation of perfect novelty; for of such a thing as a *community of paupers*, I believe no human being ever before heard. *Political Register*, August 2, 1817.

3 WILLIAM LOVETT

(a)   When Mr. Owen first came over from America he looked somewhat coolly on those 'Trading Associations', and very candidly declared that their mere buying and selling formed no part of his grand 'co-operatice scheme'; but when he found that great numbers among them were disposed to entertain many of his views, he took them more in favour, and ultimately took an active part among them. And here I think it is necessary to state that I entertain the highest respect for Mr. Owen's warm benevolence and generous intentions, however I may differ from many of his views; and this respect, I think, most people will be disposed to accord him, who know that he devoted a large fortune and a long life in reiterated efforts to improve the condition of his fellow men. I must confess, also, that I was one of those who, at one time, was favourably impressed with many of Mr. Owen's views, and, more especially, with those of a community of property. This notion has a peculiar attraction for the plodding, toiling, ill-remunerated sons and daughters of labour.

Life and Struggles, 44-5.

(b)   And here I must give a couple of anecdotes regarding Mr. Owen, showing how anti-democratic he was notwithstanding the extreme doctrines he advocated. Having resolved to call the Co-operative Congress referred to, we issued, among other invitations, a circular inviting the attendance of Members of Parliament. Mr. Owen, having seen a copy of the circular drawn up, conceived that it did not sufficiently express his peculiar views. He therefore sent an amendment, which he wished added to it. . . . The committee having discussed the amendment, rejected it. [Owen then, behind the backs of the committee, had the circular printed with his amendment. A deputation was sent to him to protest.]

We went, and were shown into Mr. Owen's room at the bazaar, and after briefly introducing our business, he told us to be seated, as he had something very important to communicate to us. This something was the *proof* of a publication he had just started, called the *Crisis*. After he had read to us a large portion of what he had written in it, I found my patience giving way, and at the next pause I took the opportunity of asking him what that had to do with the business we had come about? I began by telling him of his having submitted an amendment to our circular, of the committee having rejected it by a large majority, and of his taking it upon himself to authorize its insertion in the circular notwithstanding; and concluded by asking him whether such conduct was not highly despotic? With the greatest composure he answered that it evidently was despotic; but as we, as well as the committee that sent us, were all ignorant of his plans, and of the objects he had in view, we must consent to be ruled by despots till we had acquired sufficient knowledge to govern ourselves. After such a vain-glorious avowal, what could we say but to report—in the phraseology of one of the deputation— that we had been flabbergasted by him?

In a previous page I have stated that the proposal to establish an incipient community upon Mr. Thompson's plan was opposed and marred by Mr. Owen. It was in this curious manner. After the proposal had been discussed for some time . . . our friend Owen told us very solemnly, in the course of a long speech, that if we were resolved to go into a community upon Mr. Thompson's plan, we must make up our minds *to dissolve our present marriage connections, and go into it as single men and women.* This was like the bursting of a bomb-shell in the midst of us. . . . Nothing could have been better devised than this speech of Mr. Owen to sow the seeds of doubt and to cause the scheme to be abortive; and when we retired Mr. Thompson expressed himself very strongly against his conduct. I may add that the reporter of our proceedings, Mr. William Carpenter, thought it wise not to embody this discussion in our printed report.

Life and Struggles 49-51.

4 GEORGE JACOB HOLYOAKE

(a) He was the first publicist among us who looked with royal eyes upon children. He regarded grown persons as being proprietors of the world—bound to extend the rites of hospitality to all arrivals in it. He considered little children as little guests, to be welcomed with gentle courtesy and tenderness, to be offered knowledge and love, and charmed with song and flowers, so that they might be glad and proud that they had come into a world which gave them happiness and only asked of them goodness.   *History of Co-operation*, 1906, I, 43.

(b) It is no part of my object to present him other than he was. Though he was an amiable, he was, doubtless, at times a somewhat tiresome reformer. When he called a meeting together, those who attended never knew when they would separate. He was endowed with great natural capacity for understanding public affairs, and was accustomed to give practical and notable opinions upon questions quite apart from his own doctrines. His society was sought as that of a man who had the key to many state difficulties. Those knew little of him who supposed he owed his distinction to his riches. A man must be wise as well as wealthy to achieve the illustrious friendships which marked his career. He had personally an air of natural nobility about him. . . . He had a voice of great compass, thorough self-possession, and becoming action.

Like many other men, he spoke much better than he wrote. *ibid*, 48-9.

(c) The impression that Mr. Owen made upon workmen of his time is best described by one who won for himself a distinguished name as a working-class poet—Ebenezer Elliott. In an address to him, sent by trade-unionists of Sheffield in 1834, Elliott says: 'You came among us as a rich man among the poor and did not call us a rabble. There was no sneer upon your lips, no covert scorn in your tone.' That this distinction struck Elliott shows us how working men were then treated.

ibid, 51

5 PHILLIPPO BUONARROTI

What the Democrats of the Year VI [Babeuf and his associates] were unable to execute in France, a generous man has recently essayed, by other means to put in practice in the British Isles and in America. Robert Owen, the Scotchman [sic], after having established in his own country, and at his own expense, some communities founded on the principles of *equal distribution of enjoyment and labours,* has just formed in the United States sundry similar establishments, where several thousand people live peaceably under the happy regime of perfect equality.

By the counsels of this friend of humanity, the co-operative society, established in London has been for some time at work, propagating the principles of community, and demonstrating, by practical examples, the possibility of their application.

Babeuf attempted to combine a numerous people into one single and grand community; Owen, placed in other circumstances, would multiply in a country small communities, which afterwards united by a general bond, might become, as it were, so many individuals of one great family. Babeuf wished his friends to seize on the

supreme authority, as by its influence he hoped to effectu-
ate the reform they had projected; Owen calculates on
success by preaching and by example. May he show to
the world that wisdom can operate so vast a good without Great Britain. If successes depended on individual
grief of seeing his noble efforts fail, and furnishing, by an
unsuccessful experience, the advocates of equality. [*sic?*
inequality] with an argument against the possibility of
establishing in any manner, a social equality, to which
violent passions oppose so formidable a resistance, and
which, as appeared in our time, could only be the result
of a strong political commotion amongst civilized nations.

6 BRONTERRE O'BRIEN

[Commenting on the above remarks]

When Buonarroti penned this remarkable passage, he
neither knew the failure of the Owenite experiments in
America, nor the successive breaking up of the various
co-operative societies established in London and throughout Great Britain. If success depended on individual
merit, on generous zeal, on indomitable perseverance, and
an unquenchable desire to make men free and happy, at
all sacrifices to the individual himself, unquestionably the
experiments of Robert Owen would have succeeded. But
alas! the materials to work upon forms as essential an element in the calculations of success, as the skill of the
architect. Robert Owen brought to the task the necessary
skill, but the demoralising effects of our institutions left
him no materials to work upon. For my part, while
I admire both Babeuf and Robert Owen and agree generally, with both as to the *end* sought, I am obliged to dis-
sent from both as regards *means*.
Buonarroti's History of Babeuf's Conspiracy. Translated
by Bronterre O'Brien, 1836, 113, note.

[Ballou was the founder of Hopedale, one of the more successful of the American Fourierist communities.]

In years nearly seventy-five; in knowledge and experience superabundant; in benevolence transcendental; in honesty without disguise; in philanthropy unlimited; in religion a sceptic; in metaphysics a Necessarian Circumstantialist; in morals a universal excursionist; in general conduct a philosophical non-resistant; in socialism a Communist; in hope a terrestial elysianist; in practical business a methodist; in deportment an unequivocal gentleman.

From Hannah Whitall Smith, *Religious Fanaticism,* ed. Ray Strachey, 69.

8 FREDERICK ENGELS

(a)   English Socialism arose with Owen, a manufacturer, and proceeds therefore with great consideration towards the bourgeoisie and great injustice towards the proletariat in its methods, although it culminates in demanding the abolition of the class antagonism between bourgeoisie and proletariat.

The Socialists are thoroughly tame and peaceable, accept the existing order, bad as it is, so far as to reject all other methods but that of winning public opinion. Yet they are so dogmatic that success by this method is for them, and for their principles as at present formulated, utterly hopeless. . . . They acknowledge only a psychological development, a development of man in the abstract, out of all relation to the Past, whereas the whole world rests upon that Past, the individual man included. Hence they are too abstract, too metaphysical, and accomplish little. They are recruited in part from the working class, of which they have enlisted but a very small fraction representing, however, its most educated and solid elements. In its present form, Socialism can never become the common creed of the working class; it must condescend to return for a moment to the Chartist standpoint. But the true proletarian Socialism, having passed through Chartism, purified of its bourgeois elements, assuming the form which it has already reached in the minds of many Socialists and Chartist leaders (who are nearly all Socialists), must, within a short time, play a weighty part in the history of the development of the English people.

Condition of the Working Class.

(b)   Then a twenty-nine-year-old manufacturer came on the scene as a reformer, a man of almost sublimely child-like simplicity of character and at the same time a born leader of men such as is rarely seen. Robert Owen had adopted the teachings of the materialist philosophers of the Enlightenment, that man's character is the product on the one hand of his hereditary constitution, and on the other, of his environment during his lifetime, and particularly during the period of his development. In the industrial revolution most of his class saw only confusion and chaos, enabling them to fish in troubled waters and get rich quickly. He saw in it the opportunity to put his favourite theory into practice, and thereby to bring order out of chaos. [Engels then describes Owen's success at New Lanark.]

In spite of it all, Owen was not content. The existence which he had contrived for his workers in his eyes fell far short of being worthy of human beings; 'the people were slaves at my mercy'; the relatively favourable conditions in which he had set them were still far removed from allowing them an all-round and rational development of character and mind, and much less a free life. 'And yet, the working part of this population of 2,500 persons was daily producing as much real wealth of society as, less than half a century before, it would have required the working part of a population of 600,000 to create. I asked myself: what became of the difference between the wealth consumed by 2,500 persons and that which would have been consumed by 600,000?' The answer was clear. It had been used to pay the owners of the concern five per cent interest on their invested capital in addition to a profit of more than £300,000 sterling. And what was true of New Lanark held good in still greater measure of all the factories in England. 'Without this new wealth created by machinery, the wars for the overthrow of Napoleon, and for maintaining the aristocratic principles of society, could not have been carried through. And yet this new power was the creation of the working class.' To them, therefore, also belonged the fruits. . . .

The Owenite Communism arose in this purely business way . . . And in his definite plan for the future the technical elaboration of details shows such practical knowledge that, once the Owenite method of social reform is accepted, from an expert's standpoint there is little to be said against the actual detailed arrangements.

His advance to communism was the turning-point in Owen's life. So long as he merely played the part of a philantropist he had reaped nothing but wealth, applause, honour and glory. He was the most popular man in Europe. Not only those of his own class, but statesmen and princes listened to him with approval. But when he came forward with his communist theories, the situation was entirely changed. There were three great obstacles which above all seemed to him to block the path of social reform: private property, religion and marriage in its present form. He knew what confronted him if he attacked them: complete outlawry from official society and the loss of his whole social position. But nothing could hold him back; he attacked them regardless of the consequences, and what he had foreseen came to pass. Banished from official society, banned by the press, impoverished by the failures of communist experiments in America in which he sacrificed his whole fortune, he turned directly to the working class and worked among them for another thirty years. All social movements, all real advance made in England in the interests of the working class were associated with Owen's name. Thus in 1819, after five years' effort, he was successful in securing the first law limiting the labour of women and children in the factories. He presided at the first Congress at which the trade unions of all England united in a single great trades association. As transition measures to the complete communist organisation of society he introduced on the one hand the co-operative societies (both consumers and productive), which have since at least given practical proof that it is very well possible to dispense with both merchants and manufacturers; and on the other hand, the labour bazaars, institutions for the exchange of the products of labour by means of labour notes with the labour hours as unit. These institutions were necessarily bound to fail, but they completely anticipated the Proudhon exchange bank of a much later period, and only differed from it in that they did not represent the panacea for all social ills, but only the first steps toward a far more radical transformation of society.

Anti-Dühring, 294-7.

Index

TREATY AT FORT LARAMIE

JOHN LEGG

ST. MARTIN'S PAPERBACKS

TREATY AT FORT LARAMIE

Copyright © 1994 by Siegel and Siegel Ltd.

The Forts of Freedom series is a creation of Siegel and Siegel Ltd.

ISBN: 0-312-95128-0

Printed in the United States of America

St. Martin's Paperbacks edition/July 1994

10 9 8 7 6 5 4 3 2 1

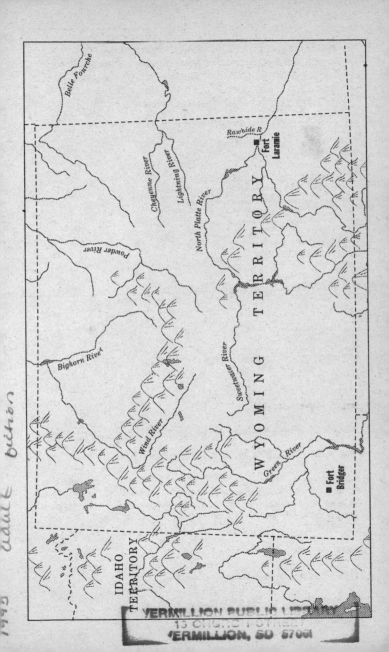

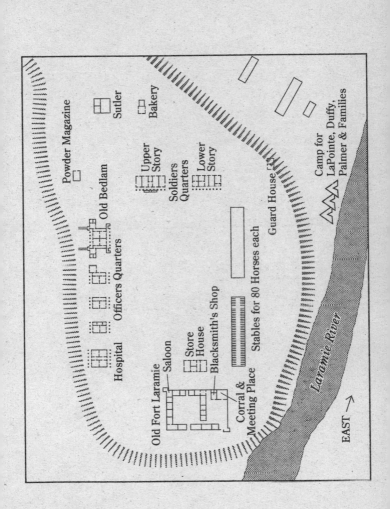

Henri LaPointe scrunched down among the thorny bushes as much as he could, hoping that none of the Crows rampaging through his small camp had seen him. One minute he, his wife, their two children, and one of his wife's brothers had been sitting at their fire, eating some freshly killed buffalo and talking idly. The next, ten Crows had swarmed in over them all.

LaPointe fired his flintlock rifle and then his single-shot flintlock pistol, before caching into the brush near the mouth of the Rawhide River. He turned and hunkered down just as his wife's twelve-year-old brother, Wolfskin, went down—his attempts to battle back futile under the power of the Crows.

As he sweated in the intense heat, LaPointe watched the massacre with dark, hate-filled eyes. His only touch of satisfaction was in noting that one of the Crows was down and it did not appear that he would get up again. It was a small thing under the weight of the horrors still going on.

LaPointe and Yellow Quiver had been together more than ten years now, and both were pleased with the other. LaPointe was not sure if what he and Yellow Quiver felt for each other was love, but he had to bite his rifle stock until his teeth felt as if they would break to prevent himself from crying out as he watched the horrifying scenes before him. Tears leaked from his eyes.

Just after LaPointe had cached, four of the Crows

grabbed Yellow Quiver. The woman fought back, but all she accomplished was to anger the warriors, one of whom finally thumped her on the side of the head. Then the four threw her to the ground. Laughing, three of them held her down while the one who had hit her brutally took her. When he was done, he replaced one of the other warriors holding her down, while that man satisfied himself in her, and then the others.

While that was going on, two other Crows had begun gleefully hacking up Wolfskin's body. The brutal mutilation of his wife's young brother meant little to LaPointe, not in the context of what was happening to his wife and children.

The last two Crows each had grabbed one of La-Pointe's children. It was hard to see, since it was dusk and the fire threw out little light, but LaPointe could see that one warrior had grabbed five-year-old Copper Kettle's hair. Holding the girl up by her long, black tresses, he slit her with a knife from belly button to sternum. The warrior laughed as he saw the girl's intestines spill out, sagging downward until they hit the ground with a soft, disgusting plop. Then the Crow flung the broken little body aside.

Little Hunter, LaPointe's nine-year-old son, had managed to get his small knife out and slashed the warrior who came at him. The Crow jerked his arm back, and then growled as he cuffed Little Hunter. The boy fell but did not cry out, not even when the Crow jumped on him and began carving Little Hunter up, angrily tossing away chunks of the boy's flesh.

Finally that Crow and his three companions joined the first four in taking their fill of Yellow Quiver. When the warriors tired of that, they grinned as one—a big, strong-looking Crow who appeared to be the war leader, and the only one LaPointe had really gotten any kind of look at—began peeling the skin from Yellow Quiver. He started at the top of Yellow Quiver's left breast, making a small precise incision along the top and then down each side. Grabbing the loosened skin with two grimy fingers, the Crow peeled it slowly down until the flap of flesh lay on Yellow Quiver's abdomen.

LaPointe could not see it happening, but he could tell from the other Crows' laughs and comments on the war leader's skills, just what was going on.

The big Crow then started on the other breast, doing the same. Yellow Quiver groaned a few times, but otherwise kept silent. She seemed to struggle less, too, as the minutes ticked by, so much so that after a while, the warriors holding her backed off.

Then she made her move, a hand flashing out to grab one warrior's knife. She jerked herself up so that she was sitting. Her breast skin hung down, exposing the raw, red flesh underneath. She whipped the knife across one Crow's face and was rearing back for another swipe when the war leader raked his fingernails across Yellow Quiver's skinless chest.

Yellow Quiver gasped, and one of the Crows snatched the knife out of her hand. The leader shoved her back down. Holding her down with a rough hand on the oozing breast flesh, he entered her again and began pumping ruthlessly. When Yellow Quiver froze, trying not to move so that the pain would lessen—and so that she would not help the Crow in his lust—the Crow ground his hard palm into her chest. Yellow Quiver groaned and gasped, wriggling uncontrollably from the pain.

After he finished, the Crow rolled back onto his haunches. Yellow Quiver once more tried to grab something, anything, to use to attack her attackers. But a warrior yanked out his tomahawk and with a strong blow hacked her right arm off just below the elbow, then did the same with the left.

That done, the war leader went back to peeling more skin off Yellow Quiver. He stopped before long, though, since Yellow Quiver had bled to death.

LaPointe remained in the midst of the thicket—unmoving though several sticks and thorns were jabbing into him—throughout the long, hot evening, his hate-filled eyes drinking in the Crows' savagery. He wanted more than anything in the world to charge out there and start laying waste the bloodthirsty Crow warriors. But that would be futile—and fatal—he knew. He might get one or two of them, but then he would go under. He didn't mind that all that much, but it would mean the Crow butchers would go unpunished. And that was something he did mind.

The same fate would result if he just sat here and tried to pick off several of the Crows. With only a single-shot rifle and a single-shot pistol, he would be able to do little damage before he, too, was dead and mutilated. So he stayed put.

After their butchery, the Crows enjoyed a small feast made with the foods of the recently deceased, feasting while sitting within feet of the victims. Finally the Crows fell asleep, sated by blood, food, and victory.

LaPointe gave it some time before he risked leaving. But finally he moved, going ever so slowly in an attempt to rustle the thorny, entwined brush as little as possible.

After what seemed like hours of movements with the rapidity of frosted molasses, LaPointe was out of the thicket. Breathing shallowly, so as not to disturb either the animals or the men, LaPointe moved toward his own horse. The beast was ungainly in looks and odd of coloration, but the gelding was a good match for the stocky Frenchman.

LaPointe patted the horse's neck softly and murmured a few words into the animal's ear. Man and beast had been together a long time, and the horse settled down as soon as it heard the familiar voice. LaPointe bent and undid the simple rawhide rope hobble. Then he leaped onto the horse's back. Leaning over the animal's neck, LaPointe whispered to the horse, *"Allons audevant. Mais lentement, mon ami. Lentement.* Let's go. But slowly, my friend. Slowly."

The horse stepped off, slow and easy. LaPointe remained lying along the horse's neck. If any of the Indians awoke, LaPointe hoped they would simply think that one of the animals was moving around in search of forage.

Some of the other animals shuffled a little nervously at LaPointe's movement, but then settled. Finally, when he was more than a hundred yards from his camp, LaPointe let the horse have its head.

He thundered across the prairie throughout the night and into the next day. It was near dark again when he rode into Fort John. He was exhausted and had not eaten since just before the massacre began. He slid off his horse and stood, an arm around the horse's neck to keep him up.

Several fort workers ran up, questions bubbling out of their mouths in concerned profusion.

Finally the fort's chief clerk, Andrew Drips, arrived. "Well?" was all he said as he stood there, a man secure in the knowledge that he was the ruler of all he saw before him.

LaPointe rattled off some French, but stopped when a glowering Drips ordered, "English, dammit. Speak English."

LaPointe nodded. "Crows come on us," he said, shaking his head to fight off the weariness weighing so heavily on him. He had little accent as a result of his parentage as well as his vocation. His father was French, but his mother American. Though Marcel LaPointe ran his home in St. Charles, Missouri, as a French home, his wife taught her son English, with her husband's permission. In addition, Henri LaPointe had spent a long time in the mountains with trappers of every breed—Americans, mulattos, French-Canadians, Mexicans, Irishmen, Scots, Germans, Indians of numerous tribes. That had served to soften his already faint accent, and now that accent appeared only when LaPointe was in the midst of a crisis. Now was not such a time; a day and a half ago was.

"Were any of my men with you?" Drips demanded.

LaPointe glowered at his boss. "No."

Drips shrugged, his interest waning. If the trouble did

not directly involve the fort, he didn't much care what happened to people, even fort employees. Still, if Crow war parties were raiding almost this far south, they could be troublesome. Such a thing might endanger the buffalo robes, wolf hides and other furs the Dakota brought into the fort to trade. And, since the American Fur Company's main objective was turning a profit, that was also Drips's foremost goal.

"You lost your wife?"

LaPointe nodded. "My two kids, too. And Yellow Quiver's brother, Wolfskin."

"I'm sorry." Drips's insincerity was obvious. "How many Crows?" he asked.

"Ten. I got one for sure, and maybe another one, too."

"Any indication of other Crow war parties in the area?" Drips asked. That was his main concern now. If there were only ten, or even a dozen Crows running around, they could not disturb the area too much. Sooner or later they would head back to their own land. Or the Dakota would catch them and solve the problem. Either way, Drips didn't much care.

LaPointe shook his head. "Hell, I never knew those Crows were around till the bastards popped up like they did. *Fils de garces.* Sons of bitches."

Drips nodded. "My sympathy for your loss," he said unctuously. He turned and walked off.

"Bastard," Otis Palmer said as he stepped up to help LaPointe. He was staring at Drips.

LaPointe shrugged, too tired and grief-stricken to care much about Drips. He would deal with that later. He allowed Palmer and another longtime friend, Rufus Duffy, to help him to a room where laborers were quartered.

As he sat in the quarters, sullenly swigging down harsh whiskey from a quart bottle, LaPointe thought back on what had brought him here, to this fort, where he tried drinking away his grief.

He had been on his own for most of the past eight

years—since the beaver trade died. His days of trapping
in the mountains had been shining times, he often remembered with a combination of loss and relief. He had
ridden with the best of the mountain men back then—
Jim Bridger, Tom Fitzpatrick, the Sublettes, Joe Meek,
Kit Carson, all of them.

The death of the beaver trade hit LaPointe hard, and
he roamed for most of a year or so trying to figure out
what to do with himself. He had no trade other than
trapping beaver, and that was out of the question now.
Some of the old mountain men had built their own
trading forts—like Bridger had done over on Black's
Fork of the Green. Others had gotten into trapping wolf
and bear and other animals for their fur or hides. Still
others had taken to guiding wagon trains or army con-
tingents. LaPointe, though, had not the money for the
first, the patience for the second, or the inclination for
the third.

He had finally gone down to Fort John and hired on
as a hunter for the American Fur Company fort. That
kept him in meat and clothes, gave him enough spending cash for whiskey and other necessities, and allowed
him to remain close to his wife's people—a band of
Brulé Dakota.

LaPointe generally worked out of the fort from the
middle of spring until the fall—as long as the weather
remained nice. He would winter with his wife's band
along the wooded banks of a river or stream in the land
of the mighty Teton Dakota.

Twice a year, LaPointe would ride out with the Brulé
bands for their big hunts—one in the spring; one just
before winter set in. He also would make occasional
forays to hunt with just a few Brulé friends or maybe
with some of his old friends from the mountain days. All
of those old friends—the ones who had remained in the
west, anyway—frequently stopped by Fort John. A few,
like Bridger and Fitzpatrick, were there more than others, but some, like Bill Sublette and Robert Campbell,
remained in Missouri. Still, there were few months that

would go by during the warmer weather when at least one of the old boys wasn't at the fort.

A week ago, LaPointe had found the routine at the fort too much for him. That was a regular occurrence, too. LaPointe hated being cooped up in the fort, or hunting with a couple of laborers. He wanted the old, free times of the mountain days. Since that was impossible, he did what he could to try to rekindle some little flicker of the old flame. Because this was one of those rare times when no old mountaineers were around, he rode off alone to Yellow Quiver's small village. He could interest no one other than his young brother-in-law, Wolfskin, to go out hunting, but he had packed up his family and gone anyway.

The small party decided to stick fairly close to their homeland, and so they rode up the Rawhide to the area near its mouth. They felt safe here, since several bands of Brulés were around, as were some bands of Hunkpapas.

The Crow war party, though, was looking for blood— Dakota blood, and they found the small party. LaPointe and Wolfskin had been a little lax in security, feeling that since they were so deep in the lands of the Dakota that they would be safe. *How wrong we were. How wrong!* LaPointe thought bitterly. And he had paid dearly for his laxity.

A few days later, LaPointe disappeared. No one saw him go, and no one knew where he had gotten himself off to. One or two friends expressed some concern for La-Pointe's safety, thinking that perhaps he had set out after the Crows by himself.

So it was with some surprise that his friends watched his arrival at Fort John again nine months later. More surprising to them was that LaPointe appeared to be a quieter man in general, and the friends were certain that he had lost some of his good cheer for all time. That was a sad thing.

However, they were nowhere near as surprised at La-Pointe's arrival, as LaPointe was himself. He sat on his horse across the wide, shallow Platte River and looked across at the fort. What he saw stunned him.

2

Before he had left, LaPointe had no more success with the men at Fort John than he had had later with the men of Yellow Quiver's village in trying to get a war party together to punish the Crows.

Andrew Drips had all but forbidden his employees from any such foolish undertaking. And it was a rare man who could afford to give up his livelihood to pursue a few Indians who were miles away just to extract vengeance for a squaw, two half-breeds and a Dakota warrior-to-be.

LaPointe had gone to the Brulés then, just after disappearing from the fort. He felt that the Dakota would be eager for revenge. After all, the hated Crows had been enemies for all time.

But the Brulés saw little sense in going to war for such a reason. Now that the winter was approaching, the hunt took precedence. After the winter, and the spring hunt, the Dakota could always find time for going to war with their longtime enemies, the Crows. But they would not restrict their searching for glory among the Crow lands to seeking out a specific few.

"You may come with us, Black Bear," Painted Bull, civil chief of the Brulé band, told LaPointe. "You're a warrior. Come with us then. We'll count many coup on the Crow."

"I don't want to count goddamn coup on those goddamn Crows. I want to kill some of them."

"Calm down, Black Bear," Painted Bull chided in English. "We will kill Crows. Many Crows. But we can't pick out some and not others. Your grief has destroyed your reason."

"Buffalo shit," LaPointe snapped. "It wasn't your wife and children killed by those sons of bitches."

Painted Bull shrugged. "All the Crows are no good," Painted Bull said in Dakota. "We all know that. So it is good to kill Crows. It doesn't matter which ones you kill."

"It does to me," LaPointe snapped.

"Then go. Go find the Crows, if that is what your heart says you should do. If your medicine is good, if your spirit helper is aware, then you will find those you seek."

LaPointe had stormed out of the village. He had never really been a passionate man, and the feeling of loss—and the accompanying obsession with revenge—were unusual to him. Now he was not really sure what to do. He paused, chest heaving as a tightness clutched at him. Then he nodded to himself.

With Brulés watching him a little nervously, LaPointe loaded some supplies on an old mule. Then he saddled his mottled horse and left the village. He rode for some days with no clear idea of where he was heading, nor even of whom he was seeking. He only knew that he had to head into the land of the Crow Indians and seek out a hatchet-faced warrior with hair that hung down past his knees. It had become apparent to LaPointe, as he had hidden from the Crows that the hatchet-faced one was the war chief for the band of raiders.

Even more insulting to LaPointe, once he had stopped to think about it, was the attitude of the Crows. He had wondered while he sat watching the savagery against his family why the warriors had not come looking for him. He had, after all, shot at least one of the war band, and most likely had killed the warrior. Yet they had not come looking for him. He had realized that they held him in such contempt that they thought him unworthy of pursuing. That bit at his insides as much as anything else.

The thought also drove him onward, up into the land of the River Crows, along the Powder River. But within a few weeks, he began to doubt his sanity. He was alone in a land inhabited by some of the fiercest warriors of the west. And, he wondered, what could he do? Alone? And against an enemy as widespread as the Crows were.

Finally he turned southwest, not stopping until he was almost in Ute land. With winter coming on, he found himself a cave. "This'll do," he muttered to himself. He spent the next several days making meat. While the meat was drying, he built a rough wall of logs across the cave mouth, leaving enough room on one side for him, his horse and his mule to go into and out of the cave.

LaPointe managed to get enough meat made and collect enough forage for the animals before the snow got too deep. Then he holed up, waiting out the fierce winter.

He was beginning to think that he would not make it out of the cave alive when the winter finally eased its grip on the mountains. He waited a few more days before coming out. When he did, it was a bright, mild day. He sucked in a long draught of fresh air, grateful after several months in the fetid cave.

As LaPointe stood enjoying the prime day, he realized that he no longer felt the pressing desire to go out killing Crows. He would not turn away the opportunity to do so if it presented itself, but he figured it would be foolish searching for the Crows.

He would miss Yellow Quiver—and his children. But death, violent death, was a way of life out here in this wide, rugged, unforgiving land. His family could have died at any time, of a thousand different things. So could he. It was something everyone lived with out here, probably everywhere, he allowed himself to think.

With spring almost arriving, the world would be renewing itself again. LaPointe figured it was about time he did, too. He had to put the past behind him and move on.

It was another few weeks before he could physically move on, though. Two days after his reemergence, another storm had swept the mountains, forcing him back inside. Spring played touch and go for a while, but finally exerted itself more or less permanently. The first thing he did was to hunt, eager to feel the life-giving meat coursing through him.

He gave the horse and the mule sufficient time to fatten up after a long winter of sparse forage. Then LaPointe loaded up his few things and rode down out of the mountains, heading northeast along the South Platte before turning eastward where the North and South branches of the Platte joined.

Instead of going straight to Fort John, LaPointe stopped off at Painted Bull's small village. The Brulés had been quite successful on their spring hunt and had celebrated considerably. Now many of the warriors—augmented by men from other Brulé bands as well as some of the Hunkpapas and Oglalas—were preparing to go to war.

"Join us, my friend," Painted Bull said in encouragement. "We will count many coup against the Crow. And we will steal many horses."

"I don't give a shit about counting coup. Or about stealing horses," LaPointe snapped. "But if you find a tomahawk-faced son of a bitch, haul his ass back here for me. I'll count coup on the bastard in ways he won't be none too fond of."

"Your heart has grown weak," Painted Bull chided.

"I'll set on you any time you want, you old bag of shit," LaPointe retorted.

Painted Bull grinned. He knew LaPointe was not serious, as he had not been serious when he had made his accusation. "I'd not want to embarrass you in front of the others," he offered.

"Embarrass me?" LaPointe said with a snort. "Hell."

"What'll you do now?" Painted Bull asked, growing serious.

LaPointe shrugged. "Go back to the fort, I suppose. A man's got to work." Suddenly he brightened. "A man needs to be married, too."

Painted Bull laughed. "This is true." He paused, then asked slyly, "You have picked someone?"

"Morning Mist," LaPointe said with a nod. "If she'll have me."

"Why wouldn't she?"

"Maybe 'cause I'm of no mind to play the flute for her and go through all the other buffalo shit that goes with courting a woman your way."

"She won't expect that," Painted Bull said with another laugh. "At least not with you. You're a big man among the white-eyes."

"Merde," LaPointe commented. "I'm nothing more than a mule to them."

Painted Bull shrugged. "Your reputation is secure among the Brulé," he said. "The People did not name you Black Bear for no reason." He sighed. "Can I help you in this matter?"

LaPointe nodded. "I'd be grateful if you were to let her know my feelings, and see if she'd be willing to respond."

"I can do that for the Black Bear," Painted Bull said solemnly. "You come to my lodge in two suns. I'll have an answer for you then." He nodded with finality.

LaPointe nodded and drifted off. He felt rather out of place here now that Yellow Quiver and his children were gone. He had no lodge to call his own. He knew he would be welcomed in many of the lodges, but he saw it as an imposition.

Making matters worse for LaPointe were the preparations for war. LaPointe was not part of them, and all the Brulé warriors knew that. He had gone on raids with them before, both southeastward against the Pawnees and northwestward against the Crow. But now he was not inclined to go with the Dakota warriors, and that made him feel even more out of place.

Because of that, he made himself a small camp off to the side of the Brulé village. He tended his animals and gathered some firewood, the latter under the watchful eyes and the tittering giggles of many of the Brulé women. Finally, with the drums of the village banging out a throbbing rhythm, LaPointe stretched out on his buffalo robe and fell asleep.

He spent most of the next day away from the village. He just rode at first, trying to keep from thinking about Yellow Quiver, Copper Kettle and Little Hunter. He was successful in it only about half the time, but at least the thoughts were not too painful now. His time in the mountains had allowed him to work out most of his grief. Besides, he was generally a pragmatic man.

Late in the afternoon, he shot a large buffalo cow and took his time butchering it. With his mule heavily laden with meat and a robe, he rode slowly back to Painted Bull's village. There he gave away the buffalo hide and most of the meat, keeping only a small portion for himself and another small portion he would give to Painted Bull as a gift for his help.

LaPointe cooked his meat and ate alone, not wanting company even if it had been offered. He turned in early, not caring now about the puzzled looks cast in his direction.

LaPointe did exhibit some signs of nervousness in the morning. He washed up in the river and then ate a small portion of buffalo meat and drank several cups of coffee. Then he figured it was time to go and see Painted Bull.

The chief was waiting in his large lodge. Before sitting across the fire from Painted Bull, LaPointe handed the old man the piece of hide with the present of buffalo meat. Painted Bull accepted it with a grave nod.

Painted Bull picked up his pipe and slowly began filling the catlinite bowl.

"Let's leave that till we're done with our parleying,

Painted Bull," LaPointe said, a note of anxiousness in his voice. "If we need to smoke."

"You're too eager, Black Bear," Painted Bull scolded mildly.

"Maybe I am," LaPointe agreed. "But I'm too old for playing games. If Morning Mist wants me, fine, let's get it done. If she doesn't, all the smoking in the world won't make a damn bit of difference."

"Such an attitude is sad, though undeniably true." Painted Bull set aside the long pipe, then grinned at LaPointe. "Morning Mist says she will become the wife of Black Bear."

LaPointe sighed in relief. He hadn't realized until just now how tense he really was. Such tenseness was uncommon in him and its effect now surprised him. But he was outwardly calm as he asked, "And how much is this going to cost me?"

"Morning Mist's brother, Spotted Horse, who has been caring for Morning Mist since her husband died, says he will take only three good ponies for his sister."

"Three good ponies for a widow?" LaPointe said, feigning shock. "Such a thing's outlandish."

"So I told him," Painted Bull muttered. "Then what will you offer to Spotted Horse?"

"One pony."

"He won't like that."

"I don't give a shit whether he likes it or not. He ought to be giving me something. After all, I'm taking three mouths off his hands all at once."

"True. But also not true."

"Something can't be true but not true. Speak your mind, Painted Bull."

"Morning Mist's children probably will stay with Spotted Horse if Morning Mist goes with you to the fort."

"All right," LaPointe said with a grin, "I'll be taking only one mouth out of his lodge. He's still getting a good deal, since the kids would've been living with him anyway."

Painted Bull nodded. "I will tell him." He grinned again. "And I'm sure he will see the wisdom of it all."

"Good. But I want it done with soon. I'm not all that eager to get back to the fort, but I need to bring in some cash money so I can get Spotted Horse his pony."

"It will be done quickly. Now, will you smoke?"

LaPointe nodded. "There's reason to now."

That night, Morning Mist came to LaPointe, who was waiting in Painted Bull's lodge. The two then left for a lodge that had been set aside for them. There was no ceremony or anything special. The couple simply moved into the lodge, spent two nights and days there, and then they left, heading for Fort John.

3

"What the hell happened here, Rufe?" LaPointe asked his friend Rufus Duffy. He had ridden down from a ridge a little northwest of the fort, awed by all the activity. Soldiers swarmed all over the area. Wood cut from upriver was being hauled into the fort on large wagons. Men were hammering or sawing. Bricks were being made. Everything was in a near chaotic state. "The Company sold the fort."

"Sold it?" LaPointe asked incredulously. "To the army?"

"Goddamn right." Duffy grinned, enjoying being the teller of such momentous news. "Lock, stock and barrel. Over the winter. Just where the hell you been anyway?"

"That's not important now, dammit," LaPointe snapped. "I need a job. The army hiring?"

"They hired nearabout all the boys that was here before."

"Nearabout?"

"A few of the boys didn't think much of workin' for the goddamn soldiers."

"Well, that doesn't bother me any," LaPointe said. "Who's doing the hiring? Drips?"

"Drips?" Duffy said with a laugh. "That sour-tempered old fart left a month ago. I don't know where he went, and I don't rightly give a good goddamn neither."

LaPointe nodded seriously. Duffy noted it sadly. He

hoped his friend would not carry his grief with him forever.

"Anyways, the head man now is Major Sanderson. He's a fair enough feller with everyone, as far as I've been able to see."

LaPointe nodded again. "So what's going on here?" he asked, waving his arm around.

"Army's gonna build a whole new fort. They've been at it near a month already. I expect it'll take 'em some time to get it all finished."

"Nothing wrong with the old fort," LaPointe commented.

"Other than the fact that the shit hole's fallin' down," Duffy said with a laugh.

LaPointe grinned. Then he sighed. "Where's this major hang his hat?"

"Drips's old quarters inside. Come on, I'll walk with you, if you don't mind."

LaPointe shrugged. He walked off alongside Duffy. He held the reins to his horse. Morning Mist's pony followed. Neither man had mentioned her. That could wait.

It did not surprise Duffy or other friends of LaPointe's that he had a new wife in tow. A man needed a woman, someone to cook his food, to make or mend his clothes, to care for their lodge, to care for him, to tan the hides and furs a man brought in. And, mostly, a man needed a woman to be a woman in the robes.

As Yellow Quiver had been, Morning Mist also was a Brulé. She was taller, slimmer and considerably younger than Yellow Quiver had been. Morning Mist was only twenty-two and a widow. She had two children, whom she had left with her sister's family while she went off to live in the odd world of white men. She was a strong woman and not unpleasing to look at, something made more obvious when she stood next to her new husband.

Henri LaPointe was in his early forties, a man of medium height and quite stocky. When he chose not to shave, his beard grew like weeds and quickly became

thick and knotted. He hated shaving, but he also hated
the tangled mass of hair when he did not shave. Unde-
cided about which he loathed more, he appeared both
ways, depending on his mood of the moment. His
weathered, round, ruddy face was marred only by a wide
scar that ran from past his hairline on the left side of his
head and arced downward past the outside of his left
eyebrow and then stopped between his left eye and temple. His eyes were dark—darker even than those of his
Dakota friends—but generally sparkling with life. He
was a strong man and hardened by years of harsh labor.

Many men noted the woman with LaPointe and Duffy
as the three walked through the gates of the bustling
adobe fort and stopped in front of Drips's former quarters. A tall, broad-shouldered officer stood just outside
the door talking to several soldiers. When the soldiers
left, the officer turned. He smiled and said, "Mister
Duffy, isn't it?"

Duffy nodded, proud that this important man remembered his name. "Yessir, Major."

"And who is this?" Sanderson asked, pointing to La-
Pointe.

"I am Henri LaPointe." It was said proudly.

"Pleased to meet you, Mister LaPointe," Sanderson
said, offering his hand. "I'm Major Winslow Sanderson."

While shaking hands, LaPointe took stock of the officer. Sanderson was a big man, but not so big as to
stand out. However, he had a commanding presence.
His face was open and honest, with a high forehead,
long, straight nose and a thin-lipped mouth. It was
topped by a mane of long brown hair. His mustache
dipped around his mouth and then angled down into a
small Vandyke beard.

"The honor is mine, Major."

Sanderson nodded. "And what can I do for you, Mister LaPointe?"

"He's looking for a job, Major," Duffy interjected.

"What kind of job?" Sanderson still looked at La-Pointe.

"Hunter."

"You're experienced, I take it?"

LaPointe nodded solemnly. *"Oui.* I was a hunter here for six, maybe seven years."

"So what happened?" Sanderson asked. "If you weren't here when I hired the other hunters."

LaPointe's face clouded a little.

Duffy answered for him. "His wife was killed almost a year ago."

"And so he went off to be by himself in his grief and mourning?" Sanderson added softly.

"Oui," LaPointe said. "I 'ave just come back."

"So who is that then?" Sanderson asked, nodding toward Morning Mist.

LaPointe glared at him, then realized that Sanderson simply was interested; that he was not moralizing. "She is Morning Mist, my new wife."

"Sioux?" Sanderson asked. He figured he should learn as much as possible of the Indians with whom he would deal the most.

LaPointe nodded. "Brulé Dakota. The Brulés are one of the seven subdivisions of the Teton Dakota—Sioux as you call them. They are the farthest west and—with the Oglala—the most warlike of all the Dakota."

"That all sounds mighty complicated," Sanderson said. "Especially the part about the Sioux being Dakota. Did I get that right?"

"Sort of. Sioux is a corruption—by my own people, sad to say—of the Ojibwa word for enemy. The people you call the Sioux call themselves 'Dakota,' or something similar. The Dakota have three major divisions—the Santee to the east, Yankton west of them, and then the Teton. Each of the three has several subdivisions." He finally shut up, figuring that Sanderson did not need a lecture.

"All very interesting, Mister LaPointe." Sanderson

sighed. "There is so much to be learned. Perhaps you could instruct me a little more in such matters."

"Be glad to, Major." LaPointe paused, then added, "But you still haven't answered me. About a job, I mean."

Sanderson stood in thought for a few moments, then asked, "Do you speak Sioux . . . I mean Dakota?"

LaPointe nodded. "French, English, sign; I'm fair in Spanish, and I can make do in Cheyenne, Arapaho and Snake."

Sanderson was astounded. He looked at Duffy. "He speaking the truth, Mister Duffy?"

"Yessir," Duffy responded with a vigorous nod.

"Why didn't Mister Drips avail himself of those talents, Mister LaPointe?" Sanderson asked, still puzzled.

LaPointe shrugged. "Me and Drips never did get along well. He thought me just an ignorant Frenchman from the backwoods."

"Such blindness is unfortunate—and stupid," Sanderson commented.

"The same can be said about many army men," LaPointe offered.

"How so?" Sanderson did not seem offended.

"Many's the chil' wearing the blue of the army can't see Indians as anything other than savages."

"Aren't they?"

"Most of them are savages—at one time or another. So're nearabout any other men. Indians aren't much different than we are, Major, underneath."

"I'm afraid you're right, Mister LaPointe," Sanderson said with a sigh. "Another common trait is our failing to see things as they are many times." He paused. "It's a pity we can't save the world by ourselves. At least not here and now. Well, I have enough hunters employed, Mister LaPointe." As he watched LaPointe growing angry, he added, "So, will you take a job as an interpreter?"

LaPointe's spreading anger suddenly came to a dead

halt and just as swiftly changed to astonishment. *"Oui!"* he said with enthusiasm. *"Mais oui,* Major!"

"Good," Sanderson said with a reassuring grin. "I . . ."

LaPointe had turned away and was chattering to Morning Mist. When he turned back, he said, "My apologies, Major. I had to explain to Morning Mist."

"No need for apologies. All I was going to say was that your pay will be sixty dollars a month. That acceptable?"

LaPointe could not believe his good fortune. *"Oui!* Yes! *Tres bon!"*

"Do you have quarters here?"

"No. I thought maybe Morning Mist and me could stay in the laborers' quarters till Morning Mist can make our own lodge."

"All the laborers' quarters are full," Duffy said.

"We could put some of the single men out," Sanderson said thoughtfully.

"Mais non," LaPointe said with a determined shake of his head. "I won't have men put out on Morning Mist's account. She is Brulé, and she will be able to live in the open for a time. It might even push her to finish our lodge quickly."

"Still, it's not right that a man in your position should be sleeping on the ground. Nor should his wife have to do that."

"We'll get by, Major."

"How about this then," Sanderson said after a moment's thought. "You can use my tent for the time being. I'm quartered here, so I have no use for it. I'll have a couple of the men put it up for you. Where would you like it?"

Sanderson's words sounded final, so LaPointe did not argue. "That wooded spot over on the bank of the Laramie." He pointed in a vague easterly direction.

"Corporal Hill," Sanderson shouted. When a tall, skinny young man ran up, Sanderson said, "Get my personal tent, Corporal. Then enlist half a dozen men to put it up."

"Where, sir?"

"Wherever Mister LaPointe here wants it."

Hill turned and looked at LaPointe and then Morning Mist. He swung back to Sanderson. "Set up the tent for a damn squaw?" he asked, stunned by the order. He hastily added, "Sir."

A snarling Henri LaPointe made a move toward Hill, but Sanderson stopped him with an upraised hand.

"I'll handle this, Mister LaPointe," Sanderson growled. He turned blazing eyes on Hill. "I'm of a good mind to let Mister LaPointe have at you, Corporal. But I won't since I need all the men I can get. However, I *can* do with one less corporal." He paused, then bellowed, "Lieutenant Bootes!" He waited more or less patiently until a fair young man with a second lieutenant's bars on his shoulders appeared. "Since Hill here is one of your men, it falls to you to remove his stripes. In addition, he will do the chore I've already ordered him to do. After which, he will be assigned to the brick-making detail."

"Until when, sir?" Bootes asked.

"Till I decide he's had enough."

"Yes, sir." Bootes turned. With a quick yank he jerked off the single stripe on Hill's left arm. He did the same on the other arm. "Now, Private," Bootes said sharply, "what was the chore you were ordered to perform?" When Hill told him, Bootes roared, "See to it at once. Any more insubordination and you'll be hanging by your thumbs. Is that clear, Private?"

"Yessir." Hill could not mask his anger.

"Move!"

Hill hustled off, and Sanderson introduced Bootes and LaPointe. Then Sanderson looked at LaPointe and said, "Your point is well taken, Mister LaPointe. About how some folks are."

LaPointe nodded. "Well, Major, I'd better get on over to where my new home's going to be." He paused. "I'm grateful for the job, Major. I hope I can do it to your satisfaction." LaPointe was bubbling with excitement inside. He had never held a job with such responsibility before. Nor one with such good, regular wages. Sure, he had made himself a thousand dollars for a season a couple of times back in the beaver days. But like many of the mountain men, he had never saved anything, always figuring there would be more years when beaver would shine, when the money would be rolling in. Then came the day when beaver didn't shine anymore, and he found himself working as a hunter for a measly dollar a day. Now, though, he had doubled that amount, and had a job in which he would not have to be smelling of blood and dung, where he had to wade in entrails day after day. He was a proud man this day.

LaPointe mounted his horse and moved slowly off, heading toward the Laramie River nearby.

All the unwanted glances and intent stares on the short journey to the site of their camp made Morning Mist ill at ease. Though she did not mention it, LaPointe could see it on her face. It bothered him, but he was not entirely sure of how to deal with it. He still felt something for Yellow Quiver—they had been together too long for him not to. And he had been with Morning Mist such a short time that they had had no time to form any kind of real relationship with each other except for a sexual one. In that, LaPointe was more than pleased. Morning Mist was attractive and well built, and made love with abandon as well as real pleasure.

Once Sanderson's tent had been set up for them, LaPointe and Morning Mist went inside. There, an excited LaPointe explained how proud he was with his new position; how proud he was that the fort's chief thought him an important man.

Morning Mist had been impressed with her new husband and expressed that in the best way she knew how.

Afterward, LaPointe lay there with Morning Mist's head resting on his shoulder. Her long, sleek black hair spread over his chest, tangling in the thick mat of his chest hair. That hair had perplexed her at first, but she had become used to it in the two weeks they had been together.

They each had made changes, most of them small. Each had been married before, so it was more a matter of settling in than in making wholesale changes. They each knew their part in the overall scheme of marriage; what they had to do was learn to fit together.

LaPointe wondered, as he and Morning Mist lay there, if he was doing right. His Catholic upbringing often caused strong pangs of guilt to sweep over him. But that was not the case this time. LaPointe sort of felt as if he were somehow being unfaithful to Yellow Quiver in spirit. That seemed odd to him, considering as how there had been a few times when he had been unfaithful to her in reality. He knew that Yellow Quiver would understand his marrying Morning Mist, but he was still uneasy about it all.

Still, it left him with a nagging sense of unease; had right from the start.

Morning Mist stirred and ran her hand along La-Pointe's chest, and then lower.

LaPointe pushed all his worrisome thoughts away and gently pulled Morning Mist atop him. He ran his callused, rough hands along Morning Mist's smooth, dark back and down onto her sleek, firm buttocks.

Morning Mist's back arched and she ground her pelvis softly against LaPointe's.

Soon they rolled until LaPointe was atop Morning Mist and thrusting hard and fast. Morning Mist matched his every stroke, until both were groaning and thrashing.

Afterward, LaPointe decided things would be all right between him and Morning Mist. The past would stay in the past. Yellow Quiver was gone, and now Morning Mist was in his life. It had been, LaPointe admitted to himself, one hell of a day.

As much as he regretted the thought, he knew he had to get up and start moving. They would need meat and firewood at least. Then there would be hides to get so that Morning Mist could make their lodge. They would also need lodgepoles for that.

For several days, LaPointe saw little of Private Hill, but when Hill was around during that time, LaPointe could feel Hill's angry eyes on him, but he ignored it for the most part. LaPointe was busy, both with fort business and private business, but he was always in and around the fort, so he could keep an eye on Hill.

A week and a half later, three families of Painted Bull's Brulé band arrived and set up camp near La-Pointe's tent, which made LaPointe a little happier. Morning Mist would be more secure—and cheerful—with her friends around.

Still, the Brulés could not stay forever, and they soon drifted off to join with the others of their band. The visiting women had, though, helped Morning Mist finish a lodge for her and LaPointe. Just before riding out, the Brulés helped raise the tipi.

LaPointe used that as another excuse to celebrate—with Morning Mist, alone. He saw it as a sort of consecration of the lodge. Morning Mist had no trouble accepting that idea, nor the festivities that went along with it.

After the Brulés left, LaPointe tried to stay closer to the tipi. He had seen more than one man casting covetous glances at Morning Mist. For her part, Morning Mist did nothing that would encourage any man but La-Pointe. Still, the soldiers and most of the civilian workers at the fort had no women; had little access to women for the most part. Fortunately, little liquor was available. Liquor had a way of making lonely men crazier than they might be otherwise.

Regardless, most of the civilians in and around the fort had enough respect for LaPointe to leave Morning Mist alone. The soldiers didn't know LaPointe, but they could see danger in his dark eyes and usually steered clear of him. More to the point, they were kept so busy building the fort that they had neither time nor energy for raising much Cain or bothering what few women were around.

There were occasional slack times in the work, and the boredom made many of the soldiers more antsy than usual. And with all his own duties, LaPointe could not be with Morning Mist every minute. When those two things coincided at one point, trouble arose.

LaPointe was a few miles away from the fort in a small Oglala village. Major Sanderson had wanted to meet Many Horses, one of the chiefs of that band. LaPointe was along to translate.

It was a dismal, rainy day, and much of the work on the fort had been halted. Even the tree cutting details had been scaled back considerably, until the weather took a change for the better.

LaPointe was bored during the dull hours of conversation between Sanderson and Many Horses. Only a continually refilled coffee cup kept him awake. Finally, though, Sanderson and Many Horses had finished their talks and the small army procession rode slowly through the thundering downpour back to the fort.

As they were nearing the fort, Otis Palmer raced up and stopped next to LaPointe. "I saw Hill and two other men headin' down to your lodge, Henri."

"When?"

"Minutes ago. I was gonna go after 'em, but then I seen you."

Without offering Sanderson any explanation, LaPointe slapped his horse with the reins and charged off. Palmer was right alongside him.

LaPointe pulled up sharply in front of his lodge. He was out of the saddle before the horse had fully stopped. He slid in the mud and went down on one knee. He heard angry words from inside the lodge, and he barged in, nearly knocking the tipi down as he tripped over the bottom of the entryway.

His eyes adjusted quickly to the dim interior of the lodge, but not fast enough. Just as he caught a glimpse of Hill and another man holding Morning Mist down, someone charged into him, knocking him backward. The two tumbled out through the flap, tearing it loose, and landed in the watery mud.

LaPointe shoved his assailant off and to the side. Leaping up, LaPointe kicked the man in the face. "Take him," he shouted at Palmer as he charged back into the tent.

He spotted Hill and another private, a man of thirty-two named Gaylord Kincaid. The latter had been busted from corporal to private at least a half-dozen times for insubordination as well as bullying his underlings. He had a reputation for being a tough man and a first-rate brawler.

LaPointe had heard that, but he did not care. He simply slammed a forearm into Kincaid's face, using his bodily momentum to add force to the blow.

Kincaid yelped as his nose broke, and he was driven backward a few steps. He fell, buttocks in the hot embers of the fire. He screeched once and shoved himself up, frantically swatting his backside where his trousers sparkled with dots of fire.

LaPointe spun, just in time to have the blade of a butcher knife slide across his ribs on the left side and then partially across his abdomen. "Bastard," he muttered. Since Hill was rearing back for another go at LaPointe with the knife, LaPointe punched Hill. He did not care where the punch went; he just wanted to prevent being stabbed.

The punch hit Hill high on his bony chest, and Hill gasped. Another punch and Hill dropped the knife. He clutched his chest, wheezing.

LaPointe grabbed Hill by the front of the shirt and jerked him forward. He half spun and then shoved Hill toward the open flap of the lodge. Hill stumbled sideways and then fell halfway outside.

LaPointe whirled to face Kincaid, who was still swiping at his rear end. "Now let's see just how tough you are, boy," he growled.

Kincaid stopped whacking himself and grinned. "You'll be sorry for this, old man," he said arrogantly. He wiped his hands on the sides of his blue wool trousers. Then he charged.

The two men slammed into each other, belly to belly,

like sumo wrestlers. They grasped each other's arms, struggling to create an advantage for themselves.

Kincaid managed to get his arms around LaPointe's middle and lock his hands. He reared back some, bringing LaPointe off the floor, and then squeezed as hard as he could.

LaPointe had only his left hand and arm free, the right had been entrapped by Kincaid's strong arms. But LaPointe figured one arm was enough—if he could use it before Kincaid squashed the life out of him. Breathing was already a difficult chore.

LaPointe brought his left hand up. Cupping it, he whacked Kincaid two hard shots on the ear.

Kincaid growled a little more fiercely and shook his head as ringing began in the ear. But he did not ease his grip. "You'll have to do a heap goddamn better'n that, gramps," Kincaid snarled.

LaPointe did not think that called for a verbal answer, so he said nothing. He wasn't sure he could've said anything even if he had wanted to. He felt like his blood would explode out his head and feet at any moment, such was the pressure around his midsection. He raised his left hand and jabbed his thumb, nail first, into Kincaid's eye as hard as he could.

Kincaid roared in pain, but kept his grip. LaPointe stabbed Kincaid's eye with the thumb again and left it there, pushing with as much leverage as he could manage. Kincaid screamed and dropped LaPointe. He staggered back, crouched and with hands clasped hard over his maimed eye. He breathed heavily and grunted steadily.

LaPointe stepped up alongside Kincaid and hammered the soldier a hard blow on the side of the face. Still crouching, Kincaid sort of half fell to the side. LaPointe pounded him another shot, pushing Kincaid to the side another few steps and driving him to his knees. Another shot to the face and Kincaid was prone on the ground.

LaPointe pulled his knife and knelt at Kincaid's side.

He grabbed Kincaid's greasy hair in his left hand and pulled the soldier's head up and back, exposing the throat. *"Adieu,"* he muttered with harsh sarcasm.

"Stop!" someone bellowed.

LaPointe dropped Kincaid's head and spun on the balls of his feet, rising at the same time.

Major Winslow Sanderson was shocked at the animal-like look on LaPointe's hard face. But he recovered himself quickly. "Put that knife away, Henri," the officer said quietly but boldly.

"No."

"You go carving up a soldier and you'll die. I promise you that."

LaPointe sort of snarled, though he said nothing.

Soldiers were moving into the lodge cautiously. They stopped, sidearms out and ready.

"I'll tell you only once more, Mister LaPointe," Sanderson said with no trace of rancor. "Put away the knife. If you don't comply, you'll be shot here and now. The army will take care of Kincaid."

Palmer slipped into the tent, a tomahawk in one hand. He stopped directly behind Sanderson and waited. Sanderson didn't know it, but he would be dead less than a second after he gave the order for his men to fire on LaPointe.

LaPointe came to his senses slowly. He finally straightened and slid the knife away. "What about the odders?"

"They're tied up and waiting out in the rain."

"You can have them, Major," LaPointe said in flat, unyielding tones. "But if I ever catch him—or any odders of your soldiers aroun' my lodge, I'll gut them."

Sanderson nodded. "Seems fair enough, Henri." He never considered asking LaPointe to move his lodge. He could not ask that of a civilian. No, his troops would have to adapt, especially since LaPointe's lodge was more than a hundred yards from the old fort.

LaPointe moved away from Kincaid's inert form and pulled Morning Mist up. "Are you all right?" he asked her in Dakota.

Morning Mist nodded. There was a little fear left in her eyes, but that was rapidly leaving her.

"Sergeant Driscoll, have a couple of men haul Kincaid out of here. Escort him and his two friends out there to the guardhouse."

"Yessir," Sergeant Max Driscoll said. He directed two men to pick Kincaid up and carry him out. The other soldiers filed out after them.

Suddenly the tipi seemed empty, with only LaPointe, Morning Mist, Palmer and Sanderson remaining.

"My apologies, Mister LaPointe," Sanderson said evenly. "And to you, ma'am."

"I don't need—nor want—your apologies, Major," LaPointe said stonily, an arm protectively around Morning Mist's shoulders.

Sanderson stood frozen a moment, then nodded. He would have felt much the same had he been in LaPointe's position. He turned and left.

"Thanks, Otis," LaPointe said to his friend.

"T'weren't nothin'."

"Buffalo shit. I'm in your debt."

"Damn, Henri, don't be so goddamn serious about it all. Ain't no thanks needed here. Not amongst friends."

LaPointe grinned. "You're goddamn right. C'mon, let's uncork us a jug."

"Now you're speakin' my language, you ol' buffler dick you." He sat at the fire.

LaPointe nodded toward the hole in the tipi where the flap should be. "Go see to the horses," he said to Morning Mist. "Then fix the lodge flap. Once you've done that, Otis and I'll be ready for filling our meatbags, eh." He got a jug and went to the fire.

5

The soldiers—and even the civilians, except for La-Pointe's friends—gave LaPointe and Morning Mist a wide berth after that. Most of them, or at least the soldiers, were quite impressed with Monsieur Henri La-Pointe after LaPointe had bested one of the toughest men in the fort. Few wanted to tangle with LaPointe now.

LaPointe was relieved. He had no desire to battle anyone, and he was pleased that he and his woman were being left alone. That suited him just fine. It also helped that his two friends—Otis Palmer and Rufus Duffy—and their families set up their lodges next to LaPointe's.

Nearly a month after the fight with Hill, Kincaid and the other man—whose name LaPointe learned was Gil Hanson—Sanderson summoned LaPointe to his office. When the interpreter was seated and both men were sipping brandy and puffing cigars, Sanderson leaned back in his chair, feet up on the desk.

"You know we've been having a hell of a time keeping men here, don't you, Henri?"

LaPointe nodded. "Once word got out about all that gold in California, these boys weren't any better than the ones back east."

"That's a fact. Damn, I'm glad I never caught the gold fever."

"Me, too. Hell, a lot of the mountaineers back a while ago found chunks of the yellow-metal devil. Not a one of them got so caught up by it, though. We just stuck those little rocks in our possibles bag and went off about our business. I know that a lot of the boys—especially ones like Bridger, who've got a big name—were being bothered regular to tell if they had found gold and if so where.

"I don't mind getting rich now, mind you," LaPointe continued after a brief pause for a sip and a puff. "It's just that panning for gold is so . . . Hell, I don't know. It just doesn't seem fitting for a grown man."

"You sound as if you think panning is beneath you," Sanderson said with a laugh.

LaPointe did not see anything funny about it. "I do," he said flatly.

"You mean that standing up to your ass in a freezing stream somewhere trapping some defenseless little animal for its fur is better than panning for gold?" Sanderson was a little surprised.

"Goddamn right. Any asshole can sit at a stream playing in the mud and get a little color. Especially if it's been shown that gold's in the river. But making beaver come, now that's a different thing."

"How so?" Sanderson asked. Inwardly he sighed. He was sure that his eternal—infernal, was more like it, he thought at times—quest for knowledge would be his downfall somehow. "I mean, how hard can it be to set a trap in the morning and pull out a drowned beaver in the evening?"

"Hell, Major, the trapping's the least difficult thing about it."

Sanderson pulled his feet down off the desk and leaned forward, forearms now on the desktop. "Tell me about it."

LaPointe was not surprised at the request. Everyone knew about Sanderson's never-ending desire to learn. "It might take a spell," he warned.

Sanderson shrugged. "I've got the time. Don't you?"

"I'm not sure," LaPointe said with a laugh. "You were the one who invited me here. I figured you had some task for me."

"I did, didn't I?" Sanderson mused. "Well, since I did, we both have the time to spare."

"In that case," LaPointe said with another small laugh, "I'll need a new dose of snakebite medicine." He held up his glass.

With refilled glass in hand, LaPointe said, "Beaver trapping's simple, but it's not easy, if that makes any sense to you?"

Sanderson nodded. "It's much like many other things in that respect."

"The hardest part of all, I sometimes think, is finding the beaver. That was most hard near the end of the trade. No one had thought it would be like that." He sighed, sorry that the old days were gone. "Even in some of the earlier days, finding beaver was difficult, what with all the men roaming all over."

"How do you find them?"

"Look for sign. There're obvious things like beaver lodges, but there're other ways, too. The way trees are cut can tell you if it was a beaver or a man. Even the kind of trees will help. The beaver he prefers willows and aspens, young cottonwoods. The first two, they make for a good beaver lodge. The third, he is for eating when the beaver can find saplings and shoots."

LaPointe paused to wet his throat. "Then you have to set the traps. Too deep and the beaver will not set it off."

"Why not?"

"You bait a cottonwood shoot or something like it, and stick it into the mud at the edge of the stream. The trap, you like him to be in half a foot of water or so. The beaver, he smells the medicine we use on the bait stick. When he comes along to see what is so enticing, he figures there is food to be had here. To get at the bait, he must step on the trap. Then, bang!" LaPointe accompanied the word with a loud hand clap. "The beaver, he doesn't like this. *Mais non*. So he dive for the bottom to see if he can get away to his lodge where he t'inks he will be safe. Soon enough the beaver, he is dead. Drowned.''

"Then what happens?''

"We check the traps in the morning and in the evening. Usually two men go as partners, but maybe some go alone, or some they take their woman. One fishes up the traps. If the trap contains a beaver, the man pitches it on the bank where his partner peels the hide. He tosses away the meat, unless they are facing starvin' times. The odder man, he resets the trap.''

"How many traps did a man carry?''

"Half a dozen or so. You might t'inks more would bring in more beaver, but that is not true, especially if you are with a large group. Places get trapped out fast in most cases anyway.''

LaPointe took another sip of brandy and set the glass down again. "In between the times we check the traps, we clean the pelts of meat and blood and fat and then we stretch the plews on willow hoops and hang them from trees.'' He laughed. "An old mountaineer's camp was some funny, I can tell you, what with plews hanging from any branch the men can reach.''

LaPointe let his chuckles fade. "We treat them with brains, which tans anything the best. Then we pack them into bales, maybe fifty or sixty plews to a pack. Each pack he weighs maybe a hundred pound.'' He smiled crookedly. "Then comes the odder hard part.''

"What's that?''

"Getting all them furs to the rendezvous.''

"Why is that difficult? Not enough horses?''

"Plenty of horses most times. Trouble is too many Indians,'' he said with a little laugh. "There isn't a warrior worth his salt who won't try to steal your plews. Even the friendly ones. Carting several thousand pounds of plews through territory used by five or six fearsome tribes isn't easy, no matter how many men're with you.''

Sanderson nodded. "My hat's off to you and your friends who did that for so long.''

LaPointe shrugged, a sudden melancholy sweeping over him. "Those days are gone forever, Major," he said, his sadness apparent in his voice and on his face.

Sanderson finished off his brandy. He refilled La-Pointe's glass but not his own. Then he sat back. "What the hell were we talking about before we got side-tracked?" he asked.

"Something about gold."

"Ah, yes, gold fever. Well, like I said, you know we've been losing men regularly; men deserting and heading for the gold fields of California country."

"Looks like you still got most of a whole compliment here, Major. So what's the problem?"

"Many of those left are in the guardhouse, or are sick. We've had almost an epidemic of dysentery, and there've been a few cases of cholera."

"That doesn't make much sense. The cholera, I mean."

"Why not? I thought cholera was one of the biggest plagues of all the immigrants."

"It is," LaPointe said with a nod. "But you're sitting on the ending point for that, Major. West of here, cholera's almost unheard of, at least among whites. Something to do with the elevation, or the dryness of the air I've been told."

Sanderson nodded. "I can understand that." He paused, thinking. "Be that as it may, both diseases have put a fair number of our men out of action for a time. All the rest are working on the fort itself, a project that looks like it'll last far longer than we had planned. That can't be helped, I figure. But because of it, we're struggling to provide vegetables for the men. Our farming efforts have been dismal, in most part because of the lack of manpower."

LaPointe looked at Sanderson in alarm. *"Merde,"* he muttered. Aloud he said, "You aren't thinking of trying to round up some Brulés to try their hand at that, are you?"

Sanderson laughed. "Good Lord, no," he said. "I

may not know much about the Indians out here, Henri, but I know enough that I would never present such a preposterous proposal."

LaPointe sighed, relieved. "Good goddamn thing. So what's all this got to do with me?"

"If I remember correctly, you said you speak Spanish?"

"Some. It's been a spell since I used it to any extent, but I can still make do. Why?" He was puzzled.

Sanderson suddenly felt like a fool, and briefly considered not mentioning his plan. But he had come too far not to. "I want you to ride down to Taos," he said, none of his uncertainty obvious.

"Sure," LaPointe said easily. He had been in Taos before and always enjoyed it. He hadn't been there in some time—since well before the Mexican War—but he figured it still retained its charm. "Why?"

Sanderson took a deep breath and let it out. "I want you to hire some Mexicans to come up here and work the fort gardens as well as do other labor." He waited for a half-feared eruption of laughter. None came. He glanced at LaPointe.

The Frenchman was lounging as much as possible in the hard-backed wood chair. His eyes were closed and his head was back. The cigar clamped between his teeth sent up a steady stream of smoke toward the ceiling.

Finally LaPointe's eyes opened and he nodded. Pulling the cigar out, he said, "That's a damn good idea, Major. A lot of folks think the Mexicans're lazy, but they aren't. Not most of them anyway. They just have a more relaxed way of doing things. They like to nap in the afternoons for a while—*siesta,* they call it. And they have fiestas for any reason they can think up. But they are good workers, hard workers, for the most part."

"Good. I was afraid you might've thought the idea ludicrous," Sanderson said frankly.

LaPointe shrugged. "I don't think that. But the timing might be crazy. Winter isn't far off."

Sanderson nodded. "I know that. But I thought that if

they came up here now, we could use them to do other work. Then they'd be here in time for the start of the spring, rather than having to send someone to Taos in the middle of winter to have them there that early.''

''Makes sense,'' LaPointe said with a nod. ''Thinking on it, it sounds better. Hiring men down there might be hard at the end of the winter. The men there will be looking to their own fields.'' He paused, then asked, ''How many men you want me to hire?''

''A dozen or so.''

''You want me to bring them back? Or just tell them they'll be hired if they come here and let them make it on their own?''

''I expect you better bring them back with you. If that's feasible.'' It was a question.

''Don't see why not. I can't see buying horses for them all. Or even letting them use army horses. But buying a wagon and team shouldn't be too costly. You could use the wagon and team here afterward.''

Sanderson nodded. ''That's the way to do it then.''

''When do you want me to leave?''

''As soon as possible. Would tomorrow be all right?''

LaPointe shook his head. ''No, sir. I'll need a couple days to get Morning Mist out to her people. Despite your promise of dealing harshly with anyone who tries to molest her again, I can't go off on a trip like this and leave her alone here. Not even with Otis and Rufe around.''

''Perfectly understandable, Henri,'' Sanderson said a little sourly. He was irked that it should be true.

''You never did say when the court-martial for Hill, Kincaid and Hanson was going to be,'' LaPointe said, suddenly harsh.

''No. No, I never did,'' Sanderson admitted. ''I'll tell you what,'' he added after some thought. ''You bring Morning Mist to her village. Can you leave to do that tomorrow?''

''First thing.''

6

It took LaPointe three days to find Painted Bull's village. He stayed the afternoon and the night there, making sure Morning Mist would be well cared for while he was gone. He moved quickly heading back to the fort, riding long hours the day he left the village. He rode into the fort just before noon the next day.

The first thing LaPointe did when he got to the fort was to go to Sanderson's office and tell the major he was back. Sanderson nodded. "The court-martial will convene at one o'clock, if that's all right with you, Henri."

"*Bon.* I will be there."

LaPointe left and put on his only new outfit—fringed buckskin trousers, black, calf-length boots, and a plain calico shirt—after shaving, having Palmer trim his hair and taking an unwelcome bath in the Laramie. He ate buffalo meat and bread at a small fire with Palmer and Duffy. While they ate, they discussed their impending trip to Taos. LaPointe had told his two friends of the plan as soon as he had walked out of Sanderson's office the day he took the job.

Finally LaPointe and his companions each had a healthy slug of whiskey from an earthen jug. Then they headed toward one of the wood fort's old storerooms. It was the only storeroom in the fort that was not loaded to the rafters with goods and supplies.

Sanderson sat at the center of a long, makeshift table. On his right was Captain Benjamin Roberts, commander of Company C, Mounted Rifles; and on his left flank was Captain Thomas Duncan, commander of Company E, Mounted Rifles.

First Lieutenant Thomas Rhett, the post-adjutant and quartermaster, was to present the army's case, while Second Lieutenant Levi Bootes, commander of Company G, Sixth Infantry, had the unenviable task of defending the three prisoners.

"You three men are charged with assault on a woman . . ."

"Indian woman," Bootes corrected.

"On a woman," Sanderson said firmly. "You also are charged with assault on a civilian employee, attempted murder, attempted rape, dereliction of duty and insubordination. How do you men plead?"

"Not guilty," Kincaid said firmly but quietly.

"Not guilty," Hill announced arrogantly.

"Guilty," Private Gil Hanson said in a whisper.

"You sure, son?" Sanderson asked Hanson.

"Yessir." Hanson's voice was more firm.

"As you wish. You'll be sentenced with the others at the end of this court-martial."

"Yessir." Hanson seemed a little relieved.

"Lieutenant Rhett, state your case," Sanderson ordered.

"Yessir. Privates Hill, Hanson and Kincaid invaded the quarters of one Henri LaPointe, a civilian employee of this post. Mister LaPointe is an interpreter and sometime hunter. He is quartered with a woman to whom he is married—as per Indian custom. In said quarters, this woman—known at this fort as Morning Mist—was attacked by the three defendants with the intention of forced fornication. Interrupted in said deviltry by Mister LaPointe and an associate, Mister Otis Palmer, the defendants then assaulted Mister LaPointe with the intent of murdering him. They were unsuccessful in that endeavor."

Sanderson nodded. "Thank you, Rhett. Lieutenant Bootes, your defense."

Bootes rose and cleared his throat nervously. "Sir, the three men were led on by that . . . that . . . that squaw." He looked at LaPointe and smiled weakly, trying to show LaPointe that he did not really mean any of this. "With Mister LaPointe away on a mission with you, Major, these three men—men who have been deprived of feminine companionship for quite some time—took advantage of the squaw's enticements and went to her primitive boudoir."

Bootes took a swift gulp of water before continuing. "While they submitted to that woman's carnal appetites, Mister LaPointe somehow learned of his wife's perfidy and barged into the scene. With reckless abandon, Mister LaPointe bodily threw Private Hanson out of the tipi. He proceeded to thrash Privates Hill and Kincaid, deforming Private Kincaid forever, and almost blinding him. My three clients were the innocent victims, first of the woman's illicit inducements, and then of Mister LaPointe's violent, jealous rage. They were not the perpetrators."

Bootes finally sat, his face coated with sweat. He finished off the water in his glass in one long gulp.

"Mister LaPointe," Sanderson said. "Take the stand here"—he pointed to a chair sitting at right angles to the desk—"and tell us what happened."

LaPointe sat in the chair and shrugged. "Not much to tell, Major. Lieutenant Rhett explained it all just the way it was." A flicker of anger rippled across his broad, dark face. "To think that Morning Mist encouraged those dickless bastards is beyond belief. She—"

"She's a fuckin' squaw," Kincaid snarled.

LaPointe looked calmly over at Kincaid, who was wearing an eye patch over the socket where his right eye had been. "And you're a fucking idiot," LaPointe said calmly.

Kincaid surged up off his chair, planning to charge LaPointe. The Frenchman stood and braced himself, waving encouragement to Kincaid.

But three armed soldiers intervened and slammed

Kincaid back into his chair. LaPointe also sat again. When Sanderson nodded at him to continue, LaPointe said, "There's not much more to say. Morning Mist would not have encouraged those men. If Otis hadn't come got me, she would've been violated by all three of those sons of bitches."

"Isn't it true that you commenced the fight?" Bootes asked in a nervous voice.

"*Oui.* I did." He smiled without humor. "And if the major and his men hadn't come in there when they did, those three would be in the ground now."

"Then you admit you tried to kill them?" Bootes asked.

"*Oui.*" Again he flashed a humorless smile. "Wouldn't you if they come to take your woman?"

Bootes froze, knowing that no answer would be right. He had thought he had found a dent in the prosecutor's armor, but now he realized he had only hurt his own position. He almost smiled, though, since he had no great desire to defend these three men anyway. He had been assigned the job and had tried to do it to the best of his abilities. He secretly was glad, though, that he was not really up to the task.

"You have anything to say in rebuttal, Lieutenant Bootes?" Sanderson asked. "Your defendants have the right to take the stand and tell their side of the story."

Bootes was aware that Sanderson had already made up his mind, and that the two other officers comprising the tribunal would follow Sanderson's lead. He also knew that if either Hill or Kincaid took the stand, they would only seal their doom. Still, he had to offer them the chance. "A moment to speak with them, Major?"

Sanderson nodded.

Bootes spoke softly with Hanson, Hill and Kincaid, the latter two of whom responded in loud, angry voices. Finally Bootes snapped at them to shut up and he turned to face the three trial officers. "Private Kincaid says he'd like a chance to defend himself on the stand, sir," Bootes said. He didn't sound as if he thought it was a good idea. "Private Hanson also would like to do the same, but he's willing to wait until the sentencing portion of this court-martial."

"Private Kincaid, take the stand," Sanderson ordered in a cold voice.

Kincaid did, and looked angrily out at the soldiers who were watching.

"State your piece, Private," Sanderson said.

"That there LaPointe is a lyin', half-breed sack of shit," Kincaid snarled. "He's an Injun-lovin' whoremonger, who shouldn't be allowed in the company of regular folks." He paused for a breath.

Before Kincaid could embark on another tirade, Sanderson asked evenly, "Do you have anything relevant to these proceedings to say?"

"Goddamn, fuckin' right I do, you mealymouth son of a bitch. I'm not gonna goddamn sit here and let that fuckin' French asshole—"

"Bind that man!" Sanderson roared. "And gag him, too."

"You can't do that, you chickenshit son of a bitch," Kincaid screamed back. But it was too late. Four husky soldiers—men who had been bullied by Kincaid because of his rank and time of service—were glad to do the job, and were a little more enthusiastic than might have been required.

Once Kincaid was silenced and tied firmly in his chair, Sanderson asked, "Does anyone else have anything to say in defense of any of the three men who have been accused?"

No one spoke, so Sanderson nodded. "Before we rule on the guilt of these men, I have a few things to say, all of them directed at Private Kincaid. You, son, are a boneheaded little snot. You're a bully and a braggart and you are unfit to wear that uniform. It is only by the most tenuous of constraints that I do not hand you over to Mister LaPointe so he can finish the job he started on you that day. But that would not be right in the army's view, much to my regret."

Sanderson surveyed the room. No one said anything. It did not take long for the three members of the tribunal to present their findings. Sanderson simply leaned to his right and said a few words, then listened for a moment. He repeated the procedure on his left. "Privates Kincaid and Hill are hereby found guilty of all charges which have been brought against them. This court-martial also accepts Private Hanson's plea of guilty —but we will accept pleas to lesser charges if that seems appropriate."

Sanderson looked over the room again. The place was silent, except for the noises the bound and gagged Kincaid made as he continued to try to free himself.

"Good. Now, Private Hanson, you have something to say to this court-martial before we announce sentencing?"

"Yessir," Hanson said meekly. "Should I take the stand?"

"That's not necessary, son. Just stand where you are and speak your mind."

Hanson nervously stood and licked his dry lips. "I'd like you to know, sir, that I didn't know what Privates Hill and Kincaid really intended. I—"

"Shut up, you fuckin' little weasel," Hill snarled.

"Open your mouth again, Private Hill, and you will join your friend there bound and gagged in your chair," Sanderson said. He turned to Hanson and said, "Continue, son."

"Elliot and Gaylord told me the woman was offerin' herself for half a dollar a man. I . . . I . . . Well, I'm mostly innocent of women—"

"Fuckin' virgin," Hill muttered.

Hanson flushed but continued. "They also said she liked it rough some, especially if someone else should find out, since then she could always say we forced her into it."

"You believed that load of shit?"

Hanson nodded. "Yessir, I'm ashamed to say. It seemed to make sense at the time. They said that if we was all caught, and she accused us of rape, there wasn't no one gonna believe her, what with her bein' a sq—— an Indian."

Sanderson nodded. It made sense in some ways, and he figured it'd be easy for a young innocent like Hanson to fall for it. "That all you have to say, Private?" he asked.

"Not quite, sir, if I might have another few moments."

Sanderson nodded.

Hanson looked at LaPointe. "I would've never gone in there if Gaylord and Elliot had told me the truth. I know it don't mean much now, but I'd like to apologize to you and to Morning . . . to Mrs. LaPointe."

"Apologize to her yourself," LaPointe said flatly.

"Oh, no, sir," Hanson said hastily. "I'd not like to face her again after what I . . . we almost done to her."

LaPointe nodded and Hanson sat.

"Anyone else have anything to say?" Sanderson asked. He did not look like he wanted an affirmative response. When none came, he said, "Mister LaPointe, do you feel a harsh penalty is necessary in Private Hanson's case?"

"No," LaPointe said after a moment's thought.

"So I thought. Private Hanson, I sentence you to have your pay withheld for two months—one month of which you will spend in the guardhouse. Following that, you will be assigned to hard labor—under the watchful eyes of guards. If you get in no further trouble, we'll put this all behind us."

"Yessir," Hanson said contritely.

"You two others," Sanderson said, "are much easier to sentence. Privates Hill and Kincaid, you will have your rank removed—just before you are executed by a firing squad. Such sentence will be carried out when Mister LaPointe returns from a job I have assigned him. I want him to be here to witness the executions. These proceedings are closed."

"**Y**ou want me to send a few men with you, Henri?"
Sanderson asked shortly after the court-martial as he
and LaPointe discussed LaPointe's trip to Taos. La-
Pointe would be leaving in the morning.

"Soldiers? No thank you. Friends? Yes."

"Who do you have in mind?"

"Otis and Rufe."

Sanderson thought about that for a moment. "Can
you trust them?" he asked.

"More than I can trust you. No offense meant, Major,
but I know them a long time."

Sanderson nodded. "Then by all means take them
with you. Tell them they'll get a five—no, make it ten—
dollar bonus each when you all get back."

"*Merci.*"

Sanderson leaned back, hands laced behind his head.
A small cigar jutted jauntily out of his mouth. "How
long you think it'll take, Henri?"

"Two months. Maybe a little less, maybe a little more.
On the way down there, we can move fast. The three of
us can ride hard and long. Coming back'll be another
thing, though, if we 'ave to bring a wagon loaded with
Mexicans."

Sanderson nodded again. "Just make it as fast as you
can, would you?" He smiled crookedly. "We lose any
more deserters and we might as well give the damn fort
to the Indians. Or back to the American Fur Company."

"Mon Dieu, no," LaPointe said with a laugh. "Not the Company." He refilled his glass with brandy from the bottle on Sanderson's desk. It was dusk, and the fort was beginning to quiet down some.

"If you disliked the Company so much, why'd you work for them?"

LaPointe shrugged. "Wasn't much else I could do. I always thought I could make my way up in the Company, but the bosses, they don' like me so much."

"Why?"

"Hell if I know. Maybe they think since I am French that I am no good for them. They always want the Englishers to run things."

"I see it's not only U.S. Army privates who think strangely."

"That's true," LaPointe said with a nod. "Too true."

"You make sure you take enough supplies, you hear me, Henri? Just because you and your two friends're used to traveling light, I want you to have enough to be able to feed those Mexicans on the trip back. I'll speak to Lieutenant Rhett about it. He'll make sure you get enough of everything, including mules."

"Merci, Major."

"You're welcome." Sanderson hesitated, unsure if he should speak, but then he decided it would hurt no one. "You think we did right today when we let Private Hanson off so easily?"

"I expect. He did seem some skittish. I don't know whether he was lucky or not that I find him first. I just t'rew him out of the lodge, where Otis tied him up quick and fast. If I wasn't to see him first, who knows, maybe I kill him. Maybe he react anodder way. Maybe he run like hell for the fort."

"How old are you, Henri?" Sanderson asked after a moment.

LaPointe shrugged. "Forty-two, I t'ink. I am not for certain. Why?"

"Just curious. You've been out here quite some time then, haven't you?"

"Oui. I come out here wit' wagons brought by Bill Sublette and his partner, Bob Campbell. That was in eighteen t'irty, I t'ink. At the rendezvous, I hire on wit' Ol' Gabe.''

"Who the hell's Old Gabe?" Sanderson asked, feeling foolish.

LaPointe smiled. "Jim Bridger. Ol' Jed Smith, who was killed by Comanches down on the Cimarron a year after I come out here, he says that Bridger looks so solemn all the time that he reminds Jed of Gabriel of the Bible. The Indians, though, they call Jim the Blanket Chief.''

Sanderson was not about to ask about that. "I would expect that you've had a hell of a lot of adventures."

"Mais oui.'' LaPointe laughed. "Too many I sometimes t'ink.''

"You miss those times, don't you?"

LaPointe nodded sadly. "It is that evident?"

"Yes, it is. But it's not something a body should be concerned about."

LaPointe nodded, thinking back on the old days. Yes, there had been a lot of shining times back then. There was money to burn for those who were industrious. There was the call of the mountains themselves. And the nubile, willing Indian women. And beaver plews that were thick and soft. And good friends to yarn with over a fire on a frigid winter morning.

There were also the bad times, though, too. Times when a band of angry Blackfoot warriors came swooping down on a man. And starving times, when a man was reduced to eating his moccasins and grubs. And times when a flash flood would wash away a camp. And when Indians would make off with a man's horses, mules and plews, running off with a whole season's catch. And early blizzards.

Yes, LaPointe knew there were enough bad times to offset the good, but he still wouldn't have changed it for all the world. He wished those times were still here. He could accept the bad with the good.

Those times had gone, though, and LaPointe was a man trying to look ahead toward his future. He had been trying that for close to ten years now, but he finally seemed to be having a little success at it.

LaPointe finished his glass of brandy. He wanted to get drunk and have himself a small spree before heading south for a long, tedious, stultifying journey. But that trek, he knew from experience, would go a whole lot easier if he started it without a crushing hangover. With a sigh, he poured himself a half portion of brandy and polished it off.

Setting the glass on the desk, LaPointe stood. He had a quiet little buzz inside his head, and he enjoyed the feeling. "I expect to be gone by first light, Major," he announced.

Sanderson nodded. He was tired. It seemed that there was something new he had to deal with every minute of the day. Desertions, sickness, weather, irritating immigrants, pestering Indians, arguments among his men, work that did not get done for want of wood or clay or bricks or . . . It was enough to drive a man crazy, Sanderson had thought more than once. He tried to shake some of the gloom away, but it was not easy. He had never had to sentence a man to execution before. That sat on him like a wagonload of rocks.

"Just remember what I told you, Henri."

"*Oui. Bon soir*, Major." He headed for the laborers' quarters. He would stay the night there with Palmer and Duffy.

Pink was just edging the eastern horizon when LaPointe and his two friends rode out of the fort. They crossed the Laramie River and followed the river southwest, moving at a leisurely pace. The men could see no reason to push the horses—and the six pack mules they had—too hard. Cutting a day or two off the total time of the trip was not worth endangering themselves by killing their horses and being stranded on foot in an area ranged by a heap of ferocious Indians.

It took just under three weeks for them to reach Taos. The first thing they did was find a *cantina* with decent *mescal* and willing *señoritas,* both of which the three men partook of fully.

The next thing they did was to recover from their hangovers. Then they went out looking for Mexican laborers and farmers to hire. Such men were easy to find. Too easy, LaPointe thought after a full day of interviewing Mexican men.

"These poor bastards must be in deep shit," Palmer said as the three sat to supper that evening. "Must be if they're this hot on takin' any work that comes along."

LaPointe nodded. When he swallowed his mouthful of tamale, he said, "Maybe we have been going about this all wrong. We should ask the people here who hire workers which workers are best."

Duffy grinned. "I'm thinkin' we ought to move real slow on this," he said, eyes sparkling with humor. "After all, we don't want to be bringin' back the wrong kind of men now, do we?"

LaPointe looked at his friend like the man had gone completely *loco.* Then a grin began to spread.

"What the hell're you two assholes grinnin' about?" Palmer asked, a tin fork frozen halfway to his mouth. The piece of enchilada he had on it fell back to the plate with a soft plop.

"You in any goddamn hurry to get back to Fort Laramie?" Duffy countered.

"Well no, but . . ." He set his fork down as understanding dawned on him. "I do believe I'd rather stay here drinkin', eatin' and fornicatin' than I would be ridin' the trail with a bunch of damn Mexican laborers. Or even you two buffler peckers."

"See, Rufe," LaPointe said with a laugh, "I told you he'd catch on sooner or later."

"Reckon so. But it took longer'n you figured."

"Eat shit, both of you," Palmer said with mock anger.

"I'd rather eat me another goddamn enchilada," Duffy said. He proceeded to do just that.

For two more days they moved around Taos, talking with vendors, craftsmen, rancho owners, nearly anyone who would have cause to hire laborers. From these talks, they came up with a list of twenty-eight names. The next day they looked up the men on their list and made their pitch. Some were eager to accept the work; others did not want to leave Taos; and still others did not want to leave but could not afford to turn down such an offer. By that night, LaPointe, Palmer and Duffy had hired sixteen men.

"You don't think that's too many, do you, Henri?" Duffy asked as they ate a late supper.

LaPointe shrugged. "Major Sanderson didn't set any limits. I think that if he's displeased with this number, he'll handle it."

"We leavin' tomorrow, Henri?" Palmer asked.

"Yes. As early as we can. We still have to hire a wagon and team. Maybe two, since we have sixteen men traveling with us. And there are some things I want to get from one of the stores I have seen."

It took longer to find a wagon than LaPointe had expected it would, and so they pulled out a day later than planned. When they did, they had one large wagon pulled by four big, dark gray mules. Fifteen men sat in the back of the wagon; the sixteenth drove. Another of the men quickly showed a small propensity for cooking and so he was entrusted with the meals on the journey.

They arrived back at Fort Laramie almost two months after they had left it. Winter was encroaching on the land. Temperatures were down considerably, and the travelers had encountered two snow squalls on the trek. LaPointe was anxious about getting back. He still needed to get to Painted Bull's village. He planned on spending the winter with the Brulé as he usually did. At this time of year, they would be ready to make their winter hunt—if they hadn't already.

Part of LaPointe's worry stemmed from the weather. It gave signs of being a bad winter. With snow coming already and the temperature as low as it was, it seemed a portent of the worst kind.

Finally, the small entourage pulled into the old fort. To LaPointe it seemed that a fair amount of progress had been made on the new fort in the short time he had been away.

The group stopped in front of Sanderson's shabby headquarters in the old fort. LaPointe dismounted and stretched, trying to get a little blood flowing in his sore buttocks and thighs. He felt as if he had not had his feet on the ground for ages. He was surprised that Sanderson had not come out to welcome him back. Not that LaPointe expected a special reception. It was just that it seemed so out of character for Sanderson. LaPointe hoped there was nothing wrong with the fort's commanding officer.

LaPointe went up the stairs and stopped. Private Dusty Moorhouse, looking blue and uncomfortable from the cold, nodded. "The major's waitin' for you inside, sir," he said, trying to keep his teeth from chattering.

"There something wrong with him, Private?"

"You'll have to ask the major that, sir."

LaPointe glanced from Moorhouse to his two friends, who shrugged. LaPointe entered the office, and immediately knew something was wrong. He stopped at the small cabinet against one wall and poured two drinks from the bottle of rye there. He carried the glasses to Sanderson's desk and put one down in front of Sanderson. He drained the other in a gulp. With a shrug, he put his empty glass down and went to get the bottle from the cabinet. He refilled his glass and then sat.

"You look like shit, Major," LaPointe said flatly. Sanderson's face was lined and tired looking. His eyes were red from lack of sleep and Sanderson's usually sharp uniform was wrinkled.

"If only I felt that good."

"What the hell happened?"

"Later. How was your trip?"

LaPointe shrugged. "About what I figured. We hired sixteen Mexicans—they all come with high recommendations."

"How'd you get them here?"

"Wagon and four mules. I got them cheap. The wagon is big enough to be of use around here." He paused. "Have your drink," LaPointe said softly. "Then tell me what the hell's going on."

Sanderson's tired face hardened. Then he relaxed and reached for the drink. He gazed into the reddish amber liquid for some moments before downing it in one swallow. "You aren't going to believe this, Henri."

"Let me decide that."

Sanderson nodded. "Yes. Of course." He poured and drank another glassful of whiskey. "Kincaid and Hill have escaped," he said with a wan smile.

"How the hell did that happen?" LaPointe asked. His face was hard as rock, his voice cold and angry.

Sanderson shook his head in annoyance. "It was Private Hanson's doing," he said quietly.

"What happened?" LaPointe asked, stunned.

Sanderson sighed and drummed his fingers on the desk for a few moments. Finally, he snapped, "Dammit all!" He sighed once more. "Hanson got out of the guardhouse after a month, just like he was supposed to," Sanderson said, anger increasing. "For a few days, he was a model soldier. One night about a week after he got out, he knifed the two men on duty—Cramer and O'Reilly—to death. He opened the guardhouse doors. Then he, Kincaid and Hill ran off, taking almost two dozen horses with them."

"You did send someone after them, no?" LaPointe asked, stone-faced.

"Of course I did."

"And?"

"And those brainless bastards either got themselves killed or they've run off themselves. Such a thing is too goddamn commonplace these days." His face smoldered with anger.

LaPointe nodded. "Your Mexicans're outside. You might want to get them quartered before they freeze to death. I'll head out as soon as I fill my meatbag and see to my horse."

"Where're you going?"

"After those bastards."

"You'll never find them now. Hell, they've been gone more than two weeks already."

LaPointe shrugged. "If I don't find them, I don't find them."

"Winter's coming, Henri. We've seen bits of it already."

"I've been out in winter before, Major," LaPointe said scornfully.

"You're being a damn fool." Sanderson wanted to smile but could not find it in him to do so now.

"It's not the first time someone says that to me." He paused. "Who'd you send out after the first three?"

"Sergeant McGinty and Privates Hampton, Lange, Dow, and Bedford."

"All infantry?"

Sanderson nodded. "G Company men."

"They fought against Mexico in the recent war?"

"Yes. It's one reason I chose them. They were hardened by the war, and I expected that this would be a hard job. They also had seemed to show no signs of gold fever. We could be wrong about that. I still think you're being a damn fool, Henri. Besides, I need you here."

"Like hell you do. The only ones going to be around here for me to interpret are those freezing Mexicans out there. No Indians're going to come around here much in the winter. If they do, there are others here who can speak to them. Especially since I don't plan to be gone more than a couple of weeks."

Sanderson sighed again, knowing there was nothing he could say or do to change LaPointe's mind. "You make sure you take whatever you need."

"I will."

"Those six-shooters?" Sanderson asked, pointing to two pistols stuck in LaPointe's belt.

"Oui." LaPointe pulled out one of the pistols and handed it butt first to Sanderson. As the officer took it, LaPointe said, "On the advice—and damn good advice, too—of the man who sold them to me, I have only loaded five of the chambers."

"And the hammer sits on the sixth—the empty one?" Sanderson asked.

"Yes. You set the hammer on a loaded chamber and you drop it—boom! Your foot, he is gone maybe."

"Heavy bastard, isn't it?" Sanderson said, hefting the weapon.

LaPointe nodded. "From what I hear, somebody named Walker took one of Colt's older pistols and tinkered with it some. Made it bigger and stronger."

"Gives you a lot of firepower, I'd expect."

"*Oui.*"

"Pain in the ass to load, though, isn't it?"

"*Comme çi, comme ça.* It helps to have these." LaPointe pulled a handful of things out of a pouch hanging from his belt and tossed them on the desk. "Paper cartridges. You can get them with linen instead of paper, too."

Sanderson set the pistol down and picked up one of the paper cartridges. "It seems complete, but how does it work?"

"Tear the end of the paper off. The end away from the ball. Pour the powder into the cylinder . . ."

"Then ram the ball down," Sanderson finished, looking up at LaPointe.

"*Oui.*"

Sanderson handed the pistol back. "Two of them, though?"

"Like you say, Major, they are hard to load. This way, I shoot ten times before I have to reload."

"Sensible. Did you get enough of these paper cartridges?" Sanderson asked as he fingered one of them.

"Otis and Rufe and me, we each bought two of these pistols. And we chipped in together for a big box of the cartridges. We will have enough for a while." LaPointe stood and shoved the pistol back into his belt. Then he gathered up the cartridges and deposited them in his pouch. "Enough stalling, Major," LaPointe said icily. "You think you can fool me, Henri LaPointe, by changing what we talk about? Hah! That will be the day. I am going now. I will be on the trail again within an hour. *Adieu.*"

Sanderson nodded, unashamed that he had been found out. He was fond of the Frenchman and did not want to see LaPointe ride off to his doom. Still, he could not morally stop LaPointe from going. He might be able to threaten some, but LaPointe then would be within his rights to quit as fort interpreter and go off on his own anyway. Sanderson only hoped now that LaPointe could not find the deserters anytime soon and would be forced by the weather to return to the fort—or at least to one of the Brulé villages.

"You taking anyone with you?" Sanderson asked.

"My two *amis*—if they want to go."

"I'd be grateful if you were to only take one of them."

"Why?" LaPointe asked, surprised.

"Because winter's almost here, we have more need now than at other times for meat. I can't have you taking half the fort's hunters with you."

LaPointe nodded; the request had been a reasonable one. He turned and left, with Sanderson bellowing for Private Moorhouse, who almost bumped into LaPointe as he burst in the door. Outside, LaPointe told Palmer and Duffy what had happened and what he planned to do.

"I'll go with you," Palmer said.

"Hell, me, too," Duffy added.

"The major asks that I take only one," LaPointe said. He explained the reasoning.

"You go, Rufe," Palmer said. "I've had enough goddamn ridin'. Shit, my ass is so sore I might not be able to sit a saddle again till spring."

"I told you, you was gettin' soft," Duffy said with a chuckle.

"It ain't what's soft that's keepin' me here, you know. It's somethin' hard." Palmer laughed. "Hell, I got to get to Gray Eagle's village. I got me an achin' for Pony Woman! My pizzle's harder'n a goddamn frozen rock."

He roared, wiping away tears of laughter before they could freeze on his face.

"Christ, you're too disgustin' for even this ol' chil'," Duffy said, unable to keep a straight face.

LaPointe just shook his head. He was angry that the three men had escaped, and he wanted more than anything to get them. Yet he could not resist the humor of his two longtime friends. Still, they did need to get a move on if they were going to get out of the fort before dark. "Let's go," he said, pulling himself into the saddle.

"What about these boys?" Palmer asked, pointing to the wagonload of shivering Mexicans.

"Hell with them," LaPointe said. "They're Sanderson's worry now." He rode to the stable and unsaddled his horse. He gave a soldier—one who was being punished for some minor infraction—orders to tend the horse, including feeding him well on grain. LaPointe also gave the soldier a silver dollar.

LaPointe and his two friends strode to the mess and ate heartily. Then LaPointe and Duffy went to grab some supplies and have them loaded on two mules. Sixty-seven minutes after LaPointe had walked out of Sanderson's office, he and Duffy were back on the trail.

Snow was falling softly as they crossed the Laramie again, but the temperature was not too bad. Buried in heavy blanket capotes and knitted wool caps, they were warm and mostly dry.

The snow stopped that night, and the morning sky was bright blue, without a cloud to be seen. But the temperature had plummeted, pushed down by a sharp wind from the northwest. It was no fun traveling in such weather, but LaPointe and Duffy had only one other choice—turning back. Both men were far too proud to do that. Besides, both had put up with far worse weather. Still, they thought it would have been nice to find some protected shelter.

The weather continued to worsen as the days passed. Within three weeks, it appeared that winter had come on strong and was determined to linger. The two men faced sleet, snow or rain nearly every day. The temperature seemed to never climb above freezing, and was often below zero. It was a thoroughly miserable journey, made worse by the many nights they had to make a cold camp, since fuel for fires was sadly lacking.

It took them almost a month, but LaPointe and Duffy finally tracked down the soldiers. The men were holed up in a cave in the Medicine Bow Mountains.

"Seems like a foolish way to go, Henri," Duffy had said when LaPointe had headed that way once they had left Fort Laramie. "They ain't gonna go southwest."

"Where else're they going to go?"

"West, dammit. West. Why'n hell would they go southwest?"

"Because, *mon ami,* they have nowhere else to go. All the wagon trains, they are gone already a long time ago. Those soldiers, they know that. And they know they can't make it across the mountains in winter. So, they need a place to hide and winter up. Once the spring comes again, the wagon trains will come again, and those bastards, they will join up with one of them and leave to California."

"I still think it's a crackpot idea, ol' friend, but what the hell, I ain't got any better ideas on where to go lookin' for them boys."

The soldiers were sloppy where security was concerned. LaPointe figured the deserters thought no one would find them here, especially if the men looking for the deserters had joined them.

LaPointe and Duffy sensed the camp before they could spot it. They weren't sure what had tipped them off, but both men had sensed it about the same time. They tied their horses to a small pine and then began creeping up the snow-covered rocky slope.

Within an hour, they were looking over the soldiers' small camp: a cave mouth covered by a large, flapping piece of canvas sewed to several buffalo skins. There was only one way to the cave—other than climbing over the rocks as LaPointe and Duffy had. But from the rocks where the two old mountain men were was a sheer drop of about fifty feet into the soldiers' camp. The only other way in was a thin trail, which LaPointe suspected was watched, if not booby-trapped.

The soldiers' horses were grouped in clumps just north of the cave mouth, where pine trees provided a little cover. The animals ate hay or other forage that had been tossed there by human hands.

"Well, ol' hoss, how're we gonna do this?" Duffy asked.

"I'm not sure."

"Well, you best make up your goddamn mind and soon, you brainless goddamn fool. My pecker's a ball hair away from goddamn frostbite."

"Merde," LaPointe grumbled in mock annoyance. "You never use that little thing anyway. It gets frostbite, we whack it off, and *voila!* You 'ave no more worries about such a useless t'ing."

"I got me a bigger pecker'n you'll ever have, you hairy-faced son of a—" He clapped his mouth shut when he spotted Private Bedford coming out of the cave. "I'm gonna drop that bastard, Henri," Duffy whispered.

"No," LaPointe hissed. "That would do nothing to help us. We'll wait and see what happens, eh. You had better make your teeny little pecker as warm and comfortable as you can."

The two settled in to wait.

"How goddamn long you expect to wait here?" Duffy asked in a whisper. He and LaPointe had been lying on the frigid rocky cliff for more than two hours.

LaPointe looked at him and grimaced in annoyance. LaPointe did not like lying here doing nothing any more than Duffy did. He nodded. "To hell with this," he said quietly. "We go."

The two slid backward along the cold stone until it was safe. They slid and scrambled down the rock-studded slope until they were standing near their horses and mules.

"I don't know about you, Frenchie, but this ol' hoss can do with a dose of Lightnin' and some goddamn hot coffee."

"Having those things wouldn't put me out any," La-Pointe agreed. "But I'm not so sure about making a fire for the coffee."

"Then I say piss on the coffee," Duffy said with a grin. "I'll just stick with some Lightnin'."

"Me, too," LaPointe said lightheartedly. Then he grew serious. "But we must make sure we don't 'ave too much of it, eh."

Duffy nodded, seemingly crestfallen. Then he grinned again. "Some's better'n none, goddammit." He pulled out a bottle, jerked the cork out, and swallowed a healthy dose of the whiskey. As he wiped his left hand across his mouth, he held out the bottle in his right.

LaPointe took it and matched Duffy's swig and then some.

"I reckon about one more of them swallows like that'll be more'n enough if we want to keep our heads," Duffy said with a small laugh.

"*Oui,*" LaPointe said almost sadly. He had his second large portion and handed the bottle back to Duffy.

He, too, had another dose and then corked the bottle. As he slid it back into a pack on the mule, he asked, "You figured out what we're gonna do about all this yet?"

LaPointe shrugged. "First we have some jerky. Then I will think."

"Christ, that oughta be interestin'—you thinkin'." Duffy chuckled and pulled some jerky out of a pack.

They sat on rocks, inwardly cursing the wind and the cold and the stonelike buffalo jerky. The food was nourishing, but it sure chewed—and tasted—like tree bark.

"It's damn near dark," Duffy said soon after they had finished eating. "You plannin' to do anything while we still got us some daylight?"

LaPointe shrugged, thinking. Then he said slowly, "I think we take them after dark."

"You're goddamn *loco!*" Duffy growled.

"Maybe I am," LaPointe said with another shrug. "But what else is there to do?"

"Shit if I know. But I'm gettin' mighty goddamn antsy just sittin' here. I expect we can move on them now."

LaPointe mulled that over for a bit, then shook his head. "No, that would be dangerous." Seeing Duffy's semiamused grin, LaPointe added, "More dangerous. But what if we take our time through the night and get into that canyon there and attack them with the dawn?"

Duffy looked out at the fast-fading daylight, considering. Then he nodded. "That'd work as well as anything else, I reckon. You aim to move out soon?"

"No," LaPointe said with a shake of his head. "Let's

wait until after midnight. Then we'll be sure they're all asleep down there.''

"Make it a heap goddamn harder to find our way in there, too," Duffy mumbled. But he grinned and stood. "We best unload them mules and unsaddle the horses."

"*Oui,*" LaPointe said as he joined his friend.

After taking care of the animals, they sat and ate a few more strips of jerky. They washed it down with a few small swallows of whiskey. Afterward, the two half-dozed for several hours. They both awoke within minutes of each other and stood. Each had another mouthful of whiskey to help them clear out the last vestiges of sleep.

"Well, *mon ami,*" LaPointe said quietly, "let's go hunting."

They walked quietly and very carefully. The moon was big, but it was playing peekaboo with long streamers of clouds. The ground was covered with broken chunks of boulders, brush in sections, and occasional stunted trees. Big boulders had to be worked around or over as LaPointe and Duffy searched to find the trail into the little canyon.

LaPointe was beginning to doubt he would ever find it, when he stumbled around a house-size boulder onto a thin trail heading northwest. The trail slithered between two sharply rising walls of rock, leaving barely enough room for a horse to make it through. A loaded mule would not make it.

LaPointe and Duffy slid cautiously up the trail until they were on the very edge of the small canyon. The soldiers' horses were toward the back of the oblong patch of land and did not seem disturbed by the newcomers.

The men stopped, taking in the scene whenever the clouds moved away long enough to allow some moonlight into the area.

"I'll take a spot over there," Duffy said, pointing to a small rock overhanging the cave on one side.

LaPointe nodded in the darkness as the moon was covered by clouds again. When the feeble light returned, he pointed to a jumble of six or seven boulders almost directly across from the cave twenty yards or so away. "I'll be over there."

Duffy nodded. "How long're we gonna wait on them boys?"

"Till it seems right to take them down. I think they'll be eager to come out early in the day, no?"

"I would. But you never can tell. Some of them ass-holes might not be bothered with pissin' their beds. Or on each other."

"In that case, we may have a problem. But I'll worry about that when the time comes."

Duffy nodded. "Won't be long before dawn."

LaPointe didn't think that needed an answer. He simply headed to his position.

They did not have long to wait. Within a quarter-hour, one of the soldiers—Private Dow—shoved aside the flapping covering from the cave mouth and walked out. He stopped, stretched, yawned. Then he went to the side of the cave to urinate—right under the slight overhang where Duffy waited.

Duffy looked across the canyon to LaPointe, who shook his head. LaPointe wanted more men to come out of the cave before he fired. Dow went back inside.

A moment later, Hill, Hampton and Bedford came out of the cave. LaPointe looked up at Duffy across the way and nodded once. LaPointe raised one of his new Colt Walker revolvers and opened fire.

Hampton went down almost immediately; and Bedford a moment later. Hill dropped to the ground at the first sound of gunfire. After a moment, he carefully lifted his head, trying to locate the source of the shooting. He spotted LaPointe, who seemed to be distracted by firing at Hampton to his left. Hill shoved himself up and ran for the cave, shouting.

Duffy, sitting on his raised platform overlooking the battleground, drilled Hill in the side of the head.

Rifles appeared sticking out of the curtain covering

the cave. The guns began shooting, slowly since the soldiers had only single-shot rifles and pistols.

LaPointe finally emptied his two big Walkers. He turned his back to the cave and slid down the rock until he was fully behind the one boulder. He braced his back against the rock and began the painstaking process of reloading the six-guns.

Private Lange pulled aside a section of the cave's covering and looked out. He turned his head back and said something to someone inside the cave. Suddenly Lange and Hanson burst from the cave, the former heading right, the latter left, toward the horses.

Each fired one pistol as he ran, planning to encircle whoever was shooting at them. Lange suddenly went flying forward, body pushed by the impact of a .44-caliber slug in the center of the back.

"Shit," Hanson muttered. He dove behind the horses and began crawling around the animals, still trying to get around the man firing from behind the pile of boulders. Then he spotted LaPointe. "That old bastard," he mumbled.

Hanson popped up and fired at LaPointe. Before he could see what effect his shot had had, bullets began banging all around Hanson. LaPointe managed to get behind a tree.

Gunfire still poured from above the cave. Hanson figured the camp was surrounded. "Best run for it, boys, while we got the chance!" he hollered. He ran and then leaped on the first horse he came to. He slapped the animal on the rump with his hand and flattened out on the horse's neck. He went flying toward the thin line of a trail.

Duffy fired frantically. He thought he had hit Hanson at least once, but the soldier did not stop.

Moments after Hanson had yelled, Kincaid and Dow charged out of the cave and managed to make the safety of the wall of horseflesh. They mounted horses bareback and fled, using the other horses as cover. The knot of horses hit the narrow neck to the trail and stopped.

Horses reared and bucked, whinnying in their nervousness.

"Come on, you sons of bitches," Kincaid roared. He lashed out with a rifle, hitting horses in an attempt to get them to move out of the way so he could get through. The action served only to put more fear into the horses.

Duffy emptied his revolvers. Kneeling on the overhang, watching the two soldiers and the group of horses, he began reloading. Just about the time he finished, the bottleneck at the trail began to give way.

"Goddammit," Duffy snapped at himself. He was worried about LaPointe, not having seen any gunsmoke coming from his friend's position. And it looked like the last two soldiers were about to get away.

Kincaid had made it onto the trail, and Dow was just about to. Duffy threw his pistol up and fired all six rounds. Dow went down amid the press of animals. Duffy figured that if a bullet hadn't killed Dow, the skittish animals would.

Slowly silence seeped over the canyon. The faint sounds of running horses could be heard, but even they faded quickly.

Growing more worried about LaPointe, Duffy nonetheless took the time to load both his pistols again. There was no telling who might still be down there. Once his pistols were reloaded, Duffy slid down the rock face and edged up to the cave. He grabbed the edge of the covering and yanked it free of the poles that held it up. The open mouth of the cave gaped at him. Warily he moved inside.

The place was rank with dampness and dirty-man smell. A small fire burned to one side, and a mass of something boiled in a pot. There were parts of army uniforms lying around, as were bedrolls, a few guns and various supplies. There was no one in there, though. With a nod, Duffy turned and ran, heading for his friend.

He skidded around the rock. LaPointe lay slumped

toward his right. Blood dropped from a hole in La-Pointe's left side. "Goddamn you, Henri, you stupid bastard," Duffy snarled. "Goddamn if you didn't go and try'n get your ass put under. Dammit."

"Shut up your blubbering," LaPointe whispered through clenched teeth. "This here is poor bull, goddammit, and I need you to get me out of here. You can't do that when you are gibbering like a fool."

"Christ, if you're gonna set there and do nothin' but nag me, I'll leave you here to bleed to death, you stupid ass Frenchman."

"Such warm words for a friend, eh?" LaPointe coughed a little, and then groaned involuntarily.

"I got to take a look at that wound, Henri," Duffy said soberly.

"I know."

With swift, sure fingers, Duffy cut LaPointe's shirt away from the wound. "It don't look good, my friend," he said.

"I know that, too."

"I don't know as if there's much I can do here. I got no medicines, hell, not even sinew to sew you up."

"I wouldn't want you sewing me up anyway," La-Pointe said, grimacing. "See if the deserters have anything in their cave to bind me up with. If you do that, and give me a little help, I can get on my horse and we can ride like hell for the fort."

"Think that'll work?"

"Who knows?" LaPointe tried to shrug but the blinding blast of pain stopped him. It took several moments for him to regain his composure. When he did, he added, "We 'ave no choice, *mon ami.*"

"Yeah, I goddamn well know that." Duffy stood. "Don't go nowhere," he said as he stalked away. He was back at LaPointe's side within minutes with a shirt sliced into something that might resemble a bandage. It was a little awkward getting the bandage around LaPointe, but it was finally done.

"I'm gonna go get our horses, Henri. You'll be all right till I get back?"

"If I'm not, it won't make any difference."

Duffy nodded. "Anything else I can do for you?"

"Not for me—for them soldiers. See if you can round up a few of the horses. We can take them deserters back to the fort."

"What in hell for?" Duffy was puzzled.

"They deserve some kind of decent burial."

"Now I know you've gone crazy." He left.

10

A few of the stolen army horses had stayed behind in the little haven, turned back by the other horses trying to get through the narrow neck on the trail. Though the horses were skittish, Duffy caught one without too much trouble. He jumped on bareback and without reins, hoping the animal would not buck too much. Since it was an army horse, it was not used to such treatment.

The horse reared, and Duffy had to grab a handful of mane to keep from being thrown off. The horse landed and then leaped and bucked a few times. Duffy continued holding on, squeezing his knees as hard as he could against the horse's sides and keeping a desperate grasp on the mane.

When the horse took a moment's breather, Duffy growled at it, "Best settle down, you knob-headed son of a bitch. You don't, and I'll go upside your goddamn fool head with a log."

Whether it was because of Duffy's calm, reasoned voice or the horse being tired, the animal calmed down some.

"Now that's better, hoss," Duffy mumbled. "Come on now, let's ride." He jammed his heels into the horse's flanks.

As he flew through the opening onto the trial, scraping the outsides of his knees in the process, Duffy was startled to see Private Dow lying on the side of the trail. The soldier was hurt bad, but alive, and was trying to crawl back into the haven. When he saw Duffy, Dow called out weakly.

Duffy paid him no mind. He simply kept racing down the trail, until he found a spot to get around the cliff edge to his and LaPointe's horses. When he did, he wasted little time in saddling both animals. Then he was leading LaPointe's horse, the army mount—now with a loop of rope around its neck—and the two pack mules hell-bent back toward the haven.

He stopped at Dow's side. One glance told him that Dow did not have long to live. Duffy picked the soldier up rather easily and threw him belly down across the army horse, ignoring the muted groans of pain Dow emitted.

Duffy climbed back into his saddle and rode into the haven. Stopping near LaPointe, Duffy slid out of the saddle and pulled Dow off the horse, letting him land heavily in a heap.

"How you doin', ol' hoss?" Duffy asked, looking worriedly at LaPointe.

"I been better." His voice was fainter than it had been, but still was not too bad.

"No shit." Duffy chuckled uneasily.

"Who'd you just dump over there?"

"Dow. He's damn near gone, but maybe he can tell us somethin' useful before he goes." Without waiting for a reply, Duffy turned and knelt at Dow's side. "You know you're next to dyin', don't you, boy?" he asked.

"Yessir." Though soft, the voice carried. Dow knew he had done wrong and was trying to atone for it in whatever small way he could—such as dying bravely.

"What happened?"

Dow coughed and it was some moments before he could speak. Duffy fretted the whole time. He wanted to get LaPointe on the trail as soon as possible; that was necessary, he figured, if LaPointe was to live. But he had to listen to what Dow had to say.

"Me and the others picked up the deserters' trail right off. We was only maybe two, three hours behind when we left Fort Laramie. Took us a few days to catch 'em, though. When we did, that feller Hanson, him and Kincaid, they tried to talk us into desertin', too. Said we'd wait out the winter somewhere and in the spring head to California and get rich diggin' up gold."

"And you decided to do that?" Duffy asked.

"All of us but Sergeant McGinty."

"What happened to him?"

"I ain't sure, but I think Kincaid killed him. The two of them walked off to chat behind some rocks. A few minutes later, we heard a horse galloping away. Kincaid came back and said Sarge wanted no part of the deal and had ridden off."

"Didn't that strike you a little odd? What the hell was McGinty going to do except go back to the fort and get more men?"

Dow shrugged and grimaced. "We were too scared at first to think straight. A few days later, me and the others from the patrol talked about it. We figured Kincaid must've killed McGinty, but there was nothin' we could do about it then. We was in too deep." He sighed and closed his eyes as pain overwhelmed him.

Duffy chafed but waited Dow out. "Where'd them others go?" he asked when Dow seemed close to alert again.

"Don't know," Dow said. The pain was intense now, and he was having trouble thinking. "Don't know. We was gonna stay . . . stay here till spring. Don't know any other place they . . ." He fell silent, eyes screwed up to prevent tears of pain from leaking out.

Duffy knew he would get nothing more of any importance from Dow. He had kept flicking glances back over his shoulder, trying to keep an eye on LaPointe, who seemed to be fading a little. With one more quick glance at LaPointe, Duffy growled, "I don't cotton to havin' folks come tryin' to kill me, boy. But seein' as how close you are to buyin' the farm, I'll not hold it against you this time. You want us to take you back and see if the sawbones at the fort can patch you up? Or you want me to finish you here and now. I can do it quick and clean.''

Dow said nothing for some seconds. Then he asked in a pain-racked voice, ''You think I got any chance of makin' it back to the fort, let alone gettin' fixed up?''

''Not a prayer, son,'' Duffy said bluntly.

''Will you bring me back there for buryin'?''

''If I can do such without endangerin' my good friend yonder.''

Dow nodded slowly. ''Why don't you see to gettin' your friend on his horse. That'll give me a couple minutes to make my peace with the Lord.''

''No skin off my ass.'' Duffy stood and walked to La-Pointe. ''You ready, ol' hoss?''

''Don't have much choice, do I?''

''Hell with 'much' choice, *amigo*. You got no goddamn choice a'tall.''

Duffy helped LaPointe onto his horse. ''Hang on, boy,'' Duffy growled.

LaPointe swayed on the horse but by force of will kept himself in the saddle. ''It will be a cold day in hell before I need your advice,'' LaPointe groaned.

''You die before I get you back to Laramie, I'm gonna carve your ass up.'' He turned and walked back to Dow. As he knelt, Duffy asked, ''You ready to meet your Maker now, boy?''

Dow was only a half-step away from dead. He moaned something that Duffy took as an affirmative.

With a sigh to steel himself, Duffy slapped a big hand over Dow's nose and mouth and clamped them off. It took less than a minute for Dow to die, and the young man offered no resistance whatsoever. Duffy held his hand in place a little longer just to make sure. Then he stood and hauled Dow's body up. With the soldier's spirit gone, Duffy felt that Dow hardly weighed anything at all.

As Duffy walked past LaPointe to put Dow's corpse on the army horse, LaPointe asked quietly, ''You all right, Rufe?''

"Don't you go worryin' your head about this ol' chil'," Duffy said gruffly. He tied Dow's body down. "Think you can hold on a bit more, Henri?"

"Yes," LaPointe said with a nod. "Why?"

"You wanted those other peckerwoods taken back to be buried like decent folk or somethin', didn't you?"

LaPointe nodded again.

In less than ten minutes Duffy was done. As he pulled himself into the saddle, he said, "Best hold on tight, ol' hoss. I ain't aimin' to ride easy."

"Then shut up and ride."

The headlong dash for Fort Laramie took just over two and a half days of virtual nonstop riding. Duffy had hardly slept the whole time, managing only some catnaps in the saddle. He had tied LaPointe onto his horse early on. But finding that even that didn't work, Duffy had stopped long enough to give the animals a couple hours rest while he fashioned a travois.

He eased LaPointe into the travois and tied him down as best he could. He also piled whatever blankets he had around LaPointe. He did not want LaPointe to be jostled about too much and start his wound bleeding again. Nor did he want his friend freezing to death. Then he mounted his horse again and once more was back on the long, tedious trail.

Duffy was moving on willpower alone by the time he rode into the fort. He slid out of the saddle and would have collapsed if his friend Otis Palmer hadn't see him arriving and rushed up in time to catch him.

Standing with Palmer's help, Duffy spotted Sanderson. "Henri's hurt bad, Major. He needs the doc."

Sanderson dispatched a man to get the post surgeon. Then he had several other men unstrap LaPointe and begin carrying him into the temporary hospital. "How about you, Rufe? You need Major Moore, too?"

"All I need's a couple day's sleep, Major," Duffy said weakly. "You can bury the rest of those assholes if you're of a mind. I'll explain later."

"Of course," Sanderson said. As Duffy headed off with Palmer's help, Sanderson turned and issued more orders. In moments, the dead soldiers were being carried off and the horses led toward the stables. Seeing that all was in order, Sanderson walked to the hospital.

Major S. P. Moore, the post surgeon, already was kneeling at LaPointe's bedside. He had cut off LaPointe's shirt and bandage. "Private Holthaus," Moore snapped, "stoke the fire in that stove. I don't want this man dying of frostbite after having made it all the way back here as badly wounded as he is."

Kurt Holthaus hurried to do the doctor's bidding. Once that was done, he came back to the bed on which LaPointe had been placed and squatted across the bed from Moore, ready to give any assistance the physician might require.

Sanderson stood quietly behind the doctor, watching but saying nothing. He knew the physician was aware of him. He also knew that the doctor was one of the best in his field and as such would not appreciate comments, even from the fort's commanding officer.

"Hey, Doc," Palmer said as he came storming into the hospital. His voice was not loud, but in the quiet hospital it sounded like the thunder of a buffalo stampede. "How's my ol' friend there?" He stopped near the bed after pushing past the soldiers who had gathered in the room.

"He'd be doing a hell of a lot better without you causing all this ruckus," Moore said without looking up at Palmer. He finished what he was doing and then looked up. "Any more outbursts like that and I can't be held responsible for what happens to my patient," he said sternly.

"I'm just lookin' out for my friend's interest, Doc," Palmer said defensively.

"So am I." Moore paused. "You want Henri to recover, I'd suggest you get the hell out of here and take the rest of those men with you." He pointed at the soldiers and a few civilians.

"Me and Henri been *amigos* a long time, Doc," Palmer said quietly but firmly. "I'd be one unhappy chil' was he to go under. I figure I'd be unhappy enough that I'd come lookin' to raise hair on the man who let him go under."

Moore stood. "Listen to me, Otis," Moore said almost urgently, "Henri's in bad shape. You want me to tend him, you'll do what I told you—get the hell out. You want to shoot me, go ahead. Then you can tend to him. And if he dies, it'll be the Lord's will for I'll have done all I can to help him. And it won't be me who's put him under. You'd be better off directing your anger at the man—or men—who shot him. Now, if you want me to go back to work, get lost."

Palmer glared at the physician, who looked calmly back at him. Very quietly, Palmer said, "Me and Henri been through a heap of shit together, Doc. From the Milk River to the Rio Grande. From Saint Louis to Santa Fe. We fought Injuns together, set traps together, faced starvin' times together. I'd be plumb put out was he to die. Not against you, mind you, but just about the happenin' of it."

Moore patted the big mountain man's shoulder. "I know you care about him, Mister Palmer. But the best thing you can do for him now is to clear out and let me do what needs doing."

Palmer stood there another moment, then nodded once, firmly. "You want everybody out?"

"That would be preferable, Mister Palmer. Except for Private Holthaus."

Palmer nodded and turned. "Everybody out!" he roared. "Now."

"Kiss my ass," somebody shouted back. "You can't order us around."

Major Sanderson spun with hot eyes glaring. "I can, goddammit. And if this room is not empty in one goddamn minute, everyone on the post will be pulling extra duty!"

There was a stampede for the door.

❦{11}❧

Morning Mist stepped tentatively into the hospital at Fort Laramie. She was timid and seemed about ready to flee. From behind her, Otis Palmer said softly, "Go on in, Morning Mist. It's all right."

"We're here to help you, Morning Mist," Duffy said, also from behind the Dakota woman.

Morning Mist looked over her shoulder. Her eyes were big and frightened looking. Palmer nodded in encouragement, and Duffy gently took her elbow. "We're right here with you," Duffy said in Dakota.

Morning Mist took heart from the words and smiled shyly. The two big white men escorted her to the bed on which LaPointe lay. LaPointe was still unconscious, as he had been since the day before Duffy had brought him to the fort. He had been abed now for five days.

In the interim, Duffy had slept nearly twenty-four hours straight, rose, ate prodigious amounts of food, and then went back to sleep. When he had finally risen and eaten again, he went to see LaPointe. Palmer was sitting on a chair next to LaPointe's bed.

"How's the ol' hoss doin', Otis?" Duffy asked.

Palmer shook his head. "Don't seem no better'n he did when you brung him in here."

"Damn. Anything I can do to help?"

"Nothin'. I just been settin' here watchin' over him. You can do the same, if you're of a mind. Doc Moore won't mind."

"That true, Doc?" Duffy asked Moore, who had just walked up.

"It is." He paused, considering. Then he nodded. "Henri has a Sioux wife, doesn't he?"

Palmer and Duffy nodded.

"How does Henri feel about her?"

The two others shrugged.

"Hell if I know," Duffy said. "He don't talk about it much. None of us do. I know he cared a heap for his first wife, Yellow Quiver, who was killed a year and a half or so ago. Don't know about Morning Mist, though. I expect he feels somethin' good for her."

"Why?" Palmer asked.

"Having her here might do Henri a world of good. Such things often do."

Palmer and Duffy looked at each other, shrugged and then nodded. Ten minutes later, both rode out of old Fort Laramie. They waved briskly at Major Sanderson, who was directing the move of his office and headquarters to the new two-story frame building that would house officers. The two headed north, to where they expected they might be able to find Painted Bull's village—and Morning Mist.

It took three days, but they finally found the camp late one afternoon. They explained their mission, and Painted Bull nodded vigorously. "Yes, Morning Mist will go. Yes," he said urgently.

"He seems mighty anxious, don't he?" Palmer said casually to Duffy.

"I reckon it's because of that time Henri pulled Painted Bull's nuts out of the fire against them Rees," Duffy responded.

"I expect so. That ol' hoss sure has a lot of faith in Henri."

"So do I," Duffy said quietly.

Palmer looked sharply at his friend, and then nodded. "Yep. He's a good man to have at your side whether you're settin' to feast or facin' starvin' times."

The two pulled out with Morning Mist just after daybreak in a heavy snowfall. They were escorted by four Dakota warriors, all friends of LaPointe—Raven Heart, Wolf Calling, Bear Dancer and Spotted Horse, the last the brother of Morning Mist.

The small group pushed hard and made it back to Fort Laramie in little more than a day and a half. As they rode into the adobe stockade, an omnipresent memento of old Fort John, soldiers scattered and bugles began. Three sergeants started issuing orders, trying to get their troops to form ranks.

Major Sanderson stepped out of his old office, wondering what the commotion was all about. He spotted the Indians through the swirling, wind-whipped snowstorm. He was all set to add his orders to the bellowing already taking place. Then he realized there were only four of them—five if you counted the woman. And the Dakota were with Otis Palmer and Rufus Duffy.

He did bellow then, to his aide to have the bugler announce that there was no fighting to be had today. Slowly the bedlam eased down, and then it stopped. Many of the soldiers stood and gaped as the four proud Dakota warriors rode up and stopped in front of the hospital.

The Dakota impressed most of the soldiers. They sat their war ponies like they had been born as part of the horse. All four men had their hair loose, lying in long cascades over their shoulders and onto their backs. Raven Heart and Spotted Horse each had two eagle feathers sticking straight up from the back of the crown of their heads. Wolf Calling had on a hat made from fox fur, and Bear Dancer wore one of badger fur. Raven Heart wore a heavy coat of buffalo hide, fur inside. The other three had blankets wrapped around them. A shield dangled from each warrior's pony, and each had a bow and quiver slung across his back.

Duffy and Palmer slipped off their horses and waited for Morning Mist, who was a little slower in getting down. The three left their horses where they were—

including the pony dragging a travois with Morning Mist's lodge and other belongings.

Morning Mist hesitated at the door to the hospital until Palmer and Duffy urged her to go inside. It was warm and stuffy, and had many strange smells, but none too offensive. Only three people were in the room—two white men and her husband lying in a bed. One of the white men—a tall man with sparse, gray hair and wearing little pieces of glass in front of his eyes—was walking toward her. Morning Mist shrank back a little, but the man had a warm, friendly smile on his face. He stopped in front of Morning Mist and said something.

"The medicine healer says he's pleased to receive the wife of Black Bear," Duffy said to Morning Mist in Dakota.

"I'm glad to be here," Morning Mist responded, voice tinny and far away.

Duffy translated for Moore, who then spoke.

"The medicine healer says he thinks the wife of Black Bear'll do her husband well and that she'll help greatly in healing him."

"And what must I do?" Morning Mist looked like she wanted to bolt, and a vein throbbed rapidly in her neck.

"The medicine healer says you need only to sit with Black Bear. Your touch, your voice will help him."

"Come," Moore said softly, smiling and touching Morning Mist gently on the elbow. "Come, it'll be all right."

Morning Mist cast frightened, dark eyes at Duffy. He, too, smiled at her. Then he nodded.

Morning Mist, still obviously scared, allowed herself to be led gently by Moore until she was at LaPointe's bedside. She sat in the chair, which felt odd to her. She was not used to such a thing, and would have preferred sitting on the floor. But the medicine healer wanted her in the chair, and so she would sit there. Besides, if she sat on the floor, she would not be able to see, or touch, her husband.

They had not been together too long, but she felt a

deep fondness for this black-bearded, hard-muscled man. No matter that he was a few winters older than her father. He was a much more kind and considerate man than her first husband had been. He was a good hunter and, if the stories told around the Brulé fires at night were true, he was also a fearless and resourceful warrior.

Morning Mist looked down at her husband. He looked worn and peaked, so unlike his usual vigorous self. She reached out slowly and took one of his big hands in her small ones. His hands were hard, the palm and fingers dotted with calluses; the knuckles oversize and knotted. The hand was warm, belying a little the wasted look that dwelt on LaPointe's creased face. She saw no change in LaPointe, but that was to be expected. She settled herself as comfortably on the chair as she could, and still holding his hand, she waited.

"You think that's gonna do Henri any good, Doc?" Palmer asked Moore.

The physician shrugged. "Can't do no harm." He smiled. "Hell, if I thought it would work, I'd have you bring in one of their medicine men."

"Now that'd be some sight. Goddamn!" Duffy said with a soft laugh.

"I'm obliged for you bringing Morning Mist," Moore said. "Like I said, I don't know if it'll do much good, but I try to remain open to things." He paused. "You two probably have better things to do right now. She'll be all right here for a while, I expect. I'm certainly not going to hurt her. Neither is Private Holthaus."

Palmer nodded. "We'll stop back for a spell later and see how things're goin'. But right now, there's several Dakota warriors out there freezin' their asses off."

"Really?" Moore asked, eyes blazing with interest.

"Yep. Why?"

"I've never seen Indians. Not close up anyway."

"I don't think they'd be too obligin' if you wanted to go pokin' and proddin' 'em."

"That's not what I . . ." Seeing the scornful looks on the faces of Palmer and Duffy, Moore suddenly laughed.

"Well, I guess it was. You think they'd mind me just meeting them?"

"Hell if I know," Duffy said. "Let's go find out."

The three walked outside and stopped next to the fierce looking warriors. "This is the white-eyes medicine healer," Duffy said in Dakota. He looked at Moore and then pointed to each warrior as he announced their names. "Doc, this is Raven Heart, Wolf Calling, Spotted Horse and Bear Dancer."

Each warrior dipped his head gravely when his name was mentioned.

"He helps Black Bear?" Raven Heart asked in Dakota. He was a somber looking man in his late twenties. He had a high forehead, glittering dark eyes, and a great, proud beak of a nose. His lips were thin and his cheekbones prominent.

Duffy nodded. "Yes. Among our people he has strong medicine."

Raven Heart looked at Moore, who felt as if the Dakota's eyes were seeing straight into his soul. "You make Black Bear better," he said in English.

Moore covered up his surprise. He had thought none of these Indians spoke English, but it only made sense that they spoke some. They had had plenty of contact with white men. Another thing puzzled him, too. "Black Bear?" he asked.

"The Brulés' name for Henri, Doc," Palmer said.

Moore nodded. "I'll do my best to help Black Bear."

The Indians and the two former mountain men chatted for a few minutes in the warriors' language. Moore, feeling the cold piercing his uniform blouse, smiled wanly at the Dakotas and then went back into his make-shift hospital, wishing his new facility was done. This room in the old fort was adequate, but barely. It was too small and too dirty.

Morning Mist had not moved. She still sat, solemn of face, holding LaPointe's hand in hers. Moore did not worry about her until supper time, when he realized she had not moved. She had had nothing to eat, nor had any chance to relieve herself. Moore was a little hesitant to try talking to her since he knew nothing of her language and was unsure that she knew any English. He also knew she was wary around him yet, something that he could understand.

After pondering it for a little, he sent Holthaus out to find either Duffy or Palmer. The latter showed up. "Somethin' wrong, Doc?" he asked.

"No, nothing wrong." He pointed to Morning Mist. "She must need to . . . take care of personal needs. And she has had no food that I'm aware of."

Palmer nodded. "I'll see to it, Doc. I'm obliged for you bein' so concerned about her welfare."

Moore shrugged. "She's a woman. A very attractive woman. And she seems to care about Henri very much."

"I suppose she does."

"You sound doubtful of that."

"Not especially." He shrugged, not figuring he had the words to explain. "They ain't had time exactly to get too close. Less'n a year is all. Most times, men like me or Henri or Rufe, we marry Injun women for convenience sake, more or less. But most of us also come to care for our women—and kids—if we're together a spell."

"You have an Indian wife, too, don't you, Otis?"

Palmer nodded. "Cheyenne. My third wife. The first two were 'Rapaho. Pony Woman and I go back five, six years. We got two kids."

"How about Henri. Any children?"

Palmer's face clouded over. "He had two with Yellow Quiver. They was killed when she was."

Moore nodded. "I'm sorry to have brought it up."

Palmer shrugged. "Those things happen out here, Doc. I expect they happen everywhere."

"Does Rufe have an Indian wife and children, too?"

"Yep. Also a Cheyenne. Him and Two Feathers got them three young 'uns."

"Do Cheyennes and Dakota get along?"

"Hell, yes. They've been allies for the longest time."

"Are their languages similar?"

"Not at all. Most of 'em speak some of the other's language. Plus they make do with signs."

"It still amazes me," Moore said with a shake of his head. "How people who have nothing in common can make do in life."

"Necessity can make a man leap a heap of gaps."

"Indeed."

12

It took Henri LaPointe most of the winter to fully recover, and because of it he was a grumbly, argumentative man for some time. Until both Palmer and Duffy told him in no uncertain terms that he was acting like an ass and that if he did not cease such behavior, they would cart his ornery hide out onto the prairie and let him cool off on the frigid plains.

Morning Mist sat at LaPointe's bedside all day, every day until he awoke. That came when he had been back at the fort for three weeks. He had floated back to consciousness slowly, and with great puzzlement. He was almost afraid to open his eyes, figuring that the first thing he would see would be old Beelzebub himself with the flames of hell flicking around his long, pointed tail.

Finally he could wait no longer. He cracked his lids, grimacing at the first tiny glimmer of light. Then he tried again. He heard a gasp and turned his head slightly. He could not believe what he saw.

Morning Mist sat on a chair, holding one of his hands in one of hers. The back of her other hand was pressed against her mouth in surprise. She had been there so long, she felt, that she had given up hope that he would ever come out of his sleep. Now that he had, she was surprised. Then she got over her shock, and she smiled after moving her hand away.

LaPointe tried to speak, but his mouth was too dry. He finally managed to croak, "Water."

Doctor Moore, who had heard Morning Mist's sudden startled gasp, was at the bedside even as LaPointe asked for liquid. Moore poured some water from the nearby pitcher into a glass. With Morning Mist's help, he half-held LaPointe up and poured water from the glass to his mouth. Most of it spilled over LaPointe's chest and neck, but some made it down his throat.

"Good," LaPointe finally mumbled.

Moore pulled the glass away. When LaPointe was re-settled, Moore asked, "How're you feeling, Henri?"

"Ready to spread my seed from here to the gold camps of California," LaPointe squawked.

"Figured so. After all, you had the finest doctoring available."

"Out here that's not saying much, eh," LaPointe whispered.

"I'm hurt," Moore said in mock anger.

"Buffalo shit." He paused, experimenting with a deep breath. It hurt like hell and he eased off right away. "How long I been out?"

"Three weeks or so. We were beginning to despair that you would ever wake."

"I suppose I did catch up on my sleep some," LaPointe said dryly.

Moore called to Holthaus and ordered him to find either Palmer or Duffy. A few minutes later, Duffy burst into the room, sliding to a stop at the side of the bed. "Well, ol' hoss," he said lightly, "it's about time you was up and about. Damn, I ain't ever seen a body lollygaggin' about for such a time."

"The hell with you," LaPointe said as pleasantly as he could manage. "You just have your nose out of joint because I got this chance to take a few minutes extra robe time."

"Minutes," Duffy hooted. "Jesus, you ain't moved in months seems like to me."

"Where's Otis?" Moore asked, fighting back a chuckle.

"Out huntin'." With winter on them, the hunters had

it somewhat easier. They could kill several dozen buffalo at a time and the meat would freeze, unlike the summer, when fresh meat had to be brought in almost daily. "Me and him've been takin' turns at it since Henri here took to lyin' around for days at a time. I tell you, Doc, it's gonna be a pleasure to have lazy ass here finally get up and around. You know, take the pressure off me and Otis some."

"I'm afraid that won't happen all that soon, Rufe. But his waking is certainly a sign of progress."

"You think he's gonna be all right now?"

Moore nodded. "I expect so." He paused. "Of course, he's not a spring chicken any longer, and that might slow his recovery some. Still, he's a strong man and should be all right after a spell."

"Christ," LaPointe croaked, "I'm alive and awake. You two goddamn fools are talking about me like I have one foot in the grave already. Henri LaPointe is not about to go under anytime soon, Messieurs."

"Feisty, isn't he?" Moore said with a laugh.

"Too damn feisty."

Moore quickly examined LaPointe and replaced the bandage. As he was finishing, he said, "You're mighty lucky, Mister LaPointe. None of your vital organs were hit, but you had a couple of broken ribs, some tissue damage and you lost a considerable amount of blood."

LaPointe nodded weakly. "I suppose I am lucky, as you say." His voice was faint. "But it doesn't feel that way right now."

"I imagine not," Moore said as he stood. But LaPointe was asleep again.

It became a little easier for LaPointe each day. He sat up after another week, and two weeks after that he actually managed to walk across the primitive hospital.

Morning Mist still sat with him virtually all the day. As LaPointe progressed, Morning Mist would help him a little more. Not so much that he would feel too dependent on her, but enough that she did not feel as if she were there for no reason.

Two days after he woke for the first time since being shot, LaPointe asked Palmer and Duffy—together at the fort for once—how they were getting along. Since Morning Mist was not there just then, he also asked what arrangements had been made for her.

"We both got our lodges set up next to yours again— where we've been puttin' 'em," Palmer said. "We put your lodge up there, too. Morning Mist's been here all day since we brought her in. Nights she spends in the lodge."

"Alone?"

Palmer nodded. "Me 'n' Rufe been keepin' an eye on her, and Major Sanderson passed word that any man came within ten feet of her was gonna be hung by his thumbs and have his nuts cut off." He grinned a little. "I ain't sure he'd actually do that, you understand, but them soldier boys believe it, which is about the same thing."

LaPointe nodded. "How long's she been here?"

"Me and Otis rode out of here a couple days after I brought you in. We picked her up from Painted Bull's village and brung her back. She's been at your bedside every day since."

"All day, every day," Palmer added. "She must care a heap for you, you old reprobate."

"You're just jealous that Pony Woman doesn't treat you so well. If you were laying here instead of me, Pony Woman would be celebrating already. She would have thrown your possibles out of the lodge and taken up with some fat ol' warrior."

"You keep up such talk and I'm gonna give you a good punch in the side. Right about here." He ever so gently touched a forefinger to LaPointe's wound.

"Then you will have my death on your conscience And I think you aren't strong enough for that." He smiled.

"That bullet might've hit you in the side, but it went and addled your brain somehow."

"Enough nonsense," Moore ordered as he walked up. He looked at LaPointe. "You seem to be feeling mighty spunky, Henri."

"I have to protect myself from them." He lifted an arm and feebly flicked a finger in the direction of Duffy and Palmer.

Moore shook his head. "Nuts. All of you are nuts." He chuckled. Then he undid LaPointe's bandage and inspected the wound. "Looks like it's healing just fine, Henri. Why, before you know it, you'll be doing a war dance with your friends the Brulés."

"That'd be somethin'," Duffy said, "since he ain't ever knew how to dance before. He's the most club-footed hoss this chil' ever met."

"I dance better than you," LaPointe said weakly. He was rapidly losing his strength.

Moore noticed. He looked at Duffy and Palmer. "You two better move on."

"Somethin' wrong, Doc?" Duffy asked, voice a little quivery with worry.

"No. It's just that Henri has had enough visiting for now. He needs more rest."

The two old mountain men nodded. "We'll be by later, Henri," Palmer said quietly.

LaPointe nodded. As Moore finished rebandaging him, LaPointe asked, "Where's Morning Mist? Otis and Rufe says she been here almost since the beginning."

"She needs to take care of herself, you know. She said she'd be back in just a little. Don't you worry over it."

LaPointe barely made a nod before he fell to sleep.

When he awoke, Morning Mist was sitting on a chair beside the bed, holding one of his hands. He smiled both in relief and in welcome. "I'm glad you're here, woman," he said softly.

Morning Mist nodded. She was proud, happy, but she did not know if she should display those feelings when others were around, even if the people were only Doctor

Moore, Private Kurt Holthaus and three troopers suffering from dysentery.

Two days afterward, LaPointe sat up in bed for the first time and managed to eat some broth with a few small pieces of meat.

His successes came more regularly after that. One of the biggest victories, at least for him, was when he was able to walk across the hospital. He had taken his first steps just days before and was ready to tackle something a little more difficult. Palmer and Duffy were there, as were Morning Mist, Moore, Sanderson and Holthaus. As they had the previous few days, both of LaPointe's old mountain men friends offered to help, but he gave them a scathing look.

LaPointe rose and then stood there a few moments, trying to give his body a little time to adjust to this still-rather-new position. Then, with his face hard with determination, he took several steps, about what he had been doing the past couple of days.

As the others mumbled words of praise, LaPointe marched off again, stiffly.

"Goddamn fool," Duffy shouted and headed toward LaPointe.

Moore held up a hand to Duffy, telling him to stop. Duffy did, but he watched closely, ready to leap to his friend's aid should his help be needed.

LaPointe kept going, lurching like a drunken stork, his motion completely unnatural. But he made it to the far wall of the hospital, a width of perhaps twenty feet. He turned and leaned back against the adobe wall. Sweat covered his face.

Palmer and Duffy watched for a few minutes, then Duffy said, "Ol' hoss there can't make it back. We best go rescue him. Again."

Palmer grinned and they headed toward LaPointe. With their help, LaPointe half walked, half was carried back to his bed. LaPointe stretched out, still sweating heavily, and blowing in and out.

"You're right, Rufe, he is a damn fool."

LaPointe tried to grin but wasn't quite successful with it. "I did it, didn't I," he commented. "Know-nothing, doubting sons of bitches." He managed a small smile this time.

LaPointe walked the length of the hospital a few days later, and the following week was allowed outside for a few minutes. It was bitter cold, with a brisk western wind, but quite sunny. LaPointe enjoyed it.

Christmas found him living in his own lodge a few yards from the old fort's wooden stockade. He had had enough strength to make love with Morning Mist his first night back. That was something he had worried about right from when he had first woke—would he be able to perform his manly duties with Morning Mist. He was quite relieved to find out that he could.

Moore had not been in favor of LaPointe moving back into the lodge. "You're not ready for such rough living yet, Henri," Moore had said.

"What rough living?" LaPointe asked, puzzled.

"Living practically out in the open."

"Christ," Duffy said from his chair across the bed from Moore, "ain't you ever been in a skin lodge?"

"No. No, can't say as I ever have."

"We'll settle this goddamn question fast enough," Palmer said. "Come on, Doc."

Ten minutes later the three had returned, the physician now convinced that there would be nothing wrong in letting LaPointe live in his tipi. Indeed, it seemed warmer and cleaner in there than it did in the makeshift hospital. The next morning, Moore directed the patient's moving.

Just after that, Moore had left. Duffy and Palmer had stayed behind. "You need any help, Henri," Duffy said, "you just call and either me or Otis'll come a-runnin'."

"I don't think that'll be necessary."

"Probably won't be. But if it is, you heed me."

LaPointe nodded. He paused a moment, then said

quietly, "I'm obliged, Rufe, for you getting me back here."

"Weren't nothin'," Duffy said flatly. He and LaPointe had been friends long enough that neither man had to pretend modesty when one thanked the other.

13

With the arrival of spring on the windy plains came the renewal of life at the fort. Construction began again, and activity picked up. Sanderson had his men begin sprucing the old fort up a little and restocking shops and storehouses. It would not be long before the immigrants began arriving in large numbers.

It had been one of the worst winters that LaPointe and his friends had ever seen. LaPointe was glad enough when it was over, too. He was just about back to normal when the first day where the temperature was above freezing came. Though the winter took a few more potshots at the people, that one day seemed to be a harbinger.

That night, LaPointe sat in his lodge with Morning Mist, Duffy and Palmer. "The Dakota ought to be making ready for the spring hunt," LaPointe said. "I think I will go with them."

"You feelin' well enough for such strenuous doin's?" Palmer asked, concern on his face.

LaPointe shrugged. "I think so, but if I'm not, I'll learn it soon enough."

"Just in time to get your ass trampled by some big fat buffler," Duffy said.

"There is that chance, eh?" LaPointe said with a little laugh. He was not afraid of such a possibility. He would know well before he got into trouble whether he could do it or not. Of course, there was always the chance that he would refuse to listen to his body telling him he was not completely healed. There was also the factor of his age. He was not old, but he was no longer a young man either. At forty-three or so, he had been in the wilds more than two decades. That had hardened him, but old wounds and what-not might've sapped him more than he would be willing to admit.

"Well, don't expect me to come help save you," Duffy said. "I've had more'n my fill of pullin' your nuts out of the fire."

"Hell, if I was to rely on you saving me, I'd be in real bad shape." He paused. "You boys going?"

Both men nodded. "Hell," Palmer said, "even if I don't go on the hunt, I'd have to take Pony Woman back to see her people or she'd get herself a heapin' dose of the sulks. And she ain't fit to live with when she's that way."

"Neither is Two Feathers," Duffy added, speaking about his own wife.

"You think the Cheyennes'll be here soon?" LaPointe asked.

Palmer shook his head. "Nah. I expect they'll still be out west somewheres. I figure they'll head east in another month or so—after they've made the hunt."

"They going to join the Dakota for the Sun Dance again this year?" LaPointe asked.

"I'd figure so," Duffy answered.

A few days later, LaPointe rode out. Palmer and Duffy had left an hour or so before, but they had a longer distance to go. LaPointe rode his motley colored horse. Morning Mist rode behind and trailed a pack mule and a horse with a travois with their lodge.

It did not take long for them to find Painted Bull's camp on the Lightning River. The band of Brulés looked gaunt and worn down by the long, harsher-than-usual winter, but the prospect of the spring hunt and full bellies gave them some cheer.

The two were welcomed into the village, and LaPointe took his place at the council fire with the other warriors.

As a man who had gone to war with his Dakota brothers against the Crow and Arikara and Pawnee, Henri La-Pointe had earned that place.

LaPointe joined the other men in preparing for the hunt. He felt a quickening of the blood, and with it came feelings of excitement tempered by worry. Doubts about his health lingered. He still tired more easily than was normal and he noticed pinches of pain when he rode too long or moved in certain ways. The hunt, he figured, would test him to the ultimate, and he hoped he was up to it.

LaPointe got caught up in the growing excitement in the village. Dances were held, and the throbbing drums entered a man's very soul. Though he was not a Dakota, LaPointe could feel it. He did not take part in the dance, but he watched intently.

Within a week, several other bands of Brulés and some of Oglalas had joined Painted Bull's village. Lodges were stretched for almost a mile along the banks of the Lightning. Hundreds of horses quickly cropped the grass down to nothing. But by that time, the scouts had reported that an immense herd of buffalo was found up north, toward the Belle Fourche River.

Three days of leisurely travel brought the Indians to the banks of the river. Standing on a low ridge, they could see the buffalo stretching out for miles.

LaPointe had Morning Mist set up their lodge a little way from the others. LaPointe always felt odd at such times. He was part of the band of Brulés, but yet not really of them. He would be a part of the hunt, every bit the equal of the warriors. At the same time, he could not really bring himself to take part in the rituals that were such an important part of the Dakota ways. He did not like being part and parcel of running roughshod over impetuous young men; or boys pursuing their independence a little. LaPointe knew the importance of keeping the youths from doing anything foolish. After all, the hunt was far more important to the tribe than to any one individual. Nor did LaPointe feel that dancing around a fire would make the buffalo wait docilely for their deaths.

LaPointe also did not like taking part in the grand hunts. Running around flapping blankets to force the buffalo into a stampede over a ridge where the fall—or the weight of later falling buffalo—killed or incapacitated them. Then the Dakota would wade in with knives and lances to kill off the survivors and begin the butchering.

LaPointe preferred running the buffalo. There was something exhilarating about rushing alongside a thundering buffalo, inches from the great hooked horns, and trying to place a lead ball into the animal's vitals.

Even more exciting was trying to reload on the back of a galloping horse. Powder generally spilled all over while he was trying to pour an unmeasured dose down the barrel of the rifle. Then a ball, wet with saliva, was rammed down. All the while, the horse was pounding along having chosen another suitable target. Then, when it came time to shoot the racing buffalo, the hunter had to hope that the lead ball would not roll out of the barrel.

Still, LaPointe knew the importance of the buffalo jumps. Right now the tribe needed food, hides and more after the winter. Especially a winter as hard and long as this one had been. LaPointe wanted meat, too, and the hides could be used, even if he just gave them away to some needy Brulé family. But he could not bring himself to stand there chasing buffalo over a cliff. And he could not jeopardize the Brulés' hunt by trying to run buffalo. So, he would go his own way during the hunt and set up a stand out of the way of the main action. He could have his five or six buffalo shot and butchered before the Indians got halfway through their hunt.

The tension and expectancy bubbled throughout the Brulé camp. LaPointe spoke to a few of his Dakota friends, but the visiting and conversation were desultory since the Indians had far more important things in mind.

LaPointe stood and watched the next morning as the nervous Dakota hunters fanned out, moving slowly and cautiously from upwind of the buffalo herd. Within half an hour came shouts and wild ululating yells followed by a rumbling roll of thunder that seemed to grow and expand until it swelled over the land like waves on a shore. It rose and rose until it blotted out all other sounds.

On the waves of noise came the dust. Great, roiling clouds of dust that spread to blot out the sun and then settle over everything. When that began happening, La-Pointe went back into his lodge, pulling the flap closed behind him. The flap and the lodge would not keep out all the dust, he knew from long experience, but it would help some. He sat a while, checking his rifle and seeing that his butcher knives were well honed.

When the thunderous noise had eased considerably, LaPointe stood and then poked his head outside. Dust still floated thick in the air, enough that it could be tasted. But the wind was blowing it away, cleansing the sky. LaPointe turned and nodded. "It's time, woman," he said quietly.

Morning Mist smiled at him and nodded. She would miss not being with all her friends during the hunt. This would be the first time she would not be with them. At first, when LaPointe told her the way the hunt would be this time—her first with him as her husband—it was enough for her to consider throwing his things out of the lodge. If she did that, she would be done with him. She was not sure, however, that she wanted that. He had treated her well, and besides, she had just spent months helping him get over the wounds he had suffered. She decided at last that she would do things his way. If, after that, she decided she could not bear life that way, then she would separate from him. In the meantime, she thought it only right that she should be of good cheer.

The two rode out, with Morning Mist trailing ten ponies behind her. She thought that perhaps ten were too many, but she would not argue over it.

They crossed the Lightning River and then rode north a few miles, before swinging a little east, back toward the river. LaPointe pulled to a stop on a small, brushy ridge on the north bank of the Lightning. The low ridge overlooked a plain to the east. Within a hundred yards were several knots of buffalo that seemed unaware that hundreds or thousands of their fellows were being run off a cliff not too many miles away.

LaPointe pulled out his heavy Plains rifle—a .50-caliber flintlock made several years before by William Craig —his powder horn, priming horn, shot pouch and a small, forged metal stand. He pounded the point of the latter into the ground and then stretched out, prone. The rifle went into the U of the stand. LaPointe pulled back the hammer and clicked the set trigger. Then he fired.

In less than an hour, he had dropped twelve cows. By then his rifle barrel was hot, and he figured he and Morning Mist would have enough butchering to do as it was. He cleaned his rifle and reloaded it. "Come on, woman," he said. "We got us work to do."

"We won't have enough ponies," Morning Mist said in Dakota as she and LaPointe rode toward the first carcass.

LaPointe shrugged. "We'll take what we can."

It took some hours to butcher out what meat they thought they could carry. Mostly they took the tongues, hump meat, ribs, hides, kidneys, livers and brains. They ate some of the organ meats as they worked.

They finished and rode back to their camp. There LaPointe passed around most of the meat to older Dakota men and women who had no sons to care for them. As LaPointe was tending his horse, the first of the Dakota hunters were moving into the village, crowing over their good fortune.

LaPointe looked forward to the feasting that would come that night. It was, to his eyes, both an exhilarating and rather grotesque event. The Dakota would stuff themselves with buffalo meat with wild abandon. Then they would vomit from overeating. That, however, did not stop the eating. The people would go right back to the fires and begin stuffing themselves all over again.

At the same time, the drums would be pounding and the men, women and children would be dancing wildly. Large fires would be crackling, their orange flames bringing out bizarre shadows that leaped and shivered.

LaPointe then became one of the Dakota. It always was so—the unwanted feeling before the big buffalo jump-off; then the acceptance as he took part in the barbarous festivities. He saw nothing odd in it.

As it always did for LaPointe—and especially so these past few years—it took him several days to recover from the bizarre celebrations. At the same time, though, it seemed to purge him. Of course, a few hours in a sweat lodge might have had something to do with that.

A week after the hunt, LaPointe and Morning Mist headed back to the fort. Most of the Dakota were planning raids, and LaPointe wanted no part of that now. A few years ago he would have been glad to join, but he figured he was getting a little too old for such young men's activities. Besides, he figured that Sanderson would want him back at the fort, though LaPointe could see no real reason why.

Several of the Brulés escorted them back, but they split off and headed northwest a mile or two away from the fort. The five warriors were on the prowl for enemies, their blood hot with the desire for honors.

⟦14⟧

"No. Absolutely not," Major Winslow Sanderson said angrily. He rose from the chair behind his desk and paced.

"There's nothing you can do about this, Major," La-Pointe said evenly.

Sanderson stopped his pacing and looked from La-Pointe to Duffy, who stood next to LaPointe. Sanderson fought his rising temper, only partly successfully. "I reckon there's not anything I can do about it, but I damn well wish you'd reconsider."

"No. I've got to go after Hanson and Kincaid. They killed one of your troopers and encouraged four others to desert. Then they damn near killed me. If I—we—don't go after them, it'll cause trouble later."

"It might. But it might not. We've had plenty of men desert. That doesn't mean any others'll get the idea. Or at least no more than were thinking about it anyway."

LaPointe shrugged. "That don't matter, Major," he said evenly. "What does matter is the fact that those boys tried to kill me and I can't let them get away with that."

"Dammit, Henri, I *need* you here. The damn wagon trains'll be rolling into here any day now."

"You don't need me for that," LaPointe said reasonably.

"That's true enough. But you know damn well

there'll be trouble between some of those idiots and the Dakota. *That's* when I'll need your help.''

"Sorry, Win," LaPointe said with no note of apology in his voice. "I've made up my mind, and I'm going. There's nothing you can say to make me change my mind."

"But where'll you look for them?"

"California. That's where they were headed. I don't expect they've changed their minds."

"There's a heap of country between here and there."

"Oui. But I have nothing better to do."

Sanderson glared at LaPointe for some moments. Then his face hardened, as if he had just come to grips with the problem and found a solution that would require harsh measures. "Private Moorhouse!" he bellowed.

Dusty Moorhouse stuck his head inside, concern wrinkling his boyish face. "Yessir?" he asked worriedly.

"Get Sergeant Driscoll and a dozen men and report back here on the double."

"Yessir." Moorhouse wanted more than anything to ask what was going on, but he knew better. As Sanderson's orderly, he had an easier life on the post than the others of his rank. He did not want to lose his privileges by getting on the wrong side of the major.

"What was that all about?" LaPointe asked. He did not sound worried.

"You'll see," Sanderson said stonily. He began pacing again, hands clasped behind his back.

Less than five minutes later—time that LaPointe and Duffy looked at each other several times and shrugged as they tried to figure out what was going on here— Sergeant Max Driscoll and his men entered Sanderson's office.

Sanderson stopped pacing and snapped, "Sergeant, arrest those two men." He pointed at LaPointe and Duffy. "Toss them in the guardhouse after you've relieved them of their weapons."

Driscoll looked at Sanderson as if he had gone mad.

Into the growing silence, LaPointe said, "You're going to lose some soldiers, Major." His voice was grim. His right hand rested on one of his Walker six-guns.

"Ready to fire, men," Driscoll said. He was not about to lose any of his men if he could help it.

LaPointe drew a pistol and cocked it. Then he aimed it at Sanderson. "Your men shoot, Major, you'll be dead a second later."

Sanderson grinned insolently. "Looks like we're in some fix, eh, Henri?" he said pleasantly.

"*Oui*. So what do we do about it, eh?"

"That's up to you now."

"Me?" LaPointe snorted. "What do you expect of me?"

"Your word that you won't go off hunting Hanson or Kincaid."

"I could lie."

"I've always taken you for a man of his word. The only thing to stop you from leaving here the moment you walk out the door is your word. I don't think you'll go back on your word, once it's given."

"And suppose I don't give you my word?"

"That should be obvious. You'll either die here and now if you try to make a fight out of it. Or you'll be thrown in the guardhouse."

"For how long?" LaPointe asked, a slight grin creeping onto his lips.

"Till winter."

"I could head out then."

"You're not that stupid, Henri," Sanderson said calmly.

LaPointe thought about that for a few moments. Everything Sanderson had said was true. So was everything he himself had said. But there was more reason in Sanderson's position than his own. It would hurt only his pride to let the two deserters get away with trying to kill him. He had suffered enough indignities to not worry too much about this slight. "What do you think, Rufe?" he asked quietly.

"It ain't me those two bastards almost kilt."

"You're a big help."

"I aim to please."

With only a moment's more thought, LaPointe lowered the pistol toward the floor and eased the hammer down. He stuck the revolver back into his belt after making sure the hammer once again was sitting on the empty chamber. "You have my word, Major," he said. He did not sound contrite.

"Rufus?" Sanderson asked.

"Hell, I ain't goin' nowhere."

"Sergeant, dismiss the detail."

"Yessir."

Before Driscoll could turn and issue orders to his men, Sanderson said, "Any of you troopers breathe a word of this to anyone—anyone—you will be flogged. Fifty lashes, administered by Mister LaPointe, Mister Duffy or both. Is that clear?" He knew how much pride men like Henri LaPointe and Rufus Duffy had. To have others see them cut down as they had just been could be fatal for anyone foolish enough to start blabbing about it. LaPointe and Duffy were not the type of men who would let such insults to their pride go unpunished.

Fourteen heads bobbed up and down. Driscoll turned and released his men.

"I think you owe Rufe and me an apology, Major," LaPointe said after the troopers had left. "There was no call for all that."

"You'll get no apology from me, Mister LaPointe," Sanderson said flatly. "You brought it all on yourself. I am sorry it did take such strong measures, but if you had acted reasonably from the beginning, this would've never occurred." He paused and sat. "Christ, Henri, give me a break. Sit down and we'll pull a cork."

LaPointe was still angry, but he stood his own ground for just a few seconds. In the meanwhile, Duffy had gone to the small sideboard and grabbed a bottle of rye and three glasses. He filled all the glasses and set them on the desk and he sat. Duffy looked up at LaPointe and grinned. He downed his glass of whiskey in one gulp. "Good stuff, Henri," he said with a chuckle. Then he refilled his glass.

"Well, goddamn you both," LaPointe said with a sudden burst of laughter. "I ain't about to walk out of here and leave you two to suck that bottle dry all by yourselves." He sat and grabbed his glass.

LaPointe, Duffy and Palmer—the latter two who had also been hired as interpreters during the winter—were kept busy enough. When things were slow at the fort, they would go out and hunt, either by themselves or with some of the fort's other hunters.

The first wagon train pulled to a stop at the fort just two days after LaPointe and Duffy had been confronted by Sanderson. Once the floodgates were open, as it were, the immigrants seemed to arrive every minute of every day. And with them came the Dakota. The Indians would sit up on the ridges and watch the anthill of activity down at the fort.

LaPointe almost always rode out to the Dakota and spoke with them. It was apparent that they did not like the many whites coming through their land. Over and over, LaPointe explained to them that these people were not here to stay. That they were traveling to far-off lands, beyond even the territory of their longtime enemies the Crow and the Blackfoot.

The Dakota were not happy with those words, but they accepted them, more or less. When they saw with their own eyes that the wagons remained at the fort only a few days before pushing on, the Indians were a little less concerned.

Some of the warriors would occasionally attack a smaller wagon train, which led to harsh words between the immigrants and Sanderson. The major and LaPointe would try to get the offending warriors and the offended parties together and work out some form of compensation. It usually worked.

But some folks, seeing how well that worked, began

making more and more outlandish claims. Those were rejected, but it took Sanderson and his interpreters time to sort things out and send the travelers on their way again. Such immigrants usually left with curses for the army on their lips.

Also coming with the influx of travelers was an increase in desertions by soldiers. Eighteen troopers deserted together, fleeing into the night. Sanderson was enraged and ordered a patrol out to try to track down the deserters. Only five men returned from that patrol. The lieutenant who had been sent to lead the patrol was wounded, and his four men told Sanderson that the deserters had tried to kill Lieutenant Cloverdale. The four had been able to protect him, but the others headed off with the deserters.

"That's the last goddamn time I send anyone out after deserters," Sanderson stormed in his office when Cloverdale and his men had explained it. Seeing that LaPointe was about to open his mouth and say something, Sanderson snapped, "And don't you give me any shit either, Henri. I'm not of a mood."

LaPointe wisely shut up.

There was always the chance of trouble with this many whites crossing Indian lands. LaPointe, Duffy and Palmer worked hectically to keep the two sides apart as much as possible. That was rare, though. The Indians—all of them—knew that the land was theirs; that they were allowing the whites simply to cross the land as quickly and with as little impact as they could.

The whites were another matter. Most of them were decent folk just trying to get to Oregon Territory or to California in peace and safety. They did not want to confront Indians any more than they wanted to encounter cholera, mountain passes, deep rushing rivers, thunderstorms or any of the other hundreds of things that were out to kill them. There were always a few, though, who felt differently. These types seemed to think that they could do with the land whatever they wanted. *After all*, they would say, *nobody's using the land. Anyone could see that.* Those were the ones who created most of the trouble. They simply could not see Indians as human beings. They insulted chiefs, went in where they had no place being; they shot at stray Indians, and did everything they could to make themselves obnoxious to any decent folk regardless of what color they were.

LaPointe hated them more than anyone. He always had. He had seen such men in the mountains in the old days. Most of the old-timers then hated some Indians and were friends with one or several tribes. About the only Indians hated universally by those men were the Blackfoot, and maybe the Apache down south. The Shoshoni, Crow, Bannock, Nez Perce, Flathead were almost invariably friendly toward whites. Or at least any whites who treated them with the respect they deserved. But there were always a few who treated Indians—any Indians—as animals, generally for no good reason.

LaPointe found that that type of person was fairly prevalent among the men with the wagon trains, and he did not know why. Some, he figured, had read the wildly false and inflammatory guides for immigrants; others probably came by it naturally and were egged on by letters from those of their own kind who had gone before.

That attitude could be found among some of the Indians, too. They were not perfect, none of them. There were always those who argued for making war on any white man who came along—including sometimes such old and valued friends as Henri LaPointe. It took a considerable amount of energy and talking to keep the rest of the warriors at peace, especially when there was good cause for the Dakota to be angry at the white travelers.

LaPointe found even more reason to dislike such folks among the whites after he returned from Painted Bull's village, where he had had to talk warriors out of attacking a wagon train over some real or imagined sleight.

He stopped at his lodge near the fort and tied the reins of his horse to the picket ring he kept in the ground nearby. He looked up, hand darting toward a pistol when a man came out of his tipi.

"What in the hell are you doing in there?" LaPointe demanded, barely managing to keep his temper in check.

"I've never seen the inside of an Indian house," the man said matter-of-factly. "What business is it of yours?"

"That's my lodge," LaPointe said tightly.

15

"I didn't know," the man said. He was not apologetic. "My name's Wilber Grimes." He held out his hand.

LaPointe ignored Grimes's outstretched hand. "That does not matter," he said, still battling his anger.

"Sure it does," the man said cautiously. He did not like being snubbed, especially by such a half-wild creature like this one. But he figured he would try to be reasonable with him. "Hell, if I'd known it was your place I'd never have gone in there. Though for the life of me I can't see why a white man—any white man— would want to live like a fuckin' savage."

LaPointe popped him a good shot in the snout.

Grimes fell on his buttocks. He scrambled up holding his suddenly bleeding nose. "What in the hell'd you go and do that for?" he asked, bewildered.

"What would you do if someone just up and walked into your house?" LaPointe countered.

"Probably the same as you just did," Grimes admitted. "But I told you, my going in there was a mistake."

"You're damn right it was."

"Hell, man, I said before I didn't know it was a white man's place."

"Meaning that if it was a Dakota lodge you would've figured it was all right for you to just barge on in?" LaPointe growled.

"Well, hell, it ain't like they're like us, you know."

"I expect any Dakota would be happy to admit he was

nothing like you—a pain in the ass. What would you have done if my woman was in there?"

"I would've apologized and got the hell out of there," Grimes said.

LaPointe could see in the man's eyes that he was lying. His first impulse was to gut the man here and now and be done with it. But there were enough problems these days that he did not want to add to the pile. "You know, boy, that if there was a warrior in there you'd be lying there with your nuts in your hand, don't you?"

Grimes blanched at the very notion. But he forced himself into bravado. "Maybe. Maybe he'd be the one carryin' his nuts in a hand."

LaPointe laughed. He could not help it.

Grimes looked offended. "Here now, what the fuck is so funny?" he demanded.

LaPointe settled down some. "The thought that you could beat a Dakota warrior in a hand-to-hand fight."

"Son of a bitch," Grimes mumbled as he pushed past LaPointe. "Miserable goddamn heathen, worse than any goddamn Injin ever was."

LaPointe turned and watched him go. LaPointe was still battling down the urge to kill the idiot. Then he wondered where Morning Mist was. He was certain that if she had been in the lodge, Grimes would not have exited it unscathed. Just to make sure, though, he poked his head inside. It seemed as if a few things had been disturbed, but it didn't appear as if anything had been taken. Morning Mist was not inside.

He swung into the saddle and rode to the old fort, stopping at the blacksmith shop. The blacksmith—Dwight Eaton—had been on the job at Fort Laramie for several years before the army had come along. His shop fronted on the Plaza of the old fort, but with the new fort going up, he had knocked a hole in the back wall of the shop and put in a door. That opened onto the parade ground of the new fort with the two newly built army stables not far away. His own stables were inside the old fort across an empty area about fifteen feet wide and twenty-five feet long. He used the area as a corral and a work area, and since the army had shown up, it also was used as an informal gathering spot for the fort's civilian workers. A hole also had been knocked in that adobe wall and a gate installed. Eaton looked up and grinned. "Hey dere, Henri," he said.

"Hey, Dwight, how's doin's?"

"Fine. Fine." He put down his hammer and the horseshoe he was working on. Wiping his hands on an old rag, he stepped out into the sunlight. Eaton was a most unlikely looking man for such a trade. He was maybe five-foot-one and wouldn't weigh a hundred pounds if he had ten pounds of iron in his pockets. His naked chest was bony, and one could count Eaton's ribs with ease. Still, he was one of the best blacksmiths La-Pointe had ever seen.

LaPointe dismounted. "I think my horse here needs a new shoe on the left foreleg."

"Well, by goddamn cracky, we'll have us one god-damn good look at it now, won't we." He leaned over and grabbed the horse's leg and bent it at the knee. One glance was enough. He let the foot down. "Sure as goddamn shootin' you need a shoe. You wanna god-damn leave him now?"

LaPointe bit back the laughter trying to escape. Eaton was a great source of amusement to LaPointe, both be-cause of his looks and the way he spoke. "How soon can you have him fixed up?"

Eaton looked up at the sun, trying to judge the time. " 'Bout a goddamn hour, I expect."

"You sure? You look like you've got a lot to do."

Eaton shrugged. "Them goddamn travelers can wait for their goddamn repairs. They goddamn never pay me enough any goddamn way. I favor folks I know."

LaPointe nodded and dropped the reins, which Ea-ton took. "I'll have a goddamn look-see at the others, too," the blacksmith said.

LaPointe nodded again. "You seen Morning Mist?"

"I goddamn think she went out with Two Feathers

and Pony Woman lookin' for some goddamn berries or somethin'. Rufe wasn't here, so Otis went wid 'em.''

LaPointe nodded, relieved. He had been mighty concerned until he had heard that Palmer was with the women.

The room just below the old fort's north-side blockhouse had been turned into a makeshift saloon, and LaPointe headed there. Like Eaton's shop, the saloon had had a new door cut into the adobe in the northwest wall to provide access from outside the old fort, rather than just from the *placita*. There was a mixture of men in the place, about equally divided between soldiers and immigrants. One of the immigrants was Wilber Grimes. LaPointe ignored him. LaPointe had several shots of whiskey and a couple of beers. When he figured about an hour had passed, he left. Feeling good, he walked to Eaton's shop.

"All done?" LaPointe asked.

The blacksmith nodded. "I replaced one of the goddamn back shoes, too, and goddamn filed the others down. Replaced a couple goddamn nails, too. That should goddamn hold you for a while."

"*Merci.*" LaPointe paid Eaton and rode back to his lodge.

Morning Mist was there. She smiled and showed LaPointe the basket of blueberries, cherries and blackberries she had found.

"They'll be tasty," LaPointe said.

"Oh," Morning Mist said in halting English, which she had been picking up from LaPointe, "Otis says meet him at . . . at . . ."

"Take your time, Morning Mist," LaPointe said gently. "Take your time."

Morning Mist nodded. "At the . . ." Her brow furrowed as she tried to remember the unfamiliar name. "Saloon!" she suddenly said with relief.

"You'll be all right here alone?"

"Yes," she answered in Dakota. "Why wouldn't I be?"

"No reason," LaPointe said evenly. He was not about

to tell her that some idiot of an immigrant had been in the lodge unannounced a few hours ago. "I'll be back before long," he promised. "My horse is outside. See to it."

He walked back to the fort in the gathering dusk, stopping occasionally to say a word or two to a friend. As he turned the corner of the saloon several men jumped him.

One of them was on his back, trying to claw out his eyes. LaPointe slammed himself backward, mashing the man on his back against the saloon's adobe wall. As LaPointe jerked forward, the man groaned and slid off his back.

A punch thrown by Wilber Grimes caught him on the cheek. It split the skin a little but did no other damage. LaPointe saw two men besides Grimes and the one that had been on his back. The two were trying to grab his arms to pin him back. They partly managed, and Grimes stepped up and slammed a punch into LaPointe's stomach. "Take that you fuckin' Injun lover," Grimes snarled.

LaPointe spit at him, hitting him in an eye. Grimes yelled angrily and moved back a couple of steps. After wiping out his eye, he snarled, "Donny, Edgar, hold that son of a bitch still!"

"We're tryin'," the man holding LaPointe's left arm gasped. He felt as if he had a hold on a big, strong snake.

"Christ, Wil, hit him or somethin'," the other one said.

"Just hold him one more goddamn second," Grimes said as he stepped up and walloped LaPointe in the stomach again.

The punch seemed to have no effect on LaPointe, but since Grimes was in reach, LaPointe kicked him in the crotch.

Grimes sucked in a breath and sank to his knees, both hands covering his pain-racked privates.

Donny Grimes, the man holding LaPointe's right

arm, swung toward the front a little, preparing to hit LaPointe in the stomach again. But the move left only one hand holding LaPointe's arm. It was not enough.

LaPointe jerked the arm free and snapped off a punch that caught Donny on the side of the face. He fell to the side and then tripped over his brother Wilber.

Edgar Grimes, the man on LaPointe's other side, suddenly looked sick. He knew he could not hold LaPointe in place by himself. He let LaPointe's arm go, hoping that LaPointe would interpret it as a bid for peace.

LaPointe didn't. He whirled and poked Edgar in the nose, knocking him down.

By this time, the fourth man—Hub Grimes—had gotten back to his feet. He was still wobbly, but he came at LaPointe with a fair-size rock.

LaPointe sensed the man coming. He ducked and snapped an elbow backward into the man's midsection. The man dropped the rock and half stood there, crouched and gasping for breath.

LaPointe grabbed Wil Grimes and jerked him upright. He spun behind Grimes and, grabbing the back of Grimes's shirt, he pushed forward, slamming Grimes's face against the saloon wall. He pulled Grimes back and did it again. Then he let Grimes fall to the ground. He turned toward Edgar Grimes.

"Hey now, ol' hoss, you need some help there?" Palmer asked sarcastically.

LaPointe looked back over his shoulder. Palmer, Sergeant Driscoll and three soldiers stood there.

"What happened here, Henri?" Driscoll asked.

LaPointe never knew quite what to think of Sergeant Max Driscoll. The soldier was as polished as a soldier could get and as hard a man as LaPointe had ever met. Yet he was well educated and could often be found reading a book when off duty.

"I'm not going to tell you that and then have to go through it all again with the major," he said.

Driscoll nodded. "Fair enough, Henri." He grinned a

little. "The major's not going to be real happy with being disturbed, you know."

LaPointe shrugged. "These goddamn fools were the ones started it."

"Like hell," Edgar Grimes said. "That heathen, Injun-lovin' son of a bitch . . ."

"You have something against Indians, friend?" Driscoll asked.

"Well, no, not really, but—"

"Then I'd advise you to shut your mouth lest I set Mister LaPointe on you again." He paused. "Now, if you gentlemen would please head to Major Sanderson's headquarters." It was a command, not a question.

The four attackers walked off, followed by the soldiers. Driscoll, LaPointe and Palmer brought up the rear.

Sanderson indeed was not happy with the interruption. He was eating his supper when the group entered the office. Driscoll knocked on the door to Sanderson's quarters and told him he was needed.

"Well, what is it?" an aggrieved Sanderson asked. He patted his mouth with a cloth napkin. In his other hand he had a cup of coffee. He was not wearing his uniform blouse, just a plain white cotton shirt. His suspenders hung loose along the sides of his pants.

"We found Mister LaPointe in a to-do with the other four gentlemen," Driscoll said.

"What caused the ruckus?"

"I don't know, sir," Driscoll said.

"Henri?"

"I found that asshole there"—LaPointe pointed at Wil Grimes—"inside my lodge when I got back here earlier today. So I popped him one on the snout."

"A reasonable response," Sanderson said flatly.

"I thought so," LaPointe responded.

"Then what?"

"I spent an hour or so over at the saloon while waiting for Dwight to replace a shoe on my horse. These four damn fools were in there but didn't bother me. I went back to my lodge, where Morning Mist told me Otis wanted me to meet him in the saloon. I was almost there when these four jumped me.''

"Well, what's your story?'' Sanderson asked, looking at Wil Grimes. He sipped coffee, his piercing eyes never wavering from Grimes.

"He's a liar,'' Grimes said. "I was nowhere near his tipi when—''

"If you were nowhere near Henri's lodge, how'd you know it was a tipi?'' Sanderson demanded.

Grimes's mouth flapped but no words came out.

"Put them in the guardhouse, Sergeant,'' Sanderson ordered. "I'll deal with them in the morning.''

16

Sanderson was back in a crisp uniform the next morning as five confused people were escorted into his headquarters. "Sit," he told them expansively.

"I'd rather stand, if you don't mind," the only man among the five said.

"Well, the ladies must certainly sit." He waved toward the chairs. "Please, ladies."

"What's this all about, Major?" the man asked.

"That will be explained in short order, Mister . . . ?"

"Hutchinson, Ralph Hutchinson."

"You're the captain of that big wagon train out there, are you not?"

"I am." He paused. "Look, Major, I don't mean to cause you no grief, but I've got a heap of things got to be seen to before we can leave the fort. And we don't have all the time in the world either. If you brought me and the ladies in here, it must be something to do with the Grimes brothers. If that's true, where are they? And what've they done?"

"That'll become clear in . . ." He paused when he heard a knock on the door. A moment later, LaPointe and Palmer entered. "Take a seat if you can find any."

"I'm not that old yet," LaPointe said as he leaned against the wall on one side of the sideboard. Palmer took a similar position on the other side.

Before Sanderson could start talking again, there was

another rap on the door and Sergeant Driscoll entered. He stood aside, holding the door open as the four Grimes brothers entered. They looked confused and more than a little frightened. They looked subdued, except for Wil, whose face was splashed with bruises. After a moment's hesitation, each went to stand next to his wife.

"Well, now that we're all gathered," Sanderson said, "we can begin." He paused. "Mister Hutchinson, since you're the captain of the wagon train with which the Grimeses are traveling, you should have final say on what happens to them. But let me tell you, sir, that I do not look favorably on those who attack men under my command or in my employ."

"He attacked me!" Wil Grimes shouted, pointing at LaPointe. "Damn Injun-lover."

"I don't doubt that's true," Sanderson said evenly. "However, as I said last night, had I been in Mister LaPointe's place, I would've walloped you one on the snout, too. Where'd you ever get the idea that you could just up and walk into another person's home?"

"It was just a damn tipi. A damn Injun tipi."

"And that gives you the right to enter it?"

"It was open and unoccupied."

"Ah, I see. So while you are traveling with Mister Hutchinson, anyone who stumbles along can crawl into your wagon and look around. Is that it?"

"Well no, but . . ."

"But what, sir? Any wagons I've seen come by here on the Oregon Trail are open back and front, and they are generally unoccupied while on the move. Ergo, you are inviting anyone to hop in and take a look around."

"That's not what I meant," Grimes snapped angrily.

"Oh, I know exactly what you meant, boy," Sanderson said coldly. "I must confess, Mister Grimes, that I dislike people like you and your brothers. You are troublemaking louts with no consideration for anyone or anything but you and yours."

"That's not such a bad thing," Hub Grimes said quietly.

"No, no, I suppose it's not," Sanderson said thoughtfully. "However, when you think you're the only ones in the world, problems arise. I know your type—and that goes for all four of you. Had that been a Dakota lodge you walked into and there had been a warrior in there, you would be dead and buried by now. And that'd raise a considerable stink among the immigrants as well as among the Dakota. Then I'd have to have my troops get between you idiots and the Indians. And if that were to happen, innocent people would get killed. Just because you couldn't keep your nose out of a place it doesn't belong!" Sanderson had built up quite a head of steam, so he stopped to let himself cool off for a few moments.

"I must say, Mister Grimes, that you are one lucky son of . . . one lucky man, seeing as how you found Henri in a good mood. Most days he would've gutted you without a thought if he had found you in his lodge. You're also mighty lucky in not having encountered Morning Mist in there."

"Who?" Wil Grimes asked. He sounded puzzled but defensive.

"Morning Mist—the wife of Mister LaPointe."

"It's not bad enough he has to live like one of 'em, he's also *married* to one of 'em?" Grimes snapped arrogantly. He felt safer with his wife and sisters-in-law there. He was certain no one would harm him.

LaPointe pushed off the wall with his shoulder and took a step toward Grimes.

"Not now, Henri," Sanderson said.

LaPointe gave him a hard look, then stepped backward and landed against the wall again. He spit some tobacco juice, which hit the spittoon with a soft, dull clang.

"Yes, Mister Grimes, you are lucky she was not there. Had she been and Henri found you there, we would still be picking up your pieces."

"All this talk's been about what Wil done," Hutchinson said. "What about his brothers? They involved in this, too?"

"After Wil's altercation with Mister LaPointe, the four Grimes boys attacked Mister LaPointe."

Hutchinson nodded. "That makes some sense, I guess."

"How come you're takin' his word for everything?" Wil Grimes said. He knew he had to deflect interest in him and move it elsewhere.

"Because," Sanderson said with a shrug, "I know Mister LaPointe and the way he is. I don't know you, but I can tell a lot about you just from this little chat. More importantly, though, is that I trust Mister LaPointe implicitly. I don't trust you at all."

"But I—"

"Shut up, Wil," Hutchinson said. He paused, sighing. "Well, what now, Major?"

"That's up to you. They spent the night in the guardhouse and I can put them back there if you want. I can keep them locked up until you pull out. I can keep them there until after you pull out, if that's what you want. Or I can release them to your custody, in which case you can deal with them as you see fit."

"Tell you the truth, Major," Hutchinson said wearily, "I ain't too fond of being in charge of these boys. They've been trouble since the beginning."

"The choice is yours. If you want, I can lock them up for a day or two, until you make up your mind."

"That might be best, Major," Hutchinson said thoughtfully. "I got too much to do to baby-sit these fools."

"Please, Major," Wil Grimes's wife said quietly, "let them go. I'll be responsible for—"

"Shut up, Olivia!" Grimes hissed.

"But I was just trying—"

"I don't give a damn what you were trying to do. I ain't about to stand here and let the world think I'm tied to your apron strings. I'm my own man, dammit, and I ain't gonna let neither you nor Hutchinson over there be my keeper.''

LaPointe watched the tableau with some interest. Olivia Grimes reminded him of a tiny, ailing bird. Too proud to give up trying but not strong enough to survive either. He figured she must have been an attractive woman once, not too long ago since she didn't appear to be much over twenty. But those few years seemed to have hung on her like a shawl. It was a pity, he thought.

Hutchinson also had watched the exchange. He nodded. ''That's made up my mind, Major. Lock 'em up. I'll be by before I leave to see if I want them back on the journey with me.''

''And so it'll be done,'' Sanderson said. ''But I am worried about the ladies.'' He looked at Hutchinson in question.

''They'll be fine with us,'' he answered. ''I'll look after 'em, and we have a few families who'll help 'em out for a spell.''

Sanderson nodded in agreement. ''Sergeant, you and your detail please escort the Grimeses back to the guard-house.''

''I ain't goin' back to no guardhouse,'' Edgar Grimes snapped. He jumped toward the desk, hands out-stretched as he headed for Sanderson's throat.

Grimes's wife, Mildred, screamed.

LaPointe took two steps and whacked Grimes on the back of the head with the butt of one of his Walker pistols. Grimes slumped, halfway across the desk, then slid back the way he had come until he lay in a heap on the floor.

''Sergeant,'' Sanderson said, nonplussed, ''your prisoners await.''

Driscoll saluted. ''Yessir.'' He looked at Wil Grimes, the oldest of the four. ''You men have the privilege of carrying your brother.''

''And what're you going to do if we don't want to?'' Hub Grimes asked.

''You other three will join your brother in unconsciousness, and then we will tie the four of you to a good, stout horse and drag you to the guardhouse," Driscoll said matter-of-factly.

The three conscious Grimes brothers snarled but they complied with the order.

"There are times when I hate this goddamn job," Sanderson said with feeling after everyone but LaPointe and Palmer had left.

"Figured you'd feel that way, Win," LaPointe said. He had filled three glasses at the sideboard. He carried one to Sanderson and set it down, then went back and got his own. "A salute," he said, raising his glass, "to every poor bastard who's been put upon by fools."

"Amen," Sanderson said before draining his glass.

The travelers never seemed to stop coming. Not at this time of year. Even before one would move on after a few days of recovering at the fort others would be pulling in. The demand on the fort's shops and supplies was endless.

Adding to the wildness of it all were the Dakota who would arrive now and again. Sometimes they came just to gawk at the weird procession of people and wagons. They might sit up on a ridge laughing and hooting at all the strange goings-on down below. Occasionally they would drop by to trade for some supplies. And once in a while just a few Brulés might stop by to visit with La-Pointe.

It all made for a lively place. It also made it an often-tense place. Many of the immigrants felt as the Grimeses did—that an Indian's lodge was somehow open to anyone who wanted to snoop around. Or that Indians were there for their amusement or servitude.

On the other side of the coin, the Indians for the most part considered the travelers intruders, and often would demand payment for crossing "their" land. To the whites, the Indians had some odd notions about private property and the thievery of such. The Indians were so curious about the whites that they would often overstep the bounds of propriety by touching people who did not want to be touched, especially by an Indian, or touching things they should not be touching. Settling disputes kept LaPointe and the other interpreters busy.

The volatile mixture included the ongoing construction of the new fort. That construction was proceeding at a snail's pace for several reasons. For one, the influx of immigrants had to be accommodated. For another, supplies and building materials were often in short supply. But probably the main problem was desertion. Soldiers were fleeing so frequently it was sometimes hard to keep track of them.

One of the few things that was working well was the addition of the Mexican farmers LaPointe and Duffy had brought back just before the past winter. They had a large garden planted with pumpkins, several kinds of beans, squash, two types of melons, potatoes, corn and yams. A small section of the garden was given over to herbs and spices.

Sanderson had taken notice of it and called LaPointe in one day. "I want you to make another trip down to Taos, Henri," he said.

"More Mexicans?"

Sanderson nodded. "They've done so well with the garden, and in general labor that I hope more of them will be able to push construction along."

"Might work. But I'm not fond of the idea of leaving just now."

"I wouldn't expect it. Not the way things've been around here lately."

LaPointe nodded. "When do you want me to leave?"

"Think you can make it down there and back if you left around the middle of August?"

"I suppose so. Why then?"

"Most, if not all, of the wagon trains should be well past here by then. If they aren't, they're not going to make it alive. You know that."

LaPointe nodded again. "Just wanted to see if our thinking was the same."

17

LaPointe stood leaning against a wall near the sideboard when Sergeant Driscoll and a detail of eight men brought the four Grimes brothers into Sanderson's office.

"Mister Hutchinson's wagons pulled out yesterday," Sanderson said without preliminary. "At his suggestion, I've kept you in the guardhouse until now. He left four mules for you to use to ride to the wagons. If that's what you wish. They've had a day and a half start, but riding unencumbered, you four should be able to catch up along about dark today."

"Gee, thanks," Wil Grimes said sarcastically.

"Were it left up to me," Sanderson said icily, "I'd give the four of you back to LaPointe. That would give him a few moments of entertainment as well as rid both this fort and Hutchinson's wagon train of four goddamn pests. It's only by the good graces of your wives—who came in here the day before yesterday with Hutchinson to plead your case—that you are being allowed to live. Those women deserve a lot better than scum like you." He paused, glaring from one to the other. "Now get the hell out of my sight. And don't ever come to this post again, gentlemen. You will not live long enough to regret it."

"What about our guns?" Wil Grimes asked sullenly.

"Mister Hutchinson has them. They'll be returned to

you when you reach the wagons. Or so he said. I'd not blame him if he did not return them. Dismissed."

After the four had stomped out, Sanderson sat back and sighed. "Damn am I glad those bastards're gone. Jesus, Henri, can you figure out why some people have to act like those fools?"

LaPointe shook his head. "No, sir. But those four aren't alone."

"I know. I know. Do the Dakota act like that?"

"Some of them. I can't figure out why they do it either."

"Well, that's the last we'll hear of those four." He chuckled ruefully. "Just think, we had a whole other wagon train pull in today and reports are that two more'll be here in the next day or so. I look so forward to the new company."

"It'd try the patience of Job himself," LaPointe agreed.

Two days later, LaPointe was back in Sanderson's headquarters. Also there were two young Oglala warriors, the captain of a wagon train and an aggrieved immigrant.

"Mister Kreutzer there," Sanderson said, pointing to the immigrant, "says the two Dakotas scared the crap out of his family—threatened them no less—and made off with a bottle of whiskey plus some other small personal items. That about right, Mister Kreutzer?"

"Yah." The bullet head bobbed once. Kreutzer had a high forehead and a gleaming dome of a head. His brushy eyebrows were gray and matched the thick mustache.

LaPointe translated it for the two Dakota. They grew agitated and spoke rapidly and with growing vehemence. LaPointe finally told them in their own language to calm down. Then he looked at Sanderson. "Up in the Sky and White Bear say Kreutzer traded them the whiskey for two buffalo robes and a badger-claw necklace."

"What about the other things they supposedly took?"

LaPointe shrugged. "They said they don't know anything about that."

"What about threatening Kreutzer's family?"

"They say they never saw any women. They said he came away from the wagons a little to entice them into a deal."

"Do you believe them, Henri?"

LaPointe shrugged. "I have no reason to doubt them. I don't know these young men but I'm inclined to believe them because of what they are. I don't have that same inclination with those two." He pointed to Kreutzer and Floyd Bennett, the wagon master.

Sanderson drummed his fingers on his desk. Either the Dakotas were lying or the immigrant was. He would not want to have to wager on which side. "Orderly!" he bellowed. When Private Dusty Moorhouse looked inside, Sanderson asked, "Were the horses of these two Indians brought in with them?"

"Yessir. They're right outside here now."

"They have bags or anything that might hold small personal items?"

"Looks to be, sir."

"Bring them in, Private." He looked back at LaPointe. "Henri, explain to your friends that we're going to look through their things to see if anything was taken that shouldn't have been."

LaPointe nodded and started to speak to the Oglalas, but Kreutzer suddenly grew very agitated and was speaking rapidly. Most of his words were in German, and the few that were in English were so heavily accented as to be no more understood than the German words.

"Best tell your man to either shut up or to speak slowly enough so that we can understand him, Mister Bennett," Sanderson said.

The wagon train captain grabbed Kreutzer by the arms and shook him a moment. Once the tirade was snapped, Bennett tried to get Kreutzer to talk coherently.

Finally Bennett turned to Sanderson. "Sorry for his

outburst, Major. From what I can gather, he don't want you goin' through the Indians' things."

"Why not?" Sanderson asked, surprised.

"You got me."

The Oglalas did not seem very perturbed that the white soldier chief was going to paw through their belongings. However, it became a moot point when Moorhouse entered the room carrying two buckskin bags.

"Which one does this belong to, Henri?" Sanderson asked, holding up one of the sacks.

After a moment's conversation with the Oglalas, La-Pointe said, "It's White Bear's."

Sanderson nodded. He opened the bag, began taking items out and spreading them out on the desk. When he was done he had found nothing that had ever belonged to any white man. What he did find were an old knife, several arrowheads, a fire-making kit, a small wood-backed mirror, some tobacco, a few pieces of sinew and an awl, and a paint pouch.

Sanderson put the items carefully back into the sack and then went through the other bag. The only thing he found in that bag that could be traced to white men was a bottle of whiskey. That he set on the desk. He put the rest of the things back into Up in the Sky's bag.

Sanderson sat quietly for a few moments, then looked at Kreutzer. "I cannot abide idiots, Mister Kreutzer," he said in a frosty voice. "Nor can I abide liars and cheats. I especially can't abide people who try to stir up trouble with the Indians for some reason they probably don't even know themselves. I don't care how recently you came here from your native land, you should've known that giving whiskey to Indians is prohibited. Your captain should have informed you of that if no one else had done so beforehand."

"He was so informed," Bennett said testily. "But he said it was stolen by those two. It seems now he probably lied about that."

"Seems?" Sanderson asked sarcastically.

"Well, now that I look at it, I guess he just flat-out lied

to me. That's what he done. And, damn, I don't like liars no more'n you do, Major. I'll run his ass up a pole for this, you can be sure."

"I can discipline him for you, Mister Bennett," Sanderson offered.

"I'd rather it be left up to me, Major," Bennett said. "To tell you the truth, I ain't got any likin' for Injuns of any kind, but I'd be some powerful put out was my wagon train to be attacked by a bunch of those red devils because of somethin' one of my immigrants did. He'll be punished, Major. Don't you doubt that for a minute."

"Then I suppose you won't mind if Mister LaPointe and I watch?"

Bennett gulped a little. "No, sir, I won't." He had hoped to punish Kreutzer leniently and then try to put the fear of God into him so as not to do it again. Now he would have to actually hurt the man some. He did not look forward to it.

"And you wouldn't mind if Up in the Sky and White Bear watched, too, no?" LaPointe said.

"I'd not like that at all," Bennett protested. He looked at Sanderson. "Ain't it enough that you and him watch? I ain't really fond of havin' those red devils in my camp, especially when I'm punishin' a white man."

"Henri?" Sanderson asked, looking at the interpreter.

"I'm going to have to tell these Oglalas that they can't have the whiskey. They're not going to like that. I'll also have to tell them Kreutzer over there will be punished. Most of the Indians don't believe much of what the white man says. To make sure they know me, you and mister train master there are speaking straight, they should watch the punishment."

"I find that a more than adequate reason, Mister Bennett, don't you?"

"Yeah," Bennett growled, more unhappy than ever.

"When will it take place?" LaPointe asked.

Bennett shrugged. "Just after dawn tomorrow all right?"

Sanderson looked at LaPointe, who nodded. Sanderson then said, "That'll be fine, Mister Bennett." As Bennett and Kreutzer turned for the door, Sanderson added, "I would not try something underhanded to get out of this, Mister Bennett. It would not advance you in my eyes."

Bennett nodded, worried. Then he and Kreutzer left.

LaPointe was explaining it to Up in the Sky and White Bear, who did not seem happy with it. Sanderson saw it and sighed, tired of the problems. There never seemed to be a winner in these things, he thought. Almost invariably both parties went away unhappy.

Finally the Oglalas left, taking their bags with them, but leaving the whiskey behind. LaPointe picked it up, pulled the cork and took a swig. "Just because the Oglalas had to leave it doesn't mean we can't drink it, Major," he said, holding the bottle out.

Sanderson took a drink. "Was this what they were so upset about?" he asked.

LaPointe nodded.

When LaPointe finally left the office, a fair portion of the whiskey was gone. LaPointe stopped outside the office, next to Moorhouse, and breathed deeply. The air was still hot, but with the sun just beginning to sink and a light breeze it didn't seem too uncomfortable. He headed back to his lodge.

The women had a fire going about centered on the three lodges. They had been doing that frequently of late. While it was nice inside the lodges, it was still close. Outside there was always something of a wind to help cool them, and help refresh them.

Morning Mist, Duffy, Palmer, Pony Woman, Two Feathers and five children—two of them the offspring of Palmer and Pony Woman, the other the progeny of Duffy and Two Feathers—were lolling about the fire. Palmer and Duffy rested against willow backrests.

A large coffeepot sat in the fire and a large iron kettle

of buffalo stew dangled over the flames from an iron bar suspended between two slightly forked iron rods. Hanging from hooks on the crossbar were several slabs of fresh buffalo meat. Two buffalo tongues roasted on the coals.

LaPointe sat against his own willow backrest and poured himself a cup of coffee. He was not drunk, not even close, but his head buzzed a little from the whiskey, the heat and the closeness in Sanderson's office. He figured the coffee would help revive him.

"How's doin's, hoss?" Palmer asked.

LaPointe told his two friends of the latest altercation.

"You think Bennett's gonna try to get out of it?" Palmer asked.

LaPointe shrugged. "I doubt it. He doesn't have the backbone to cross the commander of a fort. I suppose he could try pulling his people out tonight thinking the army won't chase him."

"Sanderson wouldn't send a patrol out after him, would he?" Duffy asked.

"Probably not," LaPointe said with a chuckle. "Not with the way so many soldiers've been deserting. However, the Oglalas might decide to take a run at the wagon train. If that happened, I don't think much damage would be done, but it'd sure scare the living shit out of all them immigrants."

"I'd like to see that," Palmer said with a small laugh.

"Me, too." Duffy added his laughter.

"Damn if I don't hate all these immigrants coming through," LaPointe said. "They're nothing but trouble."

Still laughing, Palmer rocked forward from his willow backrest, aiming his knife for one of the buffalo tongues.

Suddenly two shots rang out, one of them clanging off the iron kettle. Some of the stew spilled out through the hole, making the fire smoke and sizzle.

·❴18❵·

LaPointe shoved Morning Mist, who was next to him. Then he rolled away from the fire. Two more shots hammered out. LaPointe thought he heard a gasp of pain, but he couldn't be sure. "Rufe? Otis? You all right?" he called out softly.

"Yep," Palmer responded.

"Yeah. You see where them shots came from?" Duffy asked.

"Ain't sure. I hope they fire again, so we can—" Two more gunshots cut LaPointe's sentence off. "Got zem," he said, accent thickening in the crisis. "Near ze southwest corner of ze old fort. I go after zem."

"I'm with you," Duffy said.

LaPointe jumped up and ran for his horse, which was picketed behind his lodge. He swung up on the horse, which had neither saddle, bridle nor reins. It didn't matter, though. The horse would respond to him. He smacked the horse's flank with the palm of his hand. *"Allons!"* he snapped. The horse bolted. As he raced off, LaPointe called, "Otis, stay here."

A faint, "I will" followed LaPointe, who was aware that Duffy was only a few paces off.

The new fort was coming alive, with lanterns lighting up all over. Company commanders shouted orders. Most thought they were under an Indian attack.

Before LaPointe and Duffy reached the corner of the old fort, the moon popped out from behind a thin, lazy cloud. In the moonlight, they spotted several men galloping away.

LaPointe and Duffy flattened out along their horses' necks, letting the animals go full out. Gradually but steadily they closed the gap until each pulled up alongside one of the fleeing men. LaPointe made it first. Anger raced through his blood when he saw it was Wil Grimes.

Grimes tried to hit LaPointe with his rifle. LaPointe ducked the attempt. Straightening back up, he shoved his right foot out. He managed to hit the side of Grimes's horse with the sole of his boot. LaPointe shoved. Grimes's horse lost its stride and pitched forward whinnying. Grimes went flying.

LaPointe looked up in time to see Duffy leap off his horse and onto a man's back. The two fell off the racing animals and bounced. *"Merde,"* LaPointe muttered as he headed in that direction, hoping Duffy had not been killed. He hadn't been. He had gotten up already and was pounding the hell out of Hub Grimes.

LaPointe shrugged and rode to where he had seen Wil being dumped. He was still there, groaning as he lay on the ground. LaPointe slipped off his horse and silently glided up to Grimes. He knelt and searched Grimes, finding two single-shot pistols, a small, four-shot pepperbox, a belt knife and a small jackknife. LaPointe tossed all the weapons out into the darkness. He grabbed a handful of Grimes's shirtfront and hauled him up. "Walk," he ordered.

"Fuck you," Grimes snarled.

LaPointe splattered Grimes's nose with a fist. "You bad-mouth me again, you dickless little fart, and I'll show you a few tricks I learned from ze Dakotas. Now move."

Grimes complied, limping toward where Duffy had Hub Grimes on the ground. Duffy was casually kicking the stuffing out of Hub.

"Aren't you done yet?" LaPointe asked Duffy.

Duffy looked up and smiled grimly. "For now," he

said. He pulled Grimes up. Hub stood there weaving. "What about the other two pricks?"

"I don't think we'll 'ave to worry about zem."

"I ain't worried about 'em. I just want to kill 'em."

"Me, too. You see if anybody was hurt back there?"

"I saw Pony Woman go down, but I ain't sure if she was shot or maybe just bein' smart and duckin'. I'm worried about my younkers, though."

LaPointe nodded. Memories washed over him. "I can understand that," he said quietly.

"I know, my friend," Duffy said.

LaPointe shook off the gloom a little. "You watch these two. I'll go get your horse." LaPointe hopped onto his mottled pony and trotted off. Minutes later he was back with Duffy's horse and no others.

"Looks like you boys've got yourselves a wee bit of a walk," Duffy said as he mounted. "So best start."

The two Grimeses took a few steps, but then Wil stopped again. "I ain't goin' another step," he said defiantly.

"Me either," his brother chirped.

"I'm tired of threatening these asswipes," LaPointe said casually.

"I can understand that, ol' hoss. What I can't understand, though, is why we've let them live so long."

"There doesn't seem to be any reason for them to continue living either, is there?" LaPointe mused.

"None that I can see."

"Watch my horse, *mon ami,*" LaPointe said as he slid off the animal.

"Don't you need some help?" Duffy asked casually.

"I don't *need* any help."

"Well, maybe you *want* some help?" Duffy asked hopefully.

"I think I can handle these two by myself. After all, you softened one of them up pretty good, eh." LaPointe walked up to the Grimeses. Without a word, he kicked Hub in the stomach, then slammed a forearm against Wil's head. Wil fell, but Hub was only doubled over.

LaPointe grabbed Hub's hair and pulled his head up. Hub spit at him. "You'll be sorry, Henry, you don't let us go."

"My name, he is pronounced On-Re."

"I don't give a fuck how you pronounce it. You don't let us go, you're gonna be one sorry son of a bitch."

"Ah, then zat will make us even, eh." LaPointe balled up a hard fist and smashed Hub in the mouth five times. By the fifth, the only thing holding Hub up was La-Pointe's grip on his hair. LaPointe let him fall. Hub lay there spitting out his teeth.

As LaPointe turned, Wil barreled into him. Wil was so weak, though, that he could not knock LaPointe down. LaPointe shoved Wil away and down. "You're a pathetic piece of shit, boy," LaPointe said scornfully. "A puling little puke with no balls and no brains."

"Eat shit, Henry."

"I told your brudder there, my name he is say ON-RE! ON-RE, you goddamn moron."

"I don't give a fuck what your name is. You're still a festering pile of shit."

"Ah, such words should not be say to me, eh." His accent grew a little thicker. "But since you say these things to me, then I must teach you a lesson."

"Goddammit, you pusillanimous snot, if you're gonna kill me get it over with, chickenshit frog."

"Oh, I will kill you. Never fear. But not so fast. *Mais non!* Slow, like ze Dakota do. I will peel ze skin off you a strip at a time. I will cut things from your body. You ears first, eh. Then maybe some fingers and ze nose. Then ze toes. And I save for last *les bijoux des famille*—the family jewels, eh. But maybe you don't have any and such a t'ing doesn't bother you, eh." He sighed. "Well, we'll have to see."

LaPointe hauled Grimes up by the shirtfront again, then turned him and shoved him some. Grimes's back bounced on the side of Duffy's horse.

Duffy reached out and grabbed Grimes's hair. "Have at him, hoss," he said almost cheerfully.

LaPointe pounded Grimes unmercifully, beating mainly his chest and stomach at first, breaking ribs and certainly injuring some internal organs. After the first few moments, only Duffy's grip on him kept Grimes from falling.

Suddenly a patrol rode up with Sergeant Driscoll in charge. "What the hell's going on here, Henri?" Driscoll asked.

"What does it look like, eh?"

"It looks like you're pounding a man to death."

LaPointe was of no mood for Driscoll's slightly mocking tone. "You're very observant, Sergeant."

Driscoll ignored the attempted insult. "I don't think Major Sanderson's going to be very happy about this."

"Then go back to the goddamn fort," Duffy snapped. "We'll be back directly. Soon's we've got done with these two. And their two brothers."

Driscoll had no liking for the Grimeses, and he wasn't really all that sure if Sanderson would be upset. Then he grinned a little. "You mind if we watch?" he asked.

LaPointe looked up at him, surprised. He did not see any sarcasm reflected on Driscoll's face. "I thought this bothered you, Sergeant?" he probed.

"After what I saw in the Mexican War, this isn't so bad," Driscoll commented.

"What about Major Sanderson?"

"What about him, Henri?" Driscoll countered.

LaPointe grinned and nodded. Then he went back to working over Grimes. After some minutes, he finally stepped back.

Duffy let Grimes's hair go, and Grimes slumped to the ground.

"I don't believe he'll be going anywhere under his own power," Driscoll said.

"Bon." LaPointe headed for Hub Grimes. He was still on the ground and looked only half-conscious. LaPointe stomped on him several times, until he was certain he had broken both of Grimes's arms and legs. Then he went and jumped on his horse.

"Aren't you going to finish them?" one of the soldiers asked.

"No."

They rode back to the fort. Major Sanderson was at the camp LaPointe, Duffy and Palmer called home these days.

"Where's Otis?" LaPointe asked straight off.

Sanderson pointed toward Palmer's lodge. "He's seeing to Pony Woman."

"She gone under?" Duffy asked.

Sanderson nodded. "No one else was hurt, though," he added lamely. He looked at Driscoll. "Your report, Sergeant?" He felt better being officious.

"Two attackers dead. None of the patrol was hurt."

"Why didn't you bring in the bodies, Sergeant?" Sanderson asked. He hoped he did not get the answer he thought he was going to get.

"They don't deserve to be brought back, sir," Driscoll said flatly.

Sanderson stared at him a moment, then nodded.

LaPointe and Duffy had gone into Palmer's lodge. "How's doin's, ol' hoss?" Duffy asked quietly.

"Looks like my medicine's gone south," Palmer said, voice thick with emotion.

"Anything we can do, Otis?" LaPointe asked.

"Just help me find the bastards that done this."

"Two of 'em's been put under already," Duffy said. "Henri broke two of 'em into pieces and left 'em out there for the buzzards and the wolves."

"Good. Who were they?"

"The Grimes brothers," LaPointe said.

Palmer looked up over his shoulder. "Then two of 'em's still out there somewhere?"

"Oui. They were riding hard west. I t'ink they will try to get back to the wagon train and see if they can convince the people there that they should be protected."

"You think any wagon master'll buy that load of shit?" Palmer asked harshly.

LaPointe shrugged. "They have wives who'll have to

be cared for if their husbands are gone under. Children, too. The wagon captain might t'ink protecting them from us is the best thing."

"Bastard'll find out he's wrong in a big goddamn hurry, then, won't he."

"*Oui.*"

"Yep."

"You boys mind leavin' straight off?"

"Not me," LaPointe said.

"Me neither, goddammit."

"What're you going to do about Pony Woman?" LaPointe asked.

"Just leave her here for the time bein'. You think Two Feathers'll mind looking after her—and my young 'uns—for a bit, Rufe?"

"Nope. I suspect she'll be glad to do it. Since she's Cheyenne, too, she'll know what to do about Pony Woman."

"That's what I figured." Palmer rose. His face was stony with loss and determination. "Let's ride."

The three stepped out of the lodge.

"Is there anything I can do, Mister Palmer?" Sanderson said.

"Just keep the hell out of the way."

"What do you mean?" Sanderson was puzzled.

"We're going after the other two."

"But I can't allow—"

"Nobody's asked you to allow any goddamn thing," Palmer snapped. "We'll be takin' care of these doin's ourselves. We don't need nor want no goddamn help from the army."

Sanderson nodded. He was no fool. "You need anything? Powder? Shot? Food?"

"We 'ave all we need, Major," LaPointe said. "We won't be gone long."

Sanderson nodded again. "You mind if I send a few of my men along with you? Sort of make things official?"

Palmer shrugged.

"That'd be fine, Major," LaPointe said. "Just 'ave

them ready to ride in a few minutes. And you'd better order them to keep themselves out of our way."

"I'd like to go, Major," Driscoll said firmly.

"How about you others?" Sanderson asked, looking at the rest of the patrol. Four of the five men nodded. "Good luck, men," Sanderson said.

19

LaPointe, Duffy and Palmer led the way as the small detail left Fort Laramie. The three friends rode abreast. Behind them rode Sergeant Max Driscoll by himself. His four troopers brought up the rear.

A long, thin streamer of a cloud had covered the moon, and the men at first had trouble seeing even their comrades. Then the cloud drifted on, and silvery light splashed across the plains, giving the landscape a ghostly appearance.

They rode at a pace that covered ground well but would not overtax the horses. They caught up to the wagon train shortly after dawn after having ridden throughout the night. The immigrants were loading supplies, hitching teams to wagons and saddling horses in preparation of the day's journey.

The soldiers were surprised that they had caught the wagon train so quickly, seeing as how the immigrants had two full days of travel from the fort behind them.

"It takes a wagon train a long time to get anywhere," LaPointe said when Driscoll had asked about it. "They don't go very fast at the best of times. To tell you the truth, though, I'm a little surprised myself we found them quite so soon. I had expected we'd catch them somewhere on the move today. Maybe they had trouble with some of the wagons."

"All the better for us, goddammit," Palmer snarled.

They were about the first words he had spoken on the trek.

They rode down a small, grassy slope toward the wagons. People slowly became aware of the newcomers and stopped what they were doing to watch the procession.

Ralph Hutchinson, the wagon master, was in the midst of hitching up his team when someone tapped him on the shoulder, spoke to him a moment and then pointed. Hutchinson turned to watch as the avenging party rode into the sprawling, noisy camp, which was quickly quieting down. After a moment, Hutchinson walked slowly toward the newcomers, stopping a few feet from where LaPointe and his party had pulled up.

"What can I do for you all?" Hutchinson asked. He was a little worried.

"Bring out the Grimeses," Palmer said harshly.

"Why?" Hutchinson's nervousness grew. He had no desire to challenge these men, even if most of the men in the camp were armed.

"Just bring those bastards out," Palmer snapped, face tight with anger. "Or I'll go through every goddamn wagon in this goddamn camp to root 'em out."

"You can't do—"

"I can do any goddamn thing I want, boy," Palmer said sharply. "And the consequences be damned."

"What's this all about, Sergeant?" Hutchinson asked, looking at Driscoll.

"Your Grimes brothers got a little frisky along about sundown last night. As a result, Mister Palmer's wife is dead. While nothing can bring her back, Mister Palmer justifiably feels that vengeance is both right and proper."

"I haven't seen them today," Hutchinson said. He felt like he would piss his pants.

"Two of 'em you ain't ever gonna see again," Duffy tossed in. "Wil and Hub're worm food already."

Hutchinson blanched. He was scared, but he did not get to be the captain of such a large wagon train by running from trouble because of fear. He was not stupid either. He stood for a few moments, very conscious of Palmer's burning, unwavering eyes on him. Then he made his decision. "This way, gentlemen," he said. He turned, trying to ignore the fear of taking a bullet in the back any moment, and walked swiftly off.

Hutchinson stopped near two wagons sitting tightly near each other. "Two brothers shared a wagon," he explained over his shoulder to LaPointe and his friends. "You Grimes boys," Hutchinson shouted at the wagons. "You come on out here now."

There was no response. "You ain't gonna get but this one more chance," Palmer roared. "Now come on out before some innocent folks get hurt."

Olivia Grimes suddenly looked out the back of the nearest wagon. She was plainly nervous. "They're not here," she almost whispered. Her face was drawn, her lips pale.

"Then you'd have no objection if we took a look for ourselves, would you, *madame?*" LaPointe asked. He had been polite, but it was clear in his voice that he was determined.

"Well, yes. Yes, I would mind," Olivia said. She licked her dry lips. "I don't think that's right."

"Listen to me, *madame,*" LaPointe said. "Your husband and his brothers attacked our small camp at Fort Laramie last night. Mister Palmer's wife was laid low by a bullet from your husband or one of his brothers. Your husband, I am sad to say, was killed after the attack. So was Hub. We want the other two. They must pay for what they have done." He paused. "Now I expect you might be afraid something'll happen to you if you tell us where they are, but let me reassure you, *madame,* that is not the case. Indeed, you will be in danger if you do not tell us where they are."

"I don't know," an obviously frightened Olivia said. "I don't know where they are."

"I hate to call a woman a liar, *madame,*" LaPointe said. "But I'm afraid I must do so in this case."

"But . . . but what will I do now, with my husband

dead? What will the others do if their husbands are dead.''

"You'll all be a heap better off, ma'am," Duffy said.

"How is that possible?"

"Easy, *madame*," LaPointe said. "You're not 'appy with your husbands. That is plain to see. With them dead, you'll be free to marry others."

"But folks'll look poorly on us, won't they?" She was desperate in her concern. Her husband and his brothers had drummed it into the four women time and time again that they were used goods, and that no other man would ever want them for wives because they were so tainted. Having married young, barely fifteen, she knew no better, really. It was the same with the other three Grimes wives.

Besides, she had often thought while wondering what life would be like without Wil Grimes, what man would want a woman who came along used *and* with several children? She had four; Edgar's wife, Mildred, had two; Donny's wife, Ellen, had three; and Hub's wife, Esther, had two, with another on the way.

"Mais non!" LaPointe said enthusiastically. "There are men here in the wagon train who might make good husbands. If that doesn't please you, then wait until you get to California, where there are a hundred men, a thousand men, for every woman. *Mais oui!* You will 'ave your pick of men. They will be fighting over you, each of them eager to marry such a beautiful woman."

"Even with children?" Olivia asked, dumbfounded at the possibility.

"Yes, ma'am," Duffy answered. "Those boys out in those minin' camps ain't real particular when it comes to women. Not when there's so precious few of them out there. And with ones as beauteous as you all, well, like Henri said, they'll be fightin' over you. Some'd even be interested because you've proved fertile. That's an important thing to some men."

"Let's quit the goddamn jabberin'," Palmer snapped. "We got business to see to."

Olivia, who had been joined at the back of the wagon by Edgar's wife, Mildred, sat thinking. Mildred bent and whispered a few words to her.

"I hate to be so impatient, ladies," Palmer said, trying to keep the annoyance out of his voice, "but I ain't aimin' to wait much longer."

"We must press on," LaPointe added. "Since your husband is dead, *madame*, perhaps it is to the others that we should speak?"

"As the wife of the oldest brother, I'm sort of the one who speaks for all the wives."

LaPointe nodded. "I understand. But you really must decide soon."

Olivia and Mildred chatted a few moments more, and then conversed with someone inside the wagon. Finally Olivia looked back at the newcomers. She looked much relieved. "Edgar and Donny aren't here. They came in about an hour ago. They changed clothes, took some things and ran off. They took two of Mister Carleton's horses, but they left theirs in place."

"What kind of horses?" LaPointe asked.

"A big bay gelding with three white stockings and a white blaze; and a cinnamon-colored mare with a black tail and mane."

"Which way did they go?" LaPointe asked.

"Southwest. They said they'd make a big loop and meet us a couple days up the trail."

"Merci," LaPointe said. He looked at Hutchinson. "You'll see that the ladies are taken care of, eh?" It wasn't really a question.

Hutchinson nodded. Having the four Grimes brothers out from under his feet would make things a lot easier for him.

"You don't," Duffy said, "and we'll find you."

Hutchinson nodded again, hating the fear that trickled up and down his spine.

"Mister LaPointe?" Mildred said quietly. When LaPointe looked at her, she asked, "Would you come by here and let us know what happened."

"*Oui.*"

"Just one more thing?" Mildred pleaded.

"What is that, *madame?*"

"My husband—Edgar—carries a locket. A heart-shaped locket. It's the only real thing of value I have. It was given to me by my grandmother. I . . . I'd like . . . I'd . . ."

"You want it back, yes?"

"Yes." Her eyes were wet with tears, and LaPointe was not sure if the tears were ones of pain because her husband was going to die soon or ones of joy because she would soon be free.

The eight men rode out of the camp heading southwest, pushing the horses only a little harder than they had earlier. But since the two remaining Grimes brothers had fresh horses, the hunters were not sure they could catch their prey quickly.

But just before noon, the group was moving southward near the southern edge of the Laramie Mountains. LaPointe, who was out ahead of the group a little, stopped and held up a hand, warning the others to stop, too. All did, except Palmer, who rode slowly up and stopped beside LaPointe. The Frenchman pointed.

Palmer nodded when he saw the thin spiral of smoke coming from behind some rocks a mile or so ahead. "I reckon that'd be them," Palmer said.

"*Oui.* But we should make sure. I will do it."

"Why you and not me?" Palmer demanded angrily.

"Because you're too hotheaded right now. You wouldn't be thinking straight."

"Dammit, Henri, I hate you when you're right."

LaPointe smiled just a bit. "You must hate me all the time, then, eh." He moved on ahead.

By the time LaPointe returned, Driscoll and his troopers had a camp set up in a small copse of stunted cedars, with everything in order. Two fires were going, and the supplies were stacked neatly under one of the trees.

"That them?" Palmer asked right off.

"*Oui.*"

"You sure?"

"I didn't see them, but I saw the horses."

"That's good enough for me."

"Why in hell did they stop here?" Driscoll interjected. "It doesn't make any sense."

"Assholes like them generally think they're smarter'n everybody else," Duffy said flatly. "They get overconfident. I figure that they figured nobody'd be chasin' 'em. Or if someone was, that they'd be hard to find."

"It's rather startling how stupid some people can be," Driscoll remarked.

"Nobody gives a shit about that," Palmer growled. "Them fuckers ain't gettin' no younger settin' out there. And neither am I. Let's go."

20

"**Y**ou boys can stay out of zis, Sergeant," LaPointe said. "Unless God wants to make a joke and have us three drop dead all at ze same time, me and my two *amis* won't have any trouble with zem two."

Driscoll shook his head. He enjoyed battle, but having his soldiers take part in what would more or less be cold-blooded murder would not sit well with Sanderson. Then again, they had come all this way now. Driscoll decided that Sanderson wouldn't be too upset, considering that the major had approved Driscoll and his troopers coming along. If he didn't expect them to fight, he would've never allowed the soldiers on the expedition. "We're comin'," he said flatly.

LaPointe nodded.

"Just remember, though, soldier boys," Palmer said with an angry rasp in his voice, "I get first crack at them assholes."

The men split up and moved on the camp from different directions, creeping toward it over boulders and across rock-slippery ground. Palmer entered the camp, a pistol in each hand.

LaPointe, Duffy and the soldiers held back a little. Since Pony Woman had been slain, Palmer should have the honor of taking care of her killers, and all the men knew it.

But the Grimeses were nowhere to be seen. By the

time Palmer and his companions realized that, it was almost too late.

LaPointe caught a movement off to his left, from a position where none of his companions were. "Otis!" he roared.

Palmer began to spin, going into a crouch at the same time. Halfway through the maneuver, a shot rang out, and Palmer fell to his side. Several more shots were fired. At least one more hit Palmer, but the others whined away off rocks, or dug up small clots of soil.

LaPointe snapped off two shots in the direction of the man who was firing at Palmer. He didn't think he had hit the man, but the shooting stopped.

"Those bastards," Duffy said. He was really aggrieved that he and his friends had been suckered into a trap so easily.

LaPointe felt the same. He was angry at himself, too. Only by being lax had he and the others been drawn into the snare. LaPointe took much of the blame himself. Had he been more careful in scouting out the Grimeses' camp, they might have averted all this.

But it was too late for them to be dwelling on blame. That could come later, if necessary.

"Otis!" LaPointe yelled. "You all right?"

"Yes, I'm all right, goddammit." He pushed up, ignoring the bloodstains on his shirt. Then he darted toward the rocks that almost ringed the small clearing. Someone popped up to LaPointe's right this time and popped off two quick shots at Palmer. But Palmer was in the safety of the rocks now.

LaPointe almost chuckled at the stream of curses that emanated from Palmer's haven. LaPointe moved away from the rock. "You keep a watch out, Rufe," LaPointe said.

"Where the hell're you goin'?"

"See what I can find out. I don't think whoever was shooting is still setting where he was. He'll have to be on the move."

"Just watch your ass, ol' friend."

Moving slowly and silently, LaPointe made his way around the camp. He flitted from boulder to rock to tree. He stopped every few feet and listened for anything that would tell him where the Grimeses were. He was beginning to think that either he was getting old and couldn't see plain signs or that the Grimes brothers were a lot more skillful at hiding than he had ever suspected. Then he heard a hammer being cocked.

Inching forward, he finally saw a blue shirt against the dirt brown of a boulder. LaPointe took the last few steps in a silent rush. Then he was standing there with the muzzle of one of his Walkers brushing the back of Edgar Grimes's head. "Lay down your piece, *monsieur*. If not, well, *mon Dieu*, a .44 will make a ghastly mess of you from here, eh."

Edgar set down his pistol on the boulder he was leaning against.

LaPointe moved back two steps. "Stand," he ordered. When Grimes had done so, LaPointe commanded, "Turn."

With Grimes facing him, LaPointe said, "It would give me great pleasure to shoot you right between ze eyes here and now. But, alas, zat honor shall go to my great friend Otis. Now, strip down."

"What?"

"If you are hard of hearing, I can offer a little persuasion, eh." He waggled the gun.

"I can hear just fine," Grimes said with bravado. "But I can't help but wonder why you'd want me stripped down. You don't seem like a man who likes men, if you know what I mean." He smirked a little.

LaPointe's gun hand moved like a striking snake and whacked Grimes in the center of the forehead with the pistol. Grimes sagged and almost fell. His eyes rolled. "I am not one of them men," LaPointe said matter-of-factly. "But it will be hard for you to hide a weapon when all you are wearing is your hide, eh. Now, begin, or I will start shooting pieces off you."

Still reeling from the blow to the head, Grimes moved

as fast as possible in shucking his clothes. When he was done, three pistols and two knives littered the ground at Grimes's feet.

"Now, *monsieur,* call your brother."

"Or?" Grimes seemed cockier than ever.

"Or I will shoot you."

"I thought that honor was to go to your 'great' friend."

"Oui. But you don't have to be in one piece when he finishes ze job, no? Do as I say."

"Sure." The smirk on Grimes's face grew. "Hey, Donny," he called not very loudly, "come on out."

LaPointe wasn't sure just what had caused him to duck, but as he did, a bullet whistled over his head and ricocheted off the boulder. LaPointe caught a glimpse of Donny Grimes hiding between boulders and a few gnarly cedars. That took but a fleeting moment. Then he swung, half rising, and slammed a forearm across Edgar Grimes's nose, knocking him down. He swung back and fired off a quick shot toward where Donny had been.

"Merde," LaPointe muttered when he realized Donny was not there. He stood and grabbed Edgar's hair and jerked him up. "Move, asshole," LaPointe snapped. "Down toward ze camp." He released Edgar's hair and shoved him on the back.

"Donny!" Edgar suddenly called. "Donny. Toward the camp."

LaPointe let him holler, seeing no reason to stop him. He followed Edgar straight into the camp. He knew he was taking a risk, but something had to happen here, and soon. He would be the bait.

Sure enough, almost as soon as he walked into the clearing, a shot knocked his hat off. That was followed by a shot from Duffy's position. There was a screech from behind LaPointe, up in the boulders, and some rocks skittered down the slope.

LaPointe grabbed Edgar by the hair again and hauled him around, so that Grimes was between LaPointe and where the shot had come from. Another shot kicked up dirt near LaPointe's foot, and then another flew through the small space between LaPointe's front and Grimes's back.

LaPointe was worried about that, since the shot had come from a position where Donny could not have been. He wondered if the Grimeses had a confederate up in the rocks.

Then gunfire seemed to erupt all around. LaPointe slammed his pistol against Edgar's head. Edgar groaned and fell. LaPointe spun and ran for the rocks where he thought Donny was. A couple of fringes on his pants were torn away by a bullet, but he made the safety of the rocks.

As he caught his breath, LaPointe looked around. Gunfire was still sporadic, and it was coming from several places, which struck him as odd. He spotted one of the soldiers—Private Frank Underwood. "You all right, boy?" LaPointe asked, confused by the look on Underwood's face.

"I'm jus' fine, froggie," Underwood said as he raised his pistol.

LaPointe was still trying to puzzle it out when he heard a gun fire behind him. Underwood jerked and blood began staining the chest of his uniform. LaPointe whirled.

Sergeant Driscoll stood there, smoking pistol in hand. His face was etched with anger and determination.

"What the hell was that all about?" LaPointe asked.

"A couple of my men decided they'd rather help the Grimeses and desert. I found out about it. I took care of Gainesworthy, but Underwood there had taken off."

LaPointe nodded. He was about to speak when he heard Duffy shout, "I got the other." LaPointe and Driscoll headed back to the camp.

Duffy was holding a gun on Donny Grimes, who was in a rage. A moment later, Palmer came out of the rocks, and then the two other soldiers did so, too.

"Take your men—good and bad—back to our camp,

Sergeant," LaPointe said quietly. "Ze job that's left is best left to men like us."

Driscoll looked at him a moment, and then nodded. They disappeared.

"How's the wound, Otis?" LaPointe asked.

"Ain't but a scratch."

"We might best take a look at it," Duffy said with concern.

"You'd likely set it to putrefying."

The others said nothing more about it. The three waited until Edgar Grimes came to. In the interim, La-Pointe went back to Edgar's clothes and found the locket.

"He is all yours, *mon ami*," LaPointe said quietly to Palmer when Edgar regained consciousness.

Palmer finished off the two Grimes brothers without apparent anger and with brutal efficiency. It took the Grimeses more than a few minutes to die, and they did so noisily and bloodily.

Afterward, LaPointe and Duffy picked up the food the Grimes brothers had brought with them and headed back toward their camp. Just before they got there, Palmer walked away, heading onto the prairie. LaPointe and Duffy watched him for a moment. Both men had experienced Palmer's pain and knew what he was going through. Knowing him for many years like they did, they knew he wanted to be alone for a while.

"All done with?" Driscoll asked.

LaPointe nodded.

"You're not planning to bury them?"

"The wolves and buzzards'll take care of them."

"Where's Mister Palmer?"

"Out there," LaPointe said, jerking his head. "He wants solitude."

Driscoll nodded. "I see you found some food."

"It ain't much," Duffy said, "but it'll fill the holes in our bellies and taste better'n some shit I've had to eat at starvin' times."

"Try living on a soldier's rations sometime," Driscoll

said with a small laugh. His troopers nodded in agreement.

"No, thank you, Sergeant," LaPointe and Duffy said in chorus.

"Choose your fire, boys. One's for you three men. The other'll be for my troops and me."

"Very thoughtful, Sergeant," LaPointe said. "Any of your men know how to cook? Rufe and I can do it, but it'll taste like shit."

"Private Russell has a fair hand with cooking. He'll take care of your meals as well as our own."

While Private Russell set about making supper, La-Pointe and Duffy unsaddled their horses as well as Palmer's. They took some time in tending the horses.

Tired, the men went to sleep shortly after eating. La-Pointe woke sometime in the night, alerted by someone or something rustling around the camp. His hand was easing out a pistol when Palmer growled quietly, "Go back to sleep, goddammit."

"You all right, Otis?"

"I'll live. Now go back to sleep and leave me be."

LaPointe could see no reason to argue about it. Palmer would handle his grief the best way he knew how, much like LaPointe had done a couple years before. So LaPointe went back to sleep.

Palmer was gone again when the camp came alive the next morning. So was his horse.

"I take it you two know where he's gotten off to?" Driscoll asked.

LaPointe shrugged. "He's out there somewhere. Heading back to the fort. We might see him again or we might not. He won't be too far from us, though, in case we—or he—meet some Indians."

The men ate a quick breakfast and wasted no time in breaking camp. Before long they were on the trail. Before midday they found Hutchinson's wagon train. The four Grimes women were walking, as was nearly everyone else, as was usual. They stopped, using hands to aid their bonnets in blocking the sun, when they saw the riders coming. They moved a little away from the long, loud, dusty column of wagons and waited for the horsemen.

"Is it over?" Olivia asked anxiously.

"Oui." LaPointe pulled something from his small belt possibles bag. He leaned over toward Mildred. "Here, *madame,* this is yours I believe."

Mildred took it and held it tightly against her breast. She felt like she would certainly fry in hell for the feelings of relief and gladness that had swept over her at the pronouncement of her husband's death. She thought she was evil incarnate.

LaPointe looked at her. "You are not a sinner, *madame,"* he said softly. *"Mais non!"*

The men rode off, and Mildred stood gaping, wondering how LaPointe had known what she was thinking. She couldn't puzzle it out, but realized that it did not matter. For a few moments more, she watched the horsemen riding away. Then she turned and hurried to catch up to her wagon.

21

LaPointe stood by for a while as Sergeant Driscoll tried to explain to Major Sanderson why he had returned with two dead soldiers. He was having a hell of a hard time at it, too.

Finally LaPointe could stand it no longer. "Jesus Christ, Major," he snapped. "The man did his job. Those two assholes were going to run off. One of them was about ready to put a bullet in this ol' carcass. I'd have come back here across a saddle if it wasn't for Max."

Sanderson thought about that for a while. LaPointe let him stew a few more moments, then added, "Was it left up to me, those two would still be out there with the Grimes boys feeding the ravens and coyotes."

LaPointe could not believe that Sanderson had carried it even this far, and he was growing angry. "What the hell's got into you, Win?" he finally asked. "You've never been like this before."

"Ah, hell, I know." Sanderson slumped into his chair. "But, Christ, there's always something going on. Plus we're still having every other goddamn trooper take off on us. I figure that sooner rather than later, General Twiggs is going to wonder what we're doing with all the men we've had here."

"Jesus, Win," LaPointe said in annoyance, "you think this is the only post in the west with lots of men deserting? I've talked to some men who work other forts. They have the same problem.''

"Yeah, I've checked on that, too. It's just that . . . well, goddammit, I just hate sitting here wondering whether anytime I send a patrol out if the men'll come back. Damn, that's frustrating.''

"I expect it is,'' LaPointe said flatly. "But taking your ire out on your best noncom doesn't make any sense.''

Sanderson glared at LaPointe for a moment, then he grinned. "Lord, I ought to throw you out of here, Henri. Sergeant, let me thank you for a job well done. And give yourself a couple days off.''

Driscoll saluted and left.

"As for you, Henri,'' Sanderson said, "I still need you to make that trip to Taos. And I suspect you'd better be leaving soon.''

LaPointe nodded. In some ways he looked forward to the trip. Taos was a pleasant town, its people generally warm and friendly. Or so they had been before the Americans came along after the war several years ago. LaPointe had found in the trip he had made the previous year that the people weren't quite as hospitable as they used to be. Still, they were friendlier than fellow Americans in many a city back in the States.

In some ways, though, he did not look forward to going. He had spent enough time away from Morning Mist recently. And, while he looked forward to a few days in Taos, he did not look forward to the trip itself. Especially the ride back.

LaPointe sighed. It had to be done and fretting over it would do him no good. "I'll head out for Painted Bull's in the morning. Once I've left Morning Mist there, I can head south.''

"You planning to take Rufe with you again?''

"If you don't mind.''

"Should be all right. Most of the wagon trains're long gone, so we should have little trouble with the Sioux. I can get by with Otis for any translating.''

"No you won't,'' LaPointe said flatly.

"He gone?" Sanderson asked.

LaPointe nodded. "He took off just after we got back. Picked up his kids and his lodge and skedaddled. He's gone to the Cheyennes. I figure he wants to leave the kids there."

"Won't he be back soon then?"

"I doubt it. He has to deal with his grief. I think he'll leave the kids and go off by himself for a bit. He might winter with the Cheyennes, though he's likely to stay by himself somewhere for the winter."

"Sounds like someone else I know," Sanderson said with a knowing glance at LaPointe.

"You found out about that, eh?" LaPointe said in a monotone. He was not ashamed of having spent a winter holed up in the far mountains while he mourned Yellow Quiver and his two children. It was not something he enjoyed talking about either, though.

Sanderson nodded. "Rufe told me about it a while back. Come to think of it, Otis was there, too. Funny how things turn out."

"That's not so funny."

Sanderson looked at LaPointe, a little startled. Then he nodded. "You're right, Henri. I meant funny-odd, though." He rubbed a hand over his broad, tired face. "You think Otis'll be all right?"

LaPointe shrugged. "There's no way to tell. Otis is his own man. We all are. He's quiet usually and as strong a man as I've ever seen. Strong inside as well as on the outside. I've never seen him take something as hard as he's taking Pony Woman's death. But he'll get over it."

Sanderson nodded. "Let's hope so." He paused. "Well, since the flood of immigrants is about near an end, maybe we can get some work done on this damned place while you're gone."

"Would be nice," LaPointe said with a little grin.

Sanderson glared at him a moment, then returned the smile. "Yes, indeed."

* * *

As promised, LaPointe left the next morning with Morning Mist. Duffy also left, taking Two Feathers and his children, heading for Cheyenne country. LaPointe made it back to Fort Laramie first, since he had not had as far to go. Duffy pulled in late the next day.

Taking only one mule for their supplies, the two set out for Taos the morning after Duffy had returned to the fort. Just across the Laramie, they were joined by half a dozen Cheyennes and four Dakotas who felt like visiting the Southern Cheyennes for a bit down along the Arkansas.

As they had the last time, LaPointe and Duffy spent a few extra days in Taos, enjoying the hotly spiced food, the harsh Taos Lightning, the festival spirit of the place and the warm, willing companionship of dark, seductive *señoritas*.

They finally hired almost two dozen laborers and bought two wagons and teams. Just before dawn, they pulled out of Taos, the old wagons creaking and screeching in impudent protest.

Just across the Arkansas River, a band of Indians popped up on the horizon and charged down the grassy ridge. LaPointe and Duffy sat on their horses doing nothing but watching. Most of the laborers looked as if they would faint.

The Dakota and Northern Cheyennes—with a few Southern Cheyennes and Arapahos—circled the wagons. The warriors whooped and shouted. The two Mexicans driving the wagons were having the devil's own time keeping the mules from bolting at the noise, color and confusion.

Finally the Indians pulled to a stop and exchanged greetings with LaPointe and Duffy. All laughed at the consternation they had induced in the Mexicans. They camped where they were for the night. The Southern Cheyennes and the Arapahos headed toward their homes in the morning, while the others escorted the party of laborers.

Snow fell once or twice on the ride, but never more

han flurries. Still, LaPointe and Duffy knew winter was
not far off. So they pushed the laborers some, wanting
to make time, since they wanted to winter with their
Indian friends, and having to find the village in the dead
of winter would not be much fun.

The Indians broke off just before reaching the fort,
and headed east. LaPointe and Duffy left the
wagonloads of Mexicans at the fort and spent the night
in the fort. They were gone by the time the fort woke
the next morning. A few miles away, they met up with
the warriors again. Duffy and the six Cheyennes headed
west while LaPointe and the Dakotas went north and a
little east.

As usual, Morning Mist had her lodge set up and her
two children—Badger and Spirit Grass—living there
with her. It was the way of things and LaPointe accepted
it. Indeed, he had come to like the children. He had
even mentioned to Morning Mist the possibility of
bringing them to the fort to live with Morning Mist and
LaPointe. Morning Mist had not made up her mind
about that, though. Not yet. While she would like being
with her children, she was not happy with the thought of
having them in such proximity of so many white men.
She wanted her children to learn the old ways; the true
ways as she thought of them.

One thing that was a little different this time was the
fact that Morning Mist was pregnant. LaPointe saw it as
soon as he stepped into the lodge. His first thoughts
were of joy. Such feelings were quickly dampened by
anger; an anger bred of fear. He had lost Little Hunter
and Copper Kettle, his children with Yellow Quiver,
when the three were killed by the Crows. He was certain
he did not want to face that possibility again.

Morning Mist saw LaPointe's emotions on his face
and she grew worried. She had married Henri LaPointe
as a matter of convenience. She was a young widow with
two young children. She needed a man to care for her
and the children—even if the children were to spend
most of their time with aunts and uncles. Then LaPointe

had arrived. He was not an unpleasant man to look at, though his sometimes very hairy face was bothersome to Morning Mist. Still, Morning Mist knew she could have done a lot worse than marrying this broad-shouldered, leather-tough white man.

But in the two years since he had come into her life, Morning Mist had learned to care, indeed even love, LaPointe. Now she worried that she had somehow disappointed him by being pregnant. Perhaps, she thought, he didn't want any more children. Morning Mist knew what had happened to Yellow Quiver, Little Hunter and Copper Kettle. What she didn't know was if that had colored his vision of having more children. Morning Mist had not thought so, given LaPointe's liking of her children. Still, one could never be sure with such a man.

With one look at Morning Mist, LaPointe spun and stomped out of the lodge. He considered just mounting his horse and riding back to the fort, but then decided he was not angry enough to do that. All he really wanted was a little time to think this thing through some. He walked down to the river and sat on the bank, idly pitching pebbles into the water.

He wasn't sure how long he had been there, but he became aware of someone stealthily sneaking up on him. He smiled but did not let on that he knew. Suddenly there was a small shout and a rush.

LaPointe spun on his buttocks. Spreading his arms wide, he let loose a ferocious roar. Seven-year-old Badger and four-year-old Spirit Grass screeched and tumbled into LaPointe's arms. LaPointe fell lightly backward, pulling the two children with him and he began to tickle them, eliciting delighted shrieks.

Finally the children went scampering off. Still smiling, LaPointe looked up to see Morning Mist. She had stood watching for some minutes, delighting in seeing the play, but saddened, too, that LaPointe might not want his own children.

LaPointe stood. Still smiling he went to Morning Mist

and pulled her close to him. "I am 'appy we are to have a child. *Oui. Tres content.*"

Morning Mist was greatly relieved.

The winter was not nearly as harsh as the previous one had been, but LaPointe was still happy to see it pass. As the days began getting longer and warmer, he wondered how his two friends were, especially Otis Palmer. And with the thoughts came an eagerness to be on the trail heading toward the fort. He missed his two close friends, and would be happy to see them again.

The spring hunt took place a little earlier this year than most, as spring made an early debut. LaPointe took part in it, and then in the feasting afterward. It took him a couple of days to recover from the excesses. He growled at that, seeing it as a concession to age.

Then he prepared to leave the village. There was not really all that much to do. He had to make sure that Morning Mist had enough hides and such for clothing, and that they both had enough meat for the trip back to the fort. Mostly, though, he had to be certain that Spotted Horse, Morning Mist's brother, had enough food for the children. Not that Spotted Horse was a poor hunter—to the contrary, he was among the best hunters and warriors in the band. However, it was expected of LaPointe to provide for "his" children.

22

Duffy and Two Feathers were at the fort already, and LaPointe and Morning Mist pulled to a stop next to their lodge. Duffy wasn't around, though. LaPointe rode off, looking for Duffy and to see what was new and who was around. He left Morning Mist there to set up the lodge.

He had stopped in front of Major Sanderson's headquarters and started to dismount when a rough hand grabbed the back of his shirt and jerked him down. A low, gravelly voice said, "Hyar now, boy, what'n hell're you doing there with my goddamn horse?"

LaPointe felt his feet hit the ground. When they did, he yanked his left arm up and around to break the grip on his shirt. He reared back with a big right hand, ready to pulverize whoever had been foolish enough to try such a thing with him.

He stood there, fist hanging in the air looking into the broad, grinning face of old Blanket Chief Jim Bridger. "Why you crusty old reprobate," LaPointe said, laughing. He dropped his fist. "What're you doing here?"

"Come to see ol' Broken Hand."

"Fitzpatrick's here?"

"Yep. Playin' at Injun agent again."

"So what's he here about?"

"I'll let him tell you. I expect you're gonna be a goddamn part of it anyways."

"Where is he?"

"Hell if I know," Bridger said with a healthy laugh. Everything he did seemed bigger than life. "Last I seen that white-haired ol' son of a bitch he was runnin' 'round like that feller we seen that one time to rendezvous. You remember that fool sat on a nest of red ants and had them nasty little critters crawling all up and 'round his pecker."

"I remember," LaPointe said, joining Bridger in his laughter. "Did the best war dance this chil' ever saw anyway."

"That's the full truth," Bridger acknowledged. "Anyways, Broken Hand reminded me of that ol' hoss the way he was hoppin' and skippin' 'round." He paused. "How's about you and me go pull a cork and talk of the ol' times, eh?" His deep blue eyes were shining with merriment.

"*Bon,*" LaPointe said. "But I want to find Rufe. You seen him?"

Bridger nodded. "But not since yesterday."

"I also want to let Major Sanderson know I'm back."

"You still got that Dakota woman livin' with you, boy? Damn, now, what the hell was her name?"

"Yellow Quiver."

"Yep. That was it. A pert little thing she were, too." Bridger suddenly saw the look on LaPointe's face. "She's gone under, ol' hoss? That can't be so."

"Her and my two kids, too. Crow."

"Damn notional critters, them goddamn Crows. Can't trust 'em for nothin'." He paused. "Well, son, you got my sympathy. You got yourself another woman yet?"

LaPointe brightened a little. "Morning Mist. Another Brulé. She was widowed and has two kids of her own, plus we got one in the oven."

"Well, hot damn, you shinin' son of a bitch you. Well, you never was a one to delay in plantin' his seed if I was to recall right."

LaPointe laughed, his momentary sadness at remembering his wife and two children fleeing before the assault of Bridger's joviality. "There's some things a man shouldn't wait on, eh."

"Sure as shit."

"You still with that Snake woman? Washakie's daughter, wasn't she?"

"Yep. I call her Mary. She's the best woman I've married—so far." His eyes danced with humor.

"She here?"

"Nope," Bridger said with a firm shake of his head. "She might be a damn good woman, but I ain't of a mind to travel with her more'n necessary. I left her back there with her ol' man and the rest of the band. I'll be headin' back there soon, though."

"Well, let me go talk to the major a few minutes and then try to hunt up Rufe. I'll meet you over behind Dwight's blacksmith shop."

"Hyar now, boy, don't you delay or there'll not be enough awerdenty left to get a skeeter drunk." Bridger marched off, big, broad back straight.

LaPointe went up the few stairs. Private Moorhouse was there—he always seemed to be on duty outside Sanderson's door, and LaPointe sometimes wondered if the young man ever slept. Moorhouse didn't even announce him, he just opened the door. "Go on in, Mister LaPointe. The major's expectin' you."

"Henri," Sanderson said with real pleasure in his voice. "Welcome back."

"Good to be back, Major." He looked a little puzzled. "Kind of active around here these days, isn't it?"

"You could say that, yes. What the hell's going on? I saw Ol' Gabe out there and he tells me Broken Hand has something up his sleeve, but he won't tell me, no he don't."

"There are, as you and some of your friends have been heard to say, some big doin's going to be held here."

"Like what?"

"I'll let Tom tell you that."

"*Merde,*" LaPointe muttered. "First Ol' Gabe, he say

wait for Broken Hand, now you tell me the same thing. I'll be dead a year before somebody tells me just what the hell is happening here."

"Bullshit, Henri," Sanderson said pleasantly.

LaPointe grinned. "Where is Fitzpatrick?"

Sanderson shrugged. "Wandered off somewhere."

"I can wait till I talk to him, I suppose. Have you seen Rufe?"

"Earlier. I think he was heading for the sutler's."

LaPointe nodded. "Have you seen Otis?"

"No. No, I haven't." Sanderson looked concerned. "Are you worried about him?"

"Mais non. I was just wondering. He'll be back soon, I figure."

"You think he's been all right out there for the winter?"

"I hope so. But no one can say for certain. You know how it is out there. Maybe not as much as men like me, but you know how man can die out there in a t'ousand ways. Otis is well equipped to survive out there. We all are in our own ways, but that can't stop an act of God or a big party of Blackfoot." He paused. "Now you 'ave made me gloomy."

"Christ, knowing you, you'll be laughing your ass off at nothing ten minutes from now."

LaPointe grinned. "That is true." Still grinning, he said, "It doesn't look like much was accomplished here since I was gone."

"No, dammit all, we have not finished much. Still, many of the barracks are done, and other buildings're in progress. Once we get past this coming summer, we ought to be able to pick up the pace."

LaPointe laughed. "I think you've lost your head, Major."

"That might well be so, Henri," Sanderson said, also laughing. "I sometimes doubt my own sanity."

"Well, Major, I better be going. I promised to meet Ol' Gabe over at Dwight's. If you see Rufe, you tell him me and Bridger are there."

Not only did LaPointe find Bridger next to Dwight Eaton's blacksmith shop, he also found Rufus Duffy and Tom Fitzpatrick. "Goddamn," LaPointe said, "this's like the old days."

"Shit," Fitzpatrick said, "we're all a hundred goddamn years older'n we were back then." The brogue was still obvious, though Fitzpatrick had left his native Ireland thirty years or so ago. He had headed west with General Ashley's men back in '23 and within a few years had—along with men like Bridger, Jed Smith, Bill Sublette and others—become an owner of a fur company. Over the years, he had become one of the most well respected of the mountain men. When the fur trade had died, he became a guide for both military and civilian parties. And now, in the late spring of 1851, he had been the Indian agent for the tribes of the upper Platte and Arkansas rivers for five years.

"Speak for yourself, you old fart," Bridger said. Fitzpatrick was the oldest of the four men, beating even Bridger by five years.

"*Oui,*" LaPointe threw in with reckless abandon. "You might be so old to not be able to do more than sit on a porch somewhere sucking on your ol' pipe."

Fitzpatrick laughed. "Damn, you boys're right. It is like old times. You two windbags sitting there on your fat asses making pusillanimous noises."

"You're a fine one to accuse people of such things," Duffy chortled. "You who can't do shit so you flap your goddamn gums all the day and night."

"Jesus, you're all windbags," LaPointe said in mock offense. "Now pass me that jug before it all evaporates."

After the jug had made a few rounds, and the men were comfortable, smoking pipes, lolling on the still-cold ground, LaPointe asked, "So what's this big doin's you have planned, Tom? Ol' Gabe tells me to ask you. Major Sanderson tells me to ask you. I am the only one in the whole damned country who doesn't know why you're here."

Fitzpatrick grinned. Then he grew serious. "It'll be

the biggest goddamn doin's ever been seen west of Saint Louis.''

"This is sounding suspiciously like one of our old mountain yarns, Tom," LaPointe said cautiously.

"It seems like it's a yarn. Makes it hard to believe it even myself."

"Well, then, what the hell is it?" LaPointe asked in exasperation.

"The president wants to make peace with the Indians. All of 'em in my purview anyway. So we are going to have us one big, whoppin', whizbang of a parley. I aim to bring together the Dakota, Cheyenne, Arapaho, Snake and Crow and have us a peace parley."

"You're out of your goddamn mind," LaPointe said, astounded. *"Vous êtes fou. Tres, tres fou."* He made a small circle around his temple with his right index finger.

The others, except for Fitzpatrick, laughed. Fitzpatrick started smoking with anger. "Goddammit, quit laughin'. I'm serious about this."

"You can't be serious about somethin' so goddamn loony, Tom," Duffy said, still chuckling.

"As much as I hate to say this, dammit, I'll need you boys."

"What'n hell for?" Bridger asked. Between the drink he was trying to take and the laughter that was still percolating in him, Bridger spilled whiskey all over the front of his shirt.

"Jesus, Gabe," LaPointe said, sounding horrified, "don't waste it." He grabbed the jug. Or rescued it, as he saw it.

"I need you pusillanimous bastards to help me bring it together."

"The only goddamn thing you're gonna have here," Bridger said, "is a shinin' goddamn massa-cree."

"He's right, Tom," LaPointe said. "You know goddamn well you can't have Dakotas and Crows in the same country let alone sitting together at the same council."

"It'll be a bloodbath," Duffy added. "The Platte'll run red for miles."

"Those things'll happen for sure if you boys don't help," Fitzpatrick said. He paused for a long swig of whiskey. When he passed the jug on, he continued. "If the Indians're going to survive, there must be peace among them. And peace with the immigrants. If not, there will be a real bloodbath."

"Jesus, Tom," Bridger griped, "you sure know how to put a damper on a goddamn good time."

LaPointe sighed. "I still think you're crazy, Tom, but if I can help, I will. It won't hurt to try it."

"Like hell it won't," Duffy tossed in. "Just the idea of gettin' all those enemies together in one spot is enough to have the whole area go up in flames."

Fitzpatrick pointed the mangled hand that had given him his nickname at Duffy. "If you're afraid, Rufe, just own up to it. I'll find someone else who can help me."

"Goddammit, Tom, I've killed men for sayin' such things." His eyes were hot with anger.

But Tom Fitzpatrick was not a man to back down from anyone. "I've said my piece, Rufe. Now you either join up with me or head on."

"If you weren't such an earnest son of a bitch, I'd gut you here and now," Duffy said with a small grin. "I'm in."

23

Morning Mist stoically began taking down her lodge. It had only been up three days at Fort Laramie, but LaPointe had told her that they must leave. Today. So with Two Feathers' help she took down the lodge, and then she helped Two Feathers with her tipi. Both women would've thought their men crazy, except that they knew as well as anyone in the fort what was up. And they knew that their men were to have an important place in the big parley to be held here at the white man's fort just before the summer would flee.

LaPointe was saddling his horse—that mottle-colored beast with the thick mane and thick tail—nearby. Next to him were Duffy and Palmer.

The latter had returned to the fort the night before last, slipping into LaPointe's lodge as quietly as death. Or so he had thought. LaPointe woke and rolled partly out of his buffalo robe, a pistol in hand. "You ought not to make so much noise, eh, you with those goddamn big feet of yours."

"I didn't mean to wake you," Palmer said softly, lamely.

"With you making all that noise, how could I not wake, eh. There are robes over there."

"*Merci, amigo,*" Palmer muttered, not thinking it odd that he had mixed two languages, neither of which was his own first tongue. He slumped into the robes, broke wind and then sighed in relief and was asleep in seconds.

The next morning, as they sat at LaPointe's fire, LaPointe asked, "So, how're you doing, old hoss?"

"I been better." He tore off a piece of buffalo meat and chewed noisily. "Then, again," he added with a small smile, "I been a hell of a lot worse, too."

"You find yourself a new woman yet? It's not good for a man to not have a woman."

"Damn but I know that," Palmer said as he spit out a piece of gristle. "I was aimin' to head for Gray Eagle's village, see if there was some nubile young thing fool enough to let herself be led astray by an ol' coon like me. Then I caught wind that there was gonna be some goddamn big doin's down here. So's I rode on this way instead. I figured I could always go back to Gray Eagle's before fall and try to snare me one of them Cheyenne squaws."

"Sounds reasonable enough."

"So what's the big doin's? I see folks runnin' around like they're holdin' their asses tryin' to find a place to shit. But I ain't seen nothin' to say big goin' on."

LaPointe laughed. He carved off another chunk of buffalo meat and tossed it to Palmer. "Broken Hand's fixing to have himself a whizbang of a parley."

"That don't sound like big doin's to this chil'."

LaPointe grinned widely. "He aims to have the Dakota, Cheyenne and Arapaho here—plus the Snakes and Crows."

Palmer stopped with a piece of meat dangling from the tip of a knife several inches from his gaping mouth. Finally he shut his mouth, licked his lips, and then said, "He's gone *loco*. That run-in with the Blackfeet that time there back in '30, '31, must've done more to his head than just turn his hair white all to a sudden."

"That's what I told him. Rufe, too. And Ol' Gabe. Damn fool's not listening, though. He's got his head and his heart all set on it, and thinks he can have all the tribes make peace."

"Idiotic notion."

"I'm not so sure, Otis," LaPointe said thoughtfully. "I don't think it'll ever come to pass, but I can understand the need for it."

"And what's that?" The piece of meat finally made it into Palmer's mouth.

"Well, think about it some." LaPointe paused for a sip of coffee. "Look how many goddamn people are coming up the trail every year."

"All immigrants."

"All immigrants *now*. How long do you think they'll stay that way, eh? Sooner or later, some'll take a look around here or over by the Laramie Mountains or the Black Hills and decide they've gone far enough."

"The Indians'll drive 'em out."

"*Oui*. At first. How long do you think the government'll allow that? A month? A year? A decade? Certainly no more."

Palmer considered that for a bit. Then he nodded. "The Dakotas and Cheyennes, even the Crows'll end up like the Osage and Kickapoos and all the others."

"*Oui*," LaPointe said sadly. He could not help it. Whenever he thought about it, he turned sad.

"Sure's a gloomy outlook."

"*Oui*."

"But how's makin' peace with the Snakes and Crows gonna help the Cheyennes and the Dakotas?"

"Well, I figure that if Broken Hand can do what he aims to, the immigrants'll have no reason to stop here or to bother the Indians. If they're let through with no trouble, they won't be interested in killing Indians."

"Wishful thinkin', I'd be sayin'."

LaPointe shrugged. "I think most of the immigrants just want to get to California or Oregon. They don't want any troubles. They have enough troubles with cholera, accidents, snakebites, all kinds of shit. They don't want to run into any Indians."

"Reckon you're right about that." Palmer slopped more coffee into his tin mug and sipped some.

"It might help our friends in other ways, too."

"Like what?" Palmer was interested despite himself.

"Well, if he can get our friends and our enemies to agree to peace, they won't be killing each other anymore."

"So?"

"So, they might even be able to fight together."

"Fight who?" Palmer said. Then his eyebrows lifted in realization. "The ol' devil white-eyes."

"Oui. Sooner or later it'll come to that."

Palmer nodded glumly. "I just hope I'm long gone under when that comes to pass, dammit." He sighed. "But I don't reckon there's much chance the Cheyennes and the Crows'll make peace."

"The Cheyennes did it with the Comanches and Kiowas down south. Ol' Bill Bent made them shine, he did. Maybe Broken Hand can do the same up here."

"I wouldn't bet nothin' I didn't hate on it," Palmer said flatly. "I'd rather fuck a goose than try'n get the Crows and Dakotas to agree not to kill each other."

LaPointe nodded. He had had a sudden burst of anger and did not want to let it develop into anything substantial. But it was hard for him to control himself whenever the Crows were mentioned. He had never gotten along with them too badly, but he and they had had a few run-ins. His longtime standoffishness with those Indians turned to unadulterated hate after the Crows had killed Yellow Quiver, Little Hunter and Copper Kettle. He decided he would try to keep his distance as much as possible when the big parley took place.

Duffy lurched up and squatted, rubbing his hands against the morning chill. Without saying anything, LaPointe poured a cup of coffee and handed it to Duffy, who nodded gratefully.

"Jesus H. Goddamn Christ Almighty, Rufe," Palmer said in an exaggerated, loud voice, "you look like you was shit through a buffler and then pissed on by a wanderin' bear." He laughed raucously.

Duffy winced and he held the coffee cup tightly in both hands to keep from shaking.

"Goddamn, Henri, you ever see such a miserable lookin' critter?" Palmer was still laughing, knowing that each loud, deep chuckle was pounding on Duffy's head like a blacksmith's hammer on an anvil. "Jesus, I've seen maggot-infested buffler carcasses looked livelier than he is." He hooted.

LaPointe fought down the sweeping gale of laughter he could feel building up. He had been as hungover as Duffy was now. So had Palmer. And both had taken the rough, painful ribbing that Duffy was receiving.

Palmer stretched out his legs and yawned. "Ya know what, Henri," he said. It sounded innocent enough, but LaPointe could see the light of impishness in Palmer's eyes. "I could do with a heapin' pile of boudins. You know them ones I mean. About five feet of prime buffler intestine with the contents unsullied by anything other'n what nature put there her own self. Maybe a splash of gall on the outside to make 'em slide down the gullet nice and easy. Maybe . . ."

Duffy jumped up and bolted.

"Hey, Rufe, where'n hell're you goin'?" Palmer roared with laughter, big, thick gales that rumbled and shook.

LaPointe laughed hard, too, wiping away the tears of joy, as he watched Duffy, who was on hands and knees puking his guts out. He was still over there a few minutes later when LaPointe stood. "Come on, Otis, we'll go find Broken Hand and see if he can't put you to some goddamn use."

They found Fitzpatrick scribbling on papers at an old, small wood table in a cramped corner of a crowded room at the old fort. The white-haired Irishman tossed his pen down and leaned back. The white hair was the legacy of a frightening run from a pack of Blackfoot a long time ago. Men said that the episode had turned Fitzpatrick's hair white overnight. "Otis, Henri," he said tiredly. "Come on in and take a seat—if you can find one." He absentmindedly rubbed his broken hand, the result of a bursting gun barrel.

"I hear tell you got some cockamamie idea of gettin' all the Indians in the world to sit down to parley," Palmer said after he and LaPointe had found a couple of rickety chairs and perched gingerly on them.

"I've got such an idea, aye," Fitzpatrick said testily.

"Well, I don't condone such foolishness, you understand, but if you're goddamn crazy enough to try it, I'm just crazy enough to lend a hand. What can I do?"

Fitzpatrick thought for a few moments. "You feel like invitin' the Arapahos?"

"Reckon so."

"Good. Henri and Rufe're goin' out to talk to the Dakotas and the Cheyennes. You can handle the Arapahos. I got Ol' Gabe to deal with the Snakes. There's several boys I can send to talk to the Crows. Or I might even do it myself. That'll about do it."

Palmer shrugged. "When you want me to leave?"

"Henri, when're you and Rufe headin' out?"

"Tomorrow."

"That suit you, Otis?"

"Reckon it wouldn't put me out none."

"Good. Major Sanderson said you boys were to outfit yourselves from his supplies. Anyone tries to give you a hard time, come see me or Win."

"That ain't gonna be necessary," Palmer said flatly.

"No, I expect it won't," Fitzpatrick said with a laugh. "Come see me after supper. I'll give you the particulars."

"Ooh," Palmer mouthed mockingly, "the particulars. Well, ain't we gone high and goddamn mighty with our job as goddamn big chief Indian agent."

"Don't let this white hair fool you, bucko," Fitzpatrick said coldly, his icy blue eyes steady on Palmer's. "I can still knock you on your ass."

"Come on ahead and try," Palmer retorted.

"Jesus, you two," LaPointe said, stepping between

them. "You're worse than a couple of indulged children. I expect such behavior from you, Otis. But you, Tom, you *are* a big chief. You should act like it, eh."

The two men continued glaring at each other. LaPointe, still in the middle, looked from one to the other. Then he broke wind, quite loudly.

A moment later, Palmer's nose twitched. "Jesus, Frenchie," he complained, wrinkling his nose. "What the hell've you been eatin', dead skunks? Christ, you're disgustin'."

Fitzpatrick broke and began to laugh, all the while waving a hand in front of him as if trying to ward off something evil. "You mark my words, Otis," he said, moving back a few paces, "you come back here some time ten years from now, and I'll bet you a thousand dollars there ain't nothing growin' on this spot."

"I ain't takin' that bet. Nosiree."

"Now that you are fighting nicely," LaPointe said, trying to sound officious despite his laughter, "shake hands and then figure out what needs to be done, eh."

Palmer did not hesitate. He stuck out one of his big paws. "You ought to know by now, Tom, that I'm a chil' with a preponderance of mouth and a shortage of brains sometimes."

Fitzpatrick shook his friend's hand. "Hell, after spendin' so much time with those officious bastards out east, I tend to start actin' like 'em. It's a tough thing to shake, I'm thinkin'."

Palmer and LaPointe headed off to LaPointe's lodge. That night, they and Duffy met with Fitzpatrick in the large cabin tent he had had set up next to the officers' quarters. Duffy was doing somewhat better, and managed to stay awake and relatively hale.

LaPointe felt enthused about the plan as he headed to bed that night. He still thought the plan an impossibility, but he was glad to see that someone was taking the effort.

As he and his two friends walked back to the lodges,

they noticed that the wagon train that had pulled into the area that afternoon was still trying to sort itself out. LaPointe wondered what possessed people to make them travel in such a way.

24

"Maybe I'll get me a 'Rapaho woman instead,'' Palmer said as he pulled himself into the saddle. "Hell, a 'Rapaho woman's damn near as good as a Cheyenne.''

"We best get word to ol' Bloody Knife to lock up his daughters with that ol' reprobate gonna be around,'' Duffy said with a laugh.

"Watch your topknot, boys,'' Palmer said. He touched heels to horse and moved out slowly. His rifle rested across the saddle in front of him, a mule with some supplies trailed him.

"Come on, Henri,'' Duffy said impatiently.

"Hold your damn water.'' LaPointe climbed onto his horse, and the small group left. Besides LaPointe and Duffy, there were Morning Mist, Two Feathers and two of her three children—Many Arrows, a nine-year-old boy; and Fox, a six-year-old girl; the third was the oldest, and he was living with his mother's people. Both children were old enough now to have their own ponies. The group also had three pack animals.

The day was chilly, with batches of gray clouds patching the sky. Rain did not seem imminent, but the humidity was up, the temperature down and a good, stiff wind blowing in from the west.

The group moved at a leisurely pace. They were in no hurry, really. LaPointe led the way, with Morning Mist, one of the pack animals, then Duffy's two children, Two Feathers and the other two pack animals. Duffy brought up the rear, more out of habit than necessity. Out here they could ride abreast if they wanted. But their years of traveling over small trails through mountainous terrain had given them some habits they saw no need to change now.

LaPointe was contemplating a noon stop when he heard a screech from behind him. He started to turn in the saddle, but stopped when the crack of a rifle reached him. With rifle in hand, he slid off his horse on the left—the west, since the gunshot had come from the east. "Get down!" he yelled. He hurriedly repeated the command in Dakota and in Cheyenne.

One glance told him that Duffy was down. Since his friend was not moving, LaPointe figured him to be dead already. He was worried. If he faced a Crow or Arikara war party, he would be in dire straits. Within moments, though, he decided that there was no war party out there. Probably not even a lone Indian. Indians would have wanted to count coup, steal the horses and most likely steal the women, too. Even a warrior by himself would have used all his skills to creep up on the small party unseen before wreaking his havoc. No, LaPointe was quite sure he was facing a white man—or men. If there were only one, he was not too worried. More than that, though, would mean he was also in a bad spot.

Another shot rang out, and little Fox's pony went down, almost falling on the child.

Moving fast, LaPointe grabbed the girl and threw her up on his own horse. He whirled. "Morning Mist, you and Two Feathers get ze kids out of here. Ride. Quickly! To ze west. *Vite! Vite!*"

"The supplies?" Morning Mist asked calmly.

"Take zem. Ride for the fort."

"And you?"

"I have t'ings to do here. Now go."

The two women and two children turned and raced toward the west. Another shot came and LaPointe watched over his shoulder a moment, heart pounding. But no one had been hit. By the time the man reloaded,

LaPointe figured the women and children would be out of range.

LaPointe dropped onto the ground as something kicked up dirt nearby, followed a moment later by the report of the rifle. LaPointe slithered toward Duffy and Duffy's fallen horse.

Duffy was alive, which was a relief to LaPointe. "How're you doing, *mon ami?*" LaPointe asked.

LaPointe's relief turned to horror, when Duffy responded, "I can't move."

"Not at all?"

"Just my head a little. I'm numb from the neck down. Can't feel nothin', can't move nothin'." He did not sound particularly upset. He was more amazed than anything else. "I think my neck's broke somehow."

"Christ," LaPointe muttered. "I got to get you over zere by your horse. Zen you'll be out of ze line of fire."

"No!" Duffy hissed. "I'm gone under, old friend. I'm just as dead as that goddamn horse over yonder. You movin' me ain't gonna do me a goddamn bit of good and I expect it'll hurt like a son of a bitch. Besides, I'm bleedin' heavy, and that'll kill me soon enough if nothin' else does."

LaPointe didn't like it, but he knew Duffy was right. "Anything I can do for you?" he asked, bitter at his feeling of helplessness.

"Get the son of a bitch who put me under."

"*Oui, mon ami.* I will get ze bastard." He slid over to Duffy's horse and placed his rifle across the animal's flank and waited. Ten minutes later, he was uncomfortable and annoyed. The ground was cold under him, and the sun was hot above him. He was thirsty and angry, and he knew Duffy was suffering. No more shots had been fired.

Finally LaPointe realized that whoever was out there —if he even was still there—had no more targets to shoot at. Duffy had not moved and from a distance it would seem that he was dead. Everyone else had fled.

"Rufe?" LaPointe called quietly. "Rufe? You still here?"

There was no answer. Knowing what he would find, but knowing he had to make sure, LaPointe looked back over his shoulder. There was no sign of movement from Duffy; not even a faint rising and falling of the chest from breathing. *"Merde,"* LaPointe cursed. A moment later he forced himself to relax. His hands had been white-knuckled on the stock of his rifle. Then he made a decision.

He slowly rose and placed his right foot on the horse. He rested his rifle on the ground, braced against the bent leg. He crossed his arms across his chest.

"Hey, Monsieur Chickenshit!" he bellowed angrily. "You 'ave killed a good man. My great *ami.* Come, show yourself." He waited, eyes scanning the horizon. He saw no movement.

"Now look, *monsieur,"* he went on. "I know you 'ave a big puddle of duck shit where your brains should be. And you 'ave no *bijoux de famille.* I know zis. And you know zis. Still, a real man would show himself rather than hide out lying in buffalo shit and buffalo piss."

He waited again. Just as he was about to begin another spiel, he caught a small movement. He braced himself and waited a little longer. He saw a puff of gunsmoke, and he jerked his torso to the left.

It wasn't good enough. A trail of fire burned across his right side just under the ribs. It added to the impetus and knocked him down. He landed hard on the horse's shoulder bone, and then he rolled off onto his back, grateful that he had done so away from the gunman. Had he landed in front of the horse, the gunman might've shot him a couple more times just to make sure he was dead.

He looked down at his side. It was bleeding, but not too badly. He probed the wound and found out that despite the fiery feeling the wound wasn't serious. The bullet had just creased his side and had not really entered his midsection. No ribs had been broken, and so he figured he would be fine. His other side hurt a little from the hard landing, and he figured it would be discolored by morning, but it should not slow him down.

He lay awhile in the warm sun, letting his anger build until it ran through his veins just like his blood. Encouraging his rage were the buzzards that had come to make long swooping circles, the warm updrafts enticing them with the smell of death on the ground.

After about an hour, as best he could judge, LaPointe peered ever so cautiously over the dead horse. He saw no one, which he figured was a good sign in some ways. On the other hand, if whoever was out there was walking toward him, he could drop the man in a second.

But that was not the case, so LaPointe rolled cautiously over onto his stomach. *"Merde,"* he mumbled as he realized how uncomfortable he was with the two Walker six-guns in his belt now digging into his stomach. So over on his back he went again. He pulled the pistols out and set them aside. Once more he rolled. On his stomach again, he grabbed the pistols and shoved them into the belt at the small of his back.

He hoped the buzzards would leave Duffy's body alone for a while yet. He would hate to see the foul birds pecking over his flesh. If they did, though, LaPointe would not be able to do anything to send them away. Not if he wanted to retain any element of surprise against the unknown—and as yet unseen—opponent.

He began to crawl, never lifting his body more than necessary to scrape along on the rough, winter-damaged grass that was just really beginning to show signs of life. He crawled toward a coulee a little southwest of where he had started. It took him almost three-quarters of an hour, but he made it. Occasionally he had stopped and looked east, still hoping that the gunman would show himself. Whoever he was out there, he was a cagey bastard, LaPointe thought. That served to keep his anger a-boil.

LaPointe followed the coulee southwest for a bit, then crawled up and out of it. Over the next two hours or so,

LaPointe crawled and wriggled from one slight dip in the plains to another, from coulee to buffalo wallow and to another coulee. He worked south, then angled more easterly. Finally he began crawling north.

The effort was tiring and uncomfortable, but La-Pointe let his anger keep him going. Just as he thought he was making some real progress, he came to a swift halt as he stared at a hissing prairie rattlesnake. The reptile's head hung in the air as its rattle buzzed.

Sweat drizzled down LaPointe's nose as he said a silent prayer that the snake would not strike. At the same time, though, he gently laid down his rifle, and then eased out a pistol in his left hand and his big, wood-handled knife in his right. He would rather dispatch the snake—if it came to that—with the knife. A gunshot now would destroy his secrecy. On the other hand, he did not intend to get bitten by this dangerous reptile.

Afraid to move backward lest inciting the snake to strike, he lay where he was. After a tense standoff that seemed to drag on and on, the snake settled down and then slithered off through the short grass. LaPointe heaved a great sigh of relief. He put the pistol and knife away, and took up his rifle, ready to proceed.

Another rattler slinked into view. *"Sacre bleu,"* he breathed, anger getting the better of him for a moment. He set the rifle down again. Knowing he had to take the risk, he half rolled until he came up on his buttocks, sitting. He realized with some relief that he was several inches short of the top of the coulee, and he would not be seen unless he did something too crazy.

This snake, however, was not of the same mind of the previous one. With virtually no warning, the reptile struck.

"Merde," LaPointe breathed. Almost by instinct he swung his rifle and hit the rattler. The snake flew to the other side of the narrow coulee, hit the bank and began to slide down. Knowing this was going to be about his only chance, LaPointe dropped his rifle and dove toward the reptile.

He managed to get his left hand on the snake about two inches behind the head. The snake buzzed and writhed wildly. Though the rattler was not the biggest LaPointe had ever seen it was putting up one hell of a fight.

LaPointe eased up onto one knee. He bent and put the snake's head on the ground. Still holding the rattler in his left hand, he placed a boot on the thing's head, sort of flattening it, enough anyway that the snake could not bite him through the boot.

Breathing heavily and sweating buckets, he pulled his knife. Carefully maneuvering the blade between hand and foot, he quickly sliced the snake's head off. He threw the body as far as he could, then applied as much pressure as he could without standing, ground the snake's head into the earth.

He almost leaped backward, sort of half-fearing that the snake's head would have a life of its own and continue to try biting him. The thing was still moving a little but posed no danger.

"Damn devilish critters," he mumbled. He took a few moments to rest, then picked up his rifle and began anew on his long, serpentine undulations. He saw nothing humorous about it.

He was quite a ways east of where the gunman had been so long ago, it seemed now. LaPointe went north, moving a little faster. He slowed again when he got within what he thought was hearing distance of the gunman. He inched up the side of a buffalo wallow, saw nothing, went down into the dip and then back up the other side.

A frightening smile crept across LaPointe's lips. He set his rifle down and eased one of his pistols out. He could feel the excitement surge through him. Vengeance would indeed be sweet, and he quite enjoyed that idea. But then he remembered what had brought about the need for vengeance—Rufus Duffy's death. The excitement changed to rage.

LaPointe rose and stood on the elevated bank of the coulee, looking down at a man prone on the ground, facing where Duffy's body lay. *"Bonjour,"* LaPointe said in tight, deadly tones.

[25]

The man started to roll, bringing his rifle with him. He didn't get very far before LaPointe put a bullet into the back of his left thigh. The man yelped, and then rocked back to his former position.

"Keep both your hands in sight and turn around," LaPointe said harshly.

"I can't move so well with that bullet in my leg."

"You don't do just what the hell I tell you, I'll put a bullet in the other leg. Or maybe straight through your fat ass."

"Don't go gettin' nervous, mister," the man said. He held his hands out, but then moved them in to push himself over. As he came around, his right hand slid inside his shirt. By the time he landed on his buttocks, he had the hand out of the shirt. And in it was a small percussion pistol.

LaPointe gasped when he saw the eye patch, but he did not hesitate. He fired once, hitting the man in the right arm just above the elbow. The man screeched and the pistol fell.

It was hard to tell who was more surprised, Gaylord Kincaid or Henri LaPointe.

"What the hell're you doing here, Kincaid?" LaPointe asked. He was almost trembling in his desire to kill this man.

"Takin' potshots at assholes," Kincaid said arrogantly.

LaPointe let that pass, but he remembered it. "I thought you and Hanson would have been in ze gold camps of California."

"That was the plan."

"What happened?" LaPointe was not really interested, other than in the possibility of getting some information he might be able to use later. Besides, he had no intention of killing Kincaid quickly.

"We had figured on stayin' in that damn cave till spring, then hookin' on with whatever wagon train we saw come along. But then you and those other bastards come along and rooted us out early. Since it was nigh onto winter already, there was no way in hell we were gonna make California." He shifted a little, and tried to staunch the flow of blood from his leg with a bandanna.

"We rubbed out a couple Indians and took their horses and headed east." He smiled, relishing the way he and his friend Gil Hanson had fooled everyone. "We figured that if that idiot Sanderson had sent out others lookin' for us, they'd all be lookin' west.

"It was full winter when we got to Independence, and jobs were hard to come by. We decided when spring came that we'd rather head west in some style. Hell, livin' in Independence wasn't all that bad, either. So we spent the year there. Came out with a wagon train this year. As hunters and guides no less." He chuckled, but it was choked off by the pain of his wounds.

"Where's Hanson?"

"Hell, I've talked enough, old man. What about you? What're you doin' out here?"

"Heading for Painted Bull's village."

"That ain't what I meant."

It took LaPointe a moment to puzzle it out. "Oh, yes, now I remember. You and your asshole partners left me for dead. Rufe managed to get me back to Fort Laramie."

"Was that him I picked off out there?" Kincaid seemed not so much to be asking arrogantly as he was just plain interested.

"Oui," LaPointe said, a new wave of rage enveloping him.

Kincaid nodded. He seemed to be tiring some as his blood seeped out of the two wounds.

"You didn't know?" LaPointe asked, surprised.

Kincaid shook his head. "Nope. I was hopin' though."

"You mean you gunned a man down just on the chance it might be me or one of my friends?" LaPointe was almost incredulous.

"Hell, I figured you were dead and gone. Still, any son of a bitch I come by out here travelin' with a squaw and a couple of squallin' half-breed brats couldn't be all good. I was figurin' there might be a good chance it was your two pals."

"Where's Hanson?" LaPointe asked again.

Kincaid shrugged. "I don't know as if I'll tell. Hell, what makes you think I know anyway?"

"Any couple of men who have their noses stuck up each other's asses the way you two did aren't going to go their separate ways voluntarily."

"You're a fuckin' fine one to talk. Christ, you and them other two assholes been livin' together in close proximity—*real* close proximity, I'd say—for years."

"That doesn't answer my question."

"My heart bleeds for you."

LaPointe took a few steps and kicked Kincaid in the chest, right over the heart.

Kincaid gasped and jerked, which sent spasms of pain through his wounded arm and wounded leg. Pain seemed to be all over him, and there was no escape from it. If he moved one way, the arm hurt, another and the leg snapped with agony, still another and his chest would feel as if it were on fire.

"Where's Hanson?" LaPointe asked again. His voice was even colder now than it had been.

"Fort Laramie," Kincaid gasped.

"Tell me," LaPointe commanded.

Kincaid considered refusing, but he decided that he

was in quite enough pain. He was sure he was going to die, and knowing that, he wanted to make sure the death came as quickly and as painlessly as possible. If that meant talking, he would talk.

"I'm waiting," LaPointe said by way of warning.

"Like I said, we headed out for California with a wagon train. We knew the day before yesterday that we'd be at Fort Laramie soon, so Gil sent me off. He told the wagon folks I was off scoutin' a new trail or somethin'."

"Why?" LaPointe was a little confused.

"Hell, I couldn't walk back into the fort. Everybody there'd know me." He lightly touched the eye patch with a finger. "No thanks to you." His voice had suddenly turned bitter.

LaPointe was nonplussed. "And Hanson went to the fort?" He could not believe someone would do something so foolish.

"Sure did. Gutsy little bastard. He had all you peckerwoods fooled into thinkin' he was just some dumb farm boy. Damn, pulled the wool over your eyes but goddamn good."

"He doesn't think he'll be found out at the fort?"

"There's always a chance. But we found before we parted ways with the army that the only ones who look at you good are your immediate cronies. Mess mates and such. Officers and all those hoity-toity bastards don't take no notice. Not even during a court-martial. Gil looks a mite different than he did last time you saw him."

"Different? How?"

"Grew himself a beard and put on twenty pounds or so. I'd bet good money there ain't a one at Fort Laramie'd know it was him. And if, by some chance someone does figure out who it is, it'll probably be one of the poor bastards like us who want to take off. Such men ain't gonna let on. Besides, he wanted to press his luck a little. Almost like he wanted to dare Sanderson to find out about him and try to do something about it."

"Had it all figured out, didn't you?" LaPointe still

burned for revenge, but in some way he did not feel like himself. He seemed to be a disembodied spirit floating above, watching himself standing coolly and calmly there discussing duplicity, treason and murder with Kincaid as if they were simply jawing about the weather.

"Sure did. I swung up this way and was gonna head west tomorrow. Me and Gil figured I could meet the wagons up around Mexican Hill."

"You're going to miss zat rendezvous, boy."

"Looks like. Still, I ain't dead yet."

"You will be soon enough." There was no doubt that he meant the words.

"Then I suppose you'll try'n go after Gil, huh?"

"I'll go after him, yes. And he will meet ze same fate as you. Be sure of zat."

"To get to Gil, you're gonna have to go through Ox Mobrey."

"Who or what is an Ox Mobrey?"

"Friend we made down in Independence. His real name's Gus Mobrey. Folks call him Ox 'cause he's as big and strong as an ox."

"About as stupid as one, too, eh?"

"What makes you think that?"

"If he's thrown in with you and Hanson, he's got to be one of ze stupidest bastards to walk on two legs."

Kincaid couldn't help but grin. He was weak, but the pain had lessened some. He assumed it was because he was losing feeling in his limbs.

"Tell me more about zis Ox."

"Not much to tell. Like you figured, he's as dumb as a ox. But he's loyal to Gil. Real loyal. So loyal that he'd be more'n happy to tear off your head and then use your neck for a spittoon if Gil tells him to."

"Sounds like a prince among men," LaPointe said sarcastically. "I take it he is ze biggest person along with ze wagon train?"

Kincaid nodded weakly. "Ain't many livin' things bigger'n Ox Mobrey, 'cept for maybe an ox." He tried to laugh at his witticism, but the effort fizzled. "There ain't many things I'm sorry to have missed out on, but seein' Ox rip you to shreds is one of 'em. Damn, I sure will miss it." His voice was faint.

LaPointe half suspected Kincaid was faking being so weak. LaPointe thought that Kincaid might think that he would come up close to see how Kincaid was doing, and then be vulnerable. LaPointe could shoot Kincaid dead here and now, but that did not strike him as satisfactory. No, the man who had killed Rufus Duffy deserved something more horrible than a simple bullet in the brain.

LaPointe pondered the dilemma for a little. He was in no hurry, and Kincaid certainly wasn't going anywhere. Not now, not ever. Then an idea was born, and he gave it some moments to grow, until he figured it was worthy of attention.

"Where's your horse?" LaPointe suddenly asked. He had just realized that Kincaid must have a horse around somewhere. Hanson wouldn't be so thoughtless as to let his good friend walk several days on foot through hostile Indian territory.

"Back up over that way a bit," Kincaid said with a jerk of his head.

LaPointe nodded. He stepped forward warily, though he was fairly certain that Kincaid posed no danger to him now. He picked up the small pocket pistol and fired it into the dirt an inch from Kincaid's head. Then he picked up Kincaid's rifle and pitched it.

"Strip," LaPointe ordered.

"No." Kincaid looked adamant. "There's nothin' you can do to me that'll make me do that."

"Yes there is," LaPointe said flatly.

Kincaid believed him, and he shuddered with fear a little. He tugged his shirt over his head, groaning with the pain as his wounded arm kept getting jostled. Removing one boot was easy, but the other was torture. He finally managed though. He unbuttoned his pants and gingerly stood. His pants fell around his ankles, and he sat again, to pull them the last few inches off.

"I didn't know you were that kind of man," Kincaid said sarcastically.

"If I was, you sure as hell wouldn't be ze one I would pick. Head for your horse."

Kincaid limped off, holding his right arm as tightly against the body as he could with his left hand. When LaPointe saw the horse, he ordered Kincaid to stop. LaPointe slid his pistol away, mounted the horse, and then pointed his rifle. "Walk."

"Why don't you just kill me now and get it over with."

"Because Rufe deserves more."

For the first time, Gaylord Kincaid was utterly, unequivocally scared. He turned and limped forward.

They stopped near Duffy's body. LaPointe took the coiled rope hanging from Kincaid's saddle. It took some effort, but he got it under the dead horse and tied it. Then he tied the rope around Kincaid's chest, holding his arms tight to his sides.

"What the hell're you doin'?" Kincaid demanded.

LaPointe ignored him. He picked Duffy's body up as gently as he could and heaved it across Kincaid's saddle. He picked up Duffy's rifle and shoved it into the saddle scabbard.

"*Au revoir,*" LaPointe finally said. With rifle in one hand and the horse's reins in the other, he walked off, leaving Kincaid tied, arms bound, to a dead horse.

The buzzards swooped a little lower as Kincaid screamed imprecations at LaPointe. But LaPointe paid him no mind. He was too filled with remorse at his friend's death. He did think, however, that he had taken care of Duffy's killer in a fashion that would have pleased Duffy.

26

LaPointe decided after a half an hour or so that Kincaid's horse could bear his weight as well as that of Duffy's corpse. So he climbed aboard, gingerly riding just behind the cantle. It was uncomfortable as all hell, and he quickly gave that idea up.

Walking again, he thought about the dilemma. It would be dark in a couple of hours, and by walking it would take him to close to dawn to get back to Fort Laramie. By riding, though, he would probably be there around dark tonight.

Finally he made his decision. He stopped and eased Duffy's body off the horse. Then he unsaddled the stout bay. In a few more minutes, he had Duffy's body across the horse, up closer to the neck than he was able to do when the animal was saddled.

Not being as spry as he used to be, it took LaPointe three times to fling himself up onto the horse, sparking a new dose of anger, this one at himself. But when he made it, he was sitting more normally on the horse. Deciding he didn't care all that much if Kincaid's horse died, he spurred the horse into a lope.

Two hours later, he rode into Fort Laramie. The horse was blowing hard and was flecked with sweat-foam. He stopped in front of Sanderson's headquarters. Private Moorhouse, the orderly, saw him, and leaned inside the door. A moment later, Major Sanderson stepped outside, concern etched on his face.

"Get the others, Private," he ordered.

LaPointe slid off the horse and wiped a sleeve across his sweating face.

"You men there," Sanderson roared. "Come take Mister Duffy's body to be cared for. Move!"

Three privates rushed over and began taking Duffy's corpse off the horse.

"Easy with him, boys," Sanderson cautioned. "He was a good man and a good friend. He deserves consideration."

When the men moved off with Duffy's body, Sanderson clapped a hand on LaPointe's shoulder. "You have my sympathies, Henri. I know that Rufe was a close friend."

"You know?" LaPointe asked, stony-faced.

"Yes. Morning Mist and Two Feathers rode in with one of the children a couple hours ago. I managed to get Morning Mist to speak enough English that I got the drift."

LaPointe nodded. Then looked sharply at Sanderson. "One child?" he asked.

Sanderson nodded. "The little girl. What's her name?"

"Fox." LaPointe paused. "Where was Many Arrows, the boy?" he asked.

"We sent him for Big Hands," Morning Mist said in Dakota from behind LaPointe, using the Cheyenne's name for Otis Palmer.

He turned to look at his wife. "When?"

"Soon after we left you. We turned south for here, and sent Many Arrows west to look for Big Hands."

Merde, LaPointe muttered.

"What did she say, Henri?" Sanderson asked, annoyed that he could not understand. "What is it?"

LaPointe explained it to Sanderson. Then he stood, scratched his burgeoning beard absentmindedly as he thought about things. "Zat is not good," he finally said. "I am afraid for Many Arrows."

"He'll be fine," Morning Mist assured him, using English.

"If he's not back by morning, I'll send out a patrol to look for him, and for Otis," Sanderson said firmly.

LaPointe looked at him, and then nodded. "Zere's little we can do now."

"Come on into the office," Sanderson said. "There's more to this than's been said. I can see it on your face."

LaPointe nodded again, then turned to Morning Mist. "Set up the lodge," he told her in Dakota. "I will be with the soldier chief. If Big Hands or Many Arrows comes in, send him to see me."

"Yes," Morning Mist whispered. She was a little frightened. She had never seen her man this angry, this hard, this cold. There was the certainty of death in his smoldering dark eyes, and she knew more blood would be spilled soon. She just hoped that it would not be his blood that ran into the ground until he was no more. Sadly she turned. With Two Feathers and Fox, she left, heading for the familiar ground where their lodge would stand once again.

LaPointe and Sanderson went into the major's office. Sanderson poured them both a good stiff drink, and then he sat. He reached into a drawer, pulled out a buckskin pouch of tobacco and threw it to LaPointe. "That's the good stuff," Sanderson said. "Not that goddamn kinnik-kinnik the Indians smoke."

LaPointe nodded and filled his pipe. Tossing the pouch onto the desk, he fired up the pipe.

"So, tell me what happened," Sanderson said softly.

"We were riding. I heard a shot and Rufe fell off his horse. I sent ze women and children off. Then I took after ze killer."

"You get him?"

LaPointe nodded. "Took a while since I had to creep up on him. But I got him."

"You know who it was?"

"Gaylord Kincaid," LaPointe said flatly.

Surprised, Sanderson spat out a mouthful of whiskey,

then tried to mop up after himself. "The son of a bitch whose eye you put out that time? The one who deserted afterward?"

"Ze very same." His voice was icy.

"But how? Why?" Sanderson had never been quite so puzzled.

LaPointe explained what Kincaid had told him.

"Then Hanson's here? With this wagon train?"

"If Kincaid was talking straight, *oui.*" He paused, then added, "It still doesn't make any sense."

"It does to me," Sanderson said thoughtfully. "Hanson was always an arrogant little bastard. I never noticed that about him until I stopped to think about it after he deserted. While you were lyin' in the hospital, I gave him and the others a lot of thought. We had treated him fairly easily, since he seemed to be little of a trouble-maker. Then he led the breakout from the guardhouse. That put him in a hell of a lot worse light. It was then that I began to see a pattern in him."

Sanderson sighed. "A man in my position doesn't often get to know most of his men. Just the fellow officers, and maybe a few like Dusty Moorhouse. So it's hard for us to see when one of them's going bad. Their noncoms are supposed to do that. Maybe Hanson's did, but if so, they kept it to themselves."

Sanderson smiled wanly and took a sip of whiskey. "Anyway, he struck me as being an arrogant bastard, once I had thought about it, and I can see him pulling a goddamn stunt like this. He'd be the kind to come on in here and dare us to discover him."

"It will be ze last arrogant thing he does," LaPointe said.

Sanderson nodded. "I'll have him rooted out and arrested. He'll be hanging from a gallows before the sun sets tomorrow."

"No."

The single word sent a chill up Sanderson's spine, and he was not a man who frightened easily. "This has got to be done properly, Henri," Sanderson insisted, hoping his nervousness wasn't evident. "We'll do this by the book so no one can question it later."

"Fuck your book," LaPointe said, eyes narrowed. The rage was building in him again, and he allowed it.

"Be reasonable, Henri," Sanderson protested. He felt odd being defensive with LaPointe. The man was rough, rude and uneducated. He had few refinements, yet Sanderson suddenly felt inferior to him.

"Zis is not a time for reason. *Mais non!* Zis is a time for killing an animal zat needs killing. Hanson is like ze rabid wolf. Dangerous if given any chance. He must be kill."

"But he will die. He must die, I don't doubt the need for that. But it should be done legally."

"Ze wolf, he knows nothing about legal. He knows only ze fight, and death."

"But the army won't—"

"I don't give a shit what ze army wants or what it'll allow. If you get in my way on zis, you will be kill."

"Then you'll die, too."

"I know. I don't say I want to kill you. I only say I will do zat if needed."

"I can call a unit in here now and have you arrested." Sanderson knew he was talking in vain, but he had to try it.

"Zen some soldiers will die. And zat's why you should stay out of zis." When Sanderson looked puzzled, LaPointe added, "If zis Ox critter is as big and mean and stupid as Kincaid said, he'll be dangerous. And if Hanson's as shrewd as you t'ink, zey will be a formidable pair."

"So? I don't get your point."

"You send a unit of troops to arrest zem, I expect at least a couple of your soldiers will die. Zese men'll be desperate. And more, zey are ze kind of men who will stop at nothing to get their ways."

"We'll just shoot them down if they don't come along peacefully. I'd rather hang Hanson after a court-martial, to make it all official. But I'm not married to the idea.

And since this Ox isn't a soldier, never has been, I suppose, he can be shot down as soon as he moves.''

"But you'll be amongst innocent people, no? A man like Hanson won't be too afraid to take hostages or something. Zen your soldiers will either have to flee, be shot down in cold blood, or have to try to kill zem two when zey are hiding behind women and children.''

"But won't they do that if you go after them?''

"I don't t'ink so. Hanson is arrogant enough—so you say—zat he will want to take me one on one. At most, he might send Ox out to fight me.''

"Doesn't that worry you? I mean if this guy's as big as he said, he's got to be one big son of a bitch.''

"I can deal with him, Major, don't you worry about zat,'' LaPointe said flatly.

"Still, it'd be two against one,'' Sanderson said, skeptical of LaPointe's plan.

LaPointe shrugged.

"You put me in a very delicate position, Henri,'' Sanderson said. "I can't rightfully let you go out there and kill those men, nor can I rightly let them go. Besides, you're an employee of the United States government, and as such under my jurisdiction.'' He held up a hand to forestall any protest. "I know you can quit. But that still doesn't change much. Hanson is a deserter. He almost killed you, one of his men killed Rufe, and if he didn't kill Sergeant McGinty back when those men deserted, he most assuredly ordered it or had a hand in it. All that makes him a prime candidate for hanging by the army.''

"All zis I know. And it makes me no difference. He is mine to kill. He did more to me than he ever did to you, or to ze army. Zat gives me ze right to go after him.''

Sanderson was about to reply, but the door opened. Tom Fitzpatrick stormed in over Private Moorhouse's protest.

"It's all right, Private,'' Sanderson said. He turned hard eyes on Fitzpatrick. "You should know better than to come barging into my office, Tom,'' he chided.

Fitzpatrick shrugged. "I want to know why Henri and Rufus are back here when they should be out talking with the Dakota. There's a lot riding on this."

LaPointe was about to lay into Fitzpatrick, but Sanderson warned him off with a stern look. He stood, eyes boring into Fitzpatrick's. "You have no right barging in here like you did, Mister Fitzpatrick, and if you ever do it again, I'll have you chained in the guardhouse. As long as I am commander of this fort, you will obey the rules and regulations."

"My apologies, Major," Fitzpatrick said, not sounding at all sincere. "But the president wants this treaty badly, and I think that overrides most of your petty goddamn rules. Seeing as how Henri and Rufe are government employees, and'll be paid to interpret at the parley, I got some say in what they do and where they go."

"How'd you know he was back?" Sanderson asked.

"I have friends who tell me things."

"Did these friends bother to tell you why Henri and Rufe are back here?"

"Well, no. They just said they saw Henri coming in here, and that his lodge was going up back in the same old place. Rufe's lodge, too."

"Then next time, get the whole goddamn story before you come charging in here making goddamn stupid accusations!" Sanderson thundered.

Fitzpatrick did not back down, though. He never had; never would. "Then tell me what great catastrophe brought them back."

"Rufe is dead, shot down. Henri brought him back here for burying, and to track down a couple of men who had a hand in it," Sanderson said.

27

"This council's a heap more important than you gettin' some vengeance," Fitzpatrick said.

"Maybe to you."

"Dammit, Henri . . ."

"What the hell's eating at you, eh, Tom?" LaPointe said sharply. "You've never been like this before."

Fitzpatrick's face turned to angry red right to the roots of his snow-white hair. With a visible effort, he calmed himself some. "Dammit, Henri, this council's got me so wrought up, I like to bust from it sometimes." He sighed, almost as annoyed with himself as he was with LaPointe.

"You don't relax some, you damn well will bust," LaPointe said. "Then there'd be Irish innards all over the Scotsman major's office." A smile almost tugged at his lips.

"Damn, you're an exasperatin' man, Henri," Fitzpatrick said with another sigh.

LaPointe shrugged.

"How long's this avengin' gonna take you?"

"About as long as it takes me to find that presumptuous bastard and send him across ze divide."

"What about the other'n?"

LaPointe shrugged again. "Same thing."

"What if you get rubbed out in the doin'?" Fitzpatrick asked.

"Zen I'll be rubbed out." LaPointe did not seem at all concerned.

"And that, goddamn you, will stick me with one goddamn big problem, you dumb bastard."

"If Henri gets killed, I'll do what I damn well ought to be doing now—send my troops after Hanson and his Ox."

"I don't give a shit what happens to them two. I need him." He pointed to LaPointe.

"I didn't know you cared," LaPointe said sarcastically.

"I wouldn't piss down your throat if your innards were on fire the way I feel right now. But you're the best goddamn interpreter at Fort Laramie, and I need you around so's the treaty council can benefit from those talents. So, I'd be a hell of a lot happier if you were to put aside this yearnin' for vengeance till after the council's over and done with. After that, you can kill anyone you like—includin' yourself—anyway and anywhere you choose. It won't make no difference to me."

"Tom," LaPointe said slowly, looking with hard, glittering eyes at Fitzpatrick, "you and me, we go back a long ways together—back to ze days when you was ze *bourgeois* and I was just a man hired on with your company. But zem days're long gone now. I had always thought you were a friend, but now I see I was wrong in assuming zat, and so I apologize for presumpting something zat wasn't true." LaPointe's eyes were blazing, and he had forgotten about both his whiskey and his pipe, which smoldered in his hand.

"But now zat I see how things are," he continued. "I'll tell you ze same as I told ze major—if you get in my way, I'll tear you open like a griz rips a salmon."

"You better get yourself a goddamn lot of help, you stupid bastard," Fitzpatrick retorted.

LaPointe pushed up out of his chair and turned to face Fitzpatrick. "I won't need any help," he said flatly, jabbing his pipe at Fitzpatrick for emphasis.

"And if he needs any help, goddammit, he'll get it

from me," Otis Palmer said, stepping into the room. "No matter what that help is for."

Fitzpatrick whirled. "What the hell're you doin' back here, too?" he asked, choler plain on his face.

Palmer ignored him, shoving by so that his shoulder hit Fitzpatrick's. "You all right, Henri?" he asked, stopping by his friend.

"Oui."

"Rufe?"

LaPointe shook his head, sadness and anger gripping him.

"You know who done it?"

"Oui. He is dead now."

"Who was it?"

"Zat deserter, Gaylord Kincaid."

"Damn, I thought I'd get here in time to help you carve up the son of a bitch who rubbed out poor ol' Rufe. I figured he was gone under when Many Arrows told me what little he knew."

LaPointe nodded. "Is ze boy all right?"

"Just fine. He's with his ma and Morning Mist."

"Merci, mon ami." He paused to smack the ashes out of his pipe onto his hand, then drop them on the floor. He shoved the pipe away into a belt pouch. "But you did not get here too late for all ze doin's. There is bloody work to be done yet."

Palmer's eyes widened in question.

LaPointe explained it all—again.

When LaPointe was done, Palmer said, "Well, what'n goddamn hell're we standin' here for?"

"These two have been trying to convince me zat killing Hanson and Ox is contrary to their plans."

"That's not what—" Sanderson started.

Palmer jerked his head around toward the major. "If you're gonna drag out them ass-lickin' soldier boys of yours, best get on with it. We'll have enough time to take care of that and still go find those other two sons a bitches."

"I already caved in," Sanderson said. He was not sure whether he wanted to be angry about it or not.

"Then what's the problem?" Palmer asked.

"I am," Fitzpatrick announced.

"Shit," Palmer drawled. "Is that all?" He reached out and snagged LaPointe's drink from Sanderson's desk and downed it. He smacked his lips in satisfaction. "Come on, Henri," he said.

Palmer headed for the door but Fitzpatrick stepped in front of him. "You're not goin' anywhere," Fitzpatrick said.

Sanderson saw that Palmer was about to pound Fitzpatrick, and a man as big as Otis Palmer was not to be taken too lightly. "Let them pass, Tom," he snapped.

Fitzpatrick glared at him, then stepped out of the way. At the door, LaPointe turned back into the room. "If you want to come and watch, zat will be fine. If you want to bring some soldiers, even zat is all right. But if zey get in ze way, zey—or you—will pay for it."

They stepped outside. Private Moorhouse snapped to attention. "Your mounts, sirs," he said gravely, pointing to two saddled horses tied to the hitching rail at the foot of the stairs.

"They ain't our horses," Palmer said.

"They are for now. Your horses were too used up to be any good. You can return these when you get back."

LaPointe and Palmer nodded and mounted up. They rode hard for the wagon train which had settled in a mile west of the fort, stretched along the Platte River. They pulled up to a walk once they started working past the wagons scattered among the brush and small trees along the river. No one paid them much attention.

"Just what the hell're we lookin' for here, Henri?" Palmer asked. Now that he had had a little time to think, he was a little unsure of himself. He had always been that way—quick to act in a crisis, but finding trouble when he thought about things too much.

"You remember Hanson, don't you?"

"He that young asshole helped them others escape from the guardhouse? The one looked like a virgin?"

"*Oui,*" LaPointe said. Neither found any humor in this situation, not even when making halfhearted attempts at it.

"That's the time you was almost put under by that bullet, weren't it? The time Rufe hauled your dyin' carcass back into the fort."

"That's ze time, and ze man. Kincaid said Hanson's packing about twenty more pounds, and he has a beard now."

"That might make it tough to find him."

"I'll find him, don't you t'ink different."

"What about the other one?"

LaPointe shrugged. "If Kincaid was telling ze truth, he's as big as an ox. He'll also be wandering around with his tongue stuck up Hanson's ass, if Kincaid is to be believed."

They rode on a few more minutes. Then LaPointe stopped. Still sitting on his horse, he asked a man working on a wagon wheel, "You know where we might find a Monsieur Mobrey?"

"Ox Mobrey?"

"*Oui.*"

"Him and another feller—Gil Hendershot—got a wagon up that way a piece." He pointed upriver. "There was another feller travelin' with 'em. A heavyset feller had only one eye. But he ain't been seen since day before yesterday. I think he's gone yeller and turned back."

"Anything distinguish Mobrey's wagon from ze others?"

"Their back gate is painted red for some damn reason. Looks stupid as hell to me, but what a man does with his wagon's his business as far as I'm concerned."

"*Merci.*"

As LaPointe and Palmer began riding again, they slowly realized that people were stopping to look at something behind them. The two stopped and twisted in their saddles. Major Winslow Sanderson was trotting into the immigrants' camp at the head of a dozen troopers. Next to Sanderson rode Tom Fitzpatrick.

"Didn't waste no time, did he?" Palmer commented.

"I didn't expect him to."

Sanderson saw LaPointe and Palmer watching them, and he called a halt.

"At least he's keepin' his word to stay out of our business," Palmer said flatly.

LaPointe looked sharply at his companion. Palmer had so easily said "our" business. It angered LaPointe a little. Then he realized that Duffy and Palmer had been as much friends as had been Duffy and LaPointe.

They turned and began riding on. It was late afternoon, but there was still plenty of daylight left. A stiff breeze had come up, and it made wagon canvas snap and pop. It rustled the leaves and ruffled the river's water.

After ten minutes more of slow riding, looking at every wagon they passed, they finally stopped near a large, sloppily packed wagon sitting near the riverbank. It had a red back gate. No one was around.

LaPointe and Palmer looked at each other, wondering what to do. Then a monstrous-size man walked around the rear corner of the wagon.

"Jesus Christ all-fuckin'-mighty," Palmer breathed, "lookit the size of that son of a bitch."

LaPointe could only nod dumbly. Then he found his voice. "Would you be Mister Mobrey?"

The monster stopped and looked up at LaPointe, who noted that there was little light of intelligence or humanity in the big man's eyes. That was evident even though the eyes were squashed in among a fair portion of fat. Mobrey was perhaps six-foot-four, but LaPointe figured he had to weigh in at a minimum of three hundred fifty pounds. Maybe close to four hundred. Great piggish rolls of flab circled the man's middle, bulged up at the neck and almost obscured the dim eyes.

"A-yuh," Mobrey said, voice thickened by having to

work its way up through the many adipose bubbles of fat. He nodded his large, obese globe of a head.

"Is Mister Hanson around?"

"I don't know who dat is."

"Like hell . . ." Palmer started.

LaPointe stopped Palmer with a hand on his arm. "I meant to ask if Mister Hendershot was around?"

"Somewhere," Mobrey said with another nod.

"You know where?" LaPointe was exasperated.

The flaccid bulb of a head moved side to side.

"Kincaid lied, ol' hoss," Palmer muttered. "To say this lump of shit is as dumb as an ox is to insult the ox, a fine—if poorly reputed—critter."

LaPointe could not help but smile just a little. "You have any idea where we might go look for him?"

"Around." Mobrey stared with unblinking dim-witted eyes at the two men.

"Christ, Henri," Palmer said, "I've met trees were smarter'n this asshole." He was astounded that anything with such limited brain power could walk upright, like a man.

LaPointe shook his head. "It's amazing." He looked around, hoping to spot Hanson. When he did not, he said, "You tell Mister Hendershot that—"

"Tell me what, asshole?" a man said, coming up to the wagon from the river.

With one glance, LaPointe knew it was Hanson.

28

Hanson recovered well. "I thought you was dead," he said simply.

"Wasn't for Rufe, I would've been," LaPointe said.

"You ever catch any of the others?"

"None of ze soldiers who threw in with you back in zat gulch made it out alive." He paused. "And I put Kincaid under earlier today."

Hanson laughed. With the beard and an outward self-assurance, he looked like a completely different man than the one who had busted Kincaid and Hill out of the guardhouse more than a year ago. "Very humorous, Mister Frenchie. You don't even know where Gay is."

"He—or what's left of him—is with ze bones of a dead horse. When I left him, he was tied to ze horse's carcass. He had a bullet wound in an arm, and in a leg. He'd lost a lot of blood, and his arms were tied tight enough so he couldn't get free. It's possible, I suppose," LaPointe added almost introspectively, "zat he might still be alive, but I don't t'ink so."

LaPointe was surprised that Hanson kept his composure so well. The young man merely looked up in surprise and asked, "You did all that because he made you look like a fool that time?"

"No," LaPointe said tightly. "I did zem because he killed Rufe."

Hanson laughed again. "Well, I'll be damned."

"Mais oui!" LaPointe agreed. "You will be damned, and you'll soon be in hell, too."

"I don't think so," Hanson said, still rather amused.

"Zen think again."

"You get within five feet of me and Ox'll squash you like I would a bug."

LaPointe drew one of his Walkers, cocked it and aimed it at Hanson's chest.

Ox took a step toward LaPointe, but Palmer leveled his rifle. Mobrey hesitated, and Palmer nodded. "This rifle might be a little long in the tooth, like I am, but it's got enough punch left to put a sizable hole even in your fat carcass," he said, almost pleasantly.

"Drop your pistols, boy," LaPointe said to Hanson. "And the knife."

"You're gonna kill me, old man, go ahead and do it."

"I aim to," LaPointe growled. "And it's a job better done by hand. Still, if you want to argue, I could shoot you dead straight off."

"You gonna come at me one on one?" Hanson asked, smirking. "Hell, you're gonna be that foolish, I'll have to oblige you." He took out his two pistols and tossed them aside. The big knife followed. "There, old man, you happy now?" he asked with a sneer.

"I'll be happy when you're dead and rotted away," LaPointe said. He uncocked his pistol and dismounted. He set both his pistols and his knife on the ground. As he was beginning to straighten, Hanson suddenly charged.

LaPointe ducked back down. Instead of grabbing La-Pointe like he had planned, Hanson had to jump at the last moment. He didn't get too much lift though, and LaPointe surged upward, catching Hanson somewhere near his middle and then dumping him over and off.

Hanson landed hard, and suddenly realized he might not be as in charge as he figured he would be. He hurried to get up, humiliated that LaPointe was standing there waiting for him. On his feet, Hanson shook his arms and legs, relieved to find that he had not broken anything.

"Don't expect to get away with that shit again, old man," Hanson said, but even he could tell the bravado was false. He advanced warily on LaPointe, who seemed unworried. That made Hanson worry some, but he tried to ignore it.

LaPointe suddenly kicked out a boot, aiming for Hanson's knee, or crotch, it didn't matter much. Hanson was young and fast, while LaPointe had lost a step or two in speed. The kick hit nothing but air as Hanson dodged it.

Hanson dropped to the ground and with both feet, swept LaPointe's leg out from under him. LaPointe went down, hitting hard on his buttocks, rattling his teeth.

Hanson jumped up and aimed a kick at LaPointe's head. LaPointe dropped to the side, and the kick whistled past his head. As the leg went backward again, LaPointe popped up and grabbed the leg around the calf. He punched Hanson in the back of the thigh, along the hamstring, as hard as he could manage in his position. He did it again, but by then Hanson had grabbed a handful of his hair and jerked with all the might he could muster.

LaPointe grunted as he felt a few patches of his thinning hair rip out. LaPointe reached up and grabbed Hanson's hand—the one holding his hair—at the wrist and twisted. The fingers unlocked and LaPointe shoved the hand away. He ducked forward and rolled out of the way. Breathing heavily, he got up.

Hanson plowed into LaPointe, shoulder lowered, driving him back and back, until LaPointe's back slammed up against the side of Hanson's wagon. LaPointe grunted with the impact. He laced his hands together, raised them up and then slammed them down on the back of Hanson's neck.

Hanson let LaPointe go and shuffled backward a few steps, limping on the aching hamstring. LaPointe might have lost some speed and agility, Hanson knew, but the old mountain man certainly hadn't lost much strength.

For his part, LaPointe was beginning to regret this. He should've just shot Hanson straight off. *But, no,* he thought angrily, *I had to go and want to take him on by hand. Goddamn fool.*

As they took a moment's breather, both men became aware that many of the immigrants had gathered around Hanson's wagon. They were quiet, watching the fight with interest but a little fear. After all, no one knew where this would lead.

"Gettin' tired, old man?" Hanson asked. He tried to sound sarcastic but was having too much trouble breathing to make it work.

A surge of anger helped LaPointe shake off the tiredness and the pain. There was a reason he wanted to take Hanson on by hand. That thought would give him the strength he needed. *"Mais non,"* he responded. "You?"

"That'll be the day, when a tussle with some old fart like you makes me tired." He charged again, barreling in on LaPointe, determined to smash him once and for all.

But LaPointe was ready this time. In that split second between the time Hanson was a foot away and was about to hit him, LaPointe took a long stride backward. He latched his hands onto Hanson's shirtfront, and then spun. With Hanson's momentum helping him, LaPointe spun and jerked Hanson around. Then he drove Hanson backward with all his might.

Hanson's back slammed against the iron curve of the wagon's front wheel. Hanson groaned, and LaPointe let him go. Hanson fell straight down, his buttocks bouncing off the hub before landing on the ground.

LaPointe moved back a step or two. He was still having a little trouble breathing, and his heart pounded in his chest. He needed a moment to get his strength back before he moved in for the kill.

Hanson began trying feebly to get up, trying to pull himself up on the spokes of the wheel. He was making little progress, but LaPointe decided that he had better finish this off quick. Too much time had been expended on this quest for vengeance, and it had taken too much out of LaPointe. He should've let the army handle it, he thought, but then a picture of Duffy's rigid corpse floated before him.

Though Hanson was not the one who had killed Duffy, he had in many ways been responsible for it. If he hadn't helped Kincaid escape; if he had gone to California instead of coming back this way; if he had been killed in the Laramie Mountains. If, if if. The *ifs* were driving LaPointe mad.

Hanson was still trying to pull his way up the wheel. With a growl of anger, LaPointe moved forward, and then stomped hard on the middle of Hanson's back. Hanson screamed weakly as he was flattened to the earth again.

"Miserable, worm-fucking bastard," LaPointe muttered in French. He moved to end it.

There was a scream, a gunshot and then LaPointe got hit by a mountain. As he rolled and flopped, coming to rest against a tree, he wondered how a mountain could have fallen on him. There were no mountains here. Stopped, he shook his head. His ears buzzed and rang, and his vision was blurred.

As his eyesight cleared, LaPointe saw Palmer grappling with Ox Mobrey—the mountain that had slammed into LaPointe. Otis Palmer was a big man—six-foot, one-ninety or one-ninety-five—but he looked like a child against the massive bulk of Mobrey.

LaPointe knew he should get up and help his friend, but he just felt so peaceful here for the moment. Besides, he had no desire to tangle with that monster. He heard Sanderson's voice shouting orders, trying to get through the huge crowd. He was having little success, since he did not really want to hurt any of the immigrants.

LaPointe finally pushed himself up. He walked a little unsteadily toward where Palmer was slamming punches into the huge paunch of Mobrey while trying to keep out of Mobrey's grip.

LaPointe walked up to Hanson, who once again was trying to rise. "Here," LaPointe said sarcastically, "let me help." He grabbed a handful of the back of Hanson's shirt and hauled him up.

Hanson shook his head, trying to figure out why LaPointe had come to his aid. He found out soon enough.

LaPointe let go of Hanson's shirt and suddenly grabbed the back of his neck. He pulled Hanson's head back a little and then slammed it forward, smashing Hanson's nose against the iron rim of the wagon wheel. He did it again, and then a third time, each blow mashing more bones in Hanson's face. LaPointe let him drop.

As LaPointe turned, suddenly feeling a second wind, Palmer came flying at him, propelled by Mobrey. Palmer hit LaPointe in his low flight, and both fell— Palmer on the dirt, LaPointe atop Hanson.

"Dat ain't nice what you done to Misser Hennershot. Not nice," Mobrey mumbled.

"Jesus, Henri, how'd I ever let you talk me into somethin' this goddamn stupid?" Palmer asked softly.

"You was all fired up to go," LaPointe responded in like tones. "If I'd known you were going to have this much trouble with the man mountain, I'd have come to help you sooner."

"Buffler peckers." He glanced up. "Oh, shit, here he comes again." He began to push himself up.

"Keep him busy a while," LaPointe said as he scrambled to his feet. "I'll try to find a cannon."

Together they charged. They slammed shoulders into Mobrey's midsection and drove him back until he hit the large back wheel of the wagon. It seemed to have no effect on him. He grabbed their heads and tried to smack them together, but he didn't have a good enough grip, and Palmer slipped free.

Palmer had not been given his Cheyenne name—Big Hands—for nothing. He had two oversize paws, even for a man of his size. He balled up the right one this time and pounded Mobrey in the face three times. He thought he broke the giant's nose, but he was not sure.

LaPointe, meanwhile, began slamming punches into Mobrey's midsection in front and on the side. None of the blows—his or Palmer's—seemed to have any effect on Mobrey.

LaPointe was tiring rapidly, and his punches lost whatever little strength they had had. Mobrey suddenly reared back and pounded him one in the face. LaPointe staggered backward and then fell. *"Mon Dieu,"* he gasped. Mobrey had not even gotten him a clean shot and it felt like he had been kicked by a mule.

A moment later, Palmer ended up beside him in the dirt. "This here doin's has lost its appeal," Palmer noted, as he tried to clear the fog from his head.

"Oui," LaPointe said wearily.

"Christ, this son of a bitch's got so much fat on him we can't weaken him any 'cause we can't reach no vitals."

"Where's your pistols?" LaPointe asked.

"Hell if I know. I was on the horse. Somebody screeched. That horse I was on reared up, and my finger jerked the trigger on my rifle. That's when lard mountain there come at you. I fell off the damn horse, pistols lost somewhere in the dirt."

They charged in again, slamming hard punches to any part of Mobrey's body that they could reach. It seemed to do no more good than it had before.

Once again Mobrey took some of the blows before sending LaPointe reeling backward. LaPointe fell near the horse he had been using. Since it was not his horse, it did not know him. It reared and almost came down atop him. He rolled out of the way—and found his pistols.

LaPointe glanced up. Mobrey had Palmer around the throat and was about to squeeze the life out of him. Hoping nothing had happened to the pistol he had picked up, he cocked it and fired, praying that he would not hit Palmer.

The bullet hit Mobrey in the ribs. He did not fall; did not even seem all that hurt, but he released Palmer. Mobrey looked down and saw the blood on his side. "Not nice," he said loudly. "Not nice!" He lifted his hands, locked together, prepared to drive Palmer's head down into his shoulders.

"Otis, drop!" LaPointe roared.

Palmer did not hesitate. He just dropped.

LaPointe fired the four remaining rounds in his pistol. Each splattered through layers of fat, tearing through Mobrey's innards.

Mobrey stood weaving, and then toppled.

"Jesus Christ!" Palmer screeched. "Get him off me!"

29

LaPointe eased himself into the robes in his lodge. Morning Mist was quite pregnant, making it awkward for her to move, but she wrapped herself around La-Pointe as best she could in her condition. LaPointe smelled of blood and sweat, dirt and whiskey. She did not mind. They were man smells, and she reacted to them.

"I'm too damn sore for such doin's, woman," La-Pointe muttered. He liked Morning Mist's closeness and did not want to drive her away, but after the pounding he had taken, he was in no shape for lovemaking.

Thinking about the night was weird. There were the run-ins with Sanderson and Fitzpatrick over going after Hanson. LaPointe's blood still raged when he thought about the loss of his friend. Then there was the fight with Ox Mobrey. Despite its painfulness, it had been rather a funny episode—once it was over. LaPointe could still hear the chuckles that had erupted when he tried getting Mobrey's fat corpse off Palmer.

About that time, Sanderson and the soldiers finally broke through the lines of gawkers. Some of them laughed, too, when they saw the tableau, but Sanderson had quickly silenced them. Four troopers were ordered to help, and between them, Mobrey was moved.

Palmer stood, weaving but upright. "Jesus, Henri," he had muttered, "now I know what it's like in an ava-lanche. I thought I was rubbed out for sure this time."

As the soldiers cleaned up after the fight, Sanderson told the wagon captain what this had been all about. Meanwhile, LaPointe and Palmer limped around trying to locate their weapons. They finally did and then painfully pulled themselves into the saddles.

It was dark as they headed back to the fort, along with the soldiers. At Sanderson's headquarters, LaPointe, Palmer, Sanderson and Fitzpatrick dismounted and went inside as soldiers took their horses away. They all sat, slurping whiskey and puffing on pipes or cigars. Doctor Moore came and looked at LaPointe and Palmer, bandaged up some of their more evident wounds and then left again, after a toast or two to his health.

"Well, I hope you two damn fools've had enough fightin' for the time bein'," Fitzpatrick said sternly. "And maybe now you'll get your minds back to the business at hand. The *real* business at hand."

"Christ, Tom," LaPointe said, "are you going to be this goddamn ill-humored the rest of your life?"

"I might. At least till this council's over."

"Shit," LaPointe snorted. "I just might go tell the Dakota to come on in for the council while I stay out there with their old men and kids."

"You do and I'll set Mobrey on you again."

LaPointe and Palmer groaned in unison. Just the thought of Gus "Ox" Mobrey was enough to set all their injuries to paining again.

Suddenly Fitzpatrick laughed. "Jesus, that were some sight. The two of you assholes tangling with that thing. I ain't ever seen the likes of it, I tell you."

"Glad you enjoyed it," Palmer said defensively. "Next time you can go with Henri if he aims to tangle with a walking mountain of lard again. I'll stay out of it."

LaPointe had been growing angry again, but he suddenly felt as if a great weight had been lifted from him. He would miss Rufe Duffy. There was nothing could change that. But those who had been responsible for his death had been paid back in full. It was time to look ahead. And time to laugh. It always seemed to be that way—the intensity of the fighting, followed by the pain, and then the release of laughter as a man found out he was still alive and basically in one piece.

"Don't you worry about me," LaPointe said. "I ever hear there's a monster like that to fight, I'll head the other way. And damn fast, too."

They all laughed and then let their thoughts roam for a bit. Finally Fitzpatrick said, "I suppose you two'll want some time off to recover?"

LaPointe glanced stonily at Fitzpatrick, but then realized that Fitzpatrick was not being sarcastic. He nodded. "*Oui*. Tomorrow we return Rufe to the earth. I'll leave for the villages the day after."

"Me, too," Palmer said.

Fitzpatrick nodded, satisfied. He knew he had been wrong in riding these two men—particularly LaPointe—so hard, but he had felt it his duty. And he was not one to make apologies. LaPointe and Palmer knew that, and they would either accept it or not, as was their wont.

After three shots of whiskey and with his pipe smoked down, LaPointe got unsteadily to his feet. He felt like he would fall asleep even while standing up. It had been one hell of a day, the likes of which he hadn't encountered in some time.

"You need some help, Henri?" Sanderson asked, concerned.

"*Merci*, Major, but no. I'll be all right." LaPointe smiled weakly. "I t'ink I'm getting too old for such doin's."

"Bullshit," Sanderson snapped. "Any man's had a day like yours'd be sapped by it. A couple good nights' sleep and you'll be just fine."

LaPointe nodded. He looked at Palmer. "You comin'?"

Palmer looked up at him and tried halfheartedly to grin. "I was afraid you was gonna ask me somethin' like that. I'd be glad to come along—if I could get my ass up. I still feel like I got that giant, fat bastard lyin' on me."

LaPointe extended his hand. Palmer grinned just a little and took it. Between the two of them, Palmer made it to his feet.

"Bon soir, Major, Tom," LaPointe said. He and Palmer walked out into the dark parade ground. "You can stay in my lodge, if you're of a mind, Otis."

"I ain't so sure I wanna lay there and listen to you humpin' that pregnant little woman of yours," Palmer retorted.

"Christ, I don't have the strength to lay down let alone do any fornicating."

"Then I'll take your invite." Palmer paused, then asked, "You think we really are too old for livin' the way we do?"

"No," LaPointe answered after a moment's thought. "We might have to slow down some, but if I had to give up the way I live, I'd just as soon shoot myself in the head."

"I reckon you're right."

Despite still hurting considerably, Henri LaPointe and Otis Palmer stood straight and proud as their old friend Rufus Peabody Duffy was laid to rest in the Fort Laramie cemetery. A preacher traveling with a group of immigrants said the proper words, Sanderson praised Duffy's deeds and character, and a detachment of Sanderson's troops fired a three-gun salute.

As LaPointe, Palmer and Fitzpatrick walked slowly back toward the main part of the fort, one of the soldiers was heard to remark quietly, "I don't know why they're makin' such a big deal out of one old asshole gettin' himself killed. It ain't right, I tell you."

LaPointe stopped and turned toward the man, his eyes glinting hard.

Sanderson had been walking just behind the three former mountain men and had heard the remark. "No, Henri," he said when he saw LaPointe's flames of anger. "This one I'll deal with. Sergeant Graham!" he roared.

G Company's first sergeant snapped to attention. "Yessir?"

"You will see to it that Private Conway carries 'the log' around the fort's extreme perimeters for the next three days. Two hours on, one off, dawn to daylight. And, Sergeant."

"Yessir."

"You'll be responsible for seeing that Private Conway completes this task. If he does not, you will."

"Understood, sir!" Graham turned and barked at Conway, who had heard, of course, and had blanched. When he first heard the punishment, he decided that he would take off at the first opportunity. But with the warning issued to Graham, he realized that would not be wise. If Sergeant Isaiah Graham had to carry the forty-pound log saved for such purposes around for a day or two, he would be steaming mad, and he would come looking for him. Conway regretted having opened his mouth. His sentiments had not changed, only the knowledge that he would have been far better off to have kept them to himself.

LaPointe spent the rest of the day in and around his lodge. He was still in pain from a number of injuries, and he felt a sort of detachment from life, brought on by the loss of his friend. He saw little of Palmer, who seemed to have disappeared again. LaPointe figured Palmer could take care of himself, and he put it out of his mind.

By the next morning, LaPointe felt somewhat better. He ate a hearty breakfast and began saddling his horse while Morning Mist took down the lodge. LaPointe hadn't seen much of Two Feathers yesterday either, but she came out of her lodge now and helped Morning Mist.

LaPointe finished saddling his horse and turned. Palmer was standing there. "Hey, ol' hoss," LaPointe said halfheartedly. "How's doin's?"

Palmer shrugged.

"You all right, Otis?"

"Fine."

"Where have you been?"

"Thinkin'."

"About what?"

"A lot of things."

Anger was kindled inside LaPointe's chest. "Otis, I have a heap of shit to do. If you're feeling poorly or something, let me know and I'll do what I can to help. If you have anyt'ing to say, say it. If not, let me go about my work."

"I'm takin' Two Feathers as my woman," Palmer said flatly.

LaPointe's eyebrows arched. "You ask her how she feels about this?"

"Of course," Palmer snorted. "What kind of man do you think I am, anyway?"

"You probably won't want to hear my answer," LaPointe said with a low laugh. Palmer's face stayed stony, and LaPointe shrugged. "Did she consent?" he asked.

"Yes."

"Then what is the problem?"

"There ain't many men I respect in this world. And fewer I can call friend. You and Rufe were two of 'em." He hesitated. "And I'd not take up with Two Feathers if—"

"That's what you've been so touchy about?" LaPointe said. "That I wouldn't approve of such an arrangement?"

Palmer nodded, face flushing red with embarrassment.

"If you like the idea, and Two Feathers likes the idea, I can't say anything against it."

"But what about . . . you know . . . Rufe?"

LaPointe rested an arm on his saddle and then leaned on the horse. "Let me say this. If Two Feathers had gone under instead of Pony Woman. And then you went under instead of Rufe. Would you have thought poorly of Rufe if he had taken Pony Woman into his lodge?"

"Well, no, but—"

"Don't worry about it, *mon ami*. I t'ink Rufe is up there"—he pointed skyward—"looking down at you and Two Feathers and smiling." He paused. "Is that where you've been? Two Feathers's lodge?"

Palmer nodded. "But I ain't touched her."

"There's time for that. You sure she wants you?"

"I ain't sure she wants me, to speak of. She misses Rufe. But I think she's afraid to be alone, so she's let me latch onto her. She might get back to her village and drop me like a hot rock. But there's a few days' travelin' before we get there. Maybe I can win her over—if she needs winnin' over."

"She stays with you after you leave the village, then you will know she wants you."

Palmer nodded solemnly.

LaPointe looked at him, a question in his eyes. "Are you sure you want her?" he asked.

"I think so. I admired her for a long time. 'Course I never thought of givin' Pony Woman over so's I could try to take her away from Rufe. I'd rather have cut off my right arm than go against Rufe that way. Even after Pony Woman went under I didn't think that way."

LaPointe nodded. "That's all a person can ask for, Otis. Somebody to care for them, someone to take part in their life."

Palmer suddenly beamed. "It's somethin', ain't it," he said, "that a body can be hurtin' like a son of a bitch, but you can still feel so damn good on the inside."

"One of God's many wonders," LaPointe agreed. "Now, you better make ready to leave, eh. As Tom would say, we have important business to attend to. And soon."

"It'll be a relief to get away from that damn worry-wart, won't it?"

"Mais oui!"

Half an hour later, they left the fort. It gave LaPointe something of an eerie chill when he realized the procession was the same as it had been when Duffy had gotten killed—with the exception that Palmer was in Duffy's place.

LaPointe considered avoiding the spot where Duffy was killed, but he had to see what had happened to Kincaid. He stopped when he got there and dismounted to look over the scattered bones of man and horse. It seemed fitting. With a better spirit, he mounted his horse and rode on.

30

Early August 1851

LaPointe had never seen so many Indians at one time. He wasn't sure he had seen this many Indians in his whole life if you added up all his encounters with Indians—good and bad.

Since LaPointe had gone to them first, Painted Bull's band of Brulés were among the first to arrive for the big council. They had set their village quite near the fort, in a prime position.

LaPointe had been surprised when not only Painted Bull's band, but all the Brulés had been so willing, even eager, to attend the big council. He supposed they were aware of all the whites coming through their land and knew that someday some of them would begin stopping. By coming here, they might be able to forestall such conflict. It didn't hurt, LaPointe knew, that he had told them—as he was supposed to—that there would be a heap of presents for the Brulés.

It had been the same in the Oglala camps, too. Once he had gotten Many Horses, one of the most well-respected Oglala leaders on his side, the rest of the Oglalas quickly added their agreement to attend. The Hunkpapas were a little more reticent, but eventually they said they would join the other Dakota at the great council.

LaPointe spent more than two months out in Dakota camps, talking, cajoling, damn near threatening on one or two occasions. Finally, though, he had talked all the

Dakota bands he could find into attending the council. With the beginning of the parley only a month or so off, LaPointe had finally turned his horse toward Fort Laramie.

Within days of his return, Palmer pulled in—with Two Feathers and the two children.

"I see Two Feathers hasn't thrown your things out of the lodge," LaPointe said with a laugh as Palmer squatted at his fire and poured himself a cup of coffee.

"It were close a time or two," Palmer said, also laughing. He settled back on his haunches. " 'Specially when we got to Gray Eagle's. I even set my camp outside the village, lettin' her get on with her friends and such. Two nights later, though, she come back. Told me she couldn't do without me."

"Merde," LaPointe snorted. "It was probably you who went sneaking back to her lodge and begging her to take you back."

"Well, now, I didn't see it quite that way." Palmer laughed. He sliced off some meat and began chewing. "You have any troubles?"

LaPointe shook his head. "None to speak of. A couple of the bands were reluctant, but they didn't give me too much trouble. You?"

"About the same. Once Gray Eagle and a few of the other respected chiefs decided they'd go, most of the others fell in line. I swear, though, that I about talked myself out a few times there."

"Me, too."

Just over a week later, the Indians began arriving. Painted Bull's Brulés were among the first and chose their campsite. Within days, it seemed as if Dakota, Cheyenne and Arapaho bands were coming in nonstop.

"There's gonna be a heap of goddamn trouble we keep gettin' Indians in here," Palmer complained. "Hell, there ain't enough grass now. We get the Crows and Snakes in here, and there ain't gonna be a blade of grass for a hundred goddamn miles in any direction."

LaPointe nodded. He had already thought of that. It was particularly troublesome since some of the early arrivals were almost to the point where they would have to move just to find grazing for their many horses.

LaPointe and Palmer were kept busy. The Dakota, Cheyenne and Arapaho were allies and got along well with each other. Still, there was always some hotheaded young warrior who tried to provoke his peaceful neighbors. Then feelings had to be soothed, gifts made, apologies accepted. And with it all came talk, talk which only LaPointe, Palmer and a few others could make with any reliability.

Then, too, there were still a few straggling wagons—headed east, with people who could not make it in the harsh west and were going home. Plus there were only about two hundred soldiers at Fort Laramie. They were understandably nervous with an estimated six thousand or seven thousand Indians here already and more coming every day.

The Indians and the whites did not see eye to eye on much, but the one thing that caused the most problems was pilferage. The Indians saw theft as a game in some ways. The whites' concept of private property was alien to the warriors. It made for some tense moments.

Because of it all, LaPointe hardly ever saw Palmer. He didn't see much of Morning Mist either. She was staying with Painted Bull's people since she was close to birthing time, and there she would be with friends and family, who could take care of her. Since the camp was only a mile or two from the fort, he was able to get there most nights and stay in their lodge. But many was the night when he simply found an open patch of grass somewhere and threw his sleeping robe down.

He was several miles away in a Hunkpapa camp trying to achieve some kind of settlement between a young warrior and a soldier when a rider reached him. "Major Sanderson wants to see you, Mister LaPointe," the private said, rolling his eyes nervously.

"Tell him I'll be back as soon as I can."

"He said now, sir." Private Stankowich had known LaPointe for several years, and knew of the Frenchman's volatile temperament. He certainly didn't want to anger LaPointe unnecessarily, but Sanderson had been adamant in his orders.

LaPointe glanced at the soldier, about ready to take the young man's head off for him, but he caught himself. Stankowich would not have come out here like this unless Sanderson had ordered it. And Sanderson would not have ordered it if it had not been important.

Still, he was in a delicate position. A young warrior named Empty Horn had been inquisitive about a soldier while near the fort. He had tried to speak to the soldier, who, being afraid, had tried to brush off the Hunkpapa warrior.

Empty Horn had gotten angry and began shouting in his own language, which the soldier did not understand. Empty Horn did not understand English. The soldier—Private Matthews—had hit Empty Horn. Before the two could do any real damage to each other, LaPointe and three soldiers had gotten between them.

It took some effort, but he managed to get the two calmed down. Then he had ridden out with both of them to Empty Horn's camp. There, before several warriors and a civil chief, LaPointe was trying to work out a settlement that would soothe Empty Horn's wounded pride—something short of taking Matthews's hair.

Now this summons back to the fort. LaPointe thought for a moment, then nodded. He addressed the civil chief—Swift Hawk—in Dakota. "I give you my word, Swift Hawk, that this blue coat will be punished by the soldier chief at Fort Laramie."

Several of the warriors buzzed in annoyance, while Swift Hawk sat in quiet contemplation. "Black Bear has always spoken with a straight tongue," he finally said. "If he says that the soldier chief will punish the blue coat, then I believe him."

"But he does not speak for the soldier chief," one of the warriors protested.

"Black Bear?" Swift Hawk asked.

"It is true that I do not control the soldier chief," LaPointe said slowly, in Dakota. "Just as Running Buffalo does not control Swift Hawk. But if you know how Swift Hawk will act, then you can promise that he will act that way. I say these words to you: If the soldier chief does not punish the blue coat, then I will return here and give myself into your hands. And you shall punish me."

Swift Hawk nodded, and there were no negatives.

"Now," LaPointe said, "I must go. The soldier chief calls for me." He went outside with Matthews and Stankowich.

"What'd you tell them damn redskins?" Matthews asked.

LaPointe stopped, grabbed Matthews's arm and jerked him around. "I promised them that Major Sanderson would punish you."

"Damn, that's a relief," Matthews breathed. "Hell, the major ain't gonna worry about no little tussle with no stinkin' Injun."

"I also told them," LaPointe said tightly, "that if the major doesn't punish you, that I'll come back here and let the Dakota punish me in your stead."

"So? You ain't aimin' to keep such a stupid promise, are you?"

LaPointe fought back the impulse to jerk out his knife and shove it into Matthews's guts. "There are few things a man can truly call his own, boy," LaPointe said through tight lips. "His name, maybe. Honor. Pride. And his word. A man who doesn't keep his word is a piece of shit. Yes, I'll keep my word to Swift Hawk."

"Then you're an asshole, LaPointe," Matthews said with a swagger. "Why the hell would you keep your word to an Injun?"

"Because he'd keep his word with me."

"Christ, LaPointe, you've been livin' with the damn savages for too long. Anybody can tell you that you can't trust a thing an Injun says."

"And where did you get this knowledge, eh?"

Matthews shrugged. "It's just somethin' we all know. Or anyone who's, you know, a regular feller." He glared at LaPointe. "You've been livin' with these redskins so long it's addled your thinkin'."

LaPointe once more bit back the urge to tomahawk Matthews and be done with it. Again he was able to win that battle. "I will tell you just this one more thing," he said quietly, "then we will ride back to the fort. As we ride, you better pray that the major listens to me and punishes you."

"You're crazy, you know that, LaPointe?" He looked at Stankowich, who shook his head in disgust at Matthews's vain stupidity. "Christ, why would I pray to get punished?"

"Because if you are not punished, I will come back here and keep my word to Swift Hawk."

Matthews shrugged. "What's that got to do with me?"

"When I get back to the fort after the Hunkpapas punish me, I will come looking for you. And what I do to you will be far, far worse than what punishment Major Sanderson will give you."

"I ain't a-scared of you, goddammit . . ."

"It doesn't matter that you're not afraid of me. It only matters that you know I will keep my word. I will keep it with Swift Hawk, if that becomes necessary. And then I will keep it with you. Now, *allons,* the major awaits."

The three made the trip quickly and silently. But with each yard closer to the fort he got, Matthews looked a little more worried. When they got to the fort, LaPointe headed toward Sanderson's headquarters. So did Stankowich. But Matthews kept going straight.

"Private Matthews!" LaPointe bellowed. "Where the hell are you going?"

Other soldiers stopped what they were doing to watch. Looking sick, Matthews turned and said, "To the goddamn stables. My horse needs tendin'."

"There will be time for that later, eh. Now, come, we have to report to Major Sanderson."

"You have to report to him," Matthews snapped. "You can't order me around."

"He can't, bucko, but I sure as shit can," Sergeant Max Driscoll roared from nearby. "If Mister LaPointe says you are to go to the major's with him, then you will go, or I will kick your ass every step of the goddamn way. Now, Private, move!"

Matthews moved toward LaPointe and Stankowich, not liking it one bit.

"Is Matthews one of your men, Sergeant?" LaPointe asked.

"Yessir."

"Then you might want to come along, too. I have a feeling that Major Sanderson will want a word with you concerning Private Matthews."

"Yessir." Driscoll began walking behind LaPointe and the two soldiers. Those three stopped and tied their horses to the hitching rail, then went up the few steps. Moorhouse had seen them coming and had announced their arrival.

"What's he doing here?" Sanderson asked, pointing to Matthews.

"Learning what his punishment is," LaPointe said. He paused until Driscoll entered the room and stood quietly against a wall.

"Perhaps you'd better explain."

LaPointe explained it quickly and without frills.

When LaPointe finished, Sanderson looked at Driscoll. "Sergeant, I have no time for such trivial bullshit. Do you think you can find an appropriate punishment for Private Matthews?"

"Yes, sir," Driscoll said, almost gleefully. "He was in a hurry to get to the stables, so I think he can begin his new temporary duty there, mucking them out. I'll find some other things to occupy his time, too, sir."

"Thank you, Sergeant. Dismissed." When Driscoll and Matthews had left, Sanderson looked at Private Stankowich. "Find Mister Fitzpatrick, and bring him and his guest here on the double. Tell Mister Fitzpatrick that Mister LaPointe is here and awaiting him.''

In the interim, LaPointe and Sanderson exchanged small talk and swigged back a couple of mouthfuls of whiskey. When he heard the door open, LaPointe stood and turned to face it.

Fitzpatrick entered and was followed by a Crow, who had a hatchet thin face, a long hook of a nose and hair that hung below his knees.

31

Fitzpatrick barely managed to grab LaPointe and hold him. Sanderson swept around the side of his desk in a rush and also latched onto LaPointe. The Frenchman had been standing politely and suddenly had gone berserk. Now he fought and struggled and was screaming harsh, biting sentences in French.

Private Dusty Moorhouse, on guard at the door, heard the commotion. He cautiously opened the door. When he saw what was going on, he charged inside. Tossing his rifle aside, he joined in subduing a maniacal Henri LaPointe.

But they could not hold him for long. LaPointe managed to fling Fitzpatrick off him. The Indian agent shook his white-haired head. Seeing the crazed look in LaPointe's eyes—and where those eyes were looking— he shouted, "Hold him!" He whirled and hustled the suddenly protesting Crow outside, slamming the door closed behind him.

About the same time as the door was closing, LaPointe found another burst of fury. He shook off Moorhouse and a moment later, Sanderson. He bolted for the door, but Moorhouse tripped him up. As LaPointe scrambled to his feet, Sanderson came up behind him and thumped him a strong shot to the back of the head with his pistol butt. LaPointe dropped like a stone.

"Beggin' your pardon, sir," Moorhouse said as he stood up, "but what the hell was that all about?"

"Damned if I know, Private. All I know is that Fitzpatrick walked in here with that Crow and . . ." He paused, then nodded. "Yes, yes, that must be it."

"What's that, sir?" Moorhouse asked, puzzled.

"As soon as Henri saw that Crow, he went wild."

"So?" Moorhouse retrieved his rifle and his hat.

"Henri's first wife—Yellow Quiver was her name, I believe—and their two children were killed by Crows a few years ago. Either that Crow with Fitzpatrick was one of the war party, or maybe it was just the fact that he was a Crow set LaPointe off."

"The Crows are the enemy of the Sioux, aren't they, Major?" Moorhouse asked, looking a little pale.

Sanderson nodded.

"Again beggin' your pardon, sir, but I'm beginnin' to think this council thing is gonna lead to some big trouble."

"I am in hearty agreement, son," Sanderson said. "But it's too late to put the brakes to it now. We're committed to it, and will have to see it through as best we can." He paused. "Have someone get Doctor Moore. Right away."

"Yes, sir." Still worried, Moorhouse went outside.

A few minutes later, Major Moore, the post surgeon, entered the office. He cast a puzzled glance at Sanderson as he knelt beside LaPointe. "What the hell happened to him?" he asked.

Sanderson explained.

Moore nodded and checked the small, bloody knot at the back of LaPointe's head. Then he rolled LaPointe over. Lifting each eyelid, he peered at the eyes a moment. He took LaPointe's pulse and listened to his heart. Everything seemed to be fine. He pulled out a small vial of smelling salts. "Make yourself useful, Win," the doctor said to Sanderson, who was kneeling on the other side of LaPointe. "Hold his head up so I can get this ammonia under his nose. That'll bring him around quick enough."

Sanderson did as directed. Moore unstoppered the

vial and waved it under LaPointe's nose a few times before corking it again. LaPointe showed some signs of returning consciousness, and Moore put his instruments in his black bag. Then he stood.

LaPointe's eyes fluttered a few times and then opened, and he looked around, still dazed.

"Help me get Henri over to the chair, Win," Moore said.

The two men hauled LaPointe up as gently as they could and sat him in a chair. LaPointe shoved their hands away. "Get off me, dammit," he muttered.

"Glad to see you're your old self, Henri," Moore said sarcastically.

LaPointe ignored him. "Where's Fitzpatrick and that goddamn Crow?" he asked.

"Gone for now," Sanderson said soothingly. "Now, you want to tell me what that was all about?"

"That was the fucking Crow that butchered my family." The words were pained and coated with rage.

"I thought as much. But you . . ." He stopped when he heard the door open. He tensed when he saw Fitzpatrick, but then relaxed when he noted that Fitzpatrick was alone.

"I ought to put a lead pill in your meatbag, LaPointe, you son of a bitch. Goddamn, you're just set and determined to foul this council, ain't you?"

"I should've known I could never trust a Crow-humpin' *berdache* like you," LaPointe spit out.

Fitzpatrick blanched as white as his hair, and then grew red. "You frog-shit bastard," he hissed. "I'm nearabout of a mind to raise hair on you, goddammit."

LaPointe shoved up. His rage and the knot on his head sent throbbing pulses of pain through him, but he fought them down. "You better get a bunch of your ass-kissin' Crow friends to come help you, you peckerless son of a bitch."

Sanderson stepped between the two. "That's enough!" he roared. "Sit down, Henri." He pointed.

LaPointe glared at him for a moment, then nodded. He sat back in the chair in front of the desk.

Sanderson turned around. "Tom, over there." He pointed to another chair, this one alongside the desk. "Private Moorhouse!" he bellowed. When the orderly looked inside, Sanderson said, "Get four men—the biggest you can find—in here. On the double." He turned and went behind his desk. He pulled his pistol and laid it on the desk. Then he sat. "I'll shoot the first one of you two damn fools who moves."

Five tense minutes later, four large troopers—three privates and a corporal—entered the office.

"Two of you flank Mister Fitzpatrick," Sanderson ordered. "The other two flank Mister LaPointe. If either looks like he's going to cause trouble, you will hammer him back into his seat fast and hard. Is that clear?"

The four men eagerly answered, "Yes, sir," and took their posts.

"Now that we have some peace and quiet, maybe we can address the causes of the late ruckus. Tom, I think you should know that the Crow you brought in here was the leader of the war party that massacred Henri's family."

"I didn't know," Fitzpatrick said insincerely. "It wouldn't have made any difference, though."

LaPointe seethed but kept quiet.

"Henri," Sanderson continued, "Iron Bear is nominal leader of the Crows that'll be attending the council. He came to speak for his people and, I suspect, to make sure all's well here before allowing his people to come in. He also wanted to consult on the best place to put his camp."

"In the fiery pits of hell," LaPointe snapped.

"Dammit, LaPointe," Fitzpatrick snarled.

"Eat shit, Crow-fucker."

"Jesus goddamn Christ," Sanderson snapped. "The two of you're worse than a couple of goddamn two-year-olds. Now, much as I might hate to say it, Henri, you're going to have to change your ways. I know you hate Iron

Bear—and maybe all the Crows because of what he did. But Tom's right, far more so than the last time. This council's more important than you, me, or even him, for that matter. Now I let you get away with going after Hanson and Ox because that didn't endanger the council. All it did was make you a few days late getting back on the trail to talk with the Dakotas."

Sanderson paused while Moore handed Sanderson, Fitzpatrick and LaPointe a glass of whiskey. The physician kept one for himself. They all drank a little.

"But," Sanderson finally continued, "if you go for Iron Bear, the Platte'll run red with blood. The plains'll be awash with it. If Painted Bull, Many Horses, Red Bear and all the others have decided they can sit down with the Crows, then, by God, you will, too. Even those Oglalas who've been fighting amongst themselves for ten years, as you told me not long ago, are willing to put aside their differences for this council."

LaPointe shrugged and drained his glass. "Fill it," he snapped, holding the glass up. Moore took it, refilled it and handed it back.

"Look, Henri, the fools in Washington might be asking you or the Dakota to live in peace with the Crow. But we know better. All we want to get out of this council is a guarantee of the safety of the immigrants while they're crossing Indian Territory. Once this council's over, you can go hunting down any goddamn Crow you can find, for all I care. But until the council's done, you leave the Crows alone."

"That'll be a lot easier in saying than in doing." He unsuccessfully tried to keep the pain out of his voice.

"I know that," Sanderson said consolingly. "But if there's a man here who's strong enough to do that, it's you, Henri."

LaPointe shrugged again and swallowed his whiskey. It did not help his head hurt less, nor did it remove the feeling of loss. He set the glass down.

"There's something else you need to think of here,

Henri,'' Sanderson said. ''If you were to kill Iron Bear, or any of the Crows, there'd be a bloody war.''

''You said that.''

Sanderson nodded in acknowledgment. ''I did, but perhaps because of the knot on your head you're not thinking well. If war breaks out, a lot of Dakota will die. Probably a lot of Brulés'll die.''

''That is the price of war,'' LaPointe said philosophically. ''I know it, you know it, the Crows and the Dakota know it.''

''That's all true. But what you're not thinking about are my men.''

''What's that mean?'' LaPointe asked.

''You start a war between the Dakotas and Crows and I'll be duty-bound to try to stop it. That means a lot of my men are going to die, too. I don't like that. I've only got about two hundred men here is all. You know that. How long you think two hundred men are going to last in a battle between a couple thousand warriors?''

''Not too goddamn long,'' LaPointe acknowledged sullenly.

''You're damn right not too long. Even if we make full use of all the cannon we have.'' Sanderson paused. ''You've got to promise me, Henri, that you'll not go seeking Crow blood before the council ends.''

''If I don't?''

''You'll spend your time in the guardhouse, except when we need you for interpreting, to which you will be taken in chains.'' There was no room for doubt.

''Crows might not be the only ones I'll be looking to raise hair on,'' LaPointe said in flat tones. His eyes never left Sanderson's.

The major, though, was not a man who could be bullied easily. ''Anytime you want to come against me, I'll be there—after the council.'' He paused. ''There must be no trouble with the Crows—or the Shoshonis later—before the council ends. Is that clear?''

LaPointe hesitated only a moment, then he nodded. His head swiveled until his piercing dark eyes stabbed

Fitzpatrick. "Just keep them Crows away from me," he warned. "Especially Iron Bear."

"I'll do whatever the hell's necessary to make this council a success," Fitzpatrick said arrogantly.

"You provoke Henri, Tom, and I'll set him loose on you—and the damn Crows," Sanderson snapped. "Is that understood?"

"Reckon so."

"Is there anything else I need to clear up for either of you?" Sanderson asked.

No one said anything, and so Sanderson asked Moore to refill their glasses again. When Sanderson had his glass in hand, he raised it in a salute. Moore was the only one who returned it.

LaPointe returned to his lodge in the Brulé village. He slept through most of the afternoon and through the night. He felt refreshed when he finally awoke. Only a slight remnant of the pain buzzed in his head. Worse was the pounding of hatred for the Crow. It blinded his wisdom.

He wandered the camp, stopping to talk with a warrior here and there. He even spent some time talking with Painted Bull. And with each, he spoke of raiding the Crows.

Painted Bull did not like such talk. "You yourself, Black Bear, told us that this council was good; that we should come here to the fort for it. That it was important to the Dakota."

"All this is true," LaPointe admitted. "But—"

"Do not talk like most of the white-eyes, Black Bear," Painted Bull scolded in Dakota, which the two generally used when speaking with each other. "You have always spoken with a straight tongue. Don't change now."

LaPointe looked suitably chastised. "I have tried to change my heart, but I can't," he said quietly. "I have too much hate in my heart for the Crow. Would you ask a horse to change his color? No. And so I can't change my heart toward the Crow."

"You'll bring shame on the Dakota," Painted Bull said. Though he was trying to talk LaPointe out of this, he fully understood his hatred.

LaPointe nodded. "That might be true," he admitted. "I will give this more thought, and try to seek what's the proper thing for me to do." He stood.

Painted Bull looked up at him. "You will do what's right, Black Bear," he said.

LaPointe noticed the twinkle in Painted Bull's old eyes, and wondered what it meant.

{32}

LaPointe left the Brulé camp just before dawn. It was a cold, gray day and he was defended against the chill with a long, heavy wool capote.

Dressed in similar fashion were his four companions —Spotted Horse, who was Morning Mist's brother; Bear Dancer; Raven Heart and Wolf Calling.

The five men headed north for a few miles to avoid any patrols of soldiers, and other camps of Dakota, Cheyenne or Arapaho. Then they swung almost due west. They traveled for two days, moving unhurriedly, before they spotted signs of an Indian camp.

Stopping on a rise, they surveyed the Crow camp. It was spread out over more than a quarter of a mile, lodges standing amid the thin trees along the banks of the South Fork of the Powder River. Smoke from cook-fires drifted lazily into the sky. At the far end of the camp was the Crow horse herd. It was a sizable one.

The five men dismounted and let their horses breathe some. They waited about an hour, and then mounted up again. Dusk was imminent, and LaPointe figured they would get to the camp just before full darkness overcame them.

"Remember," LaPointe told the Brulés as they edged down the rise, "we're here to kill Crows, not count coup or steal ponies."

They stopped and tied their horses to a few trees at

the nearest fringe of the camp, and then they moved forward on foot, their moccasins making no sound.

One of the many dogs of the Crows wandered near, growling low in its throat, to investigate. Raven Heart drew the animal closer with an offering of meat, then brained the mongrel when it was in reach. They moved on again, spreading out a little.

LaPointe wanted to find Iron Bear, but he was not even sure the Crow was here. For all LaPointe knew, Iron Bear was still back at Fort Laramie. He suddenly heard a screech of warning and whirled to see a Crow woman running from Bear Dancer. The Brulé shot the woman in the back with an arrow, but the camp had been alerted.

LaPointe and his four companions each fired a few times—LaPointe, Raven Heart and Spotted Horse with pistols; Wolf Calling and Bear Dancer with arrows. They saw at least three Crow warriors go down. Then the Brulés turned and ran, yipping war cries as they did. In moments they were on their ponies and racing like hell across the prairies.

A mile on, they slowed considerably. None figured the Crows would be coming for them. Since the Crows had seen that Dakota had attacked the camp, they most likely would be afraid to send anyone out after the war party and leave the camp open to an attack by a larger force of Dakota.

They rode through the night, stopped for a hasty meal at midmorning, and then pressed on. Before dark, they were back in the Brulé village near Fort Laramie. After a long night's sleep, LaPointe headed back to the fort the next morning. As he was dismounting in front of Sanderson's, Fitzpatrick walked up. From across La-Pointe's horse, Fitzpatrick asked, "Where the hell've you been?"

"Hunting with some of the Brulés."

"Huntin' what?"

LaPointe gazed levelly at Fitzpatrick over the horse, but he said nothing.

Finally Fitzpatrick said, "I need you here."

"I'm here."

"Good, let's go."

"Where?"

"Many Horse's Oglalas are gettin' antsy because the wagonloads of presents aren't here. I'm worried about it, too."

"So we're goin' out to talk to them?"

"Yep."

"I thought you wanted me here," LaPointe said innocently.

"I didn't like your poor attempts at humor back in the old days. I certainly don't appreciate them now."

LaPointe shrugged and climbed back onto the horse. Between Many Horses's nervousness and the impending arrival of both Crows and Shoshonis, LaPointe was kept busy, going from camp to camp to explain what was going on, and why there were delays, and settling disputes. He had just finally gotten back to his own lodge in Painted Bull's village when he was summoned to the fort again. He was accompanied by Spotted Horse, his brother-in-law.

Fitzpatrick actually seemed relieved to see LaPointe for once. "The Crows pulled into the area this mornin' and set up their camps," Fitzpatrick said. "Several agitated chiefs told me there was a raid on one of their camps a few nights back. They said Dakotas did it. Brulés."

LaPointe shrugged.

"You have anything to do with it?"

"Mais non," LaPointe lied without remorse.

Fitzpatrick looked skeptical, but all he said was, "Come on."

"You mind if Spotted Horse comes along?"

Fitzpatrick shook his head.

When LaPointe, Fitzpatrick and Spotted Horse walked into Sanderson's office, several Crows there started screeching.

"Damn," Fitzpatrick muttered.

LaPointe thought for a moment that the Crows were pointing at him, but then he realized they were actually singling out Spotted Horse.

"What're they all jabberin' about?" LaPointe asked in mock innocence. He knew Spotted Horse wouldn't say anything about him having been on the raid. For one thing, he knew almost no English, and less Crow, so he was not even sure what was going on. If he did, though, he probably would have been more happy to claim leadership of the raid. He was a cocky young man.

"You know the Crow tongue as well as I do, you son of a bitch," Fitzpatrick snapped. With threats and cajoling, he managed to calm the Crows down and get them to promise they would do nothing until he could try to straighten things out. Then Fitzpatrick saw the Crows out, in the company of a white trader who was on friendly terms with them.

When the Crows had gone, Fitzpatrick turned furiously on LaPointe. "This is your doin', you goddamn fool," he screamed.

"Mais non!" LaPointe insisted. "They were pointing to Spotted Horse, not me."

"I'm aware of that. But Spotted Horse is your brother-in-law. And that raid on the Crows came when you had disappeared for a few days."

LaPointe shrugged.

"Henri," Sanderson said quietly, "I don't know if you were in on that raid or not. Or even whether you conceived the thing. Right now it doesn't matter."

"It matters to me, goddammit," Fitzpatrick interjected. "We've got almost eight thousand Indians here already, with more on the way. And you, you dumb French son of a bitch, are hellbent on ruinin' the plans of the whole goddamn government. Jesus!"

LaPointe moved fast and clubbed Fitzpatrick on the jaw with a fist, knocking Fitzpatrick down. LaPointe went to jump on Fitzpatrick, but the intervention of several soldiers kept him from continuing the attack. Others grabbed Fitzpatrick, just in case.

"Sit down, both of you," Sanderson ordered. He stood and began pacing, glaring from one man to the other. "This agitating has to stop. We're in a delicate situation. Both of you know that. Henri, you need to control yourself, and Tom, you've got to get a handle on your anger. I know you're nervous as a cat about this council, but you must temper your overriding sense of gloom and disaster. Anytime you get this many people— any kind of people—together, there're going to be problems. Especially if you have several enemies sitting down together. It's inevitable."

Sanderson paused to light a cigar. "Tom, as much as I'd like to see this council be perfect," Sanderson continued, "I know it won't. It's impossible. If you think that you can run roughshod over people—especially men who've been your friends—and that'll make this a perfect council, then you've not got the sense to make it work. You more than I should know that these Indians have age-old enmities against each other. You can't change that overnight. But if we can get them to put aside their differences for a few days or weeks, we'll have made a good start on peace."

Sanderson stopped and looked at Fitzpatrick. "I know you care a lot for the Indians, Tom, and don't want to see any of them hurt unnecessarily. It's what makes you a good agent for these peoples. But it shouldn't come at the cost of your friends."

Sanderson turned to LaPointe. "And you, you fractious bastard, know what this means to not only Tom but to the Dakotas and their allies. I threatened to throw you in chains if you did something like this, and I'm of a mind to do so, because even if you didn't take part in that raid, you probably knew about it and could've gone a long way to prevent it."

He paused again, sighing, trying to collect his thoughts. "But I'm not going to do that," he finally said. "Not yet anyway. I'm going to give you and Tom a chance to patch up your differences in the name of the

government, and for the good of all concerned. Henri
you think you can do that?"

LaPointe shrugged. "Depends on Tom."

"Tom?" Sanderson asked.

"If Henri keeps the hell away from the Crow camp
maybe."

"As the commander of Fort Laramie," Sanderson
said in warning, "I have what amounts to rule over everyone and everything in the vicinity of the fort. I can
throw you in the guardhouse, Tom, as well as I can
Henri. And I can leave you there. The government is
sending out folks to preside over the council, and you
won't be missed. Am I making myself clear?"

Fitzpatrick nodded glumly. LaPointe did the same.

Late the next day LaPointe looked Fitzpatrick up. The
Indian agent was in newer quarters assigned to him on
the growing officers' row.

"What the hell do you want now, LaPointe?" Fitzpa-
rick asked wearily.

LaPointe bit back a retort. "Put away the pen and the
paper. Such work is not good for a man, eh."

"Christ, Henri, get to the point. I've got so much
work I feel like ol' Peg-Leg Smith in an ass-kickin' session." He almost smiled.

LaPointe looked at Fitzpatrick and for the first time
really saw the strain that all this was putting on the Indian agent. He looked drawn, and his eyes were ringed
with dark circles. His leathery face appeared to be sagging and the skin had an ill pallor. "We must have a
parley, Tom. Just you and me, eh."

"No, Henri," Fitzpatrick said almost contritely. "I'm
too damn busy."

"Come with me, or I'll drag you with me."

"Like hell you will."

"The way you look, a baby could do it."

Fitzpatrick glared, then nodded. "You might be right,
Henri. All right, have a seat and let's parley."

"Not here."

"Where?" Fitzpatrick's annoyance sparked.

"You need to get away from this place. You need some fresh air, and some buffalo tongue, and some Taos Lightning."

Fitzpatrick did smile a little that time. Then he nodded firmly. He capped his ink bottle, stood and put his hat on. Outside he saw LaPointe's horse, and his own, both saddled and tied to a rail. With a shrug, Fitzpatrick mounted up and the two rode off.

They went little more than a mile, stopping at a secluded spot. Palmer and Two Feathers were there, and a fire was going. Hunks of buffalo meat hung from an iron rod over the fire.

"I didn't know you were gonna be here, Otis," Fitzpatrick said. He was not sure if he was upset about that or not.

"It's you and Henri who have to parley. I'm just here in case one or both of you get the notion to kill each other."

LaPointe and Fitzpatrick sat. Fitzpatrick took his hat off and tossed it aside. "Well?" he asked.

Palmer suddenly handed him a long, thin pipe, its bowl smoking. "Might's well get this parley off the right way, eh," Palmer said.

Fitzpatrick smiled wanly and took the pipe. He puffed and then blew some smoke north, south, east and west. Another puff was delivered to the sky above, and still another to the earth below. He handed the pipe back to Palmer, who presented it to LaPointe. He, too, went through the ritual. Finally Palmer took the pipe away.

Two Feathers gave each man exactly half a buffalo tongue on a tin plate. Each had his belt knife and would need no other eating utensil. Then Palmer brought over a quart jug and set it between the two.

Fitzpatrick looked askance at LaPointe, wondering just what LaPointe was planning. He began to suspect a trap of some kind. "Well, Henri," he said, "you wanted this parley, so speak your piece."

{33}

"**Y**ou remember that time we were up in Blackfoc country, back when the Company was hounding us? LaPointe asked. He speared his meat and then lifted th whole piece. He began eating it around the tip of th knife.

"The Company was houndin' all of us, as I recall, Fitzpatrick said flatly. The American Fur Company ha sent out brigades to shadow the brigades of the con pany Fitzpatrick owned with Jim Bridger, Milt Sublett and others. By doing so, they could find all the be trapping places. That, combined with the run-up price the Company was paying for plews, quickly crushed th competition. Indeed, Fitzpatrick, Bridger and all th others of the Rocky Mountain Fur Company who wer still alive had ended up working for the Company.

"You had that little Flathead woman . . ."

"Little Lodge."

"*Oui*. You called her Elizabeth, no?"

"Elizabeth, yes." Fitzpatrick picked up his buffal tongue in the same fashion as LaPointe had and bega eating. He thought he knew where this was going, an he wasn't sure he would like it.

"And what happened to her, eh?" LaPointe aske softly.

"She was killed by the damn Blackfoot, as you we know," Fitzpatrick said icily.

"*Oui*, the same Blackfoot war party who killed that big feller from the Company. Vanderburgh."

Fitzpatrick nodded. Vanderburgh's brigade had been tailing Fitzpatrick's men, and so Fitzpatrick had headed into Blackfoot country, hoping to throw off the Company's men. The Blackfoot had responded and killed Vanderburgh and some of his men, and sent the rest fleeing for help. But the same war party had killed his little Elizabeth. The pain of it now, twenty years later, was still intense.

"How did you feel when she was kill, eh?"

"You know goddamn full well how I felt about it, you son of a bitch," Fitzpatrick snapped.

"Zen why can't you see zat I feel ze same when my Yellow Quiver is kill, eh? I cached into ze brush and watched as Iron Bear and his Crows took and butchered Yellow Quiver after zey kill her brother, Wolfskin. And zey hack up my two children like zey was meat for ze cooking pot." He was enraged, and tears of sadness leaked from his eyes.

Fitzpatrick sat eating the buffalo tongue, no longer really tasting it. Instead, his mind wandered to a spot along some small, cold, fast-rushing stream in the Bitterroot Mountains. His mind's eye touched on the lovely face of his young Little Lodge, as sweet and nice as a young woman could be. Then he could see her battered, broken body lying among the rubble of their camp.

He realized that he, too, was weeping. He felt no more shame in it than LaPointe did. But his mind was not through painting pictures for him yet. He did not know Yellow Quiver, nor her brother or children. That did not matter, he could still see them clearly, as if in LaPointe's body, watching while the Crows did their grisly work.

Fitzpatrick sat the hunk of buffalo tongue down on the plate, his knife quivering in the meat. "I've been too harsh, perhaps, of late," he said slowly. He did not find it easy to apologize, but it was necessary. "I've been

blinded by my desire to do what's right and just for al
the Indians at this council. But to do so at the expens
of old friends, men who've been with me in shinin
times as well as in starvin' times, just ain't right."

LaPointe nodded solemnly. "I'm glad you see it tha
way, *mon ami*," he announced. Seeing the quick flash o
anger in Fitzpatrick's eyes, he said, "I, too, have beer
blinded by my desire for revenge. First against Hansor
now against the Crows. It was not right that I shoul
endanger the whole council for my purposes. My apolo
gies."

"Accepted, old friend." Fitzpatrick felt better than h
had in a long time. Still, worries tugged at his minc
"You'll stay away from the Crows, though, won't you?
he asked, smiling to take any sting out of the words.

LaPointe laughed. "I will try."

"You don't have to try for long, my friend. Just till th
council ends." He paused, then shrugged. "Hell, I'
even go with you after 'em, but I expect my *bourgeo*
back in Washington would be some put out was I to g
around chasin' some of my own charges." He laughec

LaPointe joined the laughter. "I t'ink you speak tru
on that."

They finished eating the buffalo tongue and then La
Pointe picked up the big pipe again. He lit it an
smoked a moment, then passed it to Fitzpatrick, who
when finished puffing a moment, put it down. Finally
they uncorked the jug and each took a healthy slug.

Palmer meandered up. "You two sweethearts kiss an
make up, did you?" he asked, flopping down. H
reached for the jug.

"Don't give him none of that," LaPointe commande
with a laugh. "He's had too much already."

"Bah," Palmer said as he poured some whiskey dow
his throat.

The three passed the evening with several jugs, som
buffalo meat and old stories, before all three passed ou
from their overindulgence.

* * *

Two days later, a group of Crows swept down on Painted Bull's Brulé village, seeking revenge. LaPointe was out at one of the Hunkpapa villages when Palmer rode hell-bent into it.

"Crows've hit Painted Bull's village," Palmer shouted, not even getting off his horse.

LaPointe leaped up and ran for his own horse, not bothering to say anything to the Hunkpapas. Palmer remedied that in the scant seconds before he and La-Pointe were racing out of the village.

The Crows were long gone by the time LaPointe and Palmer got there. A couple of women were wailing, and gashing themselves. LaPointe slid off his horse and tumbled into his lodge.

Several women shouted in surprise and alarm, until they saw who it was. Then they got angry, shooing him back outside with harsh words and dire imprecations.

"What the hell's goin' on in there, Henri?" Palmer asked when LaPointe came stumbling out of the lodge, followed by a barrage of angry Dakota words.

"Morning Mist's time's come. Christ, what a time to be having a baby, eh?"

They hurried to Painted Bull's lodge and entered. Several warriors, including Spotted Horse, were there.

"What happened?" LaPointe asked in Dakota.

"Crows," Painted Bull said. "About twelve, coming from the west."

"You know who was leading them?"

Painted Bull shook his head. "The one who seemed to lead was a warrior maybe a little older than Spotted Horse."

"What'd he look like?" LaPointe asked, still trying to keep his temper down.

"He had hair down below his knees."

"A mean, tomahawk looking face?" LaPointe was tense.

Painted Bull's gray-haired head nodded.

"Iron Bear," LaPointe snapped. He sat a few mo-

ments, trying to get a handle on his rapidly rising anger
When he did, he asked, "Anyone killed or hurt?"

"Two of our young men were killed," Painted Bul
said. "Wolf Calling and Red Stone."

"Damn," LaPointe muttered angrily. "You're plan
ning to go against them, aren't you?"

"We're talking about it," Painted Bull said.

"You don't want to?" LaPointe asked, suspicious.

"No. Not now. It'll bring ruin on the People. Afte
the council, we'll make the hunt, for winter will come
soon. After the cold months, when we make the hunt fo
spring, then we'll go to war against the Crows."

"That's what the hell you said when Yellow Quiver wa
killed," LaPointe snapped in English. "You see wha
that got us, don't you. Dried up old man. I don't ever
know why I bother to keep talking to you."

LaPointe stomped outside. Clouds had moved in, and
it looked like it would rain. With nowhere to go, La
Pointe walked aimlessly around the village.

"Why don't you light somewhere, goddammit?'
Palmer asked.

"Too antsy. I want to go to the fort and pick up some
supplies, then come back here and see if I can find
anyone with enough *bijoux des famille* to go with me
against the Crows."

"So go."

"Not with Morning Mist about to drop the baby."

They walked a little longer, and then LaPointe asked
"How'd you find out about the raid?"

"Badger."

LaPointe's eyes widened. "Morning Mist's Badger?"

"The very one. He wasn't really clear on it, but
figured Morning Mist sent him out of the lodge when
her birthin' time come. He must've been wanderin
around here with nothin' to do when the Crows hit.
expect he just grabbed the first pony he come on and
raced off. As best I could tell, he was lookin' for you.'

LaPointe nodded. It made sense, even if it hadn'

happened exactly like that. He would have to reward th‐
boy for his brave deed.

They walked some more, with LaPointe growing mor‐
and more angry. Finally Spotted Horse found him
"Red Plume says Morning Mist is a mother," he an‐
nounced. "You have a son."

LaPointe nodded. *"Merci."* He paused. "I'm going t‐
the fort for some powder and lead and such. Soon's ‐
get back here I'll be ready to ride for the Crows. ‐
anyone wants to ride with me, tell them to be ready."

"I'll go. I don't know who else will, except Rave‐
Heart."

Fury renewed, LaPointe galloped to the fort an‐
stopped in a flurry in front of the sutler's. Fitzpatric‐
had seen him from the window of his office. Knowin‐
about the Crow attack on the Brulés, he worried tha‐
LaPointe might be planning something, so he hurrie‐
out.

Fitzpatrick found LaPointe packing several boxes o‐
paper cartridges, as well as percussion caps in a burla‐
sack.

"You plan on leading a raid against the Crows?" Fitz‐
patrick asked.

"That's no concern of yours, Tom."

Fitzpatrick grabbed LaPointe's arm and pulled hin‐
around. Calmly, he said, "You do this and the whol‐
prairie'll go up in flames. You know that, Henri."

"What do you know about it all?" LaPointe de‐
manded.

"That the Crows raised hair on Painted Bull's Brulé‐
and that two Brulés were killed."

"You expect me to let this just lie?" LaPointe asked‐
almost incredulous.

"Nope," Fitzpatrick told him. "I do expect you t‐
wait, though, until the council's over. When all the high‐
falutin' folk from Washington go home, you can lea‐
your boys on as many raids as you like. I told you tha‐
the other day."

"Dammit, Tom, this's different."

"No it ain't. Look, Henri, I ain't aimin' to start a feud with you again. But you got to face the fact that this's your doin's."

"How the hell can you say that?"

"Easy. You either led that last raid against the Crows, or you knew about it and did nothing to stop it. I've told you those were my beliefs before. They haven't changed. In either case, if no raid had been made on the Crows, the Crows wouldn't have retaliated with a raid on the Brulés. Again, either way, it's your doin'."

LaPointe glared at Fitzpatrick, unwilling to agree. But as he thought about it, he could see that Fitzpatrick was right, that he, Henri LaPointe, great friend of the Brulé Dakota, had been responsible. Most times, that wouldn't bother him much, since the Dakota and the Crow had been at war since man could remember. But another raid now would mean a bloodbath.

"What about the Crows?" he asked. "We don't go against them, they'll think we've got no heart. That'll encourage them to more raids against the Brulés."

"I've already got them to promise to stop their raidin'."

"How do you know they aren't just lying?"

"They could be, but I think I impressed upon them the fact that if they pull another raid—provoked or not —that the army will march on them, with cannon."

"Provoked or not, eh?" LaPointe said quietly.

"Yep. And if you take advantage of that knowledge, I'll see you hanged."

"I bet you would," LaPointe said with a small grin. He sighed. "Well, Tom, I don't like it, but I'll try to keep the Brulés in line. It might not be too hard, since Painted Bull doesn't seem bent on going. A few of the younger ones are, but I guess I can talk them out of it."

He did, and it took considerably less talking and coercion by him and Painted Bull than he would have thought.

34

LaPointe might've been able to talk the young Brulé warriors into rejecting the idea of a raid on the Crows but he more than half suspected they were going to try something, somewhere, and soon. It was, he thought one of the reasons they had been so willing to agree with his suggestion of leaving the Crows alone for now.

He also noticed that the young warriors were antsy, as if they were waiting for something to happen—or planning something. LaPointe was not the only one to take note of it either. But nothing happened.

"Maybe them young Brulés of yours're just a little itchy knowin' the major's got patrols out regular keeping an eye on things," Fitzpatrick said to him one warm afternoon.

"Do you believe that?"

Fitzpatrick laughed. "I'd rather not say."

LaPointe laughed, too, and pointed. "Hell, do you think the Dakota—or even those shit-eating Crows—would be afraid of them?"

A patrol that had been out reconnoitering had just returned to the fort.

"You see anything suspicious, Lieutenant?" Fitzpatrick asked as the troops slowly walked their horses past LaPointe and Fitzpatrick, who were leaning against the wall of Dwight Eaton's blacksmith shop.

"No, Mister Fitzpatrick," Second Lieutenant Lev Bootes said. "Nothing out of the ordinary." He stopped a moment as his men rode slowly by. Bootes had lost a considerable amount of his youthful freshness in the two years he had been at Fort Laramie. He looked worn and soiled, as if wasting away.

"Where'd you reconnoiter?"

"Out among the Crows. I'm still amazed," he added thoughtfully, "at the organization shown by the savages. All of them. Their camps are laid out with perfect order, as far as their tipis go. I know it looks like a madhouse sometimes, what with all the mongrels and naked kids running around and all. But really, their organization is amazing, simply amazing." He rode off after his men, shaking his head.

Laughing, LaPointe and Fitzpatrick turned to watch him. The troopers who had just returned had stopped near the stables and dismounted. Many had rolled smokes and were stretching to get some of the kinks out of their seats and backs. After a long day of tense patrolling, they did not look forward to tending their horses.

Just about then, a small party of Brulé warriors raced into the fort from the west. Unlike the old American Fur Company fort, the new, army-owned Fort Laramie had no stockade of any kind. Buildings were simply lined up, mainly grouped around a parade ground. Since many of the buildings still were in the earliest stages of construction, the fort was open and vulnerable.

LaPointe jabbed Fitzpatrick in the ribs. "Look," LaPointe said, pointing to the Dakotas.

"Oh, shit," Fitzpatrick said, looking frantically around, wondering to whom he should shout the first warning.

"Oh shit nothing. Just watch," LaPointe said.

"You know somethin' about this?" Fitzpatrick asked suspiciously.

LaPointe shook his head. "Nope, but I think we're about to see what the Brulés've been brewing up."

"Think they'll cause any real trouble?"

"I doubt it. They know there aren't many soldiers here, but they also know Win will turn the cannon on them if they cause any real trouble. I think some of those young warriors have their blood running hot and want to do something to relieve some of their tension. And show the Crows—and everybody else for that matter—how brave they are.''

Fitzpatrick was skeptical, but it was too late to do anything about it now. He watched, worried.

The Sioux came in so fast that the soldiers were taken completely by surprise. One minute the troopers were smoking and joking, not having a care in the world. Even Bootes was taking it easy. Then next thing they knew, a screaming horde of Dakota warriors was driving off all the patrol's horses, plus a few others that had been standing nearby.

So fast was the raid that the soldiers stood flat-footed for a few moments, wondering what the hell was going on.

Then Bootes reacted. "Fire, men! Fire!" he roared.

A few men reached for their rifles.

"Merde, now this is trouble,'' LaPointe muttered. He ran forward to stop the soldiers from firing if he could.

The troopers barely got off a few shots before the Dakotas—and the horses—were gone, swept around the old fort and out across the prairie.

Bedlam ensued. Men charged out of buildings; company commanders began to rally their troops; top sergeants bellowed.

Laughing, LaPointe said, "Christ, Tom, we better put an end to this before somebody actually gets hurt.''

Fitzpatrick nodded, laughing too hard to speak.

The two trundled across the post, heading for Sanderson's office. The major was standing on his porch, looking at the madness. Three men were shouting, apparently trying to explain that the fort had been attacked by Indians.

Sanderson looked somewhat relieved when he spotted LaPointe and Fitzpatrick heading for him. He was puzzled, though, that the two were laughing. "What the hell's going on here?'' he asked as LaPointe and Fitzpatrick climbed the stairs to the porch. "Lieutenant Bootes and Sergeant Driscoll say Indians attacked the fort. Is that true?" He was worried. With only about two hundred men at his disposal against several thousand warriors within a few miles, an Indian attack could easily slay every white man at the fort.

"Call off the dogs, Major," LaPointe said, still chuckling.

"What?" Sanderson asked, confused.

"Tell your boys to go back to work."

"But the Indians—"

"Believe me, Major," LaPointe said with a shake of his head, "the Indians won't be back." He caught his breath. He hadn't seen anything quite that humorous in quite some time. It had been some spectacle.

Sanderson looked at LaPointe as if the Frenchman's mind had just come unhinged. Still, he had a lot of faith in LaPointe. And in Fitzpatrick, too. If those two men were relaxed, indeed, having a fine time by the look of them, then perhaps there really was no danger.

"Corporal," he said, "sound retreat. Lieutenant, call off the men and pass the word that the fort's in no danger. Then join me inside. And bring the other company commanders with you." He turned and looked sternly at LaPointe and Fitzpatrick. "You two," he commanded, "inside. Now."

Once they were inside the office, seated and had a drink in hand, Sanderson asked, "Now just what the hell was that all about?" He paused. "No, don't tell me. Wait till Lieutenant Bootes gets here. Then you won't have to explain it more than once. And stop snickering, dammit." His stern facade cracked a little.

It was not long before Bootes entered the office, followed by Captain Thomas Duncan, Captain Benjamin Roberts and Major S. P. Moore, the camp surgeon.

"All right, Henri, Tom, let's hear it."

"I don't know anything about this, Major," Fitzpatrick said. "It was all Henri's doin's."

Everyone's head swiveled to look at LaPointe, who

grinned. "Oh, for Christ's sake," he finally muttered, "you folks sure know how to piss on someone's parade." He finished his drink and lit his pipe. "I didn't know about it, Win. Honest. But I was certain they'd try something."

"Why?"

"Because of the raid by the Crows the other day." LaPointe's words had suddenly hardened. "Hell, the Crows were boasting and bragging about how they'd scared the Brulés with that raid. Scared them so much they would not even retaliate."

"That's crazy," Roberts said.

"No," Sanderson said slowly. "No, it isn't. You remember that time back in early '47, down in Buena Vista?"

"When we kicked Santa Ana's ass?"

"Hmm, yes, kicked his ass we did. But what happened first?"

"Well, Santa Ana was thumping us pretty good and—"

"And he and his men were taunting us, remember, Captain? You were among the junior officers who wanted to ride through Santa Ana's army by yourselves, but General Taylor held us back until we got the reinforcements."

Roberts nodded. "Yes, sir, that's right," he said thoughtfully. "And even though we were still far outnumbered, we turned their flank and soon after sent them running."

"And to what do you attribute that important victory, Captain?"

"Bravery," Roberts said with a touch of arrogance.

"Admitted. But wasn't there just a bit of something else?" Sanderson pressed.

"Well," Roberts admitted with a small laugh, "we were some pissed off. And we went charging out . . ." He paused. "Aha. Yes, now I see. We, in that case, were the Brulés."

"On the nose, Captain. On the nose." Sanderson turned back to LaPointe. "Anything else?"

"Not really. Once I saw the Brulés coming around that corner, I knew what they were up to, and I knew it wouldn't be serious."

"My men think it's serious, Mister LaPointe," Bootes said heatedly. "Not only did we lose all the patrol's horses, but my men also lost their saddles, a number of weapons and a fair amount of other gear. All of which, I might add, is government issued and not easily replaced."

"There is that," Sanderson said. "You have anything to say about that, Henri?"

LaPointe shrugged, but thought about it. "I expect," he finally said, "that I can talk the Brulés into giving back most of what they took."

"Even the horses?" Sanderson sounded skeptical.

"That'll take some doing, but I think I can talk them into it." He looked up at Sanderson. "It might help if you could think up some presents to give them in exchange."

"That might be a little hard, Henri," Sanderson said. "You know as well as I do that we're stretched mighty thin here. And, worse, as you also know, the presents we're supposed to give the Indians during the council still haven't arrived. If they don't get here soon, there might be a lot of trouble. We might have to use damn near everything in the fort at the council just to keep the peace during the talks."

"It doesn't have to be much."

Sanderson sighed. "I suppose we can come up with some things, especially if it'll get the horses back."

LaPointe grinned a little. "Hell, Major, don't look so glum. We haven't had that much entertainment around here since you soldier boys arrived."

Fitzpatrick snickered.

The humor of it finally got through to Sanderson. He smiled, then chuckled, and finally began to laugh. The others, including Bootes after some moments, joined in.

* * *

Two days later, LaPointe came into Sanderson's office.

"You got my horses back yet?" Sanderson asked, tone surly. "And just what the hell're you grinning about anyway?"

"You'll know tomorrow. Just make sure some of the Crows—some of the important ones—are out near the parade ground tomorrow. Just before noon."

Sanderson raised his eyebrows in question.

"Just do it," LaPointe said with another wide grin. "Tom can get them here. He's on good enough terms with those sons of bitches." The momentary trace of anger was melted by LaPointe's humor.

"You pull some crazy goddamn stunt, Henri, and I'll—"

"Best have Bootes and the men of his patrol there, too."

Now Sanderson was really intrigued. He had a dozen questions he wanted to ask, but knowing Henri LaPointe as he did, none would be answered now anyway. He nodded.

Almost a dozen solemn Crows were lined up on the porch of the building known as Old Bedlam. With them were Sanderson and Fitzpatrick. LaPointe was there, too, but on the other side of the porch, away from the Crows. He still could not trust himself near them. Out on the parade ground, Lieutenant Bootes and the men that had been on patrol with him waited in sweaty annoyance.

Suddenly a soft rumbling was heard. It grew in intensity and volume, until more than two dozen horses thundered over the horizon and into the fort. Most of the horses were saddled but had no riders. Pushing the empty horses along were five Brulé warriors, feathers flying, war cries proudly piercing the late summer air.

The Dakotas brought the stolen horses to a stop in a cloud of dust right in front of the soldiers. "We return these horses to you," Spotted Horse said in his own language.

LaPointe who had walked down to stand next to Bootes when he had seen the Brulés coming, translated.

"And we return all your things with them. We have no need of the blue coats' guns or equipment. Through bravery we took them, out of generosity, we give it all back." Yipping, Spotted Horse led his fellow warriors away.

On the porch nearby, the Crows were greatly impressed with their enemies. They were angry, too, that they had not thought to do it. Still, credit was given where due, and the Brulés certainly were due it.

35

"**I**'m gettin mighty damn worried about those wagons of presents not getting here, Tom," Sanderson said edgily. It was almost the first of September—the date the great treaty council was supposed to start—and the promised presents were nowhere to be seen.

It was worrisome for everyone, but none more so than Sanderson. For to him would fall the consequences if the Indians either left or began battling each other when they learned that no presents were in the offing. Sanderson was intelligent enough to know that the vast majority of the Indians were here simply because they would get presents. If none were offered, they could—and probably would—turn fractious.

The Indians had, for the most part, been coexisting peacefully. There had been feasting virtually every night, though mostly among friends. A few overtures toward old enemies had been made, and had been managed without trouble, but no one expected that the Indians would stay friendly forever.

Since the Dakotas and their allies, the Cheyennes and Arapahos, had arrived there first—beginning more than two weeks ago now—their food supplies were running very low, and they had been worried about sending out hunting parties large enough to feed all the mouths. Not with the Crows camped so nearby, and with word that the Shoshonis were on their way.

Even worse in some ways was the fact that forage for

the horses, fuel for the fires and clean water also were in dangerously short supply. The prairie around Fort Laramie was not capable of supporting the thousands of Indian horses. Not for so long a time. In addition, the army horses and mules also had to share the sparse forage.

Fort Laramie itself was all but out of food, and no one knew when more would arrive.

Tempers on all sides were heating up, and that would inevitably lead to trouble if something were not done soon to alleviate at least some of the problems.

"There's nothing I can say, Win," Fitzpatrick replied. "I don't know any more than you do."

"Can we all hold out a couple more days?" LaPointe asked.

"I suppose," Sanderson said, rubbing a hand over his tired, drawn face. "Why?"

"That Washington feller—what's his name, Tom? The superintendent, I mean."

"Mitchell. D. D. Mitchell," Fitzpatrick said sourly. "Insufferable son of a bitch."

Sanderson shrugged. "He's supposed to be here in a couple days, isn't he?"

Fitzpatrick nodded. "Yes. He had planned to arrive on the first—day after tomorrow. He might have some news of the supplies, and the presents for the Indians. We get lucky, they might have the gifts with them."

"Hell, we all three put together haven't had that good a luck in our lives," Sanderson said with a tired laugh. "Well, we'll hold out until Mitchell and his entourage get here. But I'll need you two to help keep any fires of trouble down."

Fitzpatrick nodded, but then said, "Just to make things a little merrier, Bridger sent word that he'll be in with the Snakes, probably tomorrow."

"Shit," Sanderson snapped. "It's bad enough they're enemies with everyone else here, but damn, where're we going to put them?"

"I don't know," Fitzpatrick said with a sigh. "But I'll find somewhere."

Sanderson nodded. "And you tell Bridger that he'll have to keep his Snakes in line. Just like you'll be doing with the Crows. Henri, you'll have to deal with all the Dakota. Let Otis in on what we've discussed here, too, so he can work with the Cheyennes. Now all that's left are the Arapahos."

"I can get someone to deal with them," Fitzpatrick said. "I think they're the least likely to cause trouble, but who the hell knows." He was getting testy again, what with all the problems—and potential problems.

Outside, LaPointe stood, breathing in the warm summer night's air. On the chance that he might find Palmer there, LaPointe headed for Eaton's blacksmith shop. With all the Indians around and tensions riding high, Sanderson had closed down the small saloon used for the men. The soldiers had to do without—or face severe consequences—but the civilians could make do with whatever was available, as long as the Indians didn't get so much as a drop. Because of that, LaPointe, Palmer and their friends often congregated in or next to Eaton's shop to share a jug.

Palmer and Eaton were there, along with a half a dozen other white men who LaPointe knew but not all that well.

"Finished ass kissin' the soldier chief?" Palmer asked with a wink as he handed LaPointe a jug.

LaPointe took a long swallow, ignoring the friendly jibe. When he handed the jug back, he said, "You either better lay off that shit or finish it off."

"Why?" Palmer asked, puzzled and now a little worried.

"Ol' Gabe's bringing in his Snakes tomorrow."

"Shit. I suppose Washakie's leadin' 'em?"

"Oui."

"Well," Palmer said after another swig of whiskey, "it can't be no worse than when those damn Crows showed up."

"I suppose not. But that was several days ago."

"So?"

"So, the wagons of gifts haven't shown up yet, all the tribes need to send out hunting parties but are afraid to grass is damn near gone for the horses, the fort's abou out of food, and you have to go several miles upriver t find decent water."

"Good reasons," Palmer agreed wryly. "I suppose you're headin' out to the Dakota to try and get 'em no to cause no trouble?"

LaPointe nodded and took the jug. After a swallow he said, "Tom's going out to the Crows, and he sai he'd find someone to warn the Arapahos."

"Well, then," Palmer said, standing, "I'd best be ge tin' out to Gray Eagle's and give them Cheyennes a earful." He and LaPointe had one final sip of whiske each, and then left, riding out of the fort together. The parted right afterward, though, Palmer heading mor to the west, LaPointe toward the north.

LaPointe rode slowly back to Painted Bull's villag He did not stop at his own lodge, though. He wen straight to Painted Bull's lodge and sought entrance.

"You are troubled again, Black Bear," Painted Bu said when LaPointe was sitting.

"Many Snakes will be here tomorrow," LaPointe sai flatly in Dakota.

"The Snakes have caused the People many troubles, the old warrior said with a nod.

"As if the People haven't caused any problems for th Snakes," LaPointe muttered in English under hi breath. Aloud and in Dakota, he said, "That's tru Which is why I'm worried."

"It's possible—more than possible, almost certain— that they will cause more trouble for the People. Wit the Snakes and the Crows here, the People are in muc danger."

LaPointe shook his head in annoyance. The old foo was blind to his own people's faults. All Painted Bu could see was that the Shoshonis had caused the Dako tas trouble. It was probably the main reason, LaPointe figured, that enemies among any peoples stayed that way. Neither could see any good or anything right about the other.

LaPointe sighed. "The People will not be in danger if they leave the Snakes—and the Crows—alone, Painted Bull. Your council of warriors has pledged to remain peaceful through this parley. The Snakes have made the same vow, as have the Crows."

"And what would you have us do? Let the Snakes take our women, steal our horses, kill our children?"

"You just keep your young men from doing anything foolish. Then there won't be any trouble."

"That will be hard to do."

"Not as hard as trying to defend your people from the cannons at the fort," LaPointe said bluntly.

"So now the Black Bear, a friend to the Brulé for many winters, a man we have welcomed into our lodges and treated like a brother, now you come and make threats from the soldier chief?"

LaPointe spit into the fire. "So," LaPointe countered, "now Painted Bull, the wise Brulé chief to whom all the People look for wisdom, a man who has been my friend, a man I've treated as a father, now you insult me." LaPointe pushed up, angrily. "I won't sit here and be insulted any longer." He hoped that Painted Bull would stop him, but when the words did not come, LaPointe stalked outside. He was every bit as proud as Painted Bull.

He was in a fine anger when he got to his lodge. He stormed inside. Squatting at the fire, he dished himself up a bowl of stew, not being too careful about the noise he made. As a result, the baby—named Little Stone—woke, crying. LaPointe winced, annoyed at the baby's squalling, but also irritated at himself for having caused the ruckus.

A naked Morning Mist rose, casting LaPointe a worried glance. When he ignored her, she shrugged. She

got the baby out of the cradleboard and then sat on he
bed of robes to suckle the infant.

When Little Stone was once more sleeping in th
safety and comfort of his cradleboard, Morning Mis
went to LaPointe and knelt behind him.

She said nothing for a while; she simply kneaded La
Pointe's tight shoulders with strong, sure hands. After
little while she could feel him relax some. Only then di
she ask, "What troubles you, my husband?"

"Nothing that concerns you, woman."

"Come to the robes now," Morning Mist said softly
She rose up a little and nipped his ear with her teeth.

"That's not going to get you anywhere, woman," La
Pointe growled. But his anger was beginning to fade.

"Oh, no?" Morning Mist said with a small laugh. Sh
darted forward and nipped his other ear. "And wha
will you do, then?"

LaPointe had a momentary flash of rage, then quickl
melted. With a grin, he tossed his bowl aside. He ros
swiftly, reaching back to grab one of Morning Mist
arms and pull her up with him. He tugged her unresis
ing body to the robes.

Morning Mist laughed lightly as she sank down ont
the thick, plush hides. "And now that you have me her
what will you do? You, who have all your clothes on."

"We can fix that fast," LaPointe said as he bega
flinging off his clothing. Soon he was naked and knee
ing between her legs on their bed. He ran his roug
hands along the contours of her body, thinking agai
how she was different from Yellow Quiver, but just
exciting. Morning Mist was a bit taller than Yello
Quiver had been, and with a thinner, slightly more mu
cular body. Her breasts were bigger, fuller than Yello
Quiver's had been, her hips narrower. Morning Mist wa
much more playful in the robes than Yellow Quiver ha
been. Yellow Quiver had been more shy, though not le
loving. It was more that Morning Mist knew what sh
wanted and was not shy about asking for it—and the
enjoying it to the fullest.

Like now. She was already coaxing him forward into her, urgent and insistent.

He complied and matched her movements with his own. They gradually increased the rhythm and intensity of their actions until reaching a shuddering, spasming end.

Still locked, they rolled onto their sides, not saying anything as they tried to catch their breath.

Finally, Morning Mist asked quietly. "Now, my husband, tell me what was troubling you."

LaPointe told her of his talk with Painted Bull and how it had ended. As he did, he could feel the anger building in him again. At the same time though, he felt more at peace. He thought that strange, until he realized it was because he was comfortable with the way he had acted. There was nothing wrong in a man's pride—so long as that pride did not get out of hand. LaPointe thought Painted Bull's had, and he wasn't sure why.

"You will speak with Painted Bull tomorrow?" Morning Mist asked, cradling LaPointe's head against her breast.

"Maybe. Maybe not."

"You should."

"Why? He can come see me if he wants to talk," La-Pointe grumbled though not very vehemently.

"It would show you to be the better man, maybe, if you go to him," Morning Mist said simply.

"You might have something there." With that thought in mind, LaPointe drifted to sleep. He awoke with a bright, cheery Morning Mist softly stroking him to life.

When they had finished, Morning Mist asked, "Will you go to Painted Bull?"

He grinned at her. "I think I will." He felt good and vowed that even an obstinate Painted Bull would not change that.

Inside Painted Bull's lodge, the old chief seemed thoughtful but slightly more cheerful than he had the night before. Indeed, he even seemed pleased to see LaPointe.

"Someday you will be old, Black Bear," Painted Bull said with quiet dignity masking his self-pity.

"If I live that long." LaPointe's voice was guarded.

Painted Bull nodded. "If you do live to be old like me, Black Bear, I hope you will not be such an old fool." He sighed. "Old men do many foolish things—like insult good friends."

"All men have times when they do foolish things. An old and respected chief like Painted Bull has earned the right to be contrary at times. And when that happens, young men should not pout and run away like spoiled children."

Painted Bull nodded. "You give wise counsel, Black Bear." He paused, pleased that LaPointe did not jump in to fill in the silence that should be allowed to grow for a bit because it was right. "I will talk to the warriors, and I will urge them to suffer whatever insults the Snakes and the Crows give us. That is all I can do."

"That is all I ask. I know the men of Painted Bull's village will listen to his sage counsel." He smiled a little. "Now I must hurry to the other Dakota camps and see if they have leaders as wise as you."

{36}

Word came into the fort late in the morning that the Shoshonis were almost there. Runners went out to track down men like LaPointe and Palmer, who were among the Indian bands still preaching the gospel of peace.

By the time LaPointe got to the fort, it was almost noon. He found Sanderson, Palmer and Fitzpatrick, along with a troop of men from Company G, Sixth Infantry—under the command of Lieutenant Bootes—just ready to head west to greet the Shoshonis.

They all rode out, and LaPointe noticed several young Dakotas heading in the same direction, paralleling the fort group. Then Palmer pointed to some Cheyennes and Arapahos moving to join the procession.

"I don't like this," Sanderson said, pointing to the Indians.

LaPointe shrugged. "Not much we can do about it, I suppose. Painted Bull and most of the other Dakota chiefs I talked to said they'd do their best to keep their young men in line."

"Same with the Cheyennes," Palmer added.

"That doesn't reassure me, gentlemen," Sanderson said. "I wish they had promised that they *would* keep their young men in line, rather than *trying* to do so."

"Hell, Major," LaPointe said, "you know better than that. How many times've me or Otis, or . . . Rufe, too, when he was here . . . told you there's no Indians we know of have one chief who rules the band?"

"I know, but I wish it were different. And that still

doesn't make me feel any better about those warriors out there."

A mile or so west of the fort, a lone figure appeared on the crest of a ridge. He sat there a moment, surveying the sloping land before him, sparsely grassed land that swept up to the fort. The hot noon sun beat down on the solitary Indian, wind ruffling his feathered war bonnet and the feathers on his coup stick, held upright in his right hand.

The chief shook the stick and then began riding slowly down the low hill. Moments later, hundreds of Shoshonis poured over the crest of the ridge, also moving slowly. The warriors came first. All were dressed, painted and armed for battle.

When Sanderson saw that, he sucked in a breath. Almost afraid to look, he glanced at the Dakotas and Cheyennes who had gathered. None seemed to be moving; only sitting and watching.

Then came the women and children, dressed in their finery, putting on a proud show for their enemies.

Finally Sanderson sighed. "Well, I better go welcome our new arrivals," he said. He rode off, brushing dust off his uniform as he went.

"What about you, ol' hoss?" Palmer asked with a laugh.

"*Merde,*" LaPointe muttered. "You go greet them devils if you want."

"I aim to get back to Gray Eagle's. Two Feathers is waitin' for me."

LaPointe nodded. "I want to head back to Painted Bull's, too. I might see if I can raise a few boys and go make some meat. Want to come along?"

"Nah. With what you told me, everybody'll be movin' tomorrow or the next day. Once we get settled in, I'll go make some meat."

LaPointe nodded.

"You get back, come meet me at Dwight's. We'll hoist a jug."

LaPointe nodded again.

* * *

It was just after dark when LaPointe returned to the fort. He had found no one willing to go out on the hunt, since no one was willing to leave his family with both the Crows and the Shoshonis nearby now. So he had spent most of the afternoon with Morning Mist and Little Stone.

When he got back to Fort Laramie, LaPointe stopped at Sanderson's office and checked in. The major seemed in a jovial mood.

"There've been no troubles that I've heard of, and the Snakes are settled in. I have one company between the Shoshonis and the Crows, another between the Snakes and the Dakotas, and another between the Crows and the Dakotas."

"I hope that's enough."

"Me, too," Sanderson said, some of his good humor fading. "But there's not much I can do about it anyway. I'm too thin here at the fort to send any more companies out. About all I can do is send out some small patrols to let the Dakotas, Cheyennes, Arapahos and all the rest know that we're on duty."

"You decided if you want to move everyone yet?"

Sanderson shook his head. "I'll decide that tomorrow evening, I suppose. If the commissioners get here, things ought to go a little better. If they don't . . ."

"Or if the presents don't get here . . ."

"Don't remind me, Henri." Sanderson sighed, then smiled. "Maybe I'm just an optimistic fool, but I think we'll be all right. At least for another day or two. God willing and the creek don't rise, the presents and the commissioners'll be here tomorrow or the next day and we can wrap this damn thing up."

"You're not optimistic, Win," LaPointe said with a laugh. "You're flat crazy."

"Thanks for your confidence," Sanderson responded, laughing.

"I'll stop by tomorrow to see how things're going." LaPointe left. He was riding his horse slowly across the fort grounds when someone came flying out of the dark and hit him. *"Merde,"* he muttered as he hit the ground with a thud. The fall almost knocked his breath out.

LaPointe barely managed to grab the attacker's hand as he caught a quick glint of moonlight on a tomahawk. He shoved, and the weapon's blade bit into the dirt next to LaPointe's left ear instead of his forehead.

LaPointe saw a dark face looming over him, and he jerked his own forward. His forehead crunched against the man's nose. That stunned the Indian attacker enough to allow LaPointe to be able to fling him off.

LaPointe managed to get to his feet more quickly than the Indian and he aimed a kick at the Indian's head. But the Indian—a Crow, he noticed with a fleeting glance at the upturned, bleeding face—jerked his head out of the way, grabbed LaPointe's leg and twisted it violently.

LaPointe allowed himself to go down, easing the pressure on his knee. He hit hard, then kicked with his other foot. He connected, but he didn't know where. The Crow did let go of his foot, and LaPointe rolled a few times before getting up.

He was breathing heavily, but he noticed the Indian was, too, as the Crow got up.

"Who the hell are you?" LaPointe asked.

The Crow only glared and then wiped a hand across his broken, bleeding nose.

LaPointe asked the question in Crow.

"Buffalo Walker," the Crow said arrogantly.

"And why are you trying to kill me?"

"You killed my brother."

"When?" LaPointe asked, surprised.

"Three winters ago. You were with the dirty Sioux." He spit, as if the very word had a foul taste.

LaPointe shrugged. He had been on a raid with the Dakotas into Crow territory then, and had fought hard and well. He could not remember much about that particular battle, though, but even if he did, it would have made no difference.

"Then I saw you raiding our camp while my people were on our way to this place."

"I wasn't on any raid of a Crow camp lately," LaPointe said cautiously in Crow.

"You lie! I saw you!" Buffalo Walker snapped. "None of the others did, but I saw you running like a coward."

"Coward, my ass," LaPointe snarled in English. "There were five Dakotas and me against a couple hundred of you asswipes. Why didn't you say anything to your chiefs?"

"I wanted to kill you myself."

"You're going to have a hell of a time at it."

Buffalo Walker shook his head. "It will be easy."

"In a pig's ass," LaPointe muttered. Aloud, he said in English, "Look, boy, I don't really want to kill you." *Like hell I don't,* he thought. But all the harping on him by Fitzpatrick and Sanderson had had its effect. He knew the potential apocalypse such a thing could cause.

"Your cowardly talk won't help you," Buffalo Walker said arrogantly. He was almost twenty years younger than LaPointe and, though he was giving up several pounds, he figured his youth and bravery would be more than enough to compensate.

LaPointe did not take the Crow lightly, but he hoped to avoid all the trouble by not killing Buffalo Walker. And he had no doubt that he would be able to kill the young warrior. He might not be as young and as spry as he had been. But he hadn't survived for twenty-plus years in the mountains and on the plains without learning something, and without being as tough as leather made from an old bull's neck hide. But he could see that the Crow was not about to back down.

Buffalo Walker charged again, a knife raised high in his hand.

"Damn fool," LaPointe muttered as he threw up his left arm defensively. Buffalo Walker's arm bounced, and then the knife slid down most of the length of his forearm. LaPointe ignored the blazing trail of pain and reared back. Then he hammered Buffalo Walker with a punch to the heart.

The Crow choked on his breath and staggered backward, squawking and sputtering.

LaPointe glanced down at his arm. Even in the dim moonlight he could see the blood welling up darkly. He shook his head, more annoyed than injured. He glanced at Buffalo Walker, who still looked stricken.

"Listen to me, boy," LaPointe said harshly. "This can end here. You come at me again, and I'll kill you. And I don't really want to do that, not here, not now, since it'll cause more trouble than it'd be worth. If you care about your people, you'll walk away."

"I can't," Buffalo Walker croaked.

"No one's going to know except you and me."

"That would be one too many who know." Buffalo Walker bent and picked up the knife he had dropped when LaPointe had hit him. He looked at it for a moment, almost as if he had never seen it before. Then he glanced up at LaPointe and grinned with self-assurance. He moved forward warily, lightly carrying the knife in front of him. He had underestimated this white man before, but he would not do so again.

LaPointe waited. His arm was beginning to hurt now, but he could do nothing about it, so he tried to ignore it and concentrate on Buffalo Walker. He eased out his own big knife. The weapon had been his so long that the wooden handle had worn down to fit his hand perfectly.

Buffalo Walker lunged forward, knife darting toward LaPointe's chest. LaPointe jerked himself backward and got tangled up in his feet. He fell, but he figured that was a good thing, since it had allowed Buffalo Walker's knife just to nick him on the chest.

Buffalo Walker dove at LaPointe, landing half atop him. The two men grappled, free hand to knife hand, searching for an advantage while trying to prevent his foe's knife from plunging into his vitals.

Finally, through sheer grit more than anything, La-

Pointe began to gain an advantage. He shoved Buffalo Walker off him, and then rolled a few times before getting up.

The fight, though, had sapped him a little and he was slower getting to his feet than Buffalo Walker was.

With a war cry of impending victory, the Crow flung himself at LaPointe. The Frenchman was crouched, only partway up, struggling to rise. He half turned, flinging his left arm up more instinctively to protect himself than anything. But he was fast enough to jerk his knife hand up as soon as Buffalo Walker ran into him. He also pushed up with his strong thick legs.

LaPointe's knife sank hilt deep into Buffalo Walker's abdomen. The Frenchman managed to keep his grip on the knife, twisting it, as Buffalo Walker hit on LaPointe's shoulder, and then was flipped up and over. As the Crow fell, LaPointe yanked the knife out and staggered back a step, ready for another assault.

But Buffalo Walker lay rolling from side to side, clutching his ripped open stomach. He emitted low groans, that swiftly turned into what LaPointe figured was Buffalo Walker's death song.

Two soldiers came running up from one direction. Fitzpatrick and Palmer trotted up from the blacksmith shop. All four had weapons ready, nervous.

Fitzpatrick knelt at Buffalo Walker's side and checked him over.

"Anything you can do for him, Tom?" Palmer asked.

"No," Fitzpatrick said, standing. "He's been skewered good and proper. Damn."

"We gonna be attacked?" one of the soldiers asked. He was frightened and not worried about showing it. With somewhere around twelve thousand Indians in the vicinity—perhaps three thousand or so warriors—and less than two hundred soldiers at the fort, he had every right to be scared.

"Henri?" Fitzpatrick asked. "This an attack?"

"Just on me. Not on the fort."

"What the hell is . . ." Major Sanderson asked as he

walked up. He shut up when he saw the still moaning Crow. "This your doing, Henri?" he asked tightly.

"Oui."

"In my office now," he ordered.

"No." LaPointe knelt and wiped his knife on the dirt before sheathing it. "I'm not one of your soldier boys to be ordered about."

"You two," Sanderson said angrily to the two soldiers. "Back to your post." He looked at LaPointe, who had stood. "I'd be obliged," he said in barely contained anger.

LaPointe nodded.

37

"What the hell were you trying to do, LaPointe?" Sanderson demanded when the two, plus Palmer and Fitzpatrick were in Sanderson's office. "Start a goddamn Indian war?"

"I was trying to walk across the compound to Dwight's," LaPointe said, every bit as angry as Sanderson.

Palmer snickered. Sanderson shot him a piercing glance, which stopped the snickering, but did not wipe the small grin off Palmer's face.

"Very humorous," Sanderson snapped. He got a handle on his anger. "All right, Henri, tell me what happened."

"I had left here and was heading to Dwight's, like I said. All of a sudden, this crazy Crow jumps on me and knocks me off my horse. Then he tries to brain me with a 'hawk."

"Why?"

"I asked him that. He says something about I killed his brother a couple years ago in a raid with the Brulé on his village."

"Did you?"

"Hell if I know," LaPointe said with a shrug. "I've made more than one raid on the Crow and killed more than one of those bastards."

"You expect us to believe such a tale?" Fitzpatrick demanded. "Jesus, Henri, we talked all this out, and you were gonna leave those bastards alone till after the council."

LaPointe shoved away Dr. Moore, who was trying to bandage his arm. Then he rose from his chair and turned to face Fitzpatrick, who was sitting in a chair next to Sanderson's desk. LaPointe's face was etched with rage. "I've nevair let a man call me a liar before without killing him," he said in a tightly controlled hiss of a voice. "And I will let you do so only this one time because we are old *amis*. Don' be so foolish as to do it again, or that damn Crow won't be the only one I kill tonight."

The room suddenly crackled with tension. Both La-Pointe and Fitzpatrick were hard men, long tested in the harshness of the west against all comers. Both had survived all those tests. They also had killed their share of men, and had proved their valor and deadliness more times than either might care to remember. LaPointe and Fitzpatrick were also proud men, used to living by their wiles, their wits and their weapons. Neither would want to back down.

"We all want to believe you, Henri," Sanderson said into the void. "Tell us something to *make* us believe you."

LaPointe glared at the officer, who stared coolly back. Then LaPointe nodded. "What was that Crow doing at the fort at night, eh?" he asked. "Tell me that." He paused. "Or did I ride out to the Crow villages and spirit him away in the night so I could bring him here and kill him just to start a war that would envelop the Plains? Is that what I did?"

"I didn't mean . . ." Fitzpatrick started.

But LaPointe was not finished, and overrode him. "Am I ze grand schemer, eh? One who plots to ruin ze grand council? And why would I do zis thing, eh? Am I to become ze grand chief of all ze Indians who are left after zey stop killing each other?"

"Enough, Henri!" Sanderson thundered. He looked at Fitzpatrick. "He's right, Tom. There's no damn reason for that Crow to have been here unless he was looking for Henri—or maybe for the first unfortunate son of a bitch who walked along. You, me, Henri. Maybe it didn't matter. Whatever, Henri can't be blamed for the attack. For killing the Crow, maybe, but not for the attack itself." He glanced back at LaPointe. "Was there any chance to have not killed him, Henri?"

"*Oui.* I try two times to let him walk away with his life, but that damn Crow, he don' want to listen to me. So I have to kill him."

"Sorry, Henri," Fitzpatrick said apologetically. "You had no reason to lie about this. I'm just so damned wrought up—still. Christ, waitin' for the commissioners to arrive, the lack of presents, the food, water and grass shortages, the tensions. Damn."

"All of which means you need to keep your friends, not piss 'em off," Palmer said wryly.

Fitzpatrick shot him an angry glance, then relaxed. "Aye," he said quietly. "Trouble is, you have to have common sense for that, something in which I seemed to be in mighty short supply of late."

"We all have our times, Tom," Palmer said.

Fitzpatrick nodded, then sighed. "Well, I best get that Crow back to his people."

"Wait till morning," Sanderson ordered.

Fitzpatrick nodded. "Reckon that would be best. I sure as hell hope this doesn't cause too much trouble."

"Best way to ensure that," Palmer said evenly, "is to make up a story about it for the Crow."

"A story?"

"Sure. Tell 'em you found that asshole—what'd you say his name was, Henri?"

"He called himself Buffalo Walker, as best I can understand that bastard tongue."

Palmer nodded. "You tell the Crows you found Buffalo Walker with his guts ripped open. You brought him back to the fort to see if Doc Moore there could fix him up, but it was too late, so you brung him back to his brothers so they could send him off to the happy huntin' grounds nice and proper. You ain't near as good as Ol' Gabe at tellin' tales, but give it a whirl. Hell, get inventive. Tell 'em you saw another Crow runnin' off, but couldn't see well enough to tell who it was."

"That'd go a long way to keeping the peace around here, Tom," Sanderson said after a few moments of thought.

"I reckon it would," Fitzpatrick said skeptically, but then he nodded. "I'll give that a chance. Of course, if he had friends with him, the Crows'll know I'm lyin'."

"If Buffalo Walker had friends with him, you wouldn't have the problem," LaPointe said flatly. "It'd be me layin' dead over in the hospital."

Fitzpatrick nodded. "I'll leave come first light."

"I'll send a small patrol with you. Not so much to keep you out of trouble," Sanderson said with a vacuous smile, "but to show that we are honoring that poor, dead brave."

Fitzpatrick rode into the fort and stopped at Sanderson's. LaPointe and Palmer, who had spent the night at the fort, also were there.

"Well, how'd it go?" Sanderson asked.

Fitzpatrick poured himself a whiskey and gulped it down. "Hell if I know. Them blank-faced sons a bitches just sat there and looked at me. Except his wife, of course, who set up a considerable din in her grief. The warriors council listened to what I had to say, thanked me and sent me on my way."

"Well, I'll keep the men on alert for a day or two, just in case. And I had a report just a bit ago that said a small entourage is on its way and should be here sometime this afternoon."

Fitzpatrick perked up a little. "They got the wagons with 'em?"

Sanderson shrugged. "The rider told me what I told you."

"Damn. Well, I guess I best go get myself all fancied up for when those muckety-mucks get here."

He had barely gotten himself washed off a little and donned his fancy duds—a suit of fine, soft, fringed buckskins, a colorful sash for a belt and a wide-brimmed hat—when the entourage arrived. Fitzpatrick and Sanderson stepped out onto the porch from Sanderson's office as the wagons creaked to a halt.

"Gentlemen," Sanderson said brightly, "I am Major Winslow Sanderson, post commander. Welcome to Fort Laramie. I trust your journey was not too arduous."

A tall, stooped man with iron gray hair and a thick, tobacco stained mustache, climbed carefully down off one of the wagons. He stretched and then limped up the steps.

"Superintendent Mitchell," Fitzpatrick said, stepping forward with hand outstretched. They shook, and then Fitzpatrick said, "Major Sanderson, Mister D. D. Mitchell, superintendent of Indian affairs."

"I'm honored, sir," Sanderson said smoothly.

"The pleasure is mine, Major." Mitchell's voice was as rough as his hard exterior. He half turned. "My touring companions, as it were. Colonel Sam Cooper, regular army."

Sanderson saluted smartly and then shook Cooper's hand.

"Mister—Colonel—A. B. Chambers. Colonel Chambers is the editor of the *Missouri Republican,*" Mitchell said.

"A fine newspaper, if I do say so myself, Colonel Chambers."

"Mister B. Gratz Brown, a reporter."

Sanderson nodded and shook Brown's hand.

"And last, but most assuredly not least, Major, is Mister Robert Campbell of Scotland and Saint Louis. He was one of the two partners responsible for the building of the original fort here. He and Mister Bill Sublette. Now Mister Campbell is a well-known and well-respected businessman in Saint Louis."

"I'm honored, Mister Campbell," Sanderson said. He

smiled a little. "I've heard about you from some of the men I work with here."

"Oh?" Campbell questioned, bushy eyebrows raised. "And who might they be?" He grinned a little. "Besides old Broken Hand here?" He shook hands with Fitzpatrick, and they embraced briefly. "Good to see you, Tom," Campbell said.

"And I you, old friend."

"Boy, don't he look all citified and fancy," LaPointe said loudly and sarcastically as he and Palmer stepped out of the office. Like everyone else, they were dressed in as fine clothes as they had—soft, fringed buckskin pants, beaded moccasins; LaPointe with a fringed buckskin shirt, Palmer with a white cotton shirt under a pale gray vest.

Campbell laughed. "Henri, Otis. How are you, my friends?"

They all hugged and shook hands, exchanging a few pleasantries. Then Campbell asked, "Where're some of the others? Surely Ol' Gabe'll be here? And Rufus. Where's Rufus?"

"Rufe went under a couple weeks ago. A deserter ambushed him."

"I am sorry to hear that, Henri. I know he was a good friend to you all these years."

"He was that." LaPointe smiled a little. "But nothing can be done to bring him back. As for Bridger, that ol' bastard's with the Snakes, so he'll be around the council."

"It'll be good to see him again."

"I suppose," Palmer said skeptically. Then he laughed.

"Well, gentlemen," Sanderson said, "suppose we go inside and get out of this insufferable heat."

"A fine suggestion, Major," Mitchell said.

They all filed inside and took seats that had been arranged for them. Sanderson sat behind his desk; Mitchell in a chair directly in front of the desk. Mitchell was flanked by Campbell and Chambers. Brown and

Colonel Cooper sat behind those three. Fitzpatrick had a chair alongside Sanderson's desk. LaPointe and Palmer leaned against a side wall.

As drink and cigars were being passed around, Cooper pointed to LaPointe and Palmer. "Is there a reason those two men are here, Major—other than they are Mister Campbell's friends from the old days?" Cooper did not seem pleased.

"They're interpreters for the council," Sanderson answered tightly.

"I don't see any Indians in here, Major," Cooper snapped. "Therefore, I see no need for interpreters."

"May I see your orders relieving me of command of Fort Laramie," Sanderson said sharply.

LaPointe and Palmer were angry about Cooper's words, but kept quiet, only to be surprised by Sanderson's response.

"I have no such orders, Major," Cooper said flatly.

"Then despite your rank, I am still post commander," Sanderson said icily. "As such, I will have whoever in my office that I feel like having there, and I find no reason to explain that to you or anyone else." His eyes burned at Cooper.

"I'll have you court-martialed for speaking to me in such a manner," Cooper warned.

"I don't give a good goddamn—"

"Now, now, gentlemen," Mitchell chided gently. "We're here for the purpose of a council, not to make war among ourselves. This is Major Sanderson's command, Colonel Cooper. I think it best we leave the running of it to him."

Cooper was no fool. While Mitchell held no actual sway over him, he did have the ear of the president, as well as the secretary of war. A poor account about him from Mitchell could have serious implications for his military career. "Yes, sir, Superintendent," he said. Then, "My apologies, Major. The long trek has shortened my temper."

"No apologies needed, Colonel, except mine to you.

We, too, have been under much strain of late, and it has made us edgy.''

"Well," Mitchell said expansively, "now that we are square on that, what can you tell us, Major. About the council, I mean." He sipped his whiskey and puffed on a thick cigar.

"Not much to tell, Superintendent. The Indians are here, ready and waiting. Now that you have arrived, we can get things rolling."

"One thing, though," Fitzpatrick interjected. When everyone's eyes were on him, he asked, "Have you brought the wagonloads of presents for the Indians, Superintendent?" He looked anxious. There had been several large wagons roll in with the party, and he hoped fervently that the presents were among the supplies in those wagons.

"Why no," Mitchell said. "They were late in getting out of Saint Louis. We decided to push ahead, to get started." Seeing the stricken look on Fitzpatrick's face, he asked, "Does that present a problem, Mister Fitzpatrick?"

"Yes," Fitzpatrick said sourly. "Yes, it does."

"Oh?"

"As much as we try to pretend it's not so, it's fact that most of these Indians are here at least in part because of the presents they expect. Presents they were promised."

"They'll get them, Mister Fitzpatrick," Mitchell chided gently.

"If they stay around long enough," Fitzpatrick said flatly. "There exists here a tenuous peace at best. Most of the tribes here are mortal enemies. They've come here at our behest—and with our promise that they'll be given gifts. When they learn the gifts aren't here, there's a good chance they'll pull up stakes and head home."

"All of them?" Mitchell asked, surprised.

"I'd expect so. What'll happen, is a couple of hot-heads'll tell their people they've been spoken to with forked tongues by the white man again. They'll get a few of their like-minded friends to leave. Others in the band or related bands'll not want to be left behind with smaller numbers, and so they'll leave, too. Then their enemies'll not want to look like they're kissin' our asses, so they'll begin leavin', too. Soon enough, the only ones left to have a council'll be us."

"They would do that?" Mitchell asked gruffly. This would not fit in with his plans at all.

Fitzpatrick nodded. "Part of the reason is that things're bad off here. With all these Indians, and their horses, plus the soldiers, grass is gettin' scarce. So's food and clean water. Rather than movin' downriver a ways or somethin' to have the council, as we'd planned to do in the next day or two, they might just say the hell with it and leave."

❧{38}❧

Mitchell quickly accepted the fragility of the plans for the council. He might not like it, but he was pragmatic enough to accept it as true, especially when confirmed by LaPointe and Palmer. While Cooper might object to having rough-hewn men like LaPointe and Palmer in attendance, Mitchell was not that foolish. He had even solicited their advice.

"Why are you asking them?" Cooper had demanded. "They're hardly less savage in appearance, and I would dare say, actions, than the Indians."

"Colonel Cooper," Mitchell said with a sigh. He turned in his chair to look at the officer. "These two men—along with Agent Fitzpatrick—have more knowledge of the savages we're dealing with than all of Washington put together. Now, if you do not plan to lend your energies to this enterprise, then I suggest you find a few troopers to escort you and begin making your way back to the capital." He turned forward, again, dismissing Cooper. "Now, gentlemen, is what Agent Fitzpatrick said true?"

LaPointe and Palmer nodded.

"Are we in any danger?" He smiled. "More so than normal?"

"I'd say yes, Superintendent Mitchell," LaPointe said. "There's ten, maybe twelve thousand Indians in the area, all of them looking for presents. If they don't get them—or if they don't think they'll get them—they might just go home, like Tom says. But if they think they've been bamboozled, there's no telling what some of them might do."

Mitchell mulled that over for a while. He suddenly looked up and smiled at Sanderson. "My apologies, Major. My companions and I haven't eaten since breaking our fast this morning. Would it be possible to have supper served?"

Sanderson nodded. "Private Moorhouse!" When the orderly looked inside, Sanderson said, "I, and all my guests, will be supping in here."

"Yessir."

"As soon as the meal can be prepared."

"Yessir."

"Private!" Mitchell said. When Moorhouse looked at Mitchell in question, Mitchell said, "I understand there is a scarcity of supplies here?"

"We might be low on a few things, sir," Moorhouse said cautiously.

"Well, in any case, you get a detail up directly to unload those wagons we brought in. There are food supplies aplenty. I expect you and your compatriots can do with some new stores. So once we are fed, open your mess to the men and allow them a good meal for a change."

"Yessir!" Moorhouse turned and hurried off.

"I hope you do not mind, Major," Mitchell said. "That I gave your orderly orders. I hate to impose."

"On the contrary, for a mission like that I don't mind giving up control temporarily." He smiled.

"Well, good," Mitchell said. "Now, where were we? Ah, yes, the problem. We must try to prevent the Indians from leaving. That would certainly not do us any good. Is there any chance that we can send out a force with enough horses or mules, or even wagons, to get to the gifts and split them up to get them here a little faster?"

Sanderson pondered that, then shook his head. "No, sir. I don't have that many men. Nor that many animals."

"Then we are stuck, are we not?"

"Pretty much."

"About all I can suggest," Fitzpatrick tossed in, "is that me and some of the others go spread the word to the Indians that you're here, Superintendent, and that the council is to go on. We'll tell them that the gifts are on the way and should be here by the time we end the council. That's true, isn't it?" His worry was renewed.

"I would think so," Mitchell said. "As far as I can tell, they should be here in two weeks, perhaps a little less."

"It's not certain they'll accept it, Superintendent," Fitzpatrick said.

"I understand, Tom. But it's the best we can do. I hope you and your friends can convince the Indians of that."

They all sort of mulled that over, and tried to think of something more concrete, but ideas were as sparse as the grass around the fort these days. Finally they put aside their ponderings as soldiers trooped in food for the men there. Talk turned to more general things, but with thoughts of the conference never far from their minds.

After the meal, there was little more to discuss. It was decided that LaPointe would go to Painted Bull's village that night, and then in the morning begin sweeping through the other Dakota bands. Palmer would do the same with the Cheyennes, and then one of his Cheyenne friends would do so with the Arapahos.

They were about ready to wrap things up, when Moorhouse poked his head in the door. "You might want to come see this, Major," he said, face tight with nervousness.

"Something wrong, Private?" Sanderson asked.

"Not sure, sir. But I don't think it's good."

"I'll be out in a moment, Private."

"You're mighty lax in discipline, Major," Cooper noted, nodding toward the door.

Sanderson stood and leaned forward, hands on his desk. "And you, sir, are an off-putting and pugnacious busybody. If you question my command, my methods or my tactics again, I'll have you thrown in the guardhouse.''

''You would not dare!'' Cooper snapped, jerking upward. He was short and thick and had a big chest that seemed filled with his own puffery.

''Try me,'' Sanderson said.

''Colonel Cooper,'' Mitchell said wearily, ''I won't warn you again. You are an observer in this enterprise, and as such you should keep your mouth shut and observe.''

Cooper glowered at Mitchell a few moments, then turned his malignant glare back to Sanderson. ''Your conduct will be reported to your highest superiors in Washington,'' he threatened.

Sanderson held Cooper's gaze and was about to retort when Moorhouse popped inside the door again. ''I suggest you make haste, Major,'' he said.

Sanderson looked at him, still enraged at Cooper. Then he saw the look on Moorhouse's face, and he nodded. He headed for the door, followed by everyone in the room.

''Holy shit,'' Fitzpatrick breathed.

''Amen to that,'' Sanderson added.

Several hundred angry Crow warriors were gathered in a large semicircle on the fort's parade ground, fronting on Sanderson's office. To the left and right of the office were soldiers. They looked pitifully few in the face of the mass of Crows, and as such, there were few who did not display anxiety on their faces.

Two Crow chiefs rode forward until they were less than twenty feet from the porch on which Sanderson and the others were standing.

Fitzpatrick shoved forward until he was standing on the top step. ''What do you want here?'' he asked in Crow.

''Him,'' the one chief said, pointing at LaPointe.

''Why?'' Fitzpatrick asked, flustered and trying to regain his wits.

"He must pay for killing Buffalo Walker," the chief—Strikes the Sioux—said.

"Who says he killed Buffalo Walker?"

"What're they talking about?" Mitchell asked Palmer, who was standing next to him.

Palmer translated.

"Two Drums says."

"Who's Two Drums?" Fitzpatrick questioned.

"The brother of Buffalo Walker. He knew Buffalo Walker was to come here last night to kill the white-eyes the Sioux dogs call Black Bear."

"Why would Buffalo Walker want to kill Black Bear?" Fitzpatrick asked, maintaining his calm.

"Are we in any danger?" Mitchell asked Palmer. "More so than usual."

"Them Crows decide to raise hair on us, and there ain't gonna be shit we can do to stop 'em."

"If Sanderson had any gumption," Cooper muttered, "he'd run those goddamn savages off right now."

"How many soldiers you see around here, asshole?" Palmer asked quietly. "Hundred, hundred-fifty tops. There's twice that of Crows, and there's more where they come from. The major tried to send 'em packin' without even givin' 'em a chance to speak their piece, he'd be signin' a death warrant for every white man here."

"Black Bear killed Stands in the Water two, maybe three winters ago. Stands in the Water was the brother of Buffalo Walker and Two Drums. Then Buffalo Walker says he saw the Black Bear come into our camp when we were on the trail heading here."

"That true, Henri?" Fitzpatrick asked over his shoulder.

"Nope," LaPointe lied easily.

"You've got the wrong man, Strikes the Sioux," Fitzpatrick said.

"I don't lie!"

"I didn't say you lied," Fitzpatrick said soothingly.

"All I said was you have the wrong man. Buffalo Walker must have thought Black Bear was someone else."

Brown, the reporter, was scribbling furiously on a pad of paper, while Palmer translated and his editor watched over him.

"It was Black Bear!" Strikes the Sioux insisted.

"Even if it is true, I just can't give him to you. No, Black Bear is an important man with the soldier chief and the Great Father far to the east. If we were to give him to you, the Great Father would be very angry with the Crows."

"We are not afraid of the Great Father, nor of the soldier chief," Strikes the Sioux said angrily. "If Black Bear is not given to us, my people will leave here. We will not sit at the great council."

"Then you'll suffer the consequences," Fitzpatrick said, having no real idea what the consequences might be.

"We will attack the fort," Strikes the Sioux said contemptuously, as if to say that the fort would be so easily overrun that it would be the work of only minutes.

"Then many of your warriors will die," Fitzpatrick said flatly. He pointed to where soldiers had pulled up two of their cannon and had aimed them at the great bunch of Crows.

"Oh, my Lord," Mitchell gasped, pointing. "More of them."

"Them're Brulé Dakota warriors, Superintendent," Palmer said.

"Is that good?"

"Those're the Indians Henri lives with. You see that young feller out there with black dots of paint all over his face and chest?"

"Yes. A frightening looking fellow."

"Name's Spotted Horse. He's Henri's brother-in-law. The Crows fire one shot and there ain't a one of 'em'll get out of here alive."

The Brulés, armed and painted, began forming a larger semicircle around the Crows, ringing them in.

The soldiers, who quickly grew even more worried, stood their lines, squeezed between the Crows and the Dakotas. More than one soldier thought he and all his fellows were dead for certain.

Even the Crows began to look nervous, and everyone there knew it would take only one small spark to ignite Fort Laramie.

Fitzpatrick stood there patiently trying to calm the Crows, arguing quietly but firmly with Strikes the Sioux and the other chief, Red Mountain.

Suddenly there was a shout and all the whites looked up to see beyond the Crows that a wild young Brulé was charging the massed Crows.

LaPointe, standing near the corner of the building, leaped on his horse, which was tied right there, and raced frantically through the Crow lines, heading for the Sioux warrior.

"What's going on?" Mitchell asked. He sounded almost as interested as he did frightened.

"That young fool's father was killed in a battle with the Crows, and he's lookin' for revenge and to gain glory here," Palmer answered. "And you best pray that Henri gets to him before he kills some Crow."

LaPointe slammed into the young Dakota and hauled him off his war pony. Jamming his own horse to a stop, LaPointe slid down to the ground. "You goddamn fool," he roared at the Brulé in English.

"Get away from me," Brave Dog shouted in his own language. He tried to push past LaPointe.

The Frenchman stood his ground. "You want to get past me," he hissed in Dakota, "you'll have to kill me to do it. After the council, then you can raise a war party and go after the Crows. I'll even go with you. But there's been enough trouble here. This council must go on."

"I don't care about the council," Brave Dog spat. "The Crows must die! My eyes can't even look at them without the rage coming over me. Rage that will only be quieted with Crow blood." He backed a few steps, so he could keep an eye on LaPointe.

"You stupid fool," LaPointe snarled. "You kill even one Crow here, and the land will run red with blood. Crow blood *and* Dakota blood. Your need for vengeance is not important enough to bring that."

Brave Dog pulled his knife on LaPointe, who knocked the warrior down. "Don't you even think about getting up and coming against me with that knife, Brave Dog," LaPointe warned.

Brave Dog paid him no heed. He jumped up and charged, only to be hammered to the ground again. Still the Brulé warrior was not through. Three more times he came at LaPointe, who slammed him to the ground, each time with increasing anger and force.

Finally, though, Brave Dog seemed to have had the starch knocked out of him. "Now get your ass back over there with your people and cool off," LaPointe ordered.

Embarrassed, the Dakota turned and got his pony. He mounted up and rode back to the ranks of his fellow warriors.

Feeling his own bloodlust rising at the audacity of the Crows, and unable to control himself, LaPointe spun to face the Crows. "Come on at me, you fractious bastards!" he roared. He repeated his challenge in Crow.

39

"No!" a frantic Fitzpatrick screamed.

The Crows hesitated.

Standing between the Dakotas and the Crows—who had turned to face him—LaPointe leaned on his rifle. When Strikes the Sioux and Red Mountain had come through their warriors and stopped in front of LaPointe, he said, "Send your best man out to face me. He wins, he can take my hair. What you do after that is your account. He loses, and you *fils des garces* attend the council like you're supposed to."

The Crows discussed the offer, while everyone waited in the broiling, late afternoon sun. Then Strikes the Sioux looked at LaPointe and nodded. "We will do as you say," he announced.

A large, magnificently maned Crow with a sharp, tomahawk face rode out a little way. Sneering, he dismounted. "So we meet at last," Iron Bear said with a smirk. "I'll give you the first blow," he said, none of his condescension easing.

"I don't need your kindness," LaPointe spat.

"I am a mighty warrior," Iron Bear said matter-of-factly. "And when I have been challenged by a man who hides in the bushes instead of protecting his family, I think he is a coward, and allow the first blow."

LaPointe pushed up off his rifle and then pulled the weapon into both hands. Sneering at the sudden wariness that had sprung into Iron Bear's eyes, LaPointe pitched the rifle to the side. Then he did the same with his two pistols. He stood with hands on hips, his posture a challenge to the Crow.

Iron Bear smiled and nodded. He pulled off his bow and quiver and threw them aside. He did the same with the single six-shooter he had had in his belt. Then he charged LaPointe.

The Frenchman tried to spin out of the way but was not very successful. Iron Bear hit him with a good portion of beefy shoulder, and LaPointe was spinning to the ground.

Iron Bear stopped and laughed as LaPointe got up.

LaPointe knew he was in trouble. Iron Bear outweighed him by about forty pounds and was ten years younger, in the prime of life. But LaPointe had picked up a few tricks in his forty-three years, one of them being not to get too damn cocky.

LaPointe brushed off a little dirt, realizing that Sanderson, Palmer, Fitzpatrick, Mitchell and the others had tentatively come through the Crows and were standing there watching nervously.

"Hit him again, Henri," Palmer shouted in friendly sarcasm. "A couple more good shots like that and he'll be gone beaver."

LaPointe did not even glance at Palmer.

"You're being mighty carefree with your friend's health, Mister Palmer," Mitchell said.

"Nah," Palmer said, risking a quick glance at Mitchell. He winked. "Now ol' Henri knows I'm here."

"So?"

"So, you think I'm gonna let that son of a bitch kill my ol' friend?"

Mitchell gave him a sharp glance. "Wouldn't that precipitate a war?"

"Might. But I'll worry about that when the time comes."

LaPointe drew in a long breath and charged. He counted on Iron Bear being arrogant enough to stand there and take the charge. He had judged right, and he pulled to a short stop bare inches from Iron Bear, surprising the Crow. Iron Bear had braced for the crash and relaxed when it did not come. In that instant, LaPointe smashed Iron Bear in the throat with a hard fist.

Iron Bear's look of smug superiority changed to one of strangled pain, anger and even a touch of fear.

LaPointe pounded Iron Bear with heavy fists, thumping the tall, muscular Indian's face, chest and stomach. Iron Bear's nose broke, and LaPointe could feel a couple of the Crow's teeth break.

LaPointe didn't know how, but Iron Bear managed to find some reservoir of strength, and he suddenly belted LaPointe across the face with a forearm. LaPointe stumbled back and fell. *"Mon Dieu,"* he muttered, reaching up to tap at his face with fingers. He found nothing broken, though there was some blood from split skin over his left cheekbone.

He saw Iron Bear coming toward him, his bloody face ghastly in the red afternoon. LaPointe got up slowly, suddenly wondering if he hadn't bitten off a bit much here. There weren't too many men who could take a thumping from LaPointe like he had just given Iron Bear and still be standing. LaPointe figured he had better end this fast or he might be the one getting rubbed out.

LaPointe slid out his knife and crouched a little. Still Iron Bear came on, walking unsteadily. He looked more dead than alive already, but LaPointe thought it might be an act to lull him.

Though Iron Bear was moving awkwardly, he still managed to toss a pretty good punch at LaPointe. But LaPointe blocked it and then shoved his blade home in Iron Bear's vitals. He stood there a moment, holding Iron Bear up on the blade of the knife. Then the Crow sagged, and LaPointe could not hold him up. He jerked his knife free as Iron Bear fell.

LaPointe wiped the blade of his knife on the dirt and scraps of brown grass at his feet and then slipped it into the sheath. As he retrieved his firearms, he could hear some of the Crows arguing. A few of the Crows wanted to attack, but Strikes the Sioux, Red Mountain and most of the other leaders argued against it.

One young warrior around the western end of the arc kicked his pony and charged, screeching and howling, lowering his lance to strike.

LaPointe stood there, waiting. He sensed rather than saw that some of the Dakotas were ready to kill the charging Crow, and then maybe attack the massed Crows. He angrily shouted to the Dakota that they should do nothing against the warrior or the main body of Crows. In an instant, he had realized that if his sacrifice here would allow the council to go on, it would be worth it.

He also had the fleeting thought that if he did die here, his name would be a legend in some ways around Crow as well as Dakota campfires. He stood, arms held loosely at his sides, showing no fear.

Suddenly a flurry of arrows flew from the Crow ranks, and the charging warrior fell dead.

Strikes the Sioux rode slowly out toward LaPointe and stopped only a few feet from him. With all the dignity he could muster, he apologized for his warrior's poor behavior.

"And will you attend the council peacefully like you have vowed?" he asked in Crow.

Strikes the Sioux nodded solemnly.

Two days later, the entire congregation moved thirty-some miles east, to where Horse Creek joined the Platte on the south and Spring Creek from the north. There the tribes were assigned campgrounds, with the Crows and Shoshonis separated from the Dakotas, Cheyennes and Arapahos by the troops from Fort Laramie.

Two and a half weeks of intensive talks ensued, all in a spirit of peace and friendship. Many feasts were held, including some in which a tribe would host an old enemy. At one, in which several bands of Brulés invited a number of Crows, LaPointe left. He rounded up Otis

Palmer and the two rode a couple of miles away and uncorked a jug.

Interpreting at the long, hot sessions kept LaPointe, Palmer and a number of other men busy. Their help was also important when Mitchell and his commissioners began drawing out maps of the territory in which the various tribes were to confine themselves.

Finally, though, it was done, and despite the fact that the presents promised the Indians had not arrived yet, the Indians agreed to the conditions of the treaty. Three days later, the wagonloads of presents arrived and were distributed with much fanfare.

The morning after, Mitchell and his entourage, with Fitzpatrick and several Dakota and Cheyenne chiefs left, headed east for Washington. The bands of Indians left more leisurely, drifting off a few bands at a time. Painted Bull's Brulés were one of the first to pull out. Henri LaPointe went with them, heading for buffalo country to make meat for the long winter that had already sent a few harbingers of its fullness to come.

As he rode, LaPointe wondered if the peace between the old enemies would last beyond the next spring. He vowed that he would try to bury that rage that still burned within him. He even thought he might succeed —if the Crows and the Snakes would leave him, Morning Mist and Little Stone alone. It was something to hope for anyway.